FOUCAULT'S *ASKĒSIS*

Topics in Historical Philosophy

General Editors David Kolb
John McCumber

Associate Editor Anthony J. Steinbock

FOUCAULT'S *ASKĒSIS*

An Introduction to the Philosophical Life

Edward F. McGushin

Northwestern University Press
Evanston, Illinois

Northwestern University Press
www.nupress.northwestern.edu

Copyright © 2007 by Northwestern University Press. Published 2007. All rights reserved.

Printed in the United States of America

10   9   8   7   6   5   4   3   2   1

Library of Congress Cataloging-in-Publication Data

McGushin, Edward F.
   Foucault's askesis : an introduction to the philosophical life / Edward F. McGushin.
     p. cm. — (Topics in historical philosophy)
   Includes bibliographical references and index.
   ISBN-13: 978-0-8101-2282-6 (cloth text : alk. paper)
   ISBN-10: 0-8101-2282-0 (cloth text : alk. paper)
   ISBN-13: 978-0-8101-2283-3 (pbk. : alk. paper)
   ISBN-10: 0-8101-2283-9 (pbk. : alk. paper)
   1. Foucault, Michel, 1926–1984. 2. Philosophy, Ancient. 3. Self (Philosophy)
   I. Title. II. Series: Northwestern University topics in historical philosophy.
   B2430.F724M395 2006
   194—dc22

2006015326

To my family

Contents

Acknowledgments

This book would not have been possible without the support of the Philosophy Department and the Graduate School of Arts and Sciences at Boston College. Many thanks to Richard Cobb-Stevens of the Philosophy Department, Ourida Mostefai of the Romance Language Department at Boston College, and Laurence Frabalot of the École Normale Superieure (ENS) for giving me the opportunity to spend a year at the ENS in Paris. I would also like to thank Philippe Artières of the Centre Michel Foucault, the staff of the Institut Mémoires de L'Édition Contemporaine, and the staff of the Bibliothèque du Collège de France for generously granting me access to the audio recordings of Foucault's lectures in Paris.

Many persons have contributed to this book, more than I can mention here. First of all I want to thank Jim Bernauer for guiding me through this project and for being the real inspiration for it. Taking Jim's seminar on Foucault many years ago and coming to know his approach to scholarship, to friendship, and to the intimate connection between the two is what, more than anything, has shaped my understanding of philosophy, both as an academic pursuit and as a form of friendship. Andrew Cutrofello has read more than one draft of this manuscript, and he has challenged me to improve it with his careful and penetrating questions. Frédéric Gros provided valuable insights into the later Foucault and the opportunity to share my work with his colleagues and students in Paris. I want to thank Len Lawlor for reading my manuscript so carefully and offering very useful suggestions for improving it. Thanks also to John McCumber and Rachel Delaney of Northwestern University Press. Many other friends and colleagues helped me complete this book. In particular I want to thank Scott Campbell, Paul Bruno, Jeff Ousborne, Jim Boettcher, Linda Boettcher, Richard Lynch, Tom Beaudoin, Julian Bourg, Dan Dwyer, Jeff Lyzack, Karen Yates, Stacy Drubner, Shawn Hunter, Amy Hunter, Lynn Purcell, and Joseph Tanke. While in France during the academic year of 2002–3, I lived with a truly cosmopolitan group of researchers and students at ENS at the boulevard Jourdan campus. I want to thank the "jourdaniens"—Rene Murphy-Keep, Nathalie Dupont,

Nicolas Barreyre, Martin Dumont, Christophe Imperiali, and Guillaume Pinson (among others)—for their camaraderie and inspiration. I'd especially like to thank my family, who have given me unconditional support and encouragement throughout this project. Finally, I'd like to thank Serena Parekh, who has made this a much better book through her careful readings and advice and has made me a better person through her friendship.

Introduction

The title of this book is a tangle of references. First, it alludes to a line from Foucault's preface to the book *Anti-Oedipus* by Gilles Deleuze and Félix Gauttari. Foucault wrote: "Paying a modest tribute to Saint Francis de Sales, one might say that *Anti-Oedipus* is an *Introduction to the Non-Fascist Life*."[1] *An Introduction to the Philosophical Life* is, then, a slight modification of and reference to this passage, but even more it is intended to invoke all which that passage entails. For Foucault's words are themselves a referential play on the title of Saint Francis de Sales's *Introduction to the Devout Life,* a seventeenth-century manual of spiritual practice. Further, Foucault's claim was more than a simple allusion to the title of Saint Francis de Sales's book; it was a gesture toward the whole tradition of spiritual direction and ascetic practice out of which that book emerged. What's more, Foucault was heralding the return of this tradition within which the philosophy book served as a "manual or guide to everyday life," a set of instructions in the "art of living counter to all forms of fascism."[2] I suggest that we take these words as a preface to Foucault's own project. In other words, I propose that we read Foucault's work as a sort of manual to the art of living philosophically and as a genealogy of a few of the different forms this art has taken.[3] It is in this sense that Foucault's project could be called *An Introduction to the Philosophical Life*. However, the expression "philosophical life" might seem a bit odd because we have come to think of philosophy as an academic discipline and not a way of living. What this expression means will become clear as we examine the excavations of ancient philosophy that Foucault carried out in the 1980s. Foucault's encounter with ancient philosophy allowed him to experience how the practice of philosophy is (or can be), to paraphrase Nietzsche, a way of becoming who one is.[4] My claim is that the real effect of Foucault's research and teaching was not just to develop a theory, to accumulate and transmit knowledge about the history of philosophy. Rather, as his final lectures made so clear, for Foucault philosophical activity was an exercise, an experience. Foucault's *work* in this last phase of his life was *himself* in the act of becoming a philosopher. The purpose of this exercise was to transform himself, to let himself be altered by the activity of thinking, and to offer this experience of self-transformation to those who would come into contact with this work.

An Introduction to the Philosophical Life

In the opening pages of *The Use of Pleasure,* Foucault described what he was doing in the following terms:

> As for what motivated me, it is quite simple; I would hope that in the eyes of some people it might be sufficient in itself. It was curiosity— the only kind of curiosity, in any case, that is worth acting upon with a degree of obstinacy: not the curiosity that seeks to assimilate what it is proper for one to know, but that which enables one to get free of oneself. After all, what would be the value of the passion for knowledge if it resulted only in a certain amount of knowledgeableness and not, in one way or another and to the extent possible, in the knower's straying afield of himself? . . . What is philosophy today—philosophical activity, I mean—if it is not the critical work that thought brings to bear on itself? . . . The essay—which should be understood as the assay or test by which, in the game of truth, one undergoes changes . . . is the living substance of philosophy, at least if we assume that philosophy is still what it was in times past, i.e., an "ascesis," *askēsis,* an exercise of oneself in the activity of thought.[5]

This dense and rich text merits our attention and requires unpacking. There are three points in particular that I would like to examine. First of all, Foucault uses the word curiosity to designate his motivation. We can hear the echo of an interview where he says that, to him, the word "evokes 'concern'; it evokes the care one takes for what exists and could exist; a readiness to find strange and singular what surrounds us; a certain relentlessness to break up our familiarities and to regard otherwise the same things."[6] In these passages, Foucault resists the traditional philosophical denigration of curiosity as a frivolous distraction. On the one hand (in *The Use of Pleasure*), he defines curiosity as an effort and a desire to "get free of oneself." On the other hand, he describes it as a form of *care.* In particular this form of care—a care for "what exists and could exist"—transforms the ordinary into something strange, something worthy of attention. Foucault's curiosity, then, is a mode of care that transforms the familiar into something strange and wrests one free of oneself. And finally, it is a "readiness" for this strangeness, even a "relentlessness" that drives one toward it.

Given the focus of Foucault's final project on the theme of care of the self, this is highly significant. In these passages Foucault explicitly describes his *own* philosophical practice as a form of care, a concern to transform oneself and the way one sees—"to regard otherwise the same things." Therefore, what he has to say about care of the self is not unrelated to what he is doing even when he says it.

Second, Foucault describes his philosophical activity not as a form of accumulating knowledge but as a kind of exercise—an *askēsis*. This word *askēsis* can be misleading. As Foucault assures us in many places, it does not necessarily mean the practice of self-denial. *Askēsis* came to be almost exclusively practiced as self-renunciation in the development of Christian asceticism. However, in its original Greek context the word simply meant exercise, as in training, practice, or development. Furthermore, Foucault points out that in the Greek context it always had a positive and productive meaning—exercising meant perfecting oneself, developing one's capacities, becoming who one is. It referred to physical training in athletics as well as spiritual training, that is, philosophy. Thus *askēsis* is for Foucault, just as he describes it in the passage above, an exercise of thought, a work of thought upon itself. However, while Foucault, as will be made clear in the chapters that follow, does not think of *askēsis* as something which is first and foremost a practice of self-denial, in this passage it does seem to have that implication. The work of thought, the practice of philosophy, is "an attempt to get free of oneself." Elsewhere in *The Use of Pleasure,* he describes the philosopher's activity as "straying afield of himself."[7] Is Foucault's *askēsis* another form of self-renunciation after all? One might see in Foucault's persistent and rigorous destruction of the subject and his desire to become anonymous the traces of Christian asceticism and self-renunciation. However, the picture is more complicated than that. According to Foucault, there is "irony in those efforts one makes to alter one's way of looking at things, to change the boundaries of what one knows and to venture out a ways from there."[8] Rather than denial of oneself, this philosophical *askēsis* is a kind of release from oneself, but one which does not exactly renounce the self or mortify it. To the contrary, for Foucault, *askēsis* results in a subtle transformation: "Sure of having traveled far, one finds that one is looking down on oneself from above. The journey rejuvenates things, and ages the relationship with oneself."[9] Philosophy as a practice, a work of thought upon itself, is not a denial of oneself, even if its form is a flight from oneself. A new relationship arises through this exercise—a more profound relationship marked by a broadened and elevated vision (looking down from above) and a wiser, steadier attitude ("aged" or matured).

Third, there is another surprising aspect of the text quoted above.

For most of his intellectual career Foucault maintained a highly ambivalent relation to the institution of philosophy and the title of philosopher. He sometimes claimed that the activity of philosophy, as such, no longer existed because it had been dispersed and appropriated by new disciplines—such as linguistics or ethnology—or by old ones that had reinvented themselves—such as mathematics or the history of religions.[10] When he did define a properly philosophical activity—an activity which could perhaps define a certain kind of subject, *the philosopher*—it was the practice of diagnosis.[11] He sometimes accepted the role or title of philosopher—understood as diagnostician of the present—and at other times distanced himself from such a title. In the quoted passage he does use the term "philosophy" to designate his own activity. However, he does not describe his practice as diagnostic. Neither does he characterize it as a form of theoretical knowledge. Rather, as we have just seen, it is a kind of exercise—a work of thought upon itself, and a work of oneself upon oneself.

He makes this claim with reference to what philosophy was "in times past." In other words, Foucault is calling upon a form of philosophy, an experience of philosophy, as it was practiced in the past. This experience of philosophy as exercise comes out of Foucault's encounter with Plato, Stoicism, Cynicism, and Epicureanism. According to Foucault, philosophy in the ancient world was the practice of a certain way of living and speaking, a certain way of being with oneself and with others; this way of living was defined by the care of the self. Such an experience of philosophy stands before contemporary, academic philosophical activity as a question, a challenge, and a possibility. Foucault's philosophical practice, then, appears to be both a sort of retrieval from a philosophical past and a problematization of our philosophical present. By excavating this ancient practice of philosophy, Foucault forces contemporary philosophy to come face-to-face with that which it has "neglected"—namely, itself.[12] One of the main themes of Foucault's final project is that ancient philosophy, as care of the self, was necessary to counter a tendency toward self-neglect. This theme—the struggle between care and neglect—is here invoked to describe the present of philosophical practice itself. But notice, Foucault does not restrict himself to a *diagnosis* of this contemporary neglect. This is because the neglect he addresses is not merely a theoretical blind spot or an object of inquiry to be viewed and studied from a distance. Foucault confronts philosophy's self-neglect by practicing a philosophical *askēsis*. At least, this is the conclusion we must come to if we are to take his self-description seriously; that is, if we are to understand it in terms of what he says it means to engage in philosophical *askēsis*. In other words, in order to understand what Foucault is doing in his final project, we must understand it in terms of what he says about philosophy as care of the self, as *askēsis.* What's more, in order to properly understand what Foucault says about the care of the self, we will have to see how and why he was led to this project and how it is shaped by his earlier work.

This last point can be formulated in the following questions: Why focus on this practice of freeing oneself from oneself, on care of the self, on the relationship of oneself to oneself? What is at stake in these exercises? One might even object to this project altogether by claiming that "these games with oneself would better be left backstage; or, at best, that they might properly form part of those preliminary exercises that are forgotten once they served their purpose."[13] Foucault's reply is to be found in a lecture from his 1982 course at the Collège de France:

> When one sees the meaning, or rather the near-total absence of meaning, given to all the familiar expressions, such as: come back to yourself, free yourself, be yourself, be authentic, etc. . . . one might begin to suspect the impossibility of constituting today an ethic of the self. However, it is perhaps an urgent, fundamental, and politically indispensable task, that of constituting an ethic of the self, if it is true that after all there is no other point . . . of resistance to political power than in the relation of the self to itself.[14]

The attention to, even obsession with, self-discovery, self-knowledge, and self-expression is, according to Foucault, one of the defining features of our present. Yet Foucault is skeptical about the meaning and the validity of this quest for selfhood. The modern obsession with being authentic and the modern proliferation of knowledges about the self is, in fact, a kind of prison.

What is at stake, then, is precisely the extension and intensification of power-knowledge, the problem upon which Foucault reflected, and against which he fought, with such intensity. Surprisingly, Foucault discovered, through his research in ancient philosophy, an unexpected site of resistance to power in the relationship we take up with ourselves.[15] It seems to me we can begin to understand Foucault's final project if we raise four questions with respect to the passage quoted earlier. First of all, why is there all this talk about the self and about the truth of the self? Second, why and in what way is it meaningless? Third, why is an "ethic of the self" an urgent and indispensable political task? And, finally, in what way does the final project, the study of ancient philosophical practices, offer a response to the present situation?

In order to answer these questions, I suggest that we read Foucault's work as containing two moments: a diagnostic moment and an *etho-poetic* moment. First, it is well known and I have already referred to the fact that

Foucault often characterized his intellectual work as diagnostic. I have also begun to develop the claim that he explicitly described his final project in a way that cannot be reduced to diagnosis, but is better understood as a kind of exercise, a form of care of the self. It is this philosophical *askēsis* that I am calling the etho-poetic moment of his thought. We can see the basis of such a distinction, in a provisional way, in a comment that Foucault made in 1966: "One can envision two sorts of philosophers, those who open new paths for thought, such as Heidegger, and those who in a way play the role of archaeologist, who study the space in which thought deploys itself, as well as the conditions of this thought, its mode of constitution."[16] At that point in his career Foucault was unambiguously aligning himself with the archaeologists. However, in his final project, I claim that he took up the role of etho-poetic thinker; he opened up new paths for thought. (This might suggest a different relation between Foucault and Heidegger than that which is usually seen.) In order to clarify this distinction and its significance I will begin by briefly examining what the diagnostic moment of Foucault's work is, what insight it leads to, and how this introduces us to the possibility of an etho-poetic moment.

Foucault cited three sources for his claim that modern philosophy is fundamentally a mode of diagnosing the present: Nietzsche, structuralism, and Kant. First, according to Foucault, it was Nietzsche who showed that "the philosopher is the one who diagnoses the condition [*l'état*] of thought."[17] Second, structuralism, Foucault claims, is a "philosophical activity" to the degree that "the role of the philosopher is diagnostic."[18] Foucault further links structuralism and philosophy: "One could very well speak of a sort of structuralist philosophy which would define itself as the activity that permits the diagnosis of that which is today."[19] Finally, Foucault claimed on many occasions that Kant initiated the modern critical project by giving philosophy the task of confronting its own present, its own historical reality.[20] In other words, the task of diagnosing the present originates with Kant and in the question, Who are we in our actuality? For Foucault, Nietzsche, structuralism, and Kant introduce the present moment into the heart of philosophical activity. Foucault's Nietzsche is the genealogist who sheds light on the historical emergence of the present, who reveals the *current* state of thought, not the eternal essence of reason. Structuralism makes possible an analysis of the system, in its specificity, permeating *our* culture *now*. And Kant, of course, situated philosophy itself—critical philosophy—as a response to the Age of Enlightenment. Diagnosis, in short, is an attempt to isolate that in the present moment which constitutes it in its specificity with respect to a past against which it stands out.

The first three questions posed earlier, then, are answered in Foucault's diagnosis of "who we are." (1) Our present is defined by a proliferation of discourse about individuals and about the truth of these individuals because these discourses are linked to the functioning of disciplinary power, normalization, and biopolitics. (2) Talk about the self is "meaningless" in the sense that these discourses tend to replace the political and ethical meanings of the questions, Who am I? and What is the best way to live? with disciplinary and biopolitical meanings. (3) An ethics of the self is therefore an urgent political task because the concern for the self, the formation of the self, and the truth of the self are all already permeated by relations and techniques of power—that is, the self as such is already political. The answer to the fourth question—How does care of the self respond to this situation?—is the opening of the etho-poetic moment. The etho-poetic dimension of Foucault's work was his response to the situation as it is diagnosed. But to say that Foucault's etho-poetics is a sort of response to the situation does not mean that it serves as an answer in the form of a solution. The work of thought is not to pose answers but to problematize them; it is to respond to a situation not with a solution that might end discussion or action but with a question that might open up new possibilities. Just to get our bearings and in order to provide some clarification and justification for these claims, I will present here a brief sketch of Foucault's diagnosis.

What diagnosis does Foucault give us with respect to our present relationship to ourselves? Under the influence of what is often called Cartesianism, modernity establishes the relationship between the self and itself in terms of knowledge. One becomes the object of knowledge, both of self-knowledge and of theoretical or scientific knowledge. This self-knowledge serves as the foundation of knowledge in general (for example, in the subject one will discover the conditions of possibility of theoretical knowledge) and it provides the basis of morality (in the subject one will find the conditions of possibility of moral values and laws). While it is tempting to link the modern relation of the self to itself to Descartes, Foucault complicates this picture. It is, of course, in Descartes's *Meditations* that self-knowledge takes on its modern form in the cogito, ergo sum. However, Foucault's interpretation will show that our current situation is less a matter of Descartes's *conceptualization* of the cogito than of the proliferation and elaboration of various techniques and institutions of power and knowledge which frame our concern for who we are today. Foucault diagnosed our present condition in terms of these relations of power and knowledge. His analyses of exclusions, confinements, discipline, normalization, biopolitics, and the hermeneutics of the self brought into the open the dangers inherent in our ways of being with ourselves and with others—the danger inherent in being who we are. This project displaced the liberal notion that power is essentially repressive and that the individual must be liberated from it in order to exist fully and truly. Power, according to the classic liberal view, repressed freedom, interfered with true self-knowledge. Foucault's response, his archaeologies and genealogies of relations of power and knowledge, is well known. Foucault revealed that modern individuals are the "effects" of technologies and relations of power that function by training their bodies, their thoughts, and their desires.[21] According to this schema, the self we are supposed to know and to liberate is, to a large degree, a fabrication of power and knowledge relations. These power-knowledge relations maintain themselves through leading individuals to become certain kinds of selves: normalized and well-disciplined selves. Relations of power and knowledge *subject* individuals to identities and lead them to recognize these identities as who they truly are. Therefore, the truth of the self, and the obligation to be true to oneself, cannot be accepted uncritically.

Of course, the importance of self-knowledge precedes modernity. It is the goal of the Socratic quest, the core of the examined life—it is one of the definitive themes of the history of philosophy. However, Foucault shows that the obligation to know oneself was not originally the foundation of moral or of philosophical life. Rather, the obligation to know oneself was founded upon the prior commitment to "take care of oneself."[22] The self was originally experienced through the ensemble of activities which constitute care of the self. When Foucault talked about the care of the self he insisted that care is not simply an attitude or a feeling. It is a set of practices which allow one to actively take care of oneself and others: it can involve a variety of heterogeneous techniques; for instance, meditation, dialogue, tests of endurance, vigilance over oneself, practices of writing (letters, journals, instructions to oneself), techniques of memorization, and so on. Care is a practice or an ensemble of practices, and the "self" is defined both as a material to be worked upon—that is, a concrete "ethical substance" to be cared for—and an end to be achieved, that is, a precisely defined *telos*.[23] In other words, the truth of the self, and the self as a subject capable of knowing the truth and living the true life, are attained not first and foremost through self-*discovery* but rather through the *poetics* of the self. The word "poetics," as I am using it, refers to the ancient Greek concept of *poiesis:* productive work, deliberate fabrication in which the subject employs *technē*, "craft" or "art," in order to achieve a determinate outcome. The self, in the context of care of the self, is not the object of knowledge, but rather is the work of art; it is poetic. It is this notion of *poiesis* that I have in mind when I call Foucault's work etho-poetic. It is poetic in the sense that it is a mode of fabrication; it is *etho*-poetic insofar as it is an art of *self*-fashioning (of fashioning or developing an *ēthos*—loosely speaking, a character or self, and more specifically a center of action, an orientation in the world).

In general, our present begins to take shape when the practice of, and knowledge about, the true life and the truth of the individual come to be appropriated by new institutions serving the mass formation of individuals. This process of appropriation and transformation is guided by and legitimated by a determinate teleology or strategy linked to a scientific discourse about individuals. Foucault diagnosed this situation in terms of disciplinary power, normalization, and biopolitics. On the one hand, establishing disciplinary institutions to train and shape individuals presupposes some knowledge—that is, various technologies of individuation. On the other hand, it makes possible the formation of human sciences which in turn refine and perfect the disciplines that had first made them possible. Here I will just point out what I take to be some important insights Foucault offers concerning the dangers inherent in these processes and knowledges—I will expand on these notions in the chapters that follow.

One danger inherent in our actuality is that discipline, normalization, and biopolitics have a built-in tendency to increase and spread. In other words, whatever goal discipline serves, it also brings along its internal strategy to spread and reinforce itself. Discipline structures every situation, every problem, as an occasion for more discipline. A well disciplined individual is one who has incorporated not only the specific capacities he was trained in, but has incorporated discipline as such—arts of compartmentalizing space and time in terms of economy, function, and productivity. Discipline fashions subjects of discipline—arrangers, economizers, analyzers, observers, examiners; it produces subjects who want and need discipline. The "ideal" end point of discipline would be the pathological extreme of absolute order, fascism. Normalization also becomes more and more pervasive and demanding. By defining the normal and abnormal, by proliferating discourses about them in order to judge and correct individuals, the pressure to be alert to the abnormal in ourselves and others, to correct it even before it arises, grows and becomes more integrated into our conscience and our practices. The normal individual is the goal of discipline. The abnormal, on the other hand, comes to play a powerful role in our self-understanding and self-fashioning. To be abnormal is intrinsically bad, and it is dangerous because abnormality is the basis of evil, it is a threat that needs to be contained or eliminated.

Foucault also showed that modern political rationality is biopolitical. Rather than operating according to the rationality of sovereignty in which power is represented in the image of the sword—the power to form a law and to enforce it, the right to kill those who transgress—biopower is represented in the image of a healthy population. Politics aims at the management of a population—it is the power to foster life. Biopolitics sustains the development of institutions which structure our lives and the world according to the ends of biological life—that is, toward economy in the Greek sense of the word *oeconomia,* the management of necessary, organic functions, needs, and pleasures. Life is defined in economic and biological terms rather than in ethical and political terms. All other projects are submitted to the ultimate goal of continuing and perfecting life in the biopolitical sense of the term, and the means of doing this become more and more technologically sophisticated. In the pursuit of a secure, healthy, and productive population, biopolitics deploys disciplinary, normalizing institutions. Biopolitical survival and normalization come to be mutually reinforcing.

In other words, these techniques for the mass production of individuality do not simply free us and allow us to realize our truth: they free us to be true only by fabricating a certain truth and arranging the spatial-temporal world to direct individuals toward that truth. Therefore, the modern practice of individuation is already political and the individual, as it is lived and understood, is a political construction. In other words, through our personal project of freeing ourselves from the burden of political obligations and constraints, as well as from ethical/moral constraints or laws, we are realizing the basic project of modern biopolitics. A completely biopolitical interpretation of life is a political project. In this way, discipline, biopolitics, and normalization paradoxically institute a powerful self-neglect, a pervasive thoughtlessness about the fundamental political and ethical question—How will I live?—precisely by saturating space and time, our bodies and desires, with techniques, discourses, and relationships which have the goal of taking care of us and making us happy. Our present is constituted in large part by the production of a massive discourse about the self, which however has been drained of real ethical and political significance. Therefore, there is an urgent need to create an ethics of the self.

If this is the diagnosis—that the formation of the self has been almost completely absorbed within the biopolitical project and its disciplinary techniques—then care of the self offers a possible counterpractice in the form of alternative techniques of self-fashioning. In other words, to borrow an expression from Andrew Cutrofello, it develops "disciplines of resistance."[24] As care of the self, Foucault's thinking is a practice of *conversion* to the self, a conversion of power, and a form of *salvation* in the sense that conversion frees other possibilities of fashioning our ethical subjectivity. These two terms—conversion and salvation—play a central role in Foucault's 1982 course at the Collège de France and in his understanding of philosophical practice in ancient Greece and Rome. As with the term *askēsis,* Foucault points to a pre-Christian, nonreligious, experience of conversion and salvation in Greek and Roman philosophy. Care of the self is the activity of a philosophical conversion: it resists the forms of power which structure our way of perceiving space and time, our bodies and minds. In particular, the last phase of Foucault's thought opens up the possibility of an ethics of the self in terms of care of the self, an ethic that represents a new way of practicing philosophy. The basic insight is that philosophical texts themselves can be appropriated as techniques, practical manuals, models, theories of care of the self—the activity of reading and thinking about these as such is already a practice of care, a conversion of regard toward oneself. It is not a turn inward but rather a turn toward the world as that evolving web of relations, practices, and knowledges in and through which my self manifests itself. It is also a turn toward the self as a material to be shaped and transformed, as a goal to be achieved, and as a practice articulated in the theories, models, guides, techniques, and relationships that the history of philosophy presents to us. And, most important, the conversion to the self is linked to a concern for the truth, for truthfulness; it is linked to *parrhēsia*.

The notion of *parrhēsia*, "frankness" or "free speech," is central to Foucault's understanding of the care of the self as an etho-poetic resistance to the proliferation of power-knowledge relations. Foucault examines two different forms of *parrhēsia* that map onto the two different moments of his thought. There is political *parrhēsia*—the courageous act of truth-telling, of speaking out, of resisting power with the truth. Such a discourse is a diagnosis of the present in terms of power and knowledge. But there is another form of *parrhēsia* that interested Foucault: ethical or philosophical *parrhēsia*. This practice of true, frank discourse does not take place in the political realm. Ethical/philosophical *parrhēsia* is a form of discourse that takes place in the context of care of the self. Ethical *parrhēsia* is poetic in the sense that its purpose is to transform individuals—both those who speak it and those who listen to it. But the notion of *parrhēsia*, especially in its philosophical form, challenges us to rethink the concept of truth.

Methods and Problems

While Foucault's last published works began to articulate this project, it is only in his lectures at the Collège de France that one is able to gain an understanding of the full scope of his research, because these lectures are a kind of archive of that research. One finds in his courses at the Collège de France, from 1982 to 1984, a rich array of studies, themes, insights, and suggestions about the history of the relationship between the subject and the truth. In the first lecture of his 1982 course, he goes so far as to say that his study of the ancient moral problematization of sexual morality was only one example of a much broader and richer problematization: that of care of the self and *parrhēsia*.[25] This claim reflects the fact that an understanding of the later Foucault based only on his books from the period is quite limited.[26] There are many promising lines of development to be found in Foucault's last research, but he was never able to follow these threads because of his premature death. For this reason, the overall project remains fragmented and it is impossible to know in what direction it might have led. This book attempts to develop some of the paths of thought that Foucault's final lectures open. Therefore, the present study does not attempt to be a comprehensive account of everything Foucault takes up in his final lectures. Rather, it is an interpretation of them around certain themes that seem to me most illuminating.

I take as my point of departure a number of comments Foucault made in his lectures at the Collège de France concerning the history of philosophy. First, in 1982 Foucault showed that the history of philosophy has produced two general forms of the relationship between the subject and the truth: the first is what he calls "spirituality," the second is "knowledge" (*connaissance*). Originally, according to Foucault, philosophy was structured by spirituality—the subject's access to the truth was grounded upon *askēsis*. Truth required self-transformation. In modern philosophy, the subject has access to the truth in the form of knowledge, rather than *askēsis*. Access to the truth is secured by method and by evidence. Thus, Foucault claims that one can see in the history of philosophy a process by which the relationship between the subject and the truth is despiritualized.[27] Philosophy moves from the spirituality model to the knowledge model of the relationship between subject and truth. The following chapters trace the process that led from one experience to the other and link it to other processes that Foucault identified in his earlier work, in particular the formation of discipline, normalization, and biopolitics. What I show is that the despiritualization of philosophy was linked to the rise of modern forms of power and knowledge—not that these processes were explainable in terms of each other, but that they functioned contemporaneously and often in harmony.

Second, this book takes up a set of suggestions Foucault made during his 1983 and 1984 courses at the Collège. In these courses Foucault put forward three claims which seem to me inseparable and extremely promising. First of all, in 1983 he claimed that the history of philosophy should be understood as a history of freedom, a history of different forms of freedom. By "freedom" he did not mean free will or right, but rather the capacity to invent new modes of living, new forms of subjectivity.[28] The history of philosophy would be, then, a history of the different forms of the *bios philosophicos* as it has been invented and practiced in Western culture. Second, he understood this philosophical inventiveness in terms of the fabrication of links between the subject and the truth; these inventions linked freedom to the subject's capacity and obligation to speak the truth—it is this link between the speaking subject and the truth that he or she speaks that Foucault analyzes in the Greek problematization of free speech, *parrhēsia*. In other words, the history of philosophy could be read as a history of various attempts to construct a mode of subjectivity capable of *parrhēsia*. Finally, Foucault asserted in 1983 and 1984 that this theme of *parrhēsia* becomes linked to the care of the self in the figure of Socrates. Foucault focused on this point for two reasons. First, he was astonished by the process that led Socrates to connect *parrhēsia* and care of the self. Socrates, in an act of political and ethical resistance, invented a new mode of subjectivity by linking *parrhēsia*—until then a form of political truth—to care of the self. Second, the consequence of this shift was essential to the history of Western subjectivity. This integration of *parrhēsia* and care of the self gave rise to a form of discourse about the truth of the self which was simultaneously an exercise in the formation of the subject. In other words, governing oneself and being governed by others became connected to speaking the truth about oneself, speaking it to oneself as well as to others. In sum, the history of philosophical *parrhēsia* could be read as a history of the ways in which philosophers have used the truth, true discourse, and frank, free speech in order to fashion political and ethical subjects capable of self-government and, consequently, of governing others.

The aim of this book, on the basis of these themes, is to present Foucault's unwritten genealogy of philosophy. However, to do so requires dealing with a tension in Foucault's thought. The genealogical approach, Foucault's historicism in general (whether genealogical, archaeological, or problematizing), can be understood in two different ways that are difficult, perhaps impossible, to reconcile with each other. The first way is to see Foucault as writing histories that conform to the criteria and rigors of historical science. Thus, Foucault's history of philosophy would present us with a linear narrative about what happened, as it happened, leading from the past up to the present. According to this approach, Foucault's work strives for and achieves, or at least ought to achieve, objective historical truth. To read Foucault's project in this way is to see it as a form of knowledge. But, it is also possible, and perhaps necessary, to understand Foucault's historicism as a creative work, that is, as an etho-poetic work. In this case the goal of the work is not finally to achieve objective historical truth and thereby produce knowledge. The ultimate purpose is to transform the subject engaged in historical or philosophical thinking. The production of knowledge, to the extent that it takes place in this project, is not therefore an end in itself, but is ultimately guided by a more fundamental purpose.

But then this seems to suggest that Foucault's work lacks truth. If it is not a form of knowledge, then it does not possess truth. Part of Foucault's final project was to problematize our very conception of philosophical truth. As I have indicated above, this project excavates a model of the subject-truth relation that is not reducible to the form of knowledge. My argument in this book is that by designating his philosophical activity as *askēsis,* and as care of the self, Foucault is demanding that we grasp it in those terms. Truth, in care of the self, is not experienced objectively in the form of knowledge.

Why is it preferable to read Foucault's project in this way? First of all, reading Foucault's work as a form of historical science leads to a number of different problems. Second, Foucault explicitly requests that we avoid doing so in a number of places. In fact, his insistence that the truth of his project is not objective or scientific begins well before his studies in ancient Greek philosophy. This suggests that the final project, rather than being an unexpected reversal of, or departure from, earlier work, is better understood as the explication of a problem that was already present though unthematized.

The present study takes the form of a narrative history of philosophy in order to follow a path leading from historical knowledge to ascetic transformation. The methodology is to organize what I take to be the essential claims from Foucault's unpublished lectures on philosophy, bringing them together with his earlier interpretations of Descartes and Kant to show that in his work there is a singular vision of a linear history of philosophy—from a beginning in the past to an end in the present. The purpose of this study is to follow Foucault's suggestions and to trace a succession of forms of philosophical practices beginning with Socrates and Plato, passing through the Hellenistic and Roman thinkers of the first and second centuries A.D., and culminating with Descartes and Kant. In this linear history one would see not only different forms of philosophical activity, but also the series of transformations, ruptures, developments, sedimentations, and innovations which slowly over the course of time forged our present.

I show how the later work of Foucault resituates philosophical practice within a context defined by relations of power, knowledge, and subjectivity and how that move resituates his own earlier work as well. Philosophy arises, according to Foucault, as a resistance to confining, dangerous, stagnating relations of power and knowledge. The history of philosophy in this way appears as a history of problematizations of the interpenetration of power, knowledge, and subjectivity. This history also shows that philosophical problematization is a mode of resistance to power-knowledge that takes the form of new practices of subjectivity: care of the self (*epimēleia heautou*) and ethical truth-telling (*parrhēsia*). These practices attempt to cut through the web of power and knowledge in order to forge a new bond between the subject and truth. However, according to Foucault, practices that arise as resistance in one situation can freeze, so to speak, into a new form of confinement. When these practices become detached from their agonistic source in a problematization; they no longer offer access to truth but rather function as forms of control posing as ahistorical essences or natures.

Therefore, this book offers a historical narrative. The first two chapters deal with Foucault's reading of Socrates and Plato; chapter 3 looks at his interpretation of Hellenistic and Roman philosophy; and chapter 4 takes up his discussion of the Cynics and the early Christians. These four chapters together form part 1 of the book and refer primarily to Foucault's unpublished lectures from 1982 to 1984. Part 2 is composed of chapters 5 to 7, which take up his reading of Descartes, and chapter 8, which discusses Kant. This second part of the book is essentially a rereading of certain texts from Foucault's work in the 1960s and 1970s, in particular (but not exclusively) *History of Madness, The Order of Things, Discipline and Punish,* and volume 1 of *The History of Sexuality.*

There are a number of problems inherent in this approach to Foucault's work. First of all, the chronology of this history of philosophy begins in ancient Athens in the fifth century B.C. and then moves forward. That is, it follows a linear development from past to present, beginning to end. However, Foucault's own intellectual chronology moves in the opposite direction (or even forms a sort of zigzag ramble through historical periods). His first works were his archaeologies of the classical age and modernity. (Foucault characteristically speaks of *l'âge classique.* This period, identified in the title of *Histoire de la folie à l'âge classique,* begins in 1656 and closes with the French Revolution in 1789. It should not be confused with the ancient Greek, Hellenistic, or Roman periods.) In his major works of the 1960s and 1970s Foucault looked at the period stretching from the sixteenth to the nineteenth centuries. In his lecture courses at the Collège de France during the 1970s he focused his attention on this same period, with constant reference to the contemporary forms of power and knowledge expressed in psychiatry, criminology, and juridical and political discourse. Then—just paying attention to the periodizations he demarcated and studied and without making reference to the themes of those studies—we can see that a shift takes place in his lectures of 1980 to 1982. He turned away from modernity and moved backward to the first and second centuries A.D. Finally, in 1983–84 he pushed even further into antiquity, to the fifth century B.C., to Socrates and Plato. This means that the book begins with the very end of Foucault's career—his final courses at the Collège de France in 1983 and 1984. The first chapters of my book, and of this history, represent the final chapters of Foucault's life and work. Conversely, the end of the book returns to the beginning and middle of Foucault's intellectual trajectory. Therefore, in a sense, the book might just as easily, and perhaps with better justification, have been arranged differently so that what is now part 2 would be part 1 and what is now part 1 would be part 2.

Yet simply reversing the order of the chapters would not solve the problem. To see why, it will suffice to schematically survey the internal transformations that mark Foucault's fields of inquiry and questioning. When Foucault first confronted the work of Descartes and Kant, the context was a set of questions that had to do with epistemic structures and relations of power. He had not yet isolated practices of subjectivity as an irreducible domain of inquiry. On the other hand, when he took up ancient philosophy it was first of all in the context of a limited theme—the moral problematization of pleasure in the ancient world and its singularity with respect to that of various Christian ethical practices. This study quickly led into a more general interrogation of ancient practices of subjectivity— but here we are a long way from modern epistemic formations and disciplinary relations of power. In my presentation of Foucault's readings of Descartes and Kant, I import a conceptual framework (care of the self, *parrhēsia,* governmentality) from his final period into his earlier period. On the other hand, where I take up Foucault's reading of ancient philosophy, I import concepts and interpretive tools Foucault used to investigate modern relations of power and knowledge. One would be quite justified in questioning the application of these tools to historical periods and philosophical texts they were not invented to investigate. In other words, there is a certain circularity—at best perhaps a hermeneutic circle, at worst a confused, anachronistic, and ultimately vicious circle—involved in this reading.

But the problem with this approach is not limited to the way it treats the development and meaning of Foucault's work. The readings of the history of philosophy and of major thinkers and texts in the history that Foucault's project generates are quite idiosyncratic. For example, Foucault's excavation of ancient philosophy never deals with Plato's "theory" of the forms. What's more, there is almost complete silence with respect to Aristotle. In the writing of a history of Western philosophy, especially ancient Greek philosophy, omissions such as these are hard to justify.

To begin to resolve these problems, we must listen to what Foucault has to say about the status of his historical research. And we must attempt to hear these comments in light of the developments that we see in his final project. In 1980 Foucault makes the following claim:

> I am not merely a historian. I am not a novelist. What I do is a kind of historical fiction. In a sense I know very well that what I say is not true. A historian could say of what I've said, "That's not true." . . . What I am trying to do is provoke an interference between our reality and the knowledge of our past history. If I succeed, this will have real effects in our present history. My hope is that my books become true after they have been written—not before . . . I hope that the truth of my books is in the future.[29]

According to this, Foucault's historicism, including his history of philosophy, does not aim at correspondence with a past—with that which is no longer—but rather attempts to bring into existence a new reality. In this sense, the essential reference points for Foucault are those ways in which the past interferes with the present and in so doing is able to provoke a new possibility. There is indeed a kind of circularity at work in this form of historical fiction. But it is neither a vicious circle nor a hermeneutic circle. It is what I would like to call a *genealogical circle*. The past is read, and appropriated, through the lens of a present problematic. This genealogical approach therefore does not strive for "objectivity" but rather critical effectiveness. The past that interests Foucault is the past insofar as it is alive in the present, insofar as it inhabits our actuality. In this way our present problematic is both what shapes our study of the past and is that which arises out of the past it problematizes. But historical fiction is not ultimately an attempt to explain how we got to where we are. Instead, the real purpose of this form of work is to destabilize that in our present which confines us. Foucault's reading of Plato, Seneca, Marcus Aurelius, and so on is guided by an effort to challenge the present and to produce new possibilities. In other words, the task is to free possible futures. His history is essentially futural—it seeks out potentialities and possibilities. To read philosophy in this way, to practice this form of reading and writing, is to unlock a vast deposit of philosophical potentials from confinement within a particular disciplinary practice. At the same time, it is to loosen the disciplinary grasp on our philosophical practices of reading, writing, thinking, speaking, and teaching. The point is not to eliminate theoretical, academic philosophy and its various modes of reading and writing, far from it. It is rather to begin to write what John McCumber calls the "disciplinary history" of philosophy.[30] Such a history does not seek to destroy the discipline it studies, but to allow it to see itself from a different angle and to release neglected or unconsidered potentials, to produce new disciplines. This is how I understand the following remarks by Foucault:

> It is true that the first text one writes is neither written for others, nor for who one is: one writes to become someone other than who one is. Finally there is an attempt at modifying one's way of being through the act of writing . . . Therefore, I believe that it is better to try to understand that someone who is a writer is not simply doing his work in his books, in what he publishes, but that his major work is, in the end, himself in the process of writing his books. The private life of an individual, his sexual preferences, and his work are interrelated not because his work translates his sexual life, but because the work includes the whole life as well as the text. The work is more than the work: the subject who is writing is part of the work.[31]

Foucault shows us that our very subjectivity, the truth of ourselves, is to some degree produced through techniques and relations of power. And he shows that these relations tend to capture our freedom and *freeze* it into certain forms. If he is right about this, then perhaps the history of philosophy, as "a whole rich and complex field of historicity in the way the individual is summoned to recognize himself as an ethical subject," offers us concrete alternatives to this situation.[32] Perhaps the history of philosophy contains other possible modes of self-knowledge and self-fashioning, and therefore "thaws" those forms in which we tend to confine ourselves. This practice of philosophy is not something in the past but a potential, something in a possible future. For this reason, Foucault invites us to read and write philosophy not as a process of accumulating knowledge but as part of a process of becoming subjects.

Chapter Survey

As stated previously, this book consists of two parts. In part 1 (chapters 1 to 4), I present and develop Foucault's reading of ancient philosophy as it appears in his lectures at the Collège de France from 1982 to 1984. I explicate and develop Foucault's archaeology and genealogy of "care of the self" (*epimēleia heautou*) and ethical "truth-telling" (*parrhēsia*) as these appear in ancient thought. In addition, I show how he was led from the study of disciplinary power to sexuality and the hermeneutics of desire, and finally to ancient philosophy as care of the self. This reveals the way his problematization of modern humanism in terms of relations of government and modes of veridiction shapes his approach to the ancients. That is, his problematic is the lens through which ancient philosophy comes into focus as care of the self and ethical *parrhēsia*. However, by bringing into focus the concept of *parrhēsia* in ancient philosophy, Foucault opens himself up to a transformation which he did not expect: the conception of care of the self as a work of self-transformation which could be deployed in resistance to disciplinary technologies of the self. Chapter 1 examines the problematization of democracy in Athens. The critique of democracy revolves around the problem of discourse, the problem of *parrhēsia*, "free speech." Democratic politics was dominated by flattery and rhetoric rather than by a concern for the truth or the good. Foucault shows that for Socrates and Plato the crisis of political life and language arises because the Athenians do not elaborate and practice a "care of the self." In chapter 2, I develop Foucault's interpretation of four Platonic texts: the *Seventh Letter,* the *Apology, Alcibiades,* and *Laches.* Foucault shows that Socratic-Platonic thought is a response to the crisis of democratic life and language. The way that Socrates and Plato respond to the problem is to invent practices of care of the self. These texts reveal that philosophy was not primarily a matter of knowledge but rather of self-fashioning— the goal was not so much to know the truth as to become the truth. In chapter 3, I move to Foucault's study of care of the self in Hellenistic and Roman philosophy. This reveals the fecundity of care of the self as a means of proliferating forms of subjectivity and bears witness to modes of self-care that are not dominated by modern relations of power and knowledge. However, it also becomes clear that practices which in one context resist the totalizing tendencies of power can in another context themselves become totalizing and confining. This is evident in Foucault's interpretation of the formation of the Christian pastorate. I examine this process in chapter 4. Here I examine the Cynic practice of *parrhēsia* and care of the self and how this practice opens a rift in the ancient experience of philosophy. The radical *parrhēsia* of the Cynics generates a harsh critique from more restrained philosophical schools. This rift is carried over into the Christian world. Christian ethics arise as modes of care of the self and ethical *parrhēsia* that resist prevailing power relations. But the practices of care developed in early Christianity rigidify into a new system of power relations—what Foucault calls *pastoral power.*

Having shown in part 1 that Foucault's later work arises in the context of his earlier work, in part 2 (chapters 5 to 8) I show how his earlier work can be reread in terms of the later work. That is, Foucault's earlier project takes on a new meaning in light of his later discoveries. The rise of modern relations of power and knowledge, which Foucault analyzed in the *History of Madness, The Order of Things, Discipline and Punish,* and so on, is reconceived as a response to the problem of care of the self, of self-government. This becomes clear when we read Foucault's interpretations of Descartes and Kant in light of the problematic of care of the self and *parrhēsia*. The purpose of chapters 5 to 7 is to situate Descartes's *Meditations* within the problematization of *parrhēsia*. Descartes's work is shown to be a form of resistance to the spread of pastoral power. Descartes resists this development by inventing a new practice of subjectivity. The *Meditations* are therefore not simply an argument but an exercise, a practice of self-transformation. In fact, Foucault makes this claim as early as 1972 in his famous reply to Derrida. However, it is the legacy of the Cartesian cogito that modern philosophy will come to be seen primarily as a form of knowledge rather than as a practice of self-fashioning. Chapter 5 presents a reading of the First Meditation showing that it functions as a spiritual exercise. Chapter 6 shows that Descartes's project was part of the general problematic of governmentality that arose in Europe in the classical age as a response to the spread of pastoral power. Finally, chapter 7 argues that Descartes's project is to develop a new practice of subjectivity and a new form of discourse, that is, a new philosophical *parrhēsiast*. In chapter 8 I turn to Foucault's encounter with Kant. Foucault's engagement with the thought of Kant is essential to his own self-fashioning as a critical philosopher. While Kant offers resources for defining and practicing an ethic of critique, he is not able to understand the ways his thought is confined within its historical horizon—the rise of disciplinary power and the Cartesian displacement of care of the self. Foucault is able to overcome Kant's ahistorical thinking through his experience of Nietzsche. The historical sense, which Nietzsche lends to Foucault, is precisely what allowed Foucault to experience the subject and truth as historical forms rather than as the ahistorical conditions of possibility of experience. In other words, it is his Nietzscheanism which allows Foucault to perceive in history the formation of the modern relation of subjectivity and truth, and eventually to question this relation in terms of care of the self as resistance and self-fashioning.

FOUCAULT'S *ASKĒSIS*

Part 1

Philosophy as Care of the Self

In the following chapters I will take a close look at Foucault's interpretation of Socrates, Plato, and the tradition of philosophical practice they inaugurated. This interpretation is articulated in a number of different ways, across several different projects by Foucault. In the final two volumes of *The History of Sexuality* (1984), Foucault reads Socrates and Plato, and more broadly ancient Greek, Hellenistic, and Roman philosophy, in terms of the moral problematization of pleasure.[1] However, in his lectures at the Collège de France from 1982 to 1984, Foucault finds himself concerned with ancient philosophy, as such, independently of the question of sexual ethics. What accounts for this shift? To answer this question we will have to see clearly how Foucault was initially led to the study of these texts, how his problematization of modern power and knowledge structured his reading of them, and how this very problematization allowed for the discovery in those texts of something quite unexpected which forced Foucault to rethink his project.

Despite the shift in Foucault's approach and despite the divergent themes he explored, there is a consistency and coherence to his understanding of ancient philosophy. Ultimately, for Foucault, ancient philosophy can be comprehended, if not completely, then at least in several of its fundamental characteristics, as a vast project of inventing, defining, elaborating, and *practicing* a complex "care of the self" (*epimēleia heautou*). The philosophical project of care of the self was a response to a concrete problem, the crisis of Athenian democracy.[2] The problem was the inability of democracy to practice an effective political discourse. That is to say, though democratic politics is fundamentally a discursive activity, the Athenian assembly could not practice a political discourse which articulated the *truth*—in this case "truth" refers to what is good for the city as a whole.[3] Instead of gathering and unifying the citizens in pursuit of the common good, politics was a contest of individual interests. Each individual used his freedom of speech—his *parrhēsia*—to advance his own good rather than that of the city. Socrates and Plato were not the only ones to experience democracy as being in a state of crisis. However, as Foucault points out, their perception of the problem was more radical and consequently their solution more revolutionary. For Socrates and Plato, the crisis of democratic *parrhēsia* was fundamentally rooted not in politics but in an inadequate experience of the subject who is called to *parrhēsia*. Their solution was to offer a new experience of this subject, an experience available to those able and willing to apply to themselves, to their lives, an ensemble of ascetic practices which were for Socrates and Plato the essence of philosophy. The historical-philosophical consequence of the Socratic-Platonic project is to have isolated and defined a peculiar dimension of reality, that which we might call, with caution, the *self:* a region of being which becomes intelligible for ancient philosophy in the two forms of soul (*psychē*) and of existence (*bios*). This reality was delineated as a field of truth, one in which truth is to be sought and discovered, and into which truth is to be implanted and cultivated. Philosophy appeared both as a search for self-knowledge and as an ensemble of techniques for producing one's life as a work of art, as the actualization of the truth which one has learned.

1

Truth as a Problem

Tradition assures us that in the West it was the Greeks who first made truth into a problem. Foucault's interpretation of philosophy in ancient Greece—as well as in the Hellenistic and Roman worlds—shows that the problematization of truth resulted in making a problem of the being who speaks the truth. Before turning to Foucault's treatment of Socratic-Platonic philosophy, we shall linger for a while in the historical setting of their thought and bring it into finer resolution by following Foucault's *archaeology* of the crisis of Athenian democracy and his *genealogy* of the practices, both political and ethical, which give rise to it and which are transformed through it.[1] What we shall see there is the horizon within which this philosophy unfolds, a horizon Foucault articulated in terms of a particular experience of politics (power), of truth (knowledge, discourse), and of subjectivity (ethics). In his 1981 and 1982 lecture courses at the Collège de France, Foucault interrogated ancient philosophy, exploring the concept of "care of the self," the mutations it went through, the practices it gathered together, the forms of knowledge it elaborated, and the experience of truth which permeated it—an experience Foucault called "spirituality."[2] In 1983 and 1984 Foucault drew his insights together by showing how "care of the self" is reelaborated by Plato as a response to the crisis of democracy. In other words, in order to resolve the problem of democratic *parrhēsia* Plato turns away from the political toward the ethical, embracing truth as spirituality and conceiving of a new possibility of the self which is intended to be adequate to political life.[3]

Truth and Language

At the core of Foucault's excavation of Socratic-Platonic thought is the problematization of *parrhēsia*. In the following, I will outline Foucault's analysis of the word's "original" meaning, that is, the sense of the word that Foucault reconstructs archaeologically and genealogically. Saying that Foucault gives us the original meaning of the word, then, does not mean to say that *parrhēsia* should be thought of as having a universal or univocal usage. Furthermore, Foucault's aim is to reveal the transformations in the *practices* and *institutions* to which the term refers. Therefore, the following serves as a starting point for Foucault, and essentially a *tactical* one. In other words, the way that Foucault conceives of the "original" meaning of *parrhēsia* must be understood within the problematization that guides his approach to Socrates and Plato. This is not to say that Foucault's definition of *parrhēsia* and his genealogy of its mutations are reducible to a fabrication he imposes on the texts. The sense of the word, both as a tactical point of attack and as part of his study of a historically real experience, imposes itself on him in and through his reading of it, just as much as his reading of it structures the way the word appears for him. In order to make this dynamic style of thinking clear, I will not limit myself to an explication of Foucault's lectures on *parrhēsia* in ancient Greece, but I will supplement this with an analysis that situates them within his own problematization. And I will show how Foucault's problematization is transformed as a result of his experience of ancient philosophy. This will bring into focus the complex relationship between reader and text, between "subject" and "object," which is not only an aspect of Foucault's style of reading but, as I hope to show, is essential to his understanding of what it means to practice philosophy as care of the self.

First of all, what is *parrhēsia*? Foucault refers to the etymology of the word, "to say everything."[4] He tells us that *parrhēsia* is usually rendered as "frankness," "free speech," or "license." The word is used in both a negative and a positive sense. In its negative aspect "saying everything" is a lack of restraint, as in the case of someone who cannot hold his tongue. Even worse, in its negative register, it can take on the dubious connotation of "saying whatever it takes." In other words, *parrhēsia* can mean to say "whatever is able to serve the passion or interest which motivates the one who speaks."[5] In the first, rather benignly negative aspect, one says whatever one feels like saying with no sense of shame or limit. In the second and more sinister form of negative *parrhēsia,* one says whatever one thinks will serve oneself well.

Opposed to this negative sense there is a positive aspect of *parrhēsia,* to "speak the truth." To say everything has the sense of not holding anything back through fear or humiliation, not hiding anything through the use of style, rhetoric, or dissimulation.[6] In its positive register, *parrhēsia* means "to say everything guided by the truth."[7] It means to say the whole truth and nothing but the truth. *Parrhēsia* is therefore "frankness." One freely, courageously, or impetuously speaks one's mind.

Furthermore, positive *parrhēsia* entails commitment. The *parrhēsiast* not only says the whole truth, but says the truth to which she is committed. In the act of speaking the truth the *parrhēsiast* concretizes her commitment to that truth. She gives her opinion in such a way that the fact that it is *her* opinion is clear. In other words, "the *parrhēsiast* in a way attaches his signature to the truth that he speaks, he binds himself to it."[8] The truth spoken in *parrhēsia* is one to which she is personally committed and with which she identifies herself. In frankness, one exposes oneself or reveals one's *self*. Insofar as one takes a *position* in the world with respect to a problem, one *posits* one's self.

In *parrhēsia,* furthermore, one speaks one's mind in a situation where the stakes are high. This is because one speaks a truth to someone who does not want to hear that truth—one's opinion is critical or offensive. The listener is in a position to retaliate if he is inclined to do so. The speaker, therefore, leaves himself open to the reaction of the listener. Speaking one's mind and giving one's opinion, when doing so runs a risk for the speaker, is constitutive of *parrhēsia.* "It is, therefore, truth in the risk of violence."[9] In forming a bond between oneself and the truth which one says, one introduces a distance between oneself and the listener. In a fundamental sense, *parrhēsia* stretches the relation between the speaker and listener to its limits. Because of this fact *parrhēsia* requires courage: the courage to speak the truth. The speaker must have the courage to accept the consequences of speaking and the listener must have the courage to hear the truth, which is painful. *Parrhēsia* risks, at the very least, unraveling the relationship between speaker and listener, which is the condition of possibility of speaking. But the risk can be much higher. In fact, the *parrhēsiast* may be called to risk her own life in her act of speech. She runs the risks involved because the truth to which she is committed *must* be spoken. *Parrhēsia,* then, is a duty which one is perfectly free to avoid, and which consequently requires courage to act upon.

Finally, *parrhēsia* often involves a kind of contract between the speaker and the listener which is intended to lessen the risk. The listener agrees to hear the words of the *parrhēsiast* despite the fact that they may anger him. Foucault calls this the *parrhēsiastic* game or the *parrhēsiastic* pact.[10]

Foucault captures the notion of *parrhēsia,* rich and complex as it is, in the expression, "le courage de la vérité."[11] It is the courage of the speaker to risk his life and the courage of the listener to hear the truth he does not like:

> In *parrhēsia,* the speaker uses his freedom and chooses frankness instead
> of persuasion, truth instead of falsehood or silence, the risk of death
> instead of life and security, criticism instead of flattery, and moral duty
> instead of self-interest and moral apathy.[12]

Foucault also draws out the uniqueness of *parrhēsia* by way of contrast. For example, *parrhēsia* is not rhetoric. In fact, the two are diametrically opposed.[13] Rhetoric is a technique of speaking which allows one to persuade others to believe in statements that may or may not be true, that the speaker herself may or may not believe. Therefore, while *parrhēsia* requires commitment on the part of the speaker, rhetoric implies no identification of the speaker with what is said. On the contrary, the rhetorician strives to bind the listener to what is said, "strives to establish a constraining bond, a bond of force [*un lien de pouvoir*] between what is said and the one who is addressed."[14] In other words, there is a *difference* between the speaker and what is said, but an *identity* between the listener and what is said. This identity is the desired effect of rhetoric because through this identity the listener is placed under the power of the speaker. In *parrhēsia,* on the other hand, there is an identity between the one who speaks and what is said. Precisely because of this, the particular opinion, the particular content, that the *parrhēsiast* speaks reveals a difference and the "possibility of a rupture" in the relationship between the speaker and listener, through the "sting of the truth" spoken.[15] In doing so it makes the speaker and the listener appear in their differentiation by throwing them back upon themselves.

Furthermore, rhetoric is essentially a *technē*, a savoir faire. It is what Foucault called a technology of governmentality—and often it is employed as a technology of domination. It is a systematic, deliberate technique for "conducting" individuals. Rhetorical discourse unfolds in a relationship of power.[16] *Parrhēsia*, on the other hand, is not a *technē*, it is not a craft; "it is an attitude, it is a manner of being, which is allied to virtue."[17] Rhetoric is an art one learns and uses as one wishes. *Parrhēsia* is *a way of being* in which one speaks one's mind. Rather than being a *technē*, such as rhetoric, indifferent to the truth of what is said or the commitment of the speaker, *parrhēsia* is essentially a "modality of *veridiction*."[18] *Parrhēsia* has to do with who one is.

What is a "modality of veridiction"? Foucault's introduction of this notion in his 1984 Collège de France course represents a crucial methodological advance. In his earlier studies of discourse and of statements (*énoncés*), Foucault was concerned with the systems that established certain kinds of discourses as serious, as being either true or false, while other discourses lacked meaning (the possibility of truth or falsehood) altogether. However, in his final courses, analysis takes place at the level of the relationship between discourse and the being of the subject speaking. A modality of veridiction, according to Foucault, is "in its proper conditions and forms, the type of act by which the subject speaking the truth, manifests itself . . . represents itself to itself and is recognized by others, as saying the truth."[19] It is a concrete practice according to which the subject is defined and through which she becomes actual. The subject exists for herself and for others, recognizes herself and is recognized by others, in the modality of veridiction. It is by way of the act—"in its proper conditions and forms"—that the subject appears and is able to appear. This does not entail that where the act does not take place there is no subject, but rather in that case the subject appears precisely in her failure to act. In other words, the modality of veridiction is not founded upon a subject. Rather, the modality of veridiction precedes and structures the subject. A modality of veridiction, then, is the ensemble of "conditions and forms" which articulate the acts through which subjects exist as possible "acts of truth." For Foucault the subject is not the foundation for or the condition of possibility of experience or truth; rather, as is clear here, subjects manifest themselves in certain theaters of action, which call for actors. A subject appears for herself when she is *called* to act and insofar as she can *posit* herself by taking a *position* within, and with respect to, the theater of action. The call issues from a dramatic scene—a possibility for meaningful action. In his 1983 course at the Collège, Foucault names this field of analysis the "dramatics of truth [*discours-vrai*]."[20] One's relation to oneself is organized by the dramatic scene, which calls for action. It is in terms of this drama that one is conscious of oneself as a subject, recognizing the possibility of freely acting or of failing to act for one reason or another. A modality of veridiction articulates that scene, the conditions and forms of possible action.

There are a number of constitutive moments of a modality of veridiction: the act of speaking which has its own forms and which entails a particular experience of language, of discourse; the mode of subjectivity which is capable of using language in the necessary way in order to articulate truth; and the domain or region of truth which is articulated in the act of speaking. Finally, a modality of veridiction also, at least in the case of *parrhēsia,* requires a time and place, in other words, a dramatic scene, where truth can emerge, where subjects can be recognized in the act of truth. In order to illustrate what he means by this, and to bring out the nature of *parrhēsia* by way of contrast, Foucault sketches, briefly and schematically, what he calls four "fundamental modalities of speaking the truth."[21] The four modalities of veridiction he names are prophecy, wisdom, technology, and *parrhēsia.* Each of these modes of speaking has its corresponding figure of subjectivity: the prophet, the sage, the teacher-technician, and the *parrhēsiast.* And each has a domain of truth it speaks: destiny, being, *technē,* and *ēthos.*[22]

The prophet is the speaker of truth as destiny. In other words, in order to "tell the future" one must be a prophet, one must become a prophet. Or rather, speaking the truth about the future requires the constitution of a particular kind of speaking subject. In order to speak destiny the prophet must constitute his subjectivity in the form of "mediation."[23] That is, the prophet does not speak in his own voice but is the voice of the beyond, the voice of the gods. The experience of words and language in prophecy is characterized by obscurity. The prophet's words reveal the future to human beings, but his words simultaneously hide their own true meanings. Prophecy speaks truth enigmatically and leaves the listener with the work of interpretation. *Wisdom,* on the other hand, speaks the domain of being. The sage speaks "what is," the nature (*physis*) of the cosmos and of all things in it. The sage speaks in her own name and speaks the wisdom that belongs to her, which is her own possession. Therefore the sage is not a medium as the prophet is. The sage constitutes her subjectivity through a withdrawal from the everyday world and is characterized by reticence. For this reason the sage does not feel an obligation to speak her wisdom, but chooses instead to remain silent and to live apart from the others. When petitioned the sage will speak, but like the prophet, will speak enigmatically.[24] The teacher-technician speaks the truth as *technē.* Technology is an ensemble of learned knowledges and acquired skills—it requires that one constitute one's subjectivity through the work of apprenticeship, that one become a speaker of technical truth by inserting oneself into the tradition, by having a master who passes knowledge and skill along to oneself. The teacher has an obligation to speak the truth she knows in order to maintain the tradition to which she belongs.[25] Finally, the *parrhēsiast* is the one who speaks the truth as *ēthos* and speaks in her own name. The *parrhēsiast* has an obligation to use language to articulate the truth she knows, and the language she uses is defined by its clarity and its directness. In speaking truth as *ēthos* the *parrhēsiast* says not what will be, not what is, and not the tradition, but reveals to the listener "who he is." That is, the *parrhēsiast* reveals to the listener the listener's own truth, the listener's *ēthos,* by speaking in such a way that the listener is thrown back upon himself.[26] In other words, the *parrhēsiast* does not tell the other who he is objectively. Rather, the manner of speaking in *parrhēsia* provokes the listener, brings the listener into a new relationship with himself. And unlike the prophet who leaves the others with the task of interpretation, the *parrhēsiast,* whose meaning is all too clear, leaves the others with the difficult task of accepting the truth.

The problem which Foucault takes up in 1983 and 1984 is the elucidation of precisely how *parrhēsia* constitutes a mode of subjectivity, a language, a place and a time, in and through which the truth can emerge. How does one appear for oneself and for others as a subject who speaks the truth as *ēthos?* Through the crisis of political discourse in Athens the question becomes, Who is able to use *parrhēsia* to speak the truth? Foucault shows that through the problematization of *parrhēsia* a new mode of speaking, a new manifestation of subjectivity, and consequently, a new *objectification* of the subject in discourse will result. That is, through the problem around the practice of *parrhēsia*, and the form of subjectivity it implies, the subject will appear as an object of thought. What one must keep in mind, however, is that the fundamental level is that of *being-in-the-world* and *doing*, that of the dramatic scene in which a subject appears for itself and others; the level of theoretical objectification of the subject is derivative and determined by those practices. In other words, what is objectified for knowledge is only one possibility of subjectivity: a historically real modality of veridiction. However, once this mode of subject has been constituted as an object of knowledge, it is then taken as the source of, and foundation for, the modality of veridiction. This, according to Foucault, is a mistake: modalities of veridiction cannot be traced back to or deduced from some essential subject. Rather, the subject, as it is grasped in theoretical knowledge, is a correlate to the modalities of veridiction through which it is able to appear. By defining this domain of inquiry—the modality of veridiction—Foucault is able to approach the question of subjectivity in a unique way. Rather than attempting to theorize the subject as the foundation of practices and discourses, he remains on the level of how subjects appear to themselves *as* subjects of possible actions, and he analyzes theories about human essence or subjectivity in terms of their grounding in historically real modalities of veridiction. In this way, Foucault is able to show that theoretical elaborations of the subject take as their point of departure (and point of return) concrete practices and that they are shaped by those starting points in important ways. The subject appears for itself and for others in the act of *parrhēsia* not as an object of true discourse but as a concrete way of producing the truth, as a concrete way of experiencing the truth. It is in the dramatic scene of veridiction that subjects discover and fashion themselves.

Foucault's Discovery of *Parrhēsia*

At the beginning of the previous section, I suggested that Foucault's elucidation of the "original" meaning of *parrhēsia* is to be taken in some sense as a tactical point of attack. In other words, it is to some extent what Foucault often referred to in his work as *fiction*.[27] This is not to say, however, that it is not "true" and that it has nothing to do with the actual, factual experience of the word or of the activity, virtue, technique, to which it referred. The fictional or tactical quality of Foucault's excavation has to do with his *object* of study—not historical facts, but rather the systems of thought which give historical facts their significance—and it has to do with Foucault's *objective* or aim. Therefore, in order to understand why Foucault organizes his archaeology and genealogy of ancient thought around the problem of *parrhēsia,* we must see how he was led to this project by way of his earlier work. While it is true that the status of his earlier work must be rethought in light of his last project, it is also the case that this last project is significantly shaped by his earlier work.

In his analyses of relations of power and knowledge, Foucault was searching for ways of isolating those dimensions of ourselves, our activities and our discourse, which serve as loci of power—both as effects of power and relays of power. In *Discipline and Punish* he traced the development of disciplinary power. Discipline is a mode of power which controls individuals by forming them through concrete techniques and in specific settings. This mode of power functions not so much by *repressing* individuals as by *producing* and defining them. In the first volume of *The History of Sexuality,* Foucault continues this analysis by showing that modern political power is what he calls "biopower."[28] This means that its mode of operation and its legitimacy derive from its capacity to nurture populations—to cultivate bodies and capacities, to provide them with comfort, fulfillment, pleasure, and happiness. Of course, Foucault thinks that it does this by forging individualities whose bodies, capacities, pleasures, comforts, and desires are intrinsically integrated into the productive force of institutions and networks of power-knowledge relations. One of the main sets of techniques which brings about this integration functions by inciting individuals to talk about their desire, to identify with it, to think of themselves as subjects of desire. These techniques for reflecting on oneself, for taking up a relationship to oneself, and for acquiring and expressing self-knowledge are "hermeneutical" in nature. They are ways of uncovering, in the multitude of acts, feelings, thoughts, and fantasies, the hidden truth of the individual lodged in the form of desire.

We can see in this last point that Foucault's analysis does not presuppose a passive individual entirely subjected to external measures of repressive control. Rather, Foucault conceives of subjects who participate, to a greater or lesser degree, in the processes of their own subjection (again, understood not as repression but as production).[29] Through these hermeneutic practices, and within special relationships—such as that of doctor-patient, counselor-patient, teacher-student, analyst-analysand, and so on—individuals fashion their subjectivity around the discovery, expression, liberation, and fulfillment of a truth hidden within.[30] Foucault here begins a genealogy which attempts to fix the historical horizon for this experience of subjectivity. The hermeneutical subject of desire, he learns, emerges within the confessional practices and spiritual exercises of Christian ethics.[31] What is more important is that this genealogy of the subject revealed to Foucault that prior to the formation of Christian practices, there existed a whole range of possible experiences of ethical subjectivity—relations and practices which are not hermeneutical at all—to be found in ancient texts. To put it another way, Foucault's genealogy sought to historicize our particular formulation of the imperative "know yourself" as a hermeneutics of desire. His original interest in ancient thought was that he found there a different organization of ethical subjectivity and a different formulation of self-knowledge. In the following chapters, I will explicate Foucault's archaeology and genealogy of an experience which is *aesthetic* and *etho-poetic* rather than hermeneutical. What we shall see is that the imperative to self-knowledge was not the foundation of philosophical or ethical life. It was instead one element of a broader and more fundamental task, "care of the self" (*epimēleia heautou*). It is in the context of this genealogy that Foucault discovers in Hellenistic and Roman philosophy relations of spiritual direction and self-disclosure that are different from Christian practices. And it is here that Foucault first finds the term *parrhēsia*.[32] *Parrhēsia* in this context refers to the virtue, the technique, and the attitude of the philosopher who acts as a spiritual director to his disciple. The true *parrhēsiast* is able to use true, frank discourse in order to convert the disciple to the moral life. Spiritual direction in Hellenistic and Roman philosophy, and even for early Christian ascetics, is not essentially hermeneutical.[33] However, these relationships of speaking the truth in order to fashion ethical subjectivity represent a "prehistory" of the Christian and modern practices of self-disclosure.[34]

This discovery in itself was compelling for Foucault. In disclosing relationships of spiritual direction—of governmentality—which employed techniques of poetic or productive truth-telling, Foucault was able to displace the hermeneutics of desire and the experience of ourselves as subjects of desire. Truth was spoken as a goal to be attained and as a technique for attaining that goal rather than as a pregiven nature, a static essence. Given this, Foucault began to explore the development of ethical *parrhēsia* in order to loosen the grip of hermeneutics on the subject. However, in this study of *parrhēsia* as spiritual direction and element of care of the self, Foucault made an "unexpected" discovery.[35] *Parrhēsia* was originally not a matter of *spiritual* direction or of *ethical* discourse, but rather a form of *political* discourse. In the following section, I will develop Foucault's study of the word's political roots and its role in the problem of democracy in ancient Athens. Through the problematization of democracy, *parrhēsia* will be displaced from the political to the ethical dimension. In other words, *parrhēsia* arises as a practice of governing others in a political scene and shifts to a practice of spiritual direction necessary for the proper (ethical/moral) government of oneself. The significance that Foucault gives to this movement must not be overlooked:

> With the notion of *parrhēsia,* originally rooted in political practice, and you'll recall, in the problematization of democracy, then turned toward the sphere of personal ethics and of the constitution of the moral subject, I believe that with this notion of *parrhēsia* one has the possibility—and it is for this reason that I am interested in it and which caused me to pause over it . . .—of posing the question of the subject and the truth from the point of view of the practice of what one could call the government of the self and of others . . . It seems to me that by examining more closely the notion of *parrhēsia* one can see knotting themselves together the analyses of modes of veridiction, studies of techniques of governmentality and the outline of forms, of practices of the self.[36]

Foucault organizes his genealogy and archaeology of ancient thought around the problematization of *parrhēsia* because he sees in this experience a way of isolating the dynamic interplay between relations of power, discursive or epistemic forms, and practices of ethical subjectivization. In the displacement of *parrhēsia* from politics to ethics, what is revealed is how one fashions a mode of subjectivity in order to have access to true discourse to be spoken in the game of power relations. The three axes of experience Foucault formulated and studied across the whole trajectory of his career come together in the problematization of *parrhēsia.* Furthermore, and more important still, is that the discovery of this convergence of power-knowledge-subjectivity allows Foucault to conceive of an alternative model of political ethics, or of an ethics of resistance to the proliferation of power. Foucault sees in this convergence a "resistance to political power . . . in the relation of the self to itself."[37] If it is true, as Foucault suggests, that modern disciplinary power, normalization, and biopower function by producing individualities, then the practices of the self would represent an experience of ethical life which resists those forces.

> If one takes the most general question of governmentality—governmentality understood as a field of strategic relations of power, in the largest sense of the term and not simply its political sense—. . . in the sense of relations that are mobile, transformable, reversible, I believe that reflection on this notion of governmentality cannot avoid operating, theoretically and practically, with the notion of a subject who would be defined by the rapport of the self to itself. While the theory of political power as institution ordinarily refers to a juridical conception of the subject of rights, it seems to me that the analysis of governmentality . . . must refer

to an ethic of the subject defined by the rapport of the self to itself . . .
Relations of power—governmentality of self and of others—rapport of
self to self, all this constitutes a chain, a thread, and it is there, around
these notions, that one must be able, I think, to articulate the question
of politics and the question of ethics.[38]

This passage sheds light on the status of Foucault's investigation into
ancient thought. He conceptualizes ancient philosophy in terms of practices of ethical subjectivization developed in order to respond to the intensification of relations of power and knowledge. It is this thread con-
necting power-governmentality-subjectivity which Foucault tries to follow
in his archaeology and genealogy of *parrhēsia*. This line of research is inti-
mately connected to his earlier studies of relations of power and knowledge and would be unthinkable without them. That is, we ought to read
Foucault's last project as an outgrowth of his problematization of modern
relations of power and knowledge in terms of discipline and biopower.

Truth and Power: The Problematization of *Parrhēsia*

Now that we have in mind the basic sense of the word *parrhēsia,* we are
prepared to follow Foucault's excavation of the historical site where it
originally resided. The first appearances of the word are in the work of Euripides.[39] The context in which the word appears is political. *Parrhēsia* was
a political right and activity, both a privilege and a duty of the Athenian
citizen: speaking one's mind, speaking the truth to which one is committed, in the assembly in order to guide the city. However, this right, this activity, which had long defined the free political life of Athens, had become
the source of a growing anxiety. The right to speak and to engage in the
rule of the city was, through the democratic reforms of the sixth and fifth
centuries, being extended to include not simply the aristocratic classes
but all citizens.[40] The extension of the right of *parrhēsia* to the lower classes
was perceived by the aristocrats as a breakdown in the traditional moral
and political values which provided the foundation for Athenian power
and wealth. Once *parrhēsia* was removed from the exclusive possession of
the aristocrats, they came to perceive it with suspicion. This anxiety toward *parrhēsia*, toward democratic political discourse, led to a singular experience of the difficult interrelatedness of freedom, power, and truth.
Foucault calls this kind of experience, this anxiety, a "problematization."[41]
A problematization, to put it simply, is the process by which an as-

pect of reality, of one's world, one's experience, is brought into focus as a problem in need of a response. Through a problematization "people begin to take care of something ... they become anxious about this or that."[42] This *caring-about-something* is a way of disclosing the world in light of a problem and is therefore a response to that problem. Foucault's shift from the analysis of *dispositifs* of power-knowledge to that of problematizations represents, along with the introduction of the notion of modalities of veridiction, an important methodological advance. His earlier work is not left behind, but rather displaced and complemented by this new focus. This new point of attack allows Foucault to isolate more carefully the activity of "thought."[43]

> Thought is not what inhabits a certain conduct and gives it meaning; rather, it is what allows one to step back from this way of acting and reacting, to present it to oneself as an object of thought and to question it as to its meaning, its conditions and its goals. Thought is freedom in relation to what one does, the motion by which one detaches oneself from it, establishes it as an object and reflects on it as a problem.[44]

Thought problematizes. The analysis of a problematization is therefore the analysis of historical events through which the ordinary and familiar surrounding world, practices, and relationships lose their familiarity.[45] To excavate, archaeologically, problematizations, and to trace, genealogically, their origins and effects is to do "the work of a history of thought."[46]

> This development of a given into a question, this transformation of a group of obstacles and difficulties into problems to which diverse solutions will attempt to produce a response, this is what constitutes the point of problematization and the specific work of thought.[47]

Thought does not respond to, or problematize, its world merely through a "representation" of it, that is, a theory or description of the world. Rather, thought "develops the conditions in which possible responses can be given; it defines the elements that will constitute what the different solutions attempt to respond to."[48] It does this by inventing the world anew—creating new kinds of relationships, new practices, assigning new meanings to old practices and relations. Thought reimagines the purposes and possibilities the world offers. It is a response, but not a solution. Rather, thinking is the activity that opens up a problem and prepares the conditions for many possible solutions to it. Thought, as the work of problematizing, is what opens up the dimension of the possible.

However, this dimension of the possible is not an experience of absolute freedom; thought does not make just anything possible. A problematization is precise, it responds to a concrete situation, and the possibilities it establishes are sensitive to that situation and what it demands.

In *The Use of Pleasure,* Foucault writes that problematizations are openings "through which being offers itself to be, necessarily thought."[49] Furthermore, these openings are opened up through and onto practices—ways of being-in-the-world—and these latter are transformed through their being problematized. New practices arise out of the problematization of old ones. That is, they arise out of resistance to practices and relations which appear as problems. In the analysis of problematizations, archaeology and genealogy come to play new methodological roles. The work of archaeology is to examine the "forms" of the problematizations. The work of genealogy is to show both the practices out of which problematizations arise and the transformation of those practices that the problematization brings about.[50] This new approach reveals that *dispositifs* of power and knowledge—sets of relations, practices, technologies, and strategies—arise at least in part out of problematizations, as solutions to problems. But once these solutions are detached from their source in a problematization they become frozen into rigid forms, they become the very structure of the ordinary, the familiar, the given—they become the basis for future problematization.

Given Foucault's framework, we can see that this process of sedimentation or ossification—this freezing process—poses a certain threat. First of all—and this point will be developed as we proceed—because practices, ways of being, are historical, arising out of concrete problematizations and responding to precise situations, they are not universal, natural, necessary, or inevitable. These practices and relations, these ways of being, as historical artifacts, are not intrinsic to individuals but are adopted by or imposed upon them. Given the specificity of practices and the multiplicity of individuals, there will always be the need for new ways of being that can respond to new situations. And since these ways of being are to a greater or lesser extent impositions—individuals are posited as subjects through the imposition of practices and relations upon them— there is, as we shall see, a built-in resistance to them. That is, the individual is that which comes forward in opposition to this imposition. This is not to say that individuals precede power. Rather, the individual is first posited in her individuality through the process of subjection to and by relations of power and knowledge. The individual is a relation of opposition. Individuality is the oppositional site where the process of power unfolds. The incorporation of particular modes of power and knowledge as individuals is therefore an intrinsically agonistic process. Consequently, the process of individuation—or subjection—is immediately lived by the individual as an imposition, and every such process is a site of resistance. It is the intrinsically oppositional or agonistic nature of individuation that allows any particular set of rigid practices or relations to give rise to new problems and become the objects of new problematizations, new acts of thought. The danger for Foucault—and this will also be developed as we proceed—is that along with the potential for resistance and creativity, re-lations of power have a built-in tendency to proliferate and intensify them-selves. To the extent that a relation of power, a practice of some kind or another, is not necessary and inevitable, it is fragile, vulnerable, poten-tially reversible—a relation of power and its techniques is, in light of its perpetual reversibility, always a strategy for conquest. Therefore, power does not tend to remain static—it tends to reinforce itself, tighten its grip, extend its control. Relations of power have, then, a built-in strategic ele-ment that aims at complete control.

Let's return to the historical situation in which *parrhēsia* became a problem. The word *parrhēsia* appears in Greek literature because it was a source of anxiety, because Euripides was preoccupied with this political activity which until then was "familiar and 'silent,' out of discussion."[51] In Euripides we see the first outlines of the problematization of *parrhēsia*. This, of course, is not to say that the anxiety regarding political discourse only begins with Euripides. Rather, the appearance of the word *parrhēsia* in his work coincides with and refers to a phenomenon that called for thought. In his lectures of 1983 in Paris and in California, Foucault offers interpretations of several tragedies where Euripides employs the term. However, I will focus on two in particular which serve to bring the prob-lematization into focus: *Ion* and *Orestes*. It is within the space of this prob-lematization that the thought of Socrates and Plato will come to pass. Fou-cault's analysis of this problematization, and the Socratic-Platonic place within it, will show how "philosophy was able to constitute itself, at least in certain of its fundamental traits, as a practice of true discourse—as one form of the practices of true discourse."[52]

Ion and Pericles: Problematization as Recuperation

Foucault calls Euripides' *Ion* the "tragedy du dire vrai,"[53] or "the decisive Greek *parrhēsiastic* play."[54] There are a number of reasons for this claim, but essentially Foucault means that in it we can see the dramatic enact-ment of "the movement of truth-telling from Delphi to Athens."[55] Apart from the historical and political implications of the rise of Athenian power, this drama is an event in the history of thought. By displacing Delphi, Athens displaced not merely the place of truth, but also the modality of veridiction which defined that place. At Delphi truth was culled from the reticent god and expressed in the enigmatic stammering of the oracle. At Athens truth is disclosed through the act of *parrhēsia,* a thoroughly human act of self-revelation which is clear and direct in its form. Euripides' tragedy is, therefore, a *parrhēsiastic* play because it valorizes political *parrhēsia* by dramatizing its mythic origins.

But what is this act of *parrhēsia* which displaces the oracular utterance as the modality of veridiction? In order to answer this question Foucault explicates a crucial scene in the unfolding of the tragedy. The characters in this scene are Xuthus, king of Athens, and Ion who lives in Delphi and is the son of, and a priest of, Apollo. Just before these characters meet, the oracle tells Xuthus that the next person he sees will be his own son. Of course, this is at best only partially true: Ion is the son of Xuthus's wife, Creusa, who was raped and impregnated by Apollo. In the scene we are concerned with, Xuthus, believing that he is the father of Ion, tries to persuade Ion to return to his true home, Athens. Among other things, he promises Ion that in Athens, as son of the king, he, Ion, will himself wield the power of a king.[56] Ion is unwilling to go to Athens under these conditions. Why? Because as the son of Xuthus he is the son of an outsider (Xuthus was not born in Athens). Furthermore, Xuthus believes that Ion is an illegitimate child because to his knowledge Creusa did not bear him. (Xuthus has convinced himself that Ion is the son of a slave girl.) Therefore Ion will arrive in Athens "suffering from two disadvantages": he is both illegitimate and a foreigner.[57] Because of these two disadvantages life in Athens will be impossible for Ion. On the one hand, if he engages in the public life of the city, he will be antagonized by the other citizens. Ion explains this by describing political life as a kind of struggle, an opposition of individuals who define their political identities according to the power they wield. In this struggle Ion, as an outsider and bastard, will be powerless. If, on the other hand, he decides not to enter into the political life of the city he "shall be spoken of as a nobody."[58] Concerning Xuthus's offer of kingly power, Ion has no interest. He states that "supreme rule . . . is falsely praised, it has a fair appearance but is painful within."[59] Ion does not desire absolute power; he wishes to be able to engage in democracy, he wants to take his "place in the first ranks of the city."[60] Ion experiences his freedom not in the exercise of absolute power but in the free political life of a democracy where he can strive to be among the "first ranks," those who share the power, guiding the city not through violence but through discourse. It is for this reason that he "prays" that his "mother is of Athenian stock so that . . . [he] . . . can enjoy freedom of speech . . . [*parrhēsia*]."[61] If Ion is not the child of an Athenian woman he will have "the voice of a slave and . . . [will] . . . not have freedom of speech [*parrhēsia*]."[62] Being a stranger and illegitimate, Ion can be a "citizen in theory" but he will not be able to exercise his freedom in the political field, which is the region where freedom takes on a concrete form and meaning. In order to be somebody, to be a free individual, rather than a nobody and a slave, Ion must be able to participate in the *parrhēsiastic* game.

Foucault's point is that the term *parrhēsia* refers less to a legal recognition of citizenship and the rights which that entails than to the "political game," the actual political life of the city.[63] It is in the activity of *parrhēsia,* which takes place in the political field, that Ion defines his freedom and his identity. The struggle for power in the democratic assembly is the activity of *parrhēsia;* it is through this act and in this place that one discovers and accomplishes one's freedom and duty. But unless Ion bears a certain identity, a certain status, the others will not listen to him, his "theoretical" status as a citizen will effectively mean nothing. The others will not listen, they will not possess a "will to listen" to an outsider and especially one whose birth is dishonorable. The political assembly, as the place of *parrhēsia,* is constituted by this "ethical differentiation" through which one perceives those who are able to speak, and through which one perceives oneself as a subject who is able to speak.[64] Therefore, Ion must discover who he is, he must attain knowledge of himself, his true identity, in order to be able to accomplish himself in the political field.

Foucault found the same problematization of democratic *parrhēsia* at work in Thucydides' famous portrait of Pericles.[65] Thucydides shows us the way Pericles and the assembly around him enacted the scene indicated by *Ion.* Though Thucydides does not employ the term *parrhēsia* to characterize Pericles' mode of discourse, Foucault takes his text as the construction of an ideal *parrhēsiastic* scene, the very scene Ion wished to enter. Foucault calls this scene the Periclesian moment.[66] According to Foucault, the Periclesian moment was not a period of time in history dominated by Pericles and the ideals he embodied and then recounted by Thucydides. Rather, it is an event of thought that takes place in the work of Thucydides and forms an element of the problematization of Athenian political discourse. Insofar as it is an event of thought, the Periclesian moment is an attempt to articulate and transform the structures and meanings that inhabit, propel, and define the practices and projects through which individual and collective existence unfolds.

In the Periclesian moment the Athenians assembled to speak their minds and struggle to lead the city, to see their opinion win over the others and become the one adopted by the city itself. The assembly was, in this sense, an *agon,* a contest for power. Despite this agonistic setting, the citizens were also brought together by their inclination to hear the truth; that is, to hear, accept, and do what is best for the city.[67] In other words, the assembly constitutes itself on the basis of an ethical differentiation.[68] As we have just seen, an ethical differentiation is a relationship to oneself and to others in terms of the characteristics—the *ēthos*—that single out the truth-teller as someone who must speak and must be heard. Because politics is a struggle for power, it must be tempered by a will to listen to words freely spoken and accept a truth that may be difficult to embrace; the ethical differentiation is therefore a *will to truth*. It creates an opening or an area for the emergence of the truth.

In this assembly, the *parrhēsiastic* words of Pericles emerge from the *agon* and unify the citizens around his opinion concerning what is true and right for the city. Foucault shows that the ground of Pericles' *parrhēsia* is an ethical differentiation. This ethical differentiation permits Pericles to step forward as a truth-teller and inclines the others to hear his words. Thucydides portrays Pericles in terms of the characteristics that allow him to appear to himself and others as a *parrhēsiast*. These characteristics have to do with his ethical identity. Pericles is a well-born Athenian citizen. He is courageous. He speaks his mind. His opinion does not fluctuate with trends but remains steadily focused on the good of the city. He uses powerful and persuasive language that is nonetheless direct and frank. These qualities single Pericles out as a *parrhēsiast*—someone who speaks the truth to the assembly. Because they recognize Pericles' ethical character, the assembly is inclined toward his opinion. When Pericles speaks the citizens are ready to listen. The ethical differentiation does not, however, eliminate the risks involved in speaking the truth. Rather, the consciousness of his difference incites Pericles to accept the risk—it is part of his difference from the others to accept the risk; this reflects the courage that defines his ethical identity. Therefore, when Pericles speaks in the first person the assembly is ready to be persuaded.

As long as democracy allows the best opinion to come forward and guide the city, it functions well. It does this through the courage of the best to freely say what they believe, and the courage of the others to let themselves be guided by that opinion. Furthermore, this becomes possible because of the modality of veridiction—the ethical differentiation—that constitutes the assembly and lets truth speak. Because the city needs *parrhēsia,* because it needs this activity of saying the truth, this activity of saying the truth grounds itself in an ethical differentiation. The citizens constitute their subjectivity as speakers and hearers of truth in the light of this place and this practice of *parrhēsia.*

According to Foucault, this was how Thucydides represented the ideal functioning of democratic *parrhēsia.* We must keep in mind that Foucault is showing us the way an experience of political discourse and power is being forged through the activity of thought. Much more than a historical account of Pericles, Thucydides puts forward a critique of, and a model for, political life. He is trying to respond to the problem of political discourse in Athenian democracy as this problem appears to him. It is to this same problem that Euripides responds in *Ion*. Before returning to Euripides, I will just indicate, in addition, the double game at play in Foucault's text. On the one hand, Foucault is showing precisely how relations of power and knowledge produce the possibility of resistance, of freedom, of self-invention. The Periclesian truth-teller is a construction that emerges from the play of power, subjectivity, and knowledge; it is a modulation of the relations between these three axes of experience. On the other hand, it is always within the precise problematization of modern power and knowledge relations that Foucault's text operates. In other words, just as Thucydides is re-creating the Athenian experience of politics—what it is and what it is for—and in so doing re-creating the experience of ethical and political subjectivity, Foucault is re-creating his own experience of ethical and political subjectivity in response to a modern problematic of power and knowledge. As we shall see, Foucault is problematizing the manner in which our subjectivity as truth-speakers is constituted within the framework of discipline and biopolitics. Foucault's analysis of Thucydides, and even more so his interpretation of the Platonic critique of democracy, show us a political ethic which is not reducible to the biopolitical project. The presentation of an ethics of democracy—as it appears not only in Euripides and Thucydides but also in Plato—allows us to reflect upon our own definition of democratic ethics. The problematization of *parrhēsia* poses a political ethic in which subjectivity is constituted as the courage to speak the truth and requires the ethical differentiation of political subjects in terms of this courageous truth-telling. I do not mean to suggest here that Foucault is proposing a political ethic modeled on Euripides and Thucydides. Rather, I suggest that his archaeology of this political ethic is constructed within a certain political situation and serves to bring that situation into focus. Creating an opportunity to reflect on our own situation from the "outside"—the problematization of *parrhēsia*—is the first step in creating possible responses to that situation.

Let's return to Euripides and summarize the problematization of *parrhēsia* as it appears so far. Euripides problematizes *parrhēsia*, responding to the growing disillusionment with the practice of Athenian democracy and the deterioration of its political life. The problematization arises in the absence of a Pericles, when Athens lacks a voice of truth, and when the assembly is open to all speakers, regardless of their ethical identity. There is no clear recognition in the assembly of what sets someone apart as *parrhēsiast;* there is no clear self-perception through which someone can recognize himself as *parrhēsiast.* It is this situation to which Euripides responds. How does Euripides characterize *parrhēsia,* and how does he attempt to ground it in an ethical differentiation (a relationship to oneself and others in terms of power and knowledge)? In essence, the question amounts to asking: how does Euripides invent, or reinvent, the *parrhēsiastic* subject and *parrhēsia* as a modality of speaking the truth? These are the questions Foucault brings to the texts of Euripides.

As Foucault has shown us, in *Ion* Euripides represents *parrhēsia* as an activity which the Greeks valued so much that to be without it meant to have the status of a slave.[69] Political life was the occasion for the citizen to speak his mind in the contest for power. For this reason *parrhēsia* was one manifestation of the freedom and the power of the free citizen.[70] In political *parrhēsia* the individual accomplished his subjectivity, *his freedom,* in the act of political discourse, and in the act of governing. *Who one is* was decided in the contest of political power. Here there is no question about the intrinsic value of *parrhēsia;* it is an activity in which the individual experiences himself as a subject/agent. However, because this activity is no longer limited to the aristocracy (those who are by blood linked to the good of the city), Euripides is confronted with a question: How can this activity introduce truth into the city? The way the question is formulated in the thought of Euripides is: *Who* should use *parrhēsia,* who is able to use *parrhēsia* in the assembly? To whom should the assembly listen, and who should come forward to speak? Whose voice is grounded in truth? The question of truth leads to the question of the subject who speaks, the "I" which manifests itself in a discourse with the form, "I believe . . ." or "I think . . ." Euripides handles the problem by suggesting that only certain people should have access to this activity because only certain people have the ethical quality which grounds their words in the truth and allows them to say what is truly good for the city. In *Ion* the possession of this right is secured primarily by genealogy; one must be a native of the city. As the tragedy unfolds, we see that Ion is anxious to learn the truth of his birth so that he can have an identity in Athens. Without *parrhēsia,* Ion believes he would be "a nobody."[71] In other words, his sense of self is organized around the activity of *parrhēsia;* it is through this activity that one accomplishes one's self. Moreover, to have access to this activity, one must have a good name in the city—not only must one be a native citizen, but one's family name must be honorable, as must one's own reputation.[72] Euripides suggests in these criteria a renewed ground for *parrhēsia,* a renewed mode of mutual recognition, and a renewal of the subject as a speaker of truth. Euripides' solution to the problem of *parrhēsia* is to present a form of self-perception in which *parrhēsia* is constituted as the right, duty, privilege, and characteristic virtue possessed by the best and most honorable of the citizens; it is their right and their privilege to enter into the political life of the city. This task defines the ethical subjectivity of these individuals. The others must listen to them and accept the words they speak. By grounding *parrhēsia* in an ethical differentiation, Euripides attempts to reintroduce truth into the city. He is teaching the polis how to recognize truth in the person who speaks the truth. The problematization of *parrhēsia* as it appears in Euripides and Thucydides, among others, is not the "representation" of a reality, or of a historical fact. The practice of democracy as it is depicted in Thucydides or valorized by *Ion* is a reinvention of democracy and *parrhēsia*. These texts problematize democracy by giving it a meaning, a purpose, a form it may never have had: the expression of truth in the form of *parrhēsia*.

Orestes and Plato's Democracy: Problematization as Repudiation

In Euripides' *Ion* and in Thucydides' portrait of Pericles Foucault finds two problematizations in which democratic *parrhēsia* is valorized. This attention to the practice of *parrhēsia* emerges out of the building anxiety over the functioning, or malfunctioning, of Athenian political life. The growth of democracy opens the struggle for power to everyone (relatively speaking) and is perceived as the erosion of the ethical differentiation which makes the assembly into a place of truth. The problematization, which reveals itself to us in *Ion* or in the figure of Pericles, takes the form of a recuperation of *parrhēsia* and a renewal of the ethical differentiation within the democratic assembly. However, Foucault's analysis shows that other more pessimistic views concerning democracy express themselves as the problematization deepens. An experience emerges in which *parrhēsia* itself comes to be seen in a negative light. *Parrhēsia* will no longer be immediately recognized as the manifestation of an individual's freedom and courage to speak the truth.

In Euripides' *Orestes*, Foucault sees an expression of this intensified form of problematization.[73] He refers to a passage where the term *parrhēsia* is used to describe a mode of discourse that is negative in every way.[74] Foucault's analysis of this passage brings into focus, on the one hand, the elements which characterize the mode of being of negative *parrhēsia*, and, on the other hand, the way in which someone who speaks this language constitutes his subjectivity. The first characteristic of the "negative" *parrhēsiast* who appears in *Orestes* is his lack of restraint.[75] He is unable to master himself, to know what to say and what not to say, to recognize the moment which calls for speech, or that which calls for silence.[76] This individual is not able to let his words be guided by truth, therefore his speech is characterized by its inappropriateness, its falsehood, its excessiveness. Second, this individual is arrogant. Because he lacks an ethical relationship to truth, the speaker relies on his own arrogance to give him the audacity to pronounce his opinion before the assembly.[77] Third, he is an outsider, not a true Athenian. Fourth, he relies not on the reasonableness of what he says but on "his ability to generate an emotional reaction from his audience by his strong and loud voice."[78] That is, he cannot clearly articulate the truth or the opinion which he himself believes to be true. He manipulates emotions instead of inspiring clear-sighted judgments. A fifth characteristic of the negative *parrhēsiast* and his language is the lack of *mathēsis*.[79] The individual cannot articulate truth because he has never received any kind of instruction (*mathēsis*). In this qualification Euripides shows an important, and perhaps newly emphasized, aspect of the *parrhēsiast:* wisdom which is gained from a professional teacher. "In order for *parrhēsia* to have positive political effects, it must now be linked to a good education, to intellectual and moral formation."[80] The reference to education reflects the growing importance of the power of language, the diminished importance of noble blood, and the influence of the Sophists. Finally, the speaker does not speak his own mind, but rather speaks for someone else. He says not what he believes, or what he knows, but what others want to hear. Thus *parrhēsia* in this case is not "frankness" but rather flattery. Flattery will come to be perceived as a primary danger of free political discourse. In Euripides' *Orestes* we see a thoroughly negative perception of *parrhēsia*. It is not portrayed as the act through which an individual freely and courageously confronts the assembly with the truth; rather it is flattery, excess, manipulation, and deceit.

In *Orestes* Euripides shows us an assembly which does not constitute itself through an ethical differentiation. If political discourse were grounded in such a form of self-perception, then the individual described above would never have taken the floor. He would have given himself over to a will to listen to the truth. Instead, lacking a consciousness of ethical differentiation, he acts on a will to flatter others in order to take *care of himself.* He says what those in power like to hear so that they will take care of him. Negative *parrhēsia* is the effect of the erosion of the ethical differentiation. It is a lack of restraint and a form of flattery. It is in opposition to this practice of democracy (which itself is as much a projection of the aristocratic class as it is a reality) that alternatives will appear and will allow for the invention of something like the Periclesian subject as the *ideal* structure of democracy and its accomplishment in *parrhēsia*. However, the *practice* of democracy and democratic *parrhēsia* are not experienced as a structure of differentiation but as a structure of "nondifferentiation."[81] The consciousness of difference which constituted the mutual recognition of the assembly is replaced by a new consciousness of self, a new mode of subjectivity which is associated not with the ethical character definitive of nobility, but with a lack of ethical character and an undisciplined devotion to one's private interests. While the first form of problematization represents an attempt to re-create democratic politics by giving it a new meaning, this second form results in a critique of democracy as such.[82]

Democracy and *parrhēsia* come to be seen as incompatible in two ways. First, *parrhēsia* comes to be seen as dangerous for the city.[83] This is because in post-Pericles Athens, democratic *parrhēsia* as a right and a duty tends toward flattery and manipulation.[84] Because of this, the assembly can no longer function as the place of truth, the place where the good of the city is spoken. Instead it is the place where each one struggles against the others to make the city itself the place where his personal interests are satisfied. Second, democratic *parrhēsia* also comes to be seen as dangerous for the individual. The act of saying the truth, what is best for the city, becomes dangerous to the one who speaks. The assembly will not listen to critique. It is only interested in being flattered, in being told what it wants to hear. What Foucault traces is an internal rift in the experience of *parrhēsia:* the "bad" *parrhésia* in which one flatters the assembly to serve one's own interests, which is bad for the city; and the "good" *parrhēsia* in which the courageous individual speaks the truth, which is dangerous for the individual who speaks because the crowd will not tolerate anything but flattery.[85]

It is out of this climate of anxiety concerning *parrhēsia* that the thought of Plato emerges. In the next chapter we will look at the transformations of *parrhēsia* which Plato initiates and the new experience of the self which slowly begins to take shape through his practice of philosophy. Here, however, we shall examine a well-known text in order to show Plato's involvement in the problematization of political *parrhēsia*. Foucault takes the critique of democracy which appears in the *Republic* as an explicit reference to the ineffective mode of *parrhēsia* which prevails in the assembly.[86] Plato describes the inhabitants of a democratic city, the city founded on the principle of equality. He writes: "To begin with, are they not free? And is not the city full of liberty and [*parrhēsia*]? And has not every man license to do as he likes?"[87]

Democracy is characterized as equality, liberty, and *parrhēsia*. What is essential, however, is the manner in which these elements of democracy are interpreted, or rather, lived, in the democracy described by Plato. Equality is experienced as the absence of any possibility of distinguishing any one way of life from any other in terms of their relationship to truth. Liberty is the freedom of each to choose a way of life and to live the life chosen. And *parrhēsia* is the freedom to say what one *wants* in the manner that one *wants* to say it.[88] Plato writes that given this interpretation of equality, freedom, and free speech, "it is obvious that everyone would arrange a plan for leading his own life in the way that *pleases* him."[89] The good of the polis is completely external to the individuals' freedom and fulfillment. They define their interests privately and they define their freedom as the absence of political constraint, as the ability to accomplish the private ends they set for themselves. Plato identifies these private purposes as material accumulation, reputation, power, and pleasure in general. This life of pleasure and power, of acquisition, is the one that Plato associates with the democratic regime.

An assembly of citizens who constitute their subjectivity in this way is going to listen to the discourse which *pleases* it and silence the discourse which does not. Therefore, the language of the assembly cannot be a language of truth, necessity, or critique; rather, it must be flattery. That is, the assembly does not, and cannot, distinguish between the language which is true and that which is false. The assembly listens only to the person who "says he loves the people."[90] If one wants to be heard in the assembly, if one wants to accrue power there, then one must say what the others want to hear. In this way, the democratic mode of existence constitutes the assembly as the place and the symbol of its power. Plato describes the assembly of citizens as a "great strong beast."[91] The assembly is an organic thing and its force is more animal than human. Its "full-throated clamor and clapping of hands" creates individuals, forms them, shapes them, with a mute and ruthless power that no "private teaching" can match.[92] The effect of the assembly as an apparatus (*dispositif*) of power is to "mold" the individual "so that he will affirm the same things that they . . . [the assembled citizens] . . . do to be honorable and base, and will do as they do, and even be such as they."[93] The assembly molds everyone to the same pattern, to think, to do and to *be* as "they." Inside and outside the assembly, one must not contradict the majority view, the general opinion. As Crito tactfully points out to Socrates who sits in jail awaiting execution, "one has to think of popular opinion."[94] One *must* abide by what pleases the majority—and what displeases the majority is any way of life and of speaking, any *parrhēsia*, which contradicts the democratic mode of existence. Democracy, then, is a structure of nondifferentiation which constitutes political and ethical subjects through the force of the general opinion. Individuals constitute themselves as political-ethical subjects in this pattern because of the pressure to "flatter," to articulate the general opinion as one's own, because one must think just as "they" do and be just as "they" are. If the assembly in the Periclesian moment achieves itself through a will to truth which takes the form of a consciousness of ethical difference, then the assembly of Plato's democracy accomplishes itself through a will to power which in its animal purity is a structure and a power of "nondifferentiation." Therefore, the democratic mode of existence, through the apparatus of the assembly and the power of the general opinion (the "they"), exerts itself as a force.

Furthermore, within this milieu emerges a technology of control—rhetoric. Just as the assembly is the nexus of all relationships of power, emanating force outward as a pressure which *makes* political and ethical subjects, it is itself subject to control. The one who is able to comprehend the flow of energy in the beast, to understand its moods and their causes, will possess a technology through which he can harness its power and make it his own. If flattery is the expected mode of discourse in the assembly, then rhetoric is the technology of flattering. In flattery one articulates the opinion of the other as one's own in order to seduce. To achieve this one must know the other, what he thinks and desires, what pleases him or gives him pain. This is exactly how Plato describes the knowledge which the Sophists develop.[95] The technology of the Sophists is a calculation of forces without meaning, of inertia, of impacts and reflexes. The power of rhetoric comes from its ability to work on the body and the passions—to be moving, striking. Plato shows how the Sophists study the workings of the assembly in order to learn how to use language as a power. The Sophist learns how the beast

> is to be approached and touched, and when and by what things it is made most savage or gentle, yes, and the several sounds it is wont to utter on the occasion of each, and again what sounds uttered by another make it tame or fierce and after mastering this knowledge by living with the creature and by lapse of time should call it wisdom, and should construct thereof a system and art and turn to the teaching of it.[96]

Notice that rhetoric manipulates "sounds," not words—it operates at the level of pure materiality, below the threshold of reflection, meaning, and will. It "approaches" and "touches" individuals, drawing from them a reaction. Rhetoric in this way both inhabits and cultivates the regime of ethical nondifferentiation, constructing a knowledge and an art of language which binds listeners ever more tightly to its exigencies. And, what's more, the democratic structure of nondifferentiation takes on another form—the first was the power of the general opinion which inscribes itself as the very *identity* of the subject; now it is the *artificiality* of the "I" who appears in the assembly. In the first instance the "I" is molded through the force of the assembly; in this case the "I" is a work of art, a technique, which constructs the speaking subject as a power of persuasion.

As Plato sees it, this situation has for its correlate a particular relationship to one's self which remains for the most part unarticulated. The self relates to itself in and as the immediate presence, the visceral and undeniable givenness of the desires, pleasures, and pains which present themselves in the soul. Furthermore, this self feels its freedom in the power to satisfy desires, avoid pains, and enjoy pleasures. We might say that the self is therefore a principle of pleasure and a will to power. This self-relation is first inscribed in the political practice of the assembly described above and only later reinscribed in the Sophistic theory of nature and power. Rhetoric makes individuals unfree by inscribing in them the self-relation they are already living—it subjects them to a particular interpretation of the human being. For Plato, the fundamental characteristic of this relation of the self to itself is the absence of "true discourse" in the soul which would allow it to understand the nature and meaning of desires and pleasures, to distinguish them according to their ethical values, and to master and use them in order to give the soul and one's mode of existence an ordered and beautiful form.[97]

This lack arises because the Athenians fail to develop an ethical care of the self that can produce in individuals the *ēthos* that just and effective political life, as well as just and happy private life, require. The Athenians neglect to develop and practice a care of the self because they are absorbed in the pursuits articulated by the "general opinion." Conversely, they are absorbed in the general opinion because they neglect themselves. It is this neglect of the self, and its corresponding attachment to the pleasure principle and will to power, which is the condition of possibility of rhetoric as a technology of control and the general opinion as a force. The purpose of rhetoric is to use discourse to manipulate individuals who, out of self-neglect, are absorbed in the "general opinion"; its effect is to inscribe that opinion even more deeply into their very mode of being and to perpetuate self-neglect. The effectiveness of rhetoric and the apparatus of the assembly are only possible on the basis of self-neglect.

Three dimensions are more or less explicit in Plato's problematization of democratic political life: the political dimension (power), the ethical dimension (subjectivity), and the discursive dimension (knowledge). The three fields of being which appear in this Foucauldian analysis of Plato's text mirror Foucault's threefold analysis of experience: power, knowledge, and subjectivity. In my explication I have deliberately developed this convergence in order to bring out the fact that Foucault's concern with the Platonic critique of democracy is shaped by his own project and reflects his critique of biopolitics.[98] This reading of Plato is part of his effort to comprehend and respond to the present, to problematize it, and to initiate a new political ethic, to foster a new concern for the truth. What is at stake in Foucault's analysis of Plato is the way that relations of power and knowledge implicate, play upon, depend upon, or preclude particular relations of oneself to oneself.

Foucault's interpretation of Plato in these terms reveals the complex interrelation of these three dimensions. The interaction between power, subjectivity, and knowledge can never be completely reduced to one-way causal relationships. These three dimensions of experience are equiprimordial (to borrow a term from Heidegger). Or rather, one might say that experience is overdetermined (to borrow a term from Freud) because it cannot be reduced to a causal explanation. Each field has the potential to reinforce one or both of the others, just as it has the potential to disrupt one or both of the others. Furthermore, Foucault's analysis will reveal that this instability and reversibility is what allows creative responses and resistances. Socratic-Platonic philosophy is one such response, one form of problematization of the always dangerous, but always fertile, nexus of power, knowledge, and subjectivity.

In Plato's problematization of *parrhēsia* the democratic assembly cannot speak or hear the truth because the individuals who gather there do not structure their lives according to the presence of rational discourses, the *logoi*, in their souls. For political life to fulfill its function, which is to let truth emerge in the assembly in order to govern the city, the individuals who engage in politics must first allow truth to emerge in their souls and in their lives. Now we can anticipate how Plato will reinvent *parrhēsia*. Because the political sphere is closed off as the area for frank discourse, it is in the relationship of oneself to oneself that philosophy will intervene as a cure for the failure of political and ethical life. Socratic-Platonic philosophy will offer itself as a different mode of existence, which finds its source in a different experience of the self. In order to affect the cure of the self, and cultivate true discourse in the souls of the others, philosophical practice will constitute itself as a new form of ethical *parrhēsia*. Just as the city needs *parrhēsia* in order to function well, the individual will need to hear *parrhēsia* so that true discourse can establish itself in his soul.[99]

Foucault characterizes the consequences of this shift toward ethical *parrhēsia* according to three distinctive traits. First of all, *parrhēsia* is no longer represented as the right and privilege of the best citizens to speak freely in the assembly. Rather, it will be a practice of speaking the truth which addresses not the city but the soul, the *psychē*, of the individual. The *psychē* is what *parrhēsia* will speak to and it is the place in which it will produce its effects. In other words, "one passes from the *polis* to the *psychē* as the essential correlate of *parrhēsia*."[100] At the same time, the purpose of *parrhēsia* is displaced and is no longer the realization of the good of the city, is no longer "practical life." Instead, *parrhēsia* will find its fulfillment in the "formation of a certain way of being, a certain way of doing, a certain way of conducting oneself around other people or another person. The objective of speaking the truth is not so much the salvation of the city, as the *ēthos* of the individual."[101] Third, *parrhēsia* will take its place in an ensemble of practices that aim to transform the individual soul.[102] *Parrhēsia*, through the crisis of Athenian democracy, is displaced from its original setting, purpose, and form. It becomes linked to practices of the self which have as their task the formation of an *ēthos*. This is the sociopolitical drama within which Plato's thinking unfolds. Our task now is to see precisely how Foucault conceives of Plato's philosophical reinvention of *parrhēsia* as a modality of speaking the truth. We shall see that Plato's reelaboration of the experience of the self is directly related to this historical situation. Plato's practice of philosophy will take shape outside the field of politics; it will stand in constant opposition to rhetoric; and it will take the form of an ensemble of practices of self-transformation and self-formation.

Truth and the Self: Knowledge and Spirituality

In this section, I would like to step back a bit in order to view this historical moment from a wider angle and within the unfolding of a larger drama, one in which we are still caught up, the effects of which, as Foucault sees it, we have yet to fully acknowledge. I have already outlined the political situation of Socratic-Platonic philosophy. But this is not the only aspect of their historical world involved in their thinking. Before moving on we must fix another of the coordinates which allow Foucault to map the movement of this thought. In 1982 Foucault delivered a course at the Collège de France entitled *The Hermeneutics of the Subject*. He announced the course as the continuation of a series of studies which investigated the relationship between the subject and truth. In this project he shows that this relationship is not constant through history.[103] In particular, Foucault challenges those categories of our thought that lead us to articulate the question of the relation between subjectivity and truth in the following terms: How is it possible for the subject to know itself? How is it possible to "objectify the subject in a field of knowledge?"[104] Questions concerning the relationship between subjectivity and truth are framed in these categories because of an important event in the history of thought: the eclipse of the ancient imperative to "take care of oneself" by the imperative to "know oneself." It is precisely this event and its consequences which I wish to trace in the following chapters. This will allow us to understand both the context and the purpose of Foucault's reinvention of philosophical *parrhēsia* and care of the self.

In 1982 Foucault showed that for ancient thought—Greek, Hellenistic, and Roman thought—questions concerning the relationship of subjectivity and truth were formed by a different arrangement of categories. Specifically, the notion of "care of the self" was more fundamental than that of "know yourself": "it is . . . in a sort of subordination with respect to the rule of care of the self that the rule, 'know yourself,' is formed."[105] In order to return us to this style of thinking, Foucault excavates the relationship between these two principles in ancient Greece. In ancient philosophy just until the first forms of Christian practice, care of the self was the fundamental task, and it was in light of this task that something like a self could become available to experience. Within this framework, knowing oneself was only one among many activities necessary to properly take care of oneself, and reflection on the self took form in thoroughly pragmatic knowledges.[106] The self was constituted as an object of pragmatic, not theoretical, knowledges. In fact, Foucault is cautious when he talks about the notion of a self- or subject-substance in Greek thought.[107] Rather than appearing as a unified and fundamental essence, substance, or form, the self or the subject was something dispersed among a plurality of experiential regions. In order to understand the possibility for Plato's thought, we must take account of this experience of the relationship between the subject and truth. Plato will reinvent *parrhēsia* as a modality of veridiction by delivering it from the political field to that dimension of experience which is "care of the self." In other words, if *parrhēsia* had originally been a practice of "care for the city" it would become in the hands of Plato one of "care of the self."

What is "care of the self," *epimēleia heautou*? *Epimēleia* is, undoubtedly, an attitude or state of mind which infuses all of one's comportment within the world, with others, and with respect to oneself—"a permanent principle of agitation, of movement, of anxiety in one's existence."[108] It should be noted that the translation of *souci* as "care" is perhaps a bit misleading. *Souci* is not just care in the sense of an affectionate concern for oneself, a sort of tender feeling toward oneself. *Souci* is, as the above quote makes clear, an anxiety. To care about something in this sense is to be anxious about it: in other words the self, which is the object of *souci*, is the source of an anxiety, an "agitation." Furthermore, care is a "form of attention." It is a kind of vigilance over oneself by which one keep's oneself in mind all of the time.[109] However, what is most important is that *epimēleia* is composed of activities, practices, techniques. In other words, care is not reducible to a state of being, whether that state is understood as an emotional condition or an intellectual attitude. It is an activity. In order to stress this point Foucault draws our attention to the original references of the term *epimēleia*. At first the term referred to physical actions, not intellectual or emotional states. However, even when the term does refer to spiritual, intellectual, or emotional realities, it indicates mental exercises and activities, not states of mind or forms of knowledge:

> The etymology goes back to a series of words such as *meletan, meletē,* etc. . . . *Meletai* are exercises: gymnastic exercises, military exercises, military training. *Epimeleisthai* is related more to a form of activity, an activity of continuous, applied, ordered vigilance, than to an attitude.[110]

Care is less an attitude, a cognitive or emotional relation to something, than the activities of watching over, cultivating, protecting, improving. In the following two chapters we shall see many of these practices and the role they play in well-articulated systems of care of the self. Here I will merely point to Foucault's "catalog" of some different types of practices which were extant in pre-Socratic Greece, and which can still be found in Plato's portrait of Socrates (for example, in the *Symposium*). There are "rites of purification," which prepare one for contact with the gods at the oracle or in dreams; there are "techniques for concentrating the soul," which are meant to solidify the soul, the life force, which is something easily dispersed and eliminated; there is the *retreat* by which one withdraws, not just by physically changing location, but by mentally removing oneself from one's present situation; and there are practices of endurance, tests which allow one to overcome fear of pain and the temptation of pleasure.[111] Even such a brief list provides some indication of the variety of practices of *epimēleia* and of their primarily nonintellectual form. In the following chapters we shall see in more detail the practices of care developed by Socrates, Plato, and the tradition which follows them. The primacy of practice in the notion of care of the self continues all the way into the Christian experience where *epimēleia* has "the sense of exercise, ascetic exercise."[112]

This brief catalog of practices is enough to indicate that *epimēleia* is far more than a cognitive act or attitude or an emotional state. However, even where care is described as an intellectual or mental fact, it is not primarily a form of knowing or of knowledge. Rather, care, as an intellectual activity, is still a matter of exercise, of *askēsis*. Care of the self is the practice of thinking as opposed to knowing.[113] Again, this is evident in the language used to describe this activity. Foucault outlines a few of the metaphorical registers in which *epimēleia* is often sounded and which distinguish it from knowing. First, there is the language of the conversion—

thinking is a way of converting oneself to the truth and of being saved by it. Second, care as an act of thought is often described as a "retreat" or a withdrawal from the world through which one finds restoration or rejuvenation. In addition, there are medical, juridical, and religious descriptions of the practice of care. Thinking here is therapeutic, an application of law, or an experience of transcendence. In each case thinking is not so much a way of knowing oneself as it is a way of curing, admonishing or rewarding, or freeing oneself. Finally, there is the relation of care to mastery, control, and the joy of the self in itself—thinking as pleasure or joy.[114] Therefore, whether in the form of physical exercises or in the form of practices of thought, in *epimēleia* one performs various exercises or one engages in a variety of practices which have the deliberate goal of cultivating some kind of relationship of oneself to oneself.

Who is this self that one cares for? What part of one's experience, of one's world, is marked off as the self which is an object of care in all of those senses, as an attitude, form of attention, and ensemble of practices? These questions bring us back around to the principle of self-knowledge. In order to take care of oneself one must know oneself at least enough to know what to take care of and how. Foucault makes it clear that before Socrates the notion of self-knowledge was always a matter of practical advice in a specific setting. For example, Foucault indicates that the Delphic inscription, *gnōthi seauton,* would have been understood by the Greeks as practical advice, along the lines of "do not suppose yourself to be a god," or "be aware of what you really ask when you come to consult the oracle."[115] The famous inscription does not refer to a principle of life but is a specific instruction concerning how to make proper use of the oracle. The "self" is the activity of approaching the oracle; the "self" is nothing more than a question to be posed that must be transparent to itself. With respect to a different region of praxis, in *The Use of Pleasure* and *The Care of the Self,* Foucault shows how pleasure was made into a moral problem for the Greeks; the ethical task was a matter of care of the self. One had to take up an attitude of the proper use and mastery of the pleasures, the *aphrodesia.* The Greeks did not perceive sexuality and its moral implications in terms of the nature of desire—that is, in terms of a subject- or self-substance which was at the basis of one's thoughts, feelings, and actions. Rather, the *aphrodesia*—among which sexuality was included—were a whole range of possible acts and pleasures which tended toward excess, toward a condition in which the subject lost its freedom by becoming "enslaved" to its pleasures. Sexual ethics was a matter of the proper use of pleasure, a work in which one practiced self-mastery and which led to a condition of freedom. This freedom expressed itself in a life of moderation, of power over one's pleasures. This power over oneself was what made one capable of asserting one's power over others. Through self-mastery, that is, mastery of the pleasures, one became capable of governing others, capable of political life. Politics (relations of power among equals—citizens), erotics (relations combining pleasure and power between unequal parties— lover and beloved, subject and object), economics (relations of power management between husband and wife in a household), and dietetics (relation of oneself to one's body) are all practical fields, fields of action within which the self appears and which are constituted by their possibil- ities for success and error, their dangers, their techniques and tactics for success and safety, and their rewards. From these examples, we can see that knowledge of the self was worked out as a practical matter and not in a theoretical way. In other words, we might say that knowledge of the self was developed in purely "regional ontologies" which were defined in a pragmatic way—as areas in need of work, as questions calling for answers. There was no general ontology of something like a *self* whose meaning supported these various regions and whose structure provided them with a unitary moral foundation or task.

Self-knowledge, rather than being a general and independent form of knowledge, was sought out and elaborated interior to the attitudes, forms of attention, and techniques of care of the self. In other words, self- knowledge is given its determinations by the concrete task of *epimēleia*. Self-knowledge, and the form of the self as an object of knowledge, there- fore, vary according to the mode of care of the self within which knowl- edge becomes possible. For Foucault this means:

> Within the very history of care of the self, *gnōthi seauton* does not have the same form and it does not have the same function. Consequently, the knowledge opened up and delivered by *gnōthi seauton* is not going to be the same in each case. This means that the forms themselves of the knowledge which are put to work are not the same. This also means that the subject itself, such as it is constituted by the form of reflexivity [i.e., of reflection of the self on itself] proper to such and such a type of care, is going to change.[116]

In other words, a given form of care of the self will call for a partic- ular form of reflexivity, that is, a particular relationship of oneself to one- self. The way in which the subject articulates itself as an object to be known will be determined by the form of reflexivity. For this reason, Fou- cault proceeds to an analysis of "forms of reflexivity and the history of practices which serve as their support in order to return its meaning—its variable, historical, and never universal, meaning—to the old, traditional principle of '*connais-toi toi-même*.'"[117] One does not simply "know" oneself—as if looking and seeing were an immediate disclosure of the self, as the word "theory" (*theoria*) suggests. Rather, knowing/seeing is always a distinctive style of knowing/seeing; it is a *practice*. One deploys techniques of self-interrogation, of self-manifestation or interpretation through which one becomes visible to oneself. The way one looks mediates the relation between oneself and oneself. The way one appears will depend on the way one looks, the techniques one puts to use in order to make oneself appear to oneself. Furthermore, one is not only that which appears before one's gaze when one looks, but also the activity of looking into oneself. Just as the subject, insofar as it is an *object* of knowledge, has a history, the subject insofar as it is a *subject* which can know itself, that is, insofar as it is the active deployment of certain forms of reflection on itself, also has a history. In other words, one cannot simply attempt to articulate a theory of the subject or of the self. To do so would result in accepting a certain unchallenged form of reflection on the self and would articulate an "objective" knowledge of the subject, shaped by that form of reflection, as *the* subject as such.[118] Rather, one must study the different forms of self-consciousness or self-knowledge, the different practices of "knowing" the self. But to do this requires that one resituate forms of reflection within the framing concept of care of the self which always, explicitly or implicitly, motivates the project of self-knowledge. And finally, one must be able to resituate the care of the self within the horizon of a problematization which motivates the project of care. Foucault will therefore attempt to present neither a universal theory of the subject as such, nor will he be content to show the different theories which have historically attempted an objective knowledge of the subject. He will analyze the concrete forms of thinking, of thinking about the subject, and the modes of articulating self-knowledge, which have been the concrete historical forms of subjectivity individuals have assumed in order to speak the truth about themselves.

This is an important methodological point, but it requires further elaboration. What if one raises the question, How and why is it that these practices and consequently these forms of self-knowledge undergo transformations, as is suggested by this line of historical thinking? It seems to me that Foucault addresses this question directly in his 1983 course. There we see that Plato's thought transforms care of the self as a response to the failure of democratic *parrhēsia*. As we have seen, political discourse in Athens was experienced by Plato as a crisis rooted in an insufficient mode of subjectivity. Plato's philosophical *parrhēsia* presents itself as a mode of reflection on the self, offering a *knowledge* of the self which takes the form of a practice of care. That is, it is a technique intended to transform the subject. Care, in Socratic-Platonic thought, accomplishes itself in a form of subjectivity that is fully adequate to the task of democratic political discourse. However, this new *parrhēsiastic* relationship (of philosopher and disciple) and the figures of truth (the types of subjectivity which this relationship constitutes) come to have a value and a meaning independent of the goal of forming "political" subjectivity. What the example of Plato shows is that, for Foucault, transformations in the history of subjectivity arise through the work of problematization.

In the following chapters we will see that the thought of Plato initiates, or at least indicates, two developments in the history of subjectivity: (a) a transformation in the relationship between the care of the self (*epimēleia heautou*) and the "arts of existence" (*technē tou biou*); and (b) as a consequence of this transformation, a new importance of the self as an object of knowledge, along with an ethical obligation to know oneself.[119] With respect to the first point, Foucault observes that in Greek culture prior to the appearance of Socrates—or at least the representation which Plato gives us of him—care of the self was absorbed in what he calls "arts of existence." If care of the self is an anxiety about, and a work upon, the relationship one maintains with oneself, then the arts of existence are the tools one puts to use in the determinate fields of action in order to act well. For the Greeks the self was elaborated as an object of practical knowledge within concrete parameters: sexual experience, health, political experience, and so on. The arts of existence offer responses to the questions and situations which arise in these theaters of action. Through the mastery of these arts one is able to forge a noble existence in all of the domains in which one exhibits oneself as a free, rational being. For example, the art of politics allows one to do well when it is a matter of political activity, a primary example of which would be rhetoric. In Socratic thought, the care of the self was a preparatory work through which one established the proper rapport with oneself. This relationship to oneself was what gave one the capacity to take up the arts of living, to understand their value, to be able to apply them properly. For example, care of the self in the domain of love gave one the proper mastery of passions and pleasures. It was the activity by which one established the proper relation to oneself: mastery of the passions. Once this relation was attained, one would be able to either discover, or apply to oneself and one's surrounding world, the proper techniques for loving: one would learn how to court or seduce, or how to take care of one's beloved. Once the right relationship to oneself was set up, one could take up the right relationship to one's household and master it properly, or to one's friends, to one's lover, or to others in the political realm. Care of the self was therefore a means to an end—it was a preparatory or background work which culminated in the concrete art of living that one exhibited in the theaters of action that the household and the city presented. However, in the figure of Socrates there is a new emphasis on the care of the self, on the work of establishing the proper relationship of oneself to oneself, and within this Socratic care of the self there will be an increased intensity to the obligation to know oneself. As a result, the practice of care of the self eventually will come to be not simply a means to an end, such as acquiring and deploying the proper arts of living. More and more, care of the self, the establishment and maintenance of the right self-relation, will come to be the end in itself. The arts of life will come to be incorporated into this concern for the self. One will deploy the arts of life in order to acquire the right relationship to oneself and to maintain that relationship as the *telos* of living. The emphasis which Socrates and Plato put on self-knowledge and the eventual reversal of the relation between care of the self and the arts of living will give rise to the possibility of a general ontology of the subject, a possibility which only begins to come into focus after Plato.

In the ancient world, the notion of care of the self and the theme of the arts of existence were more fundamental than knowledge of the self. They were present in the culture at large, but they also founded philosophical practice. Plato's thought itself happens in the space defined by care of the self, even though Plato gave self-knowledge a far more central place in the philosophical practice of care. However, at the beginning of this section I stated that according to Foucault self-knowledge—both the truth of the self and the relation between the subject and the truth—cannot be reduced to modern epistemological terms. Self-knowledge is not an objectifying knowledge. The subject does not acquire access to the truth, to the truth about itself, in an "objective" or theoretical way. If it is true, then, that Plato's thought moves within the orbit of care of the self, we must ask: what is the relationship between subjectivity and truth in the work of Plato? In order to answer this it is necessary to clarify a bit more in a general way the kind of relationship between subjectivity and truth which takes place in care of the self.

So far we have seen that self-knowledge arises in care of the self, not in terms of epistemology. Nor does it come about in the form of a theory about, or a general ontology of, the subject. The relationship between the subject and truth in care of the self is not dealt with as a question of how the subject is able to know the truth, including the truth about itself. In 1982 Foucault showed that this relationship as it takes place in care of the self must be seen within an experience which he calls "spirituality."[120] Foucault defines spirituality as

> the transformations necessary in order to have access to the truth . . . the ensemble of these attempts, practices, and experiments that could be

purifications, asceticism, renunciations, conversions of "regard," modifications of existence, etc., which constitute, not for knowledge but for
the subject, for the very being of the subject, the price to pay in order to
have access to the truth.[121]

Spirituality according to this definition is a special modality of care of the
self. If care of the self is, in general, the practices of self-fashioning that
one takes up in order to give one's existence a particular form, then spirituality is a care of the self which transforms one in the necessary way to
gain access to the truth. However, the truth at stake in spirituality is not
simply *a* truth. It is not truth in the sense of the quality of correctness of
a judgment; it is not a particular truth about some object to be known. In
his final courses, Foucault excavated an experience in which truth is a fullness of being which offers itself only to those individuals who have performed the proper work on themselves. Access to the truth is, then, "access to being itself."[122]

Spirituality is a particular way of experiencing the relation between
the subject and the truth or being. Foucault outlines three characteristics
of the spiritual relation between the subject and truth. First:

> Spirituality holds that the truth is never given to the subject by right.
> Spirituality postulates that the subject as such does not have the right,
> does not have the capacity to have access to the truth. It holds that the
> truth is not given to the subject by a simple act of knowing [*connais-
> sance*], which would be founded and legitimated because it is the subject
> and because it has such and such structure qua subject.[123]

The first postulate of spirituality holds that the subject does not by its very
nature and being have the "right" to the truth, to Being. Therefore, the
truth is not acquired through a simple "act of cognition." The subject, as
that which stands opposed to objects, to Being, to things, to the world,
does not by nature or its essence have access to the truth of those things,
or of itself. In other words, more fundamental than its "acts of cognition,"
the subject's looking at or reasoning about objects is its very mode of
being qua subject. It must modify its mode of being qua subject before it
is able to see things, and itself, as they are. "[Spirituality] holds that it is
necessary that the subject modify itself, transform itself, displace itself,
that it must become, in a certain measure and up to a certain point, other
than itself in order to have the right to access to truth. The truth is only
given to the subject at a price that puts into play the very being of the subject itself."[124] The subject cannot see the truth, cannot discover it through
trying to "know" things because its very being prevents it from doing so.

What appears to it is false, and this is because the subject itself prevents things from appearing to it as they are. The subject must transform its way of being, its way of letting things appear to it. In Plato, this modification will be brought about largely through exercises of thought. This will be clear, for example, in *Alcibiades*. In this dialogue, the practice of self-knowledge transforms one into the kind of subject who is able to govern the city. For the most part, however, spirituality requires practices of care of the self which are not essentially practices of *connaissance*.

The second postulate of spirituality follows from the first: "There can be no truth without a conversion or without a transformation of the subject."[125] Truth requires *conversion:* care of the self, insofar as it is a spiritual practice, aims at a conversion of the subject. The conversion is what gives the subject access to the truth because it is the transformation of the subject's very mode of being which allows things to appear to it as they truly are. Foucault defines the two main forms of conversion:

> This conversion can take place in the form of a movement which tears the subject from its status and its actual condition (movement of ascension of the subject; movement by which, on the contrary, the truth comes to him and illuminates him). Let's call, here again very conventionally, this movement, in whatever direction it goes: the movement of *erōs* (love). And then, another great form by which the subject can and must transform itself in order to have access to the truth: it is a work. It is a work of the self on itself, an elaboration of the self by itself, a progressive transformation of the self by itself for which one is responsible in the long labor which is that of asceticism (*askēsis*).[126]

The self-modification which truth requires is not a transformation of the "individual, but of the subject itself in its very being qua subject."[127] Foucault marks a clear distinction between the subject qua subject and the "individual in his concrete existence."[128] This distinction is decisive though enigmatic. Precisely what is meant by the subject in its structure, or its mode of being qua subject, will become clearer when we turn to Foucault's interpretation of *Alcibiades*. We can remark that according to this formulation one can change one's concrete existence—diet, manner of dress, leave one's family, and so on—without necessarily affecting who one is qua subject. However, is it also possible that one can change who one *is* qua subject without some transformation of one's concrete life? This will be one of the main themes of Foucault's lectures in 1984 at the Collège—the notion of the *bios philosophicos,* the philosophical life, as the true life, *alēthēs bios,* is connected to the idea that the true life is a life *other* than the normal, predominant form of life. In the West, according to Foucault, *erōs* and *askēsis* have been the primary modes of conversion that transform the subject and give one access to Being. In the following chapters we shall see these two possibilities appear in the work of Plato—in *Alcibiades* transformation will be initiated by *erōs;* in *Laches,* it will be the test (*épreuve*) and the work, *askēsis,* of testing one's mode of existence which gives one access to truth.

The third characteristic of spirituality is that truth/being has "return effects" on the subject. Truth, according to spiritual experience, "is that which illuminates the subject; the truth is that which gives the subject beatitude, the truth is that which gives the subject tranquility of soul."[129] The relation between the subject and the truth is such that conversion leads to truth. But truth is experienced as a *salvation,* not simply as "correctness." Truth is not the property of a judgment; rather, "it accomplishes the very being of the subject."[130] In other words, the subject must pay a price in its very being by converting itself, modifying itself, but the truth will also transform the subject by completing it in the experience of revelation, salvation, fulfillment. Truth rewards the subject for his work and his love.

For Plato, the subject is related to truth not by way of knowledge in the form of true judgments. Rather, the subject is related to truth as a revelation which comes to one through ascetic practices of self-transformation and which has the power to save the subject. In other words, truth is a saving power which accomplishes and completes the subject in its very being. It is in light of this experience of truth, for example, that one can comprehend the Socratic-Platonic doctrine according to which one cannot knowingly do wrong. Knowledge here is "not reducible to mere awareness of a principle."[131] It is in fact the transformation of one's being which takes place through care of the self.

According to Foucault, this aspect of Plato's thought, and the experience of truth as a spiritual practice, is difficult for us to see because of the historical event through which knowledge of the self has come to overshadow care of the self. For "modernity"—and this is what is most definitive of modernity according to Foucault—knowledge is understood as "access to a domain of objects."[132] Knowledge is objectivity. In order to acquire knowledge, even knowledge of oneself, one must apply the proper methods of thought, logic, analysis, and so on. The experience of knowledge as a spiritual work, as the struggle to win access to truth which requires not simply method but self-transformation, and the experience of truth as fulfillment of the subject illuminated by it no longer have any meaning. The handy scapegoat for all of the supposed shortcomings of modernity is Descartes. For this reason Foucault calls the shift from care of the self to knowledge or objectivity the *Cartesian moment.* However, he

is careful to point out that Descartes himself did not experience the relation between the subject and the truth in modern, *Cartesian* terms. I will
show that for Foucault the shift away from spirituality and toward objectivity is grounded more upon the spread of disciplinary technologies and
biopower than on Descartes's theory of the cogito.

In the following chapters, I will trace certain aspects of this movement by which the care of the self, and the experience of truth which dom-
inates it, are "forgotten" or "neglected."[133] It seems to me that this movement is the other side of the historical events which Foucault documented
in his major works, *History of Madness, The Order of Things, Discipline and
Punish,* and so on. And it is this "other side" which constitutes the axis of
subjectivity, of existence as an ethical-aesthetic work, an etho-poetic task,
which remains open to itself and its obligations even as it is traversed by
its historical situation.

2

The Socratic Moment

So far we have seen how Foucault articulates the problematization of political life and political discourse in fifth-century Athens. The struggle for
power in the assembly, because of the basic modes of self-perception that
prevailed there, brought about the effacement of effective political subjectivity as expressed in free and frank discourse—*parrhēsia*. The political
dimension was a space from which the true *parrhēsiast* was banished. Furthermore, the relationship between the subject and the words he speaks
was mediated by techniques of flattery and of dissimulation; in other
words, by a technology of control. Because political life takes place in the
element of language, and frank, truthful language was not tolerated, just
and effective political life was impossible. It was within the horizon of this
problem that a new experience of the *self* took shape. The need to articulate self-knowledge in order to found a just and true life came into focus
perhaps for the first time. It became necessary to confront the truth of
oneself in order to be able to speak the truth to the assembly and hear the
truth spoken there by others. This confrontation with oneself required a
particular relation to the other. Self-knowledge arises through the confrontation with the other in the experience of *parrhēsia*. The forms of self-
knowledge that emerged from this *parrhēsiastic* confrontation were closely
linked to the problematization of political *parrhēsia*. In other words, the
self was articulated as a subject who knows and as an object to be known
within the framework of this particular problem. The form of the self as
an object of knowledge and discourse, as well as the techniques of self-
contemplation and self-expression that produced self-knowledge, were
marked by this point of departure and this task. However, despite the
"pragmatic" nature of this knowledge, an experience was made possible
in which the *self* could become a field of knowledges, practices, meanings,
and values in and for itself.

In this chapter I will examine Foucault's reading of four Platonic
texts: the *Seventh Letter,* the *Apology, Alcibiades,* and *Laches.*[1] Foucault's reading of these texts shows that Socratic-Platonic philosophy is a response to
the crisis of democracy and of democratic *parrhēsia*. Furthermore, we will
see that in the thought of Socrates and Plato, *parrhēsia* is displaced from
politics to ethics. Ethical or philosophical *parrhēsia* becomes an element

of the care of the self (*epimēleia heautou*). This care will serve as a preparatory work and a constant ethical relation to the other with the goal of fashioning political subjects capable of the obligations of freedom and truth. Finally, *parrhēsia* as an ethical practice of speaking the truth will not only manifest itself as a new mode of subjectivity (a new modality of veridiction), but will also develop techniques and categories for objectifying the subject in discourse, for producing self-knowledge. It will fashion tools for directing one's attention toward the self, articulated in the forms of the soul (*psychē*) and of existence (*bios*). This practice of subjectivization through ethical *parrhēsia* and care of the self was a practice of freedom. The form of philosophical life and language that Socrates and Plato invented served to "desubjectify" the political, ethical subject. They strove to detach the subject from its experience of itself, to disconnect it from the forms of control it had incorporated through the work of the "general opinion" and the discourse of rhetoric. This means that the individual had to put his mode of existence, *bios,* to the test and examine the condition of his soul, *psychē.* The new form of subjectivity presented in these Platonic texts is defined by the effort to transform oneself through techniques of self-examination (the "ontology" of the soul) and a deliberate practice of everyday life (the testing of existence). The philosopher will define his subjectivity, his freedom to speak the truth, by the task of ethical *parrhēsia,* the obligation to incite others to take care of themselves. In other words, the subject of care, of knowledge, and of philosophy emerged as a practice of resistance to political power.

In his lectures on care of the self and *parrhēsia,* Foucault almost always remains close to the texts and the problems. He rarely steps back to tell us what he is doing or what his relationship to the texts is. In the following, while I will present an exposition of his interpretation of Plato, I also want to reveal the relation between these lectures and the problematization of discipline, normalization, hermeneutics, and biopolitics that forms the horizon for his work. I hope to make clear that Foucault's reading of Plato is guided both by his concern to diagnose his own subjection to these forms of power and by his attempt to care for himself, to open up new modes of subjectivation as a response to power. In other words, in performing his genealogy of philosophy as ethical *parrhēsia* and care of the self, Foucault is redefining and remaking himself as a philosopher, and as a political and ethical subject.

Plato's *Seventh Letter:* Autobiography of a Philosophical *Parrhēsiast*

Foucault takes up Plato's *Seventh Letter* in order to situate Plato's philosophical project within the crisis of democracy and *parrhēsia* outlined in the previous chapter. Through his reading of the *Seventh Letter,* Foucault shows that Plato constructed his philosophical identity and the style of his discourse in direct opposition to the crisis of democratic discourse. The *Seventh Letter,* therefore, is a link between the problematization of *parrhēsia* and Plato's philosophy. Furthermore, for Foucault, the main purpose of the *Seventh Letter* is to provide an account of the *mode of being* of philosophical discourse, of the conditions of possibility for the actualization of philosophical discourse and of the philosopher as a speaker of this discourse. In other words, it answers the question, In what way or form does philosophy actually exist? It presents an ontology of philosophical discourse and of the philosopher as a form of subjectivity.

Plato tells us in the *Seventh Letter* that because of the inadequacy of all actual political regimes, and particularly that of Athens, he turned his desire for self-actualization through the struggle of freedom and truth away from politics and toward philosophy.[2] Plato's life as a philosopher therefore was provoked by the failure of Athenian political *parrhēsia.* The turn to philosophy, however, was not a withdrawal from the world to a life of detachment or disinterested contemplation. Plato insisted that for philosophy to realize itself it could not remain a merely theoretical discourse. His concern for the actualization of philosophy was based on a distinction between *ergon* (work) and *logos* (words). Philosophical discourse must come to pass as *ergon.* As such it has to take shape as a concrete way of speaking and living. Plato, then, did not turn to philosophy as an escape from political life, but as the only possible way of saving truthful and effective political life, in other words, of saving political *parrhēsia.*

As Foucault sees it, Plato's philosophy arose as a consequence of the failure of *parrhēsia.* Further, it presented itself as the only possible basis of *parrhēsia.* It was therefore not just theoretical discourse existing exterior to the political field; rather, it was an intervention in the form of *parrhēsia.*[3] Plato invented a philosophical practice that would function as the foundation for political action. It would do so by correcting the pervasive self-neglect that undermines political life and language. In order to perform this function, philosophy took form as care of the self. What's more, Plato's thinking was situated in the experience of spirituality, the experience according to which, as we have already seen, truth requires practices of self-transformation.

Though Plato's thinking is set within its concrete historical horizons and draws its force from those sources available to it, there appears in it something new and unexpected. The *Seventh Letter* is in a sense an autobiography. However, what interests Foucault in this text is not the personal story of Plato. Rather, it is the outline of a new mode of subjectivity, a new form of life. Plato outlines a mode of subjectivity for whom the obligation, and accomplishment, of freedom are given expression in the form of philosophical *parrhēsia*. That is, he transfers the duty of *parrhēsia* from the political to the philosophical and in so doing reinvents what it means to be a philosopher. Plato cast philosophy as the duty to intervene in political life. But this intervention was not direct: the philosopher, in his role as philosopher, was not meant to address the assembly, to give the law, or suggest a course of action. Rather, philosophy ought to be addressed to the subject who exercises power and who makes the law. The care for the being of the subject who engages in political life is essential to Platonic philosophy. Insofar as the *Seventh Letter* is an account of philosophical subjectivity as a task and as a particular practice of living and speaking, it presents us with a new figure of truth, a new modality of veridiction: the philosophical *parrhēsiast*.

In order to escape being merely theoretical discourse, and therefore not fully philosophical, philosophy must realize itself in certain activities. For language to become philosophical it must come into being as *ergon*, as "exercise" or a "work." This is reflected in Plato's account of his trips to Syracuse. His student and friend Dion insisted that the tyrant there, Dionysius, had an inclination for philosophy. Because of this there was an opportunity for Plato to put his philosophy to use; by training the young tyrant in philosophy and justice he could see a just regime realized in Syracuse. Plato's decision to go to Syracuse turned on two interrelated points. First, he writes that he was motivated by his sense of "self-respect." He "feared to see [him]self at last altogether nothing but words, so to speak."[4] The first point is a concern for himself. By refusing this opportunity he would fail to attain himself, he would remain "nothing but words." In order to accomplish himself Plato must not be content to write and discuss philosophy. To do so would be to relegate his subjectivity to the mere production of words, *logos*. The accomplishment of his own subjectivity requires him to set himself to work.

Second, Plato writes that if he had refused such an opportune moment, he would have "proved traitor . . . to philosophy."[5] Plato felt the obligation of "reason and justice" and decided to accept the opportunity, leaving "no ground of complaint to the cause of philosophy."[6] This second point is that by refusing the moment of action Plato would fail philosophy. Again, to allow philosophy to remain at the level of mere words, *logos*, would be to forgo the task of philosophy. For philosophy to be realized it must come to pass in a deed or work. What is more, philosophy comes to be in and through the recognition and the acceptance of the moment of action. To fail in such a moment is to fail the demand of philosophy. Therefore, one accomplishes *oneself* and *philosophy* in the same moment and through the same action. In the act one manifests oneself for oneself and for others as a philosopher—one constitutes one's subjectivity, that is, one's freedom and duty to speak the truth, as a philosopher. In other words, philosophy as an activity, as a way of being, is grasped within a dramatic scene.

For Foucault's reading shows that to fashion one's subjectivity as a philosopher is to disclose oneself, the world, and the others in that world in a distinct light. It requires that one recognize the moment of action (*kairos*) that calls one to speak and to use *parrhēsia*. Philosophy does not realize itself through just any kind of discourse with just anyone and at just any time, nor does it exist in the form of theoretical discourse.[7] For philosophy to happen, as a form of *parrhēsia*, the moment of action must appear as an opportunity to engage the political dimension by addressing the subject of political action, of power. The philosopher does not manifest himself in mere discourse—in books and essays. Rather, philosophy happens, it comes into existence when it meets the test of *parrhēsia,* when the subject manifests his courage and will by speaking frankly to the subject of political power. Only then does philosophy actualize itself, and only then does the philosopher realize himself.[8] The moment of action presented itself to Plato in the person of Dionysius, the tyrant. Plato fashioned his own ethical subjectivity as a philosopher in the opportunity to address the subject of political power. He experienced his freedom in the ethical task of intervening in the political field in order to transform the mode of being of the subject who exercises political power.

Through what type of acts does philosophy realize itself? Under what conditions is philosophy given the choice to accomplish itself or neglect and forget itself? Foucault reads the *Seventh Letter* as an elaboration of, and answer to, these questions. He shows that Plato's philosophy, as *parrhēsia,* must confront the political field, but not in the form of political discourse. The philosophical *parrhēsiast* does not assert an opinion about a course of action for the city, he does not say what to do. The philosopher will intervene in order to produce an ethical discourse which aims at the transformation of the subject who rules. The philosopher says who one *is* and who one can (or must) *become.* Furthermore, philosophical *parrhēsia* will not and must not take the form of flattery or rhetoric.[9] Rhetoric intervenes in the political field and poses as the true technology of power. In this respect rhetoric pretends to teach one the art of ruling as an art of persuasion; it pretends to offer a technology of controlling others. Philosophy, on the other hand, does not teach one how to rule, how to control others. Instead it will incite one to govern oneself, to take care of oneself. Foucault's reading of the *Seventh Letter* situates it in that "thread" of relations leading from power to government to care and back.[10] Plato intervenes in this chain of relations at the level of care of the self in order to effect a resistance to practices of power and government which strive to close off free, frank political discourse.

Having shown that Plato defines philosophy in terms of the task of ethical *parrhēsia,* resistance, and care of the self, Foucault goes on to analyze the conditions which constitute the possibility of realizing this philosophical task. First, there must be a "will to listen" on the part of the potential disciple. Second, philosophy itself comes into being through the constant work of the self on itself. This work on oneself, unfolding in relations with others and within the everyday world of life and work, is what gives form to the philosophical life. And third, these practices of the self are exercises which actualize philosophical knowledge in one's soul, a form of knowledge which cannot be contained in and articulated through propositions, and which cannot be acquired through purely cognitive acts.[11]

With regard to the first condition, philosophy can only realize itself by addressing someone who has a will to listen.[12] The individual who is to become a disciple of philosophy must be able to truly hear and attend to the words of the philosopher. In order to explain this point Plato uses the metaphor of the doctor.[13] The doctor treating a patient "must first effect a reform in his way of living."[14] If the patient adopts the healthy pattern of life, then the doctor will continue to treat him. If not, there is no point in continuing the cure. Plato writes that the same rule holds for the philosopher. The will to listen is reflected in the way one attends to the words of the philosopher. Philosophical *parrhēsia* is absolutely opposed to rhetorical discourse on this point. Rhetoric operates independently of the will of the one who listens. In fact, the very essence of rhetoric is to seize the will of the other, to take it over. The purpose of rhetoric is to determine the other's will for her.[15] Plato, on the other hand, states that he will not use "constraint" nor will he "flatter" the other.[16] As soon as one must use rhetoric to persuade, seduce, and control the other, one's discourse is no longer philosophical. The difference here between the two modes of discourse is to be found in the relationship each takes to the listener. At the same time, the way one speaks, the nature of one's discourse in this situation, defines who one is; the philosopher is the one who speaks in a certain way, who produces a discourse which takes up a special relationship to those who listen. Rhetorical discourse addresses the listener outside the dimension of freedom, or on the margins of this dimension. Rhetoric attempts to determine the opinion, choice, and conduct of the listener for her. It insinuates itself between the listener and her choice, in the place where the freedom of the listener should manifest itself. Therefore, the mode of being of rhetorical discourse is, in part, to take the place of the subjectivity and freedom of the listener and to determine her opinions and conduct for her. The mode of being of rhetoric is to assume the task of freedom for the other in order to give definition to the other's life. In this way, rhetoric attains its being independently of the will to listen on the part of the other. Philosophical discourse, on the other hand, takes up a very different relationship to the other, to the listener. For discourse to be philosophical it must present itself to the listener in her freedom. This is what it means for philosophy to be heard; the other must listen, must freely attend to what is said, for the discourse *to be* philosophy and for philosophy *to become actual.*[17] Discourse attains the mode of being of philosophy on the condition that it brings the other face-to-face with her freedom. It does not attempt to insinuate itself between the other and the decision she makes or the opinion she holds, in the space where her freedom takes shape. Rather it provokes and incites the other to determine herself, to take up a deliberate relationship to herself. Philosophy does not try to think for the other or to govern her; it does not try to teach the other how to govern and persuade others. Rather, it provokes the other to take care of and govern herself. Therefore, philosophical discourse must rely on the free choice of the listener to attend and respond to it. The philosopher engages the freedom of the other, whereas rhetoric attempts to deny the other her freedom.

The realization of philosophy cannot come to pass without a second essential condition. This condition comes to light in Plato's answer to the question: How does the philosopher recognize a will to listen in the other? Plato describes his "experimental method" for testing the will of the listener, to learn if the individual possesses a philosophical will.[18] This method involves giving an account of the *pragma* of philosophy, the "activities" which constitute the being of philosophy. What is of interest here is the way Plato characterizes the *pragma* of philosophy. He lays out for the listener the long and difficult path which philosophy requires. The true listener will be enthralled and will understand that philosophy is a "path of enchantment, which he must at once strain every nerve to follow, or die in the attempt."[19] Therefore, the second condition for the realization of philosophy is that the one who hears must choose a way of life in which he "never ceases to practice philosophy."[20] The individual must take up a life in which he develops and applies his natural intelligence, steadiness, and memory, not by renouncing the everyday world but by transforming himself and his life *within* it.[21] The *pragma* which compose philosophy are a work of the self upon the self, the practices which give a certain form to one's life and which give a certain form to oneself: "[A] choice, an uninterruptible path, a development from start to finish and the grip . . . [of philosophy] . . . on everyday life constitute the character of philosophical practice."[22] Philosophy realizes itself through the choice, perpetually reconfirmed, of a practice of daily life.

The third condition for the coming into being of philosophy has to do with the nature of these practices of the self. The practices one takes up and applies to oneself in one's daily life accomplish themselves in the "sudden illumination" of philosophical knowledge in the soul.[23] Foucault offers a provisional account of these practices based on the brief and not entirely clear remarks which Plato makes in the *Seventh Letter*. First, we see that an important quality of philosophical knowledge is that it cannot take the form of a written work composed of "propositions," *mathemata*.[24] Foucault describes the *mathemata* as both the propositions or formulae that are used to transmit information from teacher to student, and the information communicated in this way.[25] Philosophical knowledge cannot be formulated in and transmitted by way of *mathemata*. This is because the path of philosophy does not follow that of the acquisition of information.[26] In other words, there is a distinction between philosophical knowledge and other forms of knowledge. In teaching (for example, in the form of the teacher-technician)[27] one speaks the truth in the form of propositions or instructions in order to transmit one's own knowledge and skill to the disciple. One "learns" through the accumulation and mastery of knowledge transmitted in propositions. To acquire philosophical knowledge, however, one must choose to live with philosophy. This is "not the deposit of ready-made phrases into the soul," but rather the constant work one performs on oneself.[28]

What is the nature of this work? We have already seen that philosophy cannot realize itself without the practice of a certain way of life. The practice of a philosophical life involves putting to work all of one's capacities for knowledge in an exercise that ultimately leads to an experience of truth, an experience in which the individual draws near to Being. In the *Seventh Letter* Plato describes in outline the activity that leads to the experience of truth. First he analyzes the elements involved in philosophical knowledge:

> For everything that exists there are three classes of objects through which knowledge about it must come; the knowledge itself is a fourth, and we must put as a fifth entity the actual object of knowledge which is the true reality.[29]

The first four elements are the name of the thing, its definition, its shape or image, and the understanding of it that one has in one's mind. Each of these elements is distinct from the being which is known by them. Furthermore, each of these four elements can be transmitted through language or symbols or representations. Therefore, one can acquire all of them without perceiving the *object itself* in its being. Someone who attains possession and mastery of all four of these elements without an experience of the true being of the object to be known does not attain philosophical knowledge and may always be exposed to error or refutation. For example, recall the inability of Thrasymachus to respond to Socrates' arguments in the *Republic.* Thrasymachus clearly possessed elements of the knowledge of justice, but what was revealed by Socrates was his lack of a philosophical understanding of the matter.[30] How does one pass beyond the level of understanding composed of the first four elements of knowledge? How does one approach the true being of the object to be known and acquire philosophical knowledge? Plato explains that one attains philosophical knowledge through an exercise (*tribē*) which is constituted by the constant movement "up and down from one to the other" of the four elements of knowledge, by "scrutinizing them in benevolent disputation by the use of question and answer without jealousy."[31] And finally "in a flash understanding of each blazes up, and the mind as it exerts all its powers to the limit of human capacity, is flooded with light."[32] Philosophy is a practice of care of the self which transforms the self and gives one access to truth. Truth in this sense is the fullness of being which offers itself in the form of an "illumination" only after long and difficult work on oneself. In the thought of Plato, philosophy is a form of spirituality.

The spirituality of philosophical knowledge is also evident in Plato's famous critique of writing which appears in the *Seventh Letter* and elsewhere. The reason why one cannot put one's true philosophical knowledge in writing is that philosophical discourse does not realize itself in the form of assertions, *mathemata.* Philosophy does not exist in the form of propositions and cannot be transmitted by way of them.[33] Foucault points out that the same critique holds for spoken language as well. Philosophical discourse does not exist at the level of theory, of pure *logos*, but at the level of *askēsis,* of living in a certain way, of *ergon.* The mode of being of philosophy and philosophical discourse is the relationship it takes to the subject who speaks and the subject who listens. On the one hand, it is actualized in the disciple as a series of practices through which he gives to his life a form that accomplishes itself through practices of thought in the illumination of his soul by philosophical knowledge. In this way the disciple becomes a subject adequate to political life and to just political action and decisions. Through taking care of himself, and governing himself, he becomes capable of taking care of and governing others. On the other hand, the mode of being of philosophical discourse is related to the philosopher as the accomplishment of his duty to use philosophical *parrhēsia* to intervene in the political dimension, not by speaking before the assembly and not through direct political advice, but by inciting those who exercise power to take care of themselves.

Foucault draws another conclusion that has an important bearing on his approach to the work of Plato. In the *Seventh Letter,* Plato writes that it is impossible to put philosophical knowledge into words and set it out as a theory.[34] He states that he has never attempted to do so, writing, "It is an inevitable conclusion from this that when anyone sees anywhere the written work of anyone . . . the subject treated cannot have been his most serious concern."[35] Foucault takes this as a clue to the meaning of the dialogues. If they do not set out philosophical knowledge in the form of theoretical knowledge, or at least if this is not the fundamental and *serious* task of the dialogues, then it must be something else. Given this, it is more likely that the writings are meant not as a theory of philosophy setting out its doctrines so much as a confrontation of the reader with the activity of philosophy portrayed in the figure of the first philosophical *parrhēsiast,* Socrates. Foucault will approach the works of Plato as portraits of Socrates which reveal who Socrates is dramatically, by giving us a representation of the dramatic scene—*the modality of veridiction*—which gave form to his words and to his life. In the *Apology* we will see Socrates' representation of himself, much as we have seen in the *Seventh Letter* Plato's autobiography. The *Apology* will provide an account of Socrates' life as a philosophical *parrhēsiast.* We shall see that he took up his activity of *parrhēsia* as a form of care of the self, avoiding the political field because of the way it closed off the possibility of true discourse. Instead of political *parrhēsia,* Socrates spoke directly to individuals, not to instruct them but to incite them to take care of themselves. In *Laches,* we are given a representation of Socratic *parrhēsia* in which the others are made to "give an account" of themselves. Philosophical *parrhēsia* appears in this dialogue as the interrogation which tests the others to reveal whether there is a harmony between their lives and their words. Therefore, the subject is led to focus attention on himself in the form of *bios,* of the choice and practice of existence. In *Alcibiades,* Socrates' *parrhēsia* appears in a different form. Here Socrates leads Alcibiades to "give an account of himself," but this time it is not an account of the harmony between his life and his words. Rather, Alcibiades is led to an account of the nature of his soul and the truth which is revealed there. In other words, the subject comes to know itself through a contemplation of the soul, *psychē.* These two dialogues manifest two different modes of philosophical *parrhēsia* and two different modes of self-knowledge to which it leads.

Before moving on, I would like to pause for a moment to suggest how Foucault's lectures on the *Seventh Letter* contribute to his *own* autobiography. First, I wish to be clear about how I understand the term "auto-biography" here. By arguing that there is an autobiographical dimension to Foucault's project, I do not mean to suggest that the key to his work is to be sought in his life. I do not wish to reduce the meaning of his project to his unconscious desires, his childhood, his love life, or any other aspect of his personal life. Rather, I want to show how Foucault's final project incites us to rethink the notion of philosophical autobiography itself. I have already outlined the autobiographical nature of Plato's *Seventh Letter.* What is at stake is not so much a narrative about the events of Plato's life. Rather, what is being written is a new form of philosophical subjectivity, a new mode of life. The kind of autobiography that I am interested in, then, has less to do with personal history and more to do with the invention of new forms of life, new kinds of subjectivity. Autobiography in this sense is not aimed at the past but rather at the future, and its purpose is not to memorialize but to transform the self. It is, in this sense, a spiritual exercise. It is what Foucault calls *etho-poetic,* borrowing from Plutarch.[36] Etho-poetic writing is a mode of the "subjectivation of discourse," a process whereby discourse comes not simply to be possessed by the subject (in memory), but rather comes *to be* the very subjectivity of the subject.[37] Therefore, I am claiming that Foucault's final project is autobiographical not in the sense that it somehow translates his life and can be reduced to his personal story. Rather, it is autobiographical in that through it a new form of philosophical subjectivity is being invented. What it means to be a philosopher is being rewritten. If Foucault is the subject of his own work, he is not so in the form of the hidden meaning that explains the work, nor is he the subject being written about; rather, he is so as the effect and product of the work.

How do we read the autobiographical dimension of this project? What form of philosophy emerges in Foucault's final project? First, in my introduction I have already made the claim that Foucault's archaeology of the problematization of *parrhēsia* and care of the self is not first of all about the past, but rather is about the future, about possibilities. However, we cannot simply assume that Foucault is reviving, intact and in whole, any ancient philosophical system of care of the self. Foucault frequently cautioned against the idea that contemporary philosophy must strive to recover its lost past or renew the ancient truths that have been forgotten. Furthermore, he made it clear that much in ancient ethics was totally reprehensible.[38] For Foucault, contact with ancient philosophy does not resurrect the past but results in "something new."[39] If Foucault is not, however, reviving the ancient philosopher as this figure appears in Plato, Seneca, Marcus Aurelius, or anywhere else, then what guide do we have to understanding the possibilities Foucault's work offers? One clue is Foucault's emphasis on the role of eclecticism in his excavation of ancient spiritual exercises.[40] Practices, modes of discourse, and forms of existence offer possibilities for choosing, borrowing, rejecting, and so on. Pierre Hadot is critical of Foucault's insistence on the heterogeneity of spiritual writing.[41] He claimed that Foucault placed too heavy an accent on this aspect of the practice of writing as spiritual exercise. The reason why Foucault did so, if Hadot's critique holds, is because Foucault's work sought to produce possibilities, not return to the past. Therefore, if Foucault is opening up a new possibility for philosophical discourse and subjectivity, then this is likely to be composed of heterogeneous elements. But what guides the choice of these heterogeneous elements? If they do not refer to some "authentic" form of philosophy, some original philosophical experience, as guide and goal, then does that mean they are arbitrary? My claim is that Foucault's project is far from arbitrary. What guides Foucault's choices is the problematization of modern relations of power, knowledge, and subjectivity that orients his work. Therefore, in order to grasp the possibilities Foucault creates, we should carefully attend to the intersections between his problematization of power/knowledge/subjectivity and what he says about ancient philosophical practices.

So what are the autobiographical dimensions of Foucault's reading of the *Seventh Letter*? He presents this reading at the beginning of his 1983 course at the Collège. As we saw in the last chapter, Foucault found his way to ancient Greece by following a long path which led from the discovery of disciplinary power to the genealogy of the hermeneutic subject, to Christian confessional practices, to the spiritual direction—*parrhēsia*—practiced by Stoic philosophers, and finally to the isolation of the political problematization of *parrhēsia* in Athens. In 1983 Foucault excavated the event by which *parrhēsia* shifted out of the political field and into the space of care of the self. According to Foucault, that event is what defined Platonic philosophy as an invention, something new, which arose as a form of resistance to relations of power and knowledge. Plato—and of course Socrates—redefine philosophy and redefine *parrhēsia* by incorporating them into the same activity: care of the self. Similarly, Foucault is, through this genealogy, reappropriating and redefining his own practice of philosophy. It is his effort to resist a certain form of power—a power which functions on the subject in its very being—that leads Foucault to the text of Plato. In the *Seventh Letter* Plato characterized philosophy as a practice that targets the subject who exercises power, as a means of provoking this subject to become aware of himself, to take care of himself. While political *parrhēsia* is a direct intervention in the field of power and politics, ethical, philosophical *parrhēsia* intervenes indirectly by speaking to the subject of power. Foucault's philosophical discourse will aim at the subject of power; that is, the individual subjected to a particular form of subjectivity through the incorporation of power and knowledge. Foucault's work, like Plato's, opens up the possibility of care of the self as a form of resistance to power and the self-neglect it feeds and feeds upon. As we have seen, care of the self serves as a point of resistance both because the self is the site where modern power operates and because of its potential for transformation through *askēsis*.

If Foucault is indeed transforming the practice of philosophy, reinventing it as a practice of ethical *parrhēsia* and as a form of care of the self, then what he has to say about the being of philosophical *parrhēsia* is significant. His ontology of philosophical discourse should allow us to understand the being of his own discourse and one possibility for future philosophical discourse. At the very least, we ought to take into account the conditions of possibility of philosophy that Foucault outlines in his analysis of the *Seventh Letter*. This is because these conditions refer not only to the discourse itself, but also to the being of the listener. In other words, for Foucault's discourse to be philosophical it must speak to someone who has a will to listen. That is, we must understand how to properly attend to the meaning of the words spoken. Second, the will to listen is manifested when the listener practices philosophy as a mode of living, as a transformation of life through *askēsis*. And third, this *askēsis* must result in some form of "return effect" on the subject who practices it. What does this mean? The modern academic practice of philosophy is the institutionalization of a particular form of subjectivity. As I have already claimed in my introduction, in modern philosophy the relation between the subject and the truth is one of *connaissance*. This means that our practice is defined in terms of methods for developing knowledge and making arguments. In part 2 of this book I will turn to Foucault's genealogy of modern power-knowledge, which shows that modern philosophical subjectivity arises along with the formation of disciplinary power. The disciplining of philosophy takes place at the level of our very subjectivity. Through the discipline of philosophy we train ourselves to experience discourse in a particular way. That is, discipline shapes how we hear—how we grasp and attend to—philosophical discourse. Our will to listen, in other words, is forged through discipline, and it is this that must be transformed in order to hear otherwise. But to transform our manner of hearing—our will to listen—is what it means to transform our subjectivity. The "return effect" of this alteration is the openness to a whole host of possible meanings at work in philosophical texts, a new world of possible "truth effects" and "games of truth." Plato's critique of writing is meant to draw our attention to this very distinction, the distinction between truth understood in terms of propositions (*mathēmata*) and truth understood in terms of *askēsis*.

Modern philosophy grasps truth and knowledge in terms of propositions. However, according to Plato, philosophical knowledge cannot take the form of propositions and is not able to be transmitted by way of them. If Foucault shows that philosophy is not simply a form of knowledge, but a style of discourse that aims at the transformation of the subject who speaks as well as the subject who listens, then that has a bearing on how we listen, how we can or ought to hear what he says. In other words, philosophical discourse can only attain its status as *ergon,* as work, where there is a proper will to listen, otherwise it remains nothing but words.

The *Apology* of Socrates

Three themes in the *Apology* form the heart of Foucault's interpretation: (1) the way Socrates differentiates his *parrhēsia* from the rhetoric of his accusers; (2) the way Socrates practices an ethical *parrhēsia* which remains external to the political field of discourse; and (3) the definition of Socratic *parrhēsia* as care of the self. As we have seen, these three themes are interconnected: *parrhēsia* is displaced from the political to the ethical dimension of care of the self in order to oppose rhetoric which insinuates itself in the heart of the political field. Foucault shows that together these three themes serve to provide a basic portrait of Socrates as a philosophical, ethical *parrhēsiast.*

Truth and Lies: The Opposition of *Parrhēsia* to Rhetoric

Socrates begins his defense in the *Apology* with an accusation. He charges his accusers of a series of crimes—crimes against Socrates and crimes against the judges and jury. These charges serve to distinguish Socrates' way of talking, and way of being, from the way his accusers talk. *They* are marked by three characteristics: they tell lies, they are seductive, and they are tricky. In other words, they speak falsely yet they are extremely persuasive. Because they lie *and* they are persuasive, the power of their words must come from some source other than the truth. The power of their speech, according to Socrates, is that it is well polished, "a set oration duly ornamented with words and phrases."[42] In other words, they use a technical mastery of language to construct an effective discourse, which *poses* as truth, without actually saying the truth. There is something else about the way they talk, about the power of their words: they are so powerful that Socrates himself was almost convinced by them. He says that "their persuasive words almost made me forget who I was."[43] Their tricks are so persuasive, so powerful, that they can even provoke one to forget the truth of one's very self, who one truly is. For Socrates this power of persuasion, which leads people to forget who they are, goes to the heart of the problem: self-forgetting and self-neglect lay at the basis of the crisis of political life in Athens. Rhetoric is the bag of tricks which is simultaneously grounded on and reinforces this self-neglect. On the other hand, *parrhēsia* as direct, unadorned speech calls one back to oneself, reminds one of who one truly is and that it is necessary to take care of one's true self: "If the skill to speak provokes the oblivion of self, then the simplicity of speech, the speech without devices and without ornamentation, the speech which is immediately true, the speech therefore of *parrhēsia,* will lead us to the truth of ourselves."[44] *Parrhēsia* is the recollection of the truth, the recollection of oneself, and the provocation to be concerned about the truth of oneself.[45]

Socrates introduces his own way of talking in direct opposition to that of his accusers. While they are polished and seductive, he is clumsy and drab. But while their power comes from lots of special effects, Socrates relies on the power of the truth. He portrays himself as someone who speaks the unadorned truth. To make his point, Socrates tells the tribunal that he has never argued a matter before the assembly or defended himself before the court and he therefore lacks any understanding of how to talk in such situations. He is like a foreigner among them, speaking in an unfamiliar language.[46] Foucault points out that this very claim was a typical defense tactic.[47] In other words, presenting oneself as a helpless foreigner who doesn't know the language, and who has to rely only on the truth of what he says so clumsily, was a common rhetorical tactic. The aim of this tactic was to gain the sympathy of the jurors and to mask "technical eloquence."[48] As a rhetorical trick, and as a common one at that, it can hardly be called unadorned, frank, and true to the individual who speaks it. It is, rather, what anyone could and might say in such a situation. Used in such a way, this claim does not and cannot be the immediate truth of the one who speaks. Socrates, however, speaks the truth here. In other words, though his claim is a standard rhetorical technique in the court, Socrates does not *use* it as such. The *use* of language is what Foucault analyzes as the "mode of being of discourse." It refers, on the one hand, to the relationship between the subject and the words he speaks; and on the other hand, to the relationship between the listener and the words spoken. The difference between the way Socrates talks and the way his accusers talk resides in the very being of the discourse they speak. It is in the way they each, respectively, use discourse to manifest or hide the truth, free or control their listeners, and care for or neglect themselves and those they talk to.

In what way is Socrates' claim to be like a foreigner more than just a trick? In fact, we can see that it is not a trick because he proceeds to talk in a way which truly is foreign to the court, in a way in fact which is intolerable for the judges. Socrates helps us understand his strange words by characterizing the way he is going to talk to the court: first, he is going to talk the same way he always talks, the way he talks when he is in the marketplace, with his friends, where he is most himself. There is no discontinuity between his everyday way of talking and the way he will talk in the court; that is, he uses no technique to alter his own habitual mode of discourse. Second, the words he uses are going to be "the first words that occur" to him.[49] His discourse will be the immediate and unaltered translation into speech of the "movement of thought."[50] He will not use any technique to rearrange the order of his thought to produce a speech which is not "immediate"; that is, there will be no rhetorical technique which mediates the passage from thought to speech. Finally, Socrates is absolutely committed to the truth and justice of what he speaks.[51] He believes in what he says, rather than in the tricks he has for saying it well. The truth will give his words power if they are to have any at all. In sum, Socrates' mode of discourse opposes that of his accusers along these three lines: it is his everyday mode of speech, not a special art of persuasion; it is an immediate translation of thought to speech, not a polished oration made to please the audience; and Socrates believes in the truth and justice of what he says, whereas his accusers tell a pack of lies.

These three characteristics not only distinguish Socrates' way of talking from the rhetorical discourse of his accusers, they also ground Socrates' words in the truth. Foucault suggests that this reflects a particular conception of language: the notion of *logos etymos,* the notion that language has an original relationship to truth.[52] Error and falsehood in language are the products of rhetorical techniques that move one's words away from their natural and original proximity to the truth. To speak truly one must abandon rhetorical ornamentation and speak naturally. However, as we shall see, to speak in this way is not simply a matter of choosing a style of discourse. Only someone who lives a natural and true life can speak the natural language of truth. Paradoxically, the natural, true life is not something that just happens.[53] The cultural rhetoric of unnecessary desires, superfluous relationships, and distracting customs and rituals interrupts life just as techniques of speaking interrupt language. Therefore, in order to live the true life and acquire the right and capacity to speak the language of truth, one needs to transform oneself. This becomes possible through the care of oneself, the movement by which one returns to oneself, to discover one's original affinity to truth. This theme was evident in the *Seventh Letter,* and it shall return in Foucault's interpretation of

Alcibiades and *Laches*. Socrates is able to speak the truth because he has taken care of himself, because he lives the true life.

Socrates' discourse is a form of *parrhēsia* because it "says everything" in the sense of saying the whole truth to which he is committed even though doing so is extremely dangerous. Furthermore, Socrates realizes that his way of speaking will not be pleasant and persuasive—he will not flatter the jury by saying what it wants to hear. The discourse of the accusers, however, is constructed through a technical manipulation of language in order to persuade the listeners, to please them, to have the listeners accept it as true. The accusers pose their discourse in a particular relationship to the listeners. It is conceived in order to determine their opinion; it is spoken in a way that is most likely to persuade and to bind (*lier*) them to a certain opinion and course of action. The accusers seek to convince the jury to accept a certain account as true in order to determine their conduct. In this case, the accusers use their technology of language to produce a guilty verdict. The discourse of Socrates has a different relation both to himself and to the judges. On the one hand, he gives no thought to what constructions of language may or may not produce belief on the part of the listeners. He does not attempt to govern them, to bind them to a certain decision by binding them to the opinion transmitted in his speech. On the other hand, his words are related immediately to himself. Rather than using a technology to take hold of the listener, he speaks words to which he binds himself. His goal is not so much to produce a particular decision on the part of the listener as it is to manifest to the listener what he, Socrates, believes, and in effect *who he is* and at the same time to reveal who they are in terms of power, knowledge, and subjectivity.

The Daimonic Voice: Socrates' Refusal of Political Life

The second aspect of the *Apology* to which Foucault draws our attention is Socrates' peculiar political choices, peculiar at least to the other citizens. Socrates says that he spent his days going from one individual to the next like a "father or older brother" advising each one to know who he is and to begin to take care of himself.[54] He realizes that this behavior appears unusual to his fellow citizens. He says, "It may seem curious that I should go round giving advice like this and busying myself in people's private affairs, and yet never venture publicly to address you as a whole and advise on matters of state."[55] Foucault sees this as an explicit reference to the *parrhēsiastic* scene. It is before the assembly that one should speak the truth that one knows in order to guide the others. Because he claims to speak the truth to each one about what is the best life, because he claims to say something which is in the best interest of the city and of each of its citizens, Socrates should go before the assembly and take up the role of *parrhēsiast*. It is in the agonistic setting of the assembly where the truth about the good, what must be done and how, is put to the test and revealed as true.

Parrhēsia, the modality of veridiction in which one asserts ethical truth, had its scene and its function. The Athenians constituted their subjectivity as speakers and hearers of truth in terms of this scene, its agonistic relations, rhetorical structures, and rules. In his defense, Socrates marks a rupture within this function of *parrhēsia.* He speaks the truth in order to guide the others, but he refuses to play the established *parrhēsiastic* game and to constitute himself as political *parrhēsiast.* Why? Because he hears a voice. His daimon turned him away from political life, from speaking truth directly in the political field.[56] His daimon prevented him from doing so because any attempt to speak the truth before the assembly would have resulted in death. Foucault sees this as a reference not simply to the *parrhēsiastic* game but to the problematization of democratic *parrhēsia. Parrhēsia* cannot serve its function of guiding the city through true discourse about the good. The assembly cannot hear and accept the truth.

There are, despite Socrates' general refusal of the *parrhēsiastic* game, two occasions where he acted in the political field. In both cases he resisted the authority of the majority because in his opinion the majority was acting unjustly. Socrates, in each case, acted in accordance with the law and chose the law over the majority view. In each case he risked death in order to avoid committing an unjust act. What marks both of these examples, however, is that he does not voluntarily enter the political scene in order to speak with the purpose of asserting himself over the others and guiding them. In fact, rather than freely taking up the role of *parrhēsiast* in order to enter the struggle for power, Socrates is in each case dragged into the political game and demanded to subsume his political subjectivity under the function given him within this system. In such situations, Socrates constituted his subjectivity as a *parrhēsiast,* he manifested his freedom and his courage, in the refusal of an inauthentic and unjust political act.

Why risk death by such a refusal? "It is out of care for himself [*souci de lui-même*], out of concerning himself with himself [*se preoccuper de lui-même*], out of care for that which is himself, that he is going to refuse to commit an unjust act."[57] The very scene where the Athenians had constituted their subjectivity and where they accomplished their freedom by courageously participating in the struggle for power and truth, Socrates now finds to be the obstacle to his own experience of freedom and duty. Socrates' modality of veridiction takes place in another scene. Rather than letting himself be bound by a political decision made to appropriate him as "anyone," as one of "them," and to determine his political, ethical self for him, he risked death. It is through the risk of death that Socrates is able to appropriate his own existence as a work and a freedom. In other words, Socrates does not feel obligated to freely enter the assembly and risk the truth there to lead the others. He does not achieve himself in his authentic freedom and courage through "care of the city." Rather, out of care for himself he evades this scene and enacts his own drama of truth. His political resistance, in both cases where he risked death, was a matter of not losing or forgetting himself by letting himself be claimed by the structure of nondifferentiation which constantly levels each individual down to the same, to the "they."

The daimon which warned Socrates away from politics did so to preserve him for the task which was his: to care for himself and to use an altogether different form of discourse to care for the others. In other words, "being dead, he would not have been able . . . to be useful to himself and to the Athenians."[58] What underlies Socrates' decision is a "certain relationship to himself and to the Athenians."[59] Socrates avoids death because he wants to preserve and fulfill a certain relationship which is beneficial to himself and to the others. His daimon, the voice which intervenes in his life, calls him back to this task by turning him away from activities which are contrary to it: "This daimonic sign which turned him away from politics . . . this daimonic sign had as its effect—and this was without a doubt its function—to protect this very task and the charge which Socrates had received [from the god]."[60] However, in a situation in which Socrates is implicated in the political field, where he must choose between the possibility of death or of binding himself to injustice, then he must, by way of his refusal, accept the risk of death and thereby reclaim himself, manifestly committing himself to his freedom and courage.

In these first two aspects of the *Apology*—the opposition to rhetoric and the evasion of politics—Foucault defines ethical *parrhēsia* and care of the self negatively: he shows primarily what it is not. Furthermore, for Foucault rhetoric and politics function together, problematically, and therefore Socratic *parrhēsia* and care appear as a form of resistance. Foucault's account of the nature of rhetoric and political domination in Athens clearly reflects his own problematic of discipline, normalization, and biopower. Rhetoric is a technology of power, a form of knowledge, which has the purpose of controlling individuals. Politics is an area dominated by this technology—it attempts to control individuals, in a sense, by defining them, by coercing them to conform. Of course, rhetoric and political power in Athens were by no means forms of discipline, normalization, or biopower. But they were a dangerous convergence of power and knowledge, and they did function through attempting to inhabit the very identity of individuals. Foucault's, and our, situation is quite different from that of Socrates. And yet, insofar as Socrates represents the formation of a resistance to power and knowledge, he shows Foucault a new possibility. Socrates resists rhetoric and the domination of the general opinion through a practice of the self. If self-neglect is what allows individuals to be manipulated by rhetoric, then fashioning a powerful care of the self opposes that manipulation. Therefore, while we should not substitute "Foucault" every time we read "Socrates," Foucault's experience of Socrates opens up a new path to follow: the exploration of care of the self as a mode of resistance to power and knowledge relations. In the following section, I will look at Foucault's analysis of the positive definition of Socratic care of the self. Here we will be able to see specific links to Foucault's diagnosis of modern power and the discovery of ways of resisting this power.

Philosophy as Care of the Self

Socrates claims in the *Apology* that though he refused to play the political game directly, he performed an activity of even greater value to the city. Besides maintaining himself in a relationship of exteriority to the political field, he exercises a positive function of *parrhēsia* in a philosophical rather than a political relationship. Foucault tells us that the task to which the divine voice calls Socrates is "a certain exercise, a certain practice of speaking the truth . . . completely different from those which can take place in the political scene."[61] Socratic philosophy appears as a new game of truth, a new modality of veridiction, a new form of *parrhēsia* whose scene is exterior to political discourse and power but whose effects are positive with respect to the political life of the city. The subject who speaks philosophical *parrhēsia* does not enter the *agon* to try to assert himself in the struggle for power, to speak his mind on the affairs of the city in order to let his interest become that of the city. Rather, he constitutes himself as a subject speaking the truth in an altogether different way.

Foucault isolates three essential "moments" of Socrates' practice of philosophy as it is described to us in the *Apology*.[62] The first moment is evident in Socrates' relationship to the words of the oracle.[63] The oracle asserts that no man is wiser than Socrates. Rather than accept in the "field of reality" the words of the oracle and try to interpret their meaning, Socrates submits them to an "investigation" (*recherche*) in order to discover their "truth." He shifts the meaning of the oracle's words from revelation of the real to the field of *logos*, assertion, and therefore to the game of true and false. The assertion of the oracle is to be tested and verified rather than accepted and interpreted. In order to test the assertion that Socrates is wisest he "submits it to questioning," to an "interrogation."[64]

He sets himself on a path of questioning and interrogating in order "to know if the prophecy can effectively become unarguable."[65] That is, the truth of this assertion will be established only when it is no longer arguable, no longer questionable. Socrates' practice of philosophy begins as an interrogation into the truth of an assertion. Later this will become the general form of Socratic *parrhēsia*. The first "moment" of Socratic philosophical practice is, then, the investigation which tests and verifies the truth of an assertion through submitting it to interrogation.

How does Socrates carry out his investigation? Where does his path lead him? This brings us to the second moment of his philosophical practice. In order to test the truth of the oracle's words, Socrates goes around the city confronting the other citizens and questioning them to see what they know, if they know more than he does. He begins by dividing the citizens into categories distinguishable in terms of knowledge. According to the general opinion, the politicians are the wisest, followed by the poets, and finally the craftsmen. Socrates can only know the truth of the oracle, which says that no man is wiser than he, by confronting and *examining* those citizens who are supposedly wisest. The interrogation of the oracle, in this way, turns into an interrogation of the other citizens, it turns into an examination in which Socrates learns what relationship the others have to truth, what knowledge or wisdom they possess. The test of the oracle takes the form, therefore, of an "examination."[66] Socrates approaches and engages individuals outside the assembly, comes into contact with them in a private relationship, and examines them with respect to the kind of knowledge they claim to have and really do not have. The ensuing exchange is a confrontation, a test of one against the other, the soul of Socrates against the soul of his interlocutor. The investigation of the truth of the oracle's assertion unfolds through a "confrontation of souls."[67] Socrates must discover who is wiser. Therefore, he confronts, examines, and interrogates the others to learn the condition of *their* souls—to learn what kind of relationship holds between their souls and the truth.

The notion of the examination plays a crucial role in both Foucault's analysis of modern operations of power-knowledge and his genealogy of care of the self. The examination is ostensibly an objectivizing technique for the production of knowledge. It is a tool used by doctors, scientists, teachers, psychiatrists, police officers, lawyers, students, and so on. However, Foucault has shown that within the modern problematic of discipline, normalization, and biopower, the examination is one of the central technologies for producing individuals as objects to be known and controlled.[68] It is a method for making individuals visible, for documenting them, and for turning them into cases. Modern forms of examination have as their genealogical source the confession. As Foucault saw it, our culture is obsessed with confession. The examination, as a mode of confession, presupposes that the self is a kind of text, hidden within, that can and must be read out loud before an audience. The confessional examination is also linked to a hermeneutical practice: the self must not only confess, but it must interpret what it says in the confession to discover the real meaning hidden in the words. In the *Apology*, Foucault excavates a mode of examination that is radically different from the asymmetrical and objectifying practices of the disciplines, confession, and hermeneutics. The Socratic examination is not exactly symmetrical, but it is also not at all objectifying. Socratic examination requires a *confrontation*, a dialogue. In order to test the statement of the oracle, Socrates must compare himself to others. In order to learn the condition of his own soul, his own mind, he must engage in dialogue. The examination is neither a solitary examination of conscience, nor is it a technique organized and managed in order to produce objective knowledge and control of individuals. Socratic examination is also neither a confessional nor a hermeneutic technique. The oracle's pronouncement is not submitted to an interpretation. Socrates' method is to question its truth, not its hidden meaning. Nor does Socrates engage in a confession of who he is, what he has done, his thoughts, or his desires. The examination does not measure his aptitude, his capability, what he has learned or whether he is capable of learning. Socratic examination is therefore different from disciplinary deployments of examination. In the context of care of the self, Foucault isolates nondisciplinary, nonhermeneutic, nonconfessional techniques of examination. One of the main problems in almost every theory and practice of care of the self that Foucault studies is to define the role and the method for the examination of conscience: is it solitary or does it require a partner; is it juridical, hermeneutic, or objectifying; is it considered a form of knowledge or is it a manner of self-formation? By reading Socratic examination through the double filter of disciplinary power and care as resistance, Foucault offers a way of converting the notion of examination from a form of power to a form of resistance and care. By loosening the disciplinary grip on the instrument of examination, Foucault makes it available as a possible tool for care for the self; he shows that it can be transformed and made to work according to different rules, toward different ends and in other contexts. Furthermore, Foucault's study of examination, both as a disciplinary technology and as an element of care, focuses on the way the practice itself defines the subject. Examination does not just produce knowledge, it produces *examining subjects*. By putting the examination within the context of care, and by focusing on its etho-poetic rather than its hermeneutic effect, Foucault gives us a variety of ways of remaking ourselves as *examining subjects*. Finally, by showing that the modern disciplinary technique of examination arose as a form of resistance and part of the care of the self, Foucault reveals something about the interrelations between power and care or power and freedom. A practice that serves as resistance in one setting can be a technology of control in another. Once practices are dislodged from the problematizations that give rise to them, they have the potential to rigidify, to become elements of control or domination rather than freedom and invention. In Foucault's own approach to Socrates and Plato, we can see this kind of displacement at work. Foucault does not simply provide an objectifying examination of Socrates, Plato, and all the rest. The Foucauldian examination of these texts is both a form of confrontation and a form of invention.

For Socrates, the purpose of this confrontation and examination is to learn whether the oracle has spoken the truth. But the truth of the oracle's words is at the same time the truth about Socrates himself. The truth the oracle reveals concerns the condition of Socrates' own soul. The path of interrogations and confrontations leads, therefore, to a kind of self-knowledge—knowledge about the relationship which one has to the truth. Of course, all the others, when questioned by Socrates, claim knowledge that they do not really possess. In the *Apology* we are not told to what kind of questions, to what kind of confrontation, Socrates subjected the others. However, it is clear from the subject of other dialogues and the *Apology* itself that the questions revolved around the themes of justice and the "best way to live." Furthermore, we can imagine the reason why the others claimed knowledge about these themes. They made a claim to such knowledge because they were *claimed by* a false opinion, the majority opinion, the one inscribed in their lives and in their souls by the force of the assembly and the words of the Sophists.[69] They claim knowledge, but in fact they are ignorant because they have never taken care of the state of their souls. Always believing they already possessed self-knowledge, they never sought out the "true education," the one through which true discourse comes to be present in the soul.[70] By revealing the ignorance, self-neglect, and self-forgetfulness characteristic of the others, this confrontation leads Socrates to the truth about himself; he learns that he is wiser than the others because he, paradoxically, knows that he knows nothing. "It is in this manner that the soul of Socrates becomes the touchstone— *basanos*—the touchstone of the souls of the others."[71] The second moment of Socratic philosophy is the self-examination which unfolds in the confrontation of souls and results in self-knowledge.

To return to Foucault's project: the examination as he defines it in his reading of the *Apology* is first of all an investigation into a statement made by an authority, the oracle. The statement presents itself as the truth, and it concerns the very identity of the individual to whom it is spoken. Socrates examines this statement not to find out what it means, but to find out if it is true or false. The examination proceeds not in a solitary reflection but in a dialogue in which one learns the truth about the statement, and therefore about oneself, in a test, a confrontation with someone else. In other words, the starting point, and in a sense the material which is under examination here, is not some inner truth, some inner text or nature, but rather a pronouncement that comes from the outside and must be tested in public, in a relationship to someone else. In the attempt to define practices of care, a subtle redefinition of one of the central practices of control offers a potentially powerful tool for self-fashioning and for alternate modes of producing self-understanding. By turning the statements of experts, like the oracle, into strange and unfamiliar objects, and by using them as starting points for our own inquiry and self-formation rather than taking them as answers and end points to our self-understanding, they no longer appear as necessities or as destinies, but rather as possibilities.

Socrates' practice of philosophy leads him to self-knowledge. This takes place not through "teaching" but through the confrontation by which his own truth is revealed to him. This brings us to the third moment of Socratic philosophy. The confrontation of souls has illuminated self-knowledge in Socrates. Foucault points out that this self-knowledge opens Socrates to another, unexpected form of knowledge, a deeper and transformative relationship to the truth. Here we see the way in which Socratic knowledge operates within the horizon of spirituality. After having confronted all those who claim to know, who claim wisdom, Socrates realized that he was indeed the wisest, but through this discovery the *meaning* of the oracle reveals itself to him and gives his (self-)knowledge its definitive form: the god spoke out of care, care for the city itself and care for each of the individuals who lives in it. The god spoke for the very purpose of setting Socrates on a path, on a *mission* of confronting and examining everyone he meets, testing each one in such a way that each one becomes aware of the negligence that defines his relationship to himself. Socrates' knowledge of his relationship to the truth, that he knows nothing, is in fact a form of truth, a new relationship to himself, that of care of the self, the form of truth through which one knows that one must care about the soul, reason, and truth.[72] The practice of care is, in a sense, the very same practice Socrates has been engaged in since receiving the Oracle, but now this practice is transformed from within; Socrates continues to confront the others, continues to examine them, to reveal the relationship which they maintain to the truth (which in fact they neglect entirely), but he no longer tests the words of the oracle. Rather, he performs the mission which the god has given to him, to take care for the care that the others must take of themselves, and this is the essence of Socratic philosophical *parrhēsia*. This spiritual transformation from within is precisely what I suggest takes place in Foucault's practice of philosophy when he confronts the texts of Plato. His practice of diagnosis takes on a new meaning and a new possibility: the practice of ethical *parrhēsia* and care of the self.

The god has put Socrates among the others like a soldier who is charged with the task of maintaining a constant *vigilance* over them.[73] The purpose of this vigilance, which unfolds as confrontation and examination, is to "incite them to occupy themselves with themselves . . . with their reason, with the truth and with their soul—*phronēsis, alētheia, psychē.*"[74] The others have neglected and forgotten themselves because of their concern for "wealth and reputation." They are ignorant, they lack *phronēsis,* because they do not know the nature of their souls. Socrates' practice of philosophy, the examination of himself and the others with respect to the knowledge they claim, is a practice of care of the self. Through the contest of souls one is led to the recognition of one's ignorance. This recognition incites one to begin to care for oneself, that is, one's soul, one's reason, and the truth. In this way care is the condition of possibility of effective political life because it detaches one from the inadequate self-interpretation which causes and is caused by self-neglect and which supports inauthentic political life.

Like "examination," the term "vigilance" has a central spot in the Foucauldian lexicon. Modern power, as biopower and disciplinary power, is essentially a mode of vigilance: it is panopticism. Always watching, power controls precisely by making individuals visible. But in his lectures on ancient philosophy as care of the self and as *parrhēsia,* Foucault analyzes vigilance as a technique of resistance to power, a way of taking care of oneself and others, guarding against self-neglect. From Socrates to the Cynics the role of the philosopher is to make himself and others visible, to reveal their self-neglect, and to show them what they need to take care of. Foucault makes vigilance into a constant theme of his study of care of the self. This vigilance with respect to vigilance is also a way of loosening the grip of power upon us; it creates a kind of torsion within the function of discipline, not just by pointing out how discipline functions, but by re-appropriating its own techniques, subtly changing them, putting them to use in the service of different ends.

The care Socrates takes for himself is a care for the care that the others must take of themselves.[75] The place of the philosopher, the activity and the life of the philosopher, therefore, is defined by its special relationship to others, to the truth and to the self. The philosopher must live a certain kind of life, he must neglect the concerns of others, not to withdraw to a life of solitude and contemplation, but rather to transform the way he inhabits the everyday world and lives among others. Socrates must neglect the everyday projects of the city. First he has to concern himself with something else, he must practice a constant vigilance over the souls of the others and the form of existence they choose. But he must also detach himself from the false self-interpretation presupposed in, and constantly reinforced by, the practice of political life in Athens. The philosophical life detaches itself from the general opinion and the control of rhetoric, from the neglect of the self, so that it can lead another kind of life, have another kind of relationship to the others.[76]

The choice of, and practice of, a certain kind of life gives one access to a truth which otherwise remains hidden. By taking up the mission the god gave to him, Socrates gains access to the truth which others cannot see because of their self-neglect. Foucault's interpretation of the spiritual truth of the dialogues takes on an almost lyrical quality at this point. He says that Socrates' practice of care, of ethical *parrhēsia*, "deploys itself in what one could call the great chain of cares and solicitudes."[77] A new meaning emerges which structures the cosmos and which gives it unity and wholeness. The relationship of the gods to human beings and of the gods to each individual is one of *care*—out of care the gods sent Socrates to the city (using the oracle at Delphi), out of care they turned Socrates away from the political scene (using the daimonic voice) in order to protect him from the assembly and to hold him to his mission of examining his fellow citizens. Conversely, out of care for the words of the god, Socrates did not content himself merely to accept the oracle's words and to *await* the truth which it indicated. Rather, he set out on a mission, he devoted himself to testing the statement of the oracle, and he learned that care is the fundamental relationship of oneself to oneself, to others, and to the gods. Socratic knowledge is a practice of care and is grounded in the relationship of the self to truth. The practice of care, in the form of philosophical *parrhēsia,* recalls one to the fundamental truth, to the interrelation of one's self, the world, the divine, and the other, the interrelatedness which is constituted by care.

Foucault shows that this theme is evoked in the *Crito* and the *Phaedo* as well, that it traverses the "cycle" of the trial and death of Socrates, and is in fact the fundamental meaning of these dialogues.[78] In the *Crito*, for instance, Socrates refuses to escape from prison and from the sentence he received in the court. He refuses to flee from death because were he to do so it would mean that he no longer cared for the laws which have cared for him all of his life. The laws are what cared for Socrates, protecting him, educating him, giving him a place and an identity in the city, and making his entire existence possible.[79] In return he owed respect in the form of a gesture of care: preserve those laws which preserve you. To flee would be an act of annihilating the laws, of neglecting them, of saying that they are binding only when it is convenient. In other words, the meaning of the laws is not just to hold the city together, but to do so by taking care of the citizens. The city itself is based upon the structure and practice of care of the self. In the *Phaedo,* Socrates argues that suicide is not permissible because we are in the care of the gods and as such are their possessions. To neglect the property of the gods, a property entrusted to us for a time, is to neglect the gods themselves.[80] Therefore, the relationship between human beings and the gods is one of care of the self. The relationship of care also binds together Socrates and his companions. In each of the dialogues, *Apology, Crito,* and *Phaedo,* Socrates insists that it has been his task to take care of the others, and in the *Phaedo,* shortly before Socrates speaks his final words, Crito asks him, "Have you no directions for the others or myself about your children or anything else? What can we do to please you best?" Socrates' response is: "Nothing new Crito . . . just what I am always telling you. If you look after yourselves, whatever you do will please me and mine and you too."[81] Foucault argues that this is the meaning of the final words of Socrates, "We owe a cock to Asclepios . . . see to it, and don't forget [*mē amelē se te*]."[82] The final instruction is in fact an instruction to "take care," *epimēleia.* The word translated as "forget" or "neglect" is the Greek *ameles.* It is etymologically tied to the word *epimēleia* in that it is the alpha-privative of the root word *melēs.*[83] Socrates' final request is therefore a double negation, the negation (*mē*) of neglect, of noncare (*a-melē*), and is in this way a call, a recall, to care. The enigmatic final words of Socrates, which refer to the ritual act of making a sacrifice to Asclepius, the god of medicine, after one has been cured of a disease, are an affirmation of the practice of philosophical *parrhēsia,* care of the self, and the "great chain of cares" which gives meaning and structure to the cosmos. These words mean, "Don't forget to perform this sacrifice to this god, to this god who helps us to heal ourselves when we take care of ourselves."[84]

It is through confrontation, philosophical *parrhēsia,* that Socrates discovers the truth about himself. Self-neglect—the absorption of the self into the nondifferentiation of the general opinion, the concern for wealth, power, and reputation—is "cured" by Socrates' *parrhēsia.* Care is therefore a therapeutic activity: it cures one of self-neglect, which is a disease of the soul. Through ethical *parrhēsia* one is led to the self-knowledge one needs to govern oneself, to conduct oneself well, to take care of oneself and therefore to heal oneself. Without this *ēthos* political life will continue to be ineffective because the citizens will lack the knowledge to "make good decisions . . . [and] . . . and avoid false ones."[85] Philosophical *parrhēsia* is a care of the self which responds to the political crisis, the crisis of political discourse and subjectivity, by producing an experience of a self, a subject, who is able to speak, and listen to, the truth. Socrates forms his own subjectivity through the confrontation with the other; his mode of life is determined by this confrontation in which he tests his soul against that of the other to see what wisdom he possesses, to test the truth of his own soul, and simultaneously to test the soul of the other. He risks his life, he forgoes wealth, power, and reputation in order to maintain his constant vigilance over the life and souls of his fellow citizens. This mode of life and of discourse is, in its effects, beneficial for the city itself because in confronting the citizens as individuals it strives to instill the truth in them, the realization that they must take care of themselves. Philosophical *parrhēsia* does not insert itself directly into the field of politics, but rather intervenes in the being of the subject who exercises power. This function is politically necessary because individuals must possess a certain kind of *ēthos*, they must first take care of themselves, in order to enter the *agon* of politics to speak and hear the truth. Through ethical *parrhēsia* and care of the self they learn how to be guided by what is true rather than by what is merely pleasant or persuasive.

Conclusion: Socrates' *Apology* and *Parrhēsia*

Foucault shows that these three themes outline the basic way Socrates portrays his mode of life and language in the *Apology*. Socratic *parrhēsia* takes shape as a recollection of oneself that opposes rhetoric. Rhetoric, the technology of flattery, functions by constructing discourses that bind listeners more tightly to the false experience of self. The power of rhetoric is based upon self-neglect. The neglect of the self as a political ethical subject was the prevailing experience determining the political life of the Athenians. Because of this neglect, the political assembly was perceived as the place where one engages in a struggle for power, a struggle that unfolds in the element of language. One desires power for wealth and reputation, and one desires wealth and reputation to increase one's power. Truth is impossible in such a setting. Therefore Socratic *parrhēsia* does not take a stand in the assembly, in the public space, but rather in private relationships. Socratic philosophy takes place exterior to the political field but it is not apolitical. It maintains itself in a constant tension with the political. This is because Socrates uses *parrhēsia* to transform the individual whom he confronts. He calls the individual back to himself and therefore away from the deficient, negligent experience that founded problematic political discourse.

Socratic *parrhēsia* does not teach by passing along a set of doctrines meant to be accepted as true. Or at least, this is not what constitutes Socrates' philosophy insofar as it is a practice of *parrhēsia*. As *parrhēsiast*,

Socrates does not persuade his listeners to accept a certain opinion in order to determine their conduct, to substitute his opinion for their own proper freedom. Rather, he confronts the other in order to lead him to the truth of himself. Socratic *parrhēsia* attempts to reveal to the interlocutor his own self-neglect, his own nonrelationship to himself. In this sense Socratic *parrhēsia* is care of the self; by provoking the listener to pay attention to himself, Socrates establishes in the listener a relationship of care for himself. The *parrhēsiastic* dialogue is in itself a mode of caring for the self. It cares for a self defined in terms of reason (*phronēsis*), in terms of the relationship between the soul and the truth. Only reason, *phronēsis*, developed through the practice of care of the self is true power because only this reason lets one choose what is best and avoid what is not. By establishing a relationship between the individual and himself, a relationship based on a concern for reason, truth and the soul, Socratic *parrhēsia* and care of the self are a therapy for self-neglect. This forms a resistance to the foundation of political domination in the form of rhetoric and the general opinion. In opposition to political subjection, care of the self constructs a subject.

Alcibiades and *Laches:* An Introduction to the *Parrhēsiastic* Life

In the *Seventh Letter* and in the *Apology*, Foucault discovers adumbrations of Socratic-Platonic philosophy as ethical *parrhēsia*. He shows that Plato and Socrates develop philosophy as an ethical relationship of speaking and hearing the truth, as a provocation through which the listener is made to begin to care for himself. In *Alcibiades* and in *Laches*, Plato sketches two forms of the philosophical practice of care of the self. These practices are meant to resist the prevailing neglect of self. In each case the "Delphic principle"—know yourself—is given a special emphasis among the activities of which care is composed. To know oneself becomes not simply a preparation for approaching the oracle, but rather an introduction to life and to the *parrhēsiastic* life in particular. Therefore, while the invocation of *epimēleia heauton* links Plato to the ancient tradition of spirituality and the practices of self-modification that *epimēleia* entails, he radically revises and reorganizes these practices by placing the obligation of self-knowledge at the center of them. Both *Alcibiades* and *Laches* illustrate the new form of *parrhēsia* and care of the self, which prepare one for political *parrhēsia*. In each case, Socrates will care for the care that the others take of themselves. But each dialogue represents a different form of ethical *parrhēsia*. In Alcibiades ethical parrhēsia proceeds in the form of an "ontology of the soul."[86] Parrhēsia and care of the self require one to give an account (*logos*) of the condition and nature of one's soul (*psychē*). In *Laches*, on the other hand, ethical *parrhēsia* is a "test of existence" in which one is made to give an account (*logos*) of one's life (*bios*).[87] In a confrontation with Socrates one is forced to pay attention to the way one lives, to examine and account for how one lives one's life. Therefore, the self is articulated as an object of discourse (*logos*) in two possible domains, the soul (*psychē*) and existence (*bios*). Ethical *parrhēsia,* as a technique of care of the self, appears as a *psychological* and *biological* art. Foucault believes that these two forms of care of the self will result in two different traditions. One tradition will place an accent on the psychological practices and will focus on the care of the self as a soul—Stoicism represents this tradition. The other tradition will develop care as a constant test of life— this is the tradition of Cynicism and Christian mysticism, according to Foucault.

Alcibiades: Eros and Care of the Self

As the dialogue opens, Socrates approaches Alcibiades and claims to be his first and last lover.[88] This is strange because the time for courting Alcibiades is over—he is at the threshold of manhood and is no longer an appropriate object of love. Socrates is therefore his last lover because all of the others have abandoned Alcibiades, realizing he is no longer to be loved. He is Alciabiades' first lover because, as he will show, none of those who chased him around before truly loved him. Furthermore, when Alcibiades was, because of his beauty and his age, an appropriate object of love, Socrates remained silent and kept at a distance. He was silenced by "a power more than human," that is, by the daimonic voice that always turned him away from harmful, self-destructive actions.[89] Therefore, the same voice which turned Socrates away from political life and silenced his political *parrhēsia* also turned him away from the erotic dimension and silenced him there as well; until, of course, the moment at which the dialogue begins, the moment where Alcibiades must no longer be an *object* of Eros but must become instead a *subject* of political life, an agent. And, we shall see, just as the daimon's negation of political *parrhēsia* had a more fundamental, positive meaning, which was to open up the dimension of ethical *parrhēsia,* here the refusal of the accepted and expected erotic game will also have another positive meaning: the possibility of a new, unexpected modality of Eros which will have for its definitive form care of the self.

It is no coincidence that Socrates' daimonic voice should intervene in both his erotic life and his political-ethical life. As Foucault showed in *The Use of Pleasure,* the erotic and the political intersect in an essential way in Plato's thought. This is in part because the erotic relationship structurally mirrors the political relationship in ancient Greece: "Pleasure practices were conceptualized using the same categories as those in the field of social rivalries and hierarchies: an analogous agonistic structure, analogous oppositions and differentiations, analogous values attributed to the respective roles of the partners."[90] But even more important, the field of erotic experience conditions the young Athenians, initiating them into a certain experience of themselves, of their relations to others and to the forms of desire and the purposes which determine those relationships. Erotic relationships in Athens were structured, according to Socrates and Plato, by the same neglect of the self that supported rhetoric and the general opinion. The erotic field, with the intensity of its involvements and identifications, the dissymmetry of its relationships owing to the difference in age and experience between the lover and the beloved, was potentially a privileged place for care of the self. But the Athenians missed this opportunity and instead took up the erotic as another place for the struggle for power and self-satisfaction. In other words, it was used as an opportunity for one individual, the lover, experienced as a principle of pleasure and a will to power, to persuade, manipulate, and seduce the other, the beloved, who was at great disadvantage in the erotic game. This relationship was especially dangerous precisely because it neglected the proper attention to the self as a subject; it initiated one into a game of controlling and objectifying others by making the beloved into an object of control. It served as a powerful indoctrination into the "general opinion," which dominated and precluded political and ethical life.

The Socratic-Platonic response to this situation was *to use* this relationship as a place of care of the self, in order to develop and give form to the beloved; the erotic relationship takes on an ethical function through the work of Socrates and Plato.[91] The figure of Socrates will represent a new kind of lover, the philosopher who cares for the soul of the beloved. Erotics will be transformed into a practice of care and the beloved will be transformed from being an *object* of love and therefore passive, to a *subject* who must take up an active relationship to himself. The erotic relationship appears, in the work of Plato, as a place of truth, where one can use ethical *parrhēsia* in order to take care of the other, to produce in him the proper *ēthos* for political life.

Socrates approaches Alcibiades and interrogates him in order to force him to recognize his current condition. Alcibiades is at that point where he is expected to become a political agent, to fulfill the expectations of his status, his wealth, his family, and the potentialities of his freedom, in the political field. It is at this moment that he finds himself abandoned by all his former suitors. Socrates confronts Alcibiades in order to force him to recognize that he is motivated by an ambition, an indefinite desire, to rule in Athens. Furthermore, Socrates challenges and interrogates Alcibiades on the problem of government to make him realize that he is completely ignorant of what it means to rule, he lacks the *technē* of governing effectively. The Socratic interrogation brings to light the situation in which the ethical function of Eros has not fulfilled itself. The Athenians who chased after Alcibiades neglected him. They did not truly love him, and the proof is the fact that they did not take care of Alcibiades in order to make him into a subject capable of governing. They abandoned him just at the moment where he had to actualize the *ēthos*, the *technē*, and the freedom that the erotic relationship was supposed to develop in him.

Socrates' aim is to take care of Alcibiades and correct his condition. He is going to exhibit a true love for Alcibiades because he is concerned about Alcibiades as a subject, not an object. That is, he is going to take care of him by helping him learn how to take care of himself. Foucault shows that Socrates' erotics invokes the principle of self-knowledge at three crucial junctures of the dialogue. The first has already taken place. It happens when Socrates confronts Alcibiades and lets him know that he has a problem. Alcibiades reflects on his situation and realizes that he is defined by two characteristics: (1) he wants to rule Athens; and (2) he has no idea what ruling entails. Socrates tells Alcibiades that he must know himself; that is, he must recognize his current condition.[92] Through the recognition of his condition, Socrates says, Alcibiades "will be more likely to take care of [him]self."[93] The purpose of the interrogation of Alcibiades is to make him anxious, to make him aware of his inadequacy and to incite a desire to correct, to *cure* himself of his condition. Socrates offers himself as a guide to Alcibiades who, realizing his situation, submits to be governed by Socrates, to follow him and learn from him. In order to become capable of governing others Alcibiades must first "be governed." Therefore, he submits to Socrates, not in order to renounce his will, but to strengthen it, to make it adequate to the tasks of political life. In other words, as Foucault sees it, the central problem of the text is the problem of the government of oneself and of others. The relationship which Alcibiades and Socrates establish is not going to be one in which Socrates transmits knowledge, a *technē* of governing, to him.[94] This is the procedure of the Sophists. They instruct students in the technology of persuading and controlling others—rhetoric. The Socratic approach, on the other hand, is based on the principle of care of the self. Socrates will not pass along a *technē* to Alcibiades but will help him to transform his mode of being in order to help him become a subject. Through this transformation in his very being, Alcibiades will discover and learn how to put to use an art of governing. Alcibiades must free himself of his current way of being, the symptom of his self-neglect. He must learn how to take care of, govern, himself before he can hope to govern others. The erotic relationship is therefore displaced from its former situation, the struggle of power (in the form of conquest and seduction) between lover and beloved, and is now realized in the relationship between the philosopher, who practices the art of care of the self, and the disciple who must begin to take care of himself.

Once Alcibiades has recognized his condition he is willing to begin to care for himself. However, a problem arises—part of his condition, his ignorance, is that he neither knows what the self is insofar as it is simultaneously the subject and object of care, nor does he know what to do in order to care for himself. Together Socrates and Alcibiades address these two questions: What is the self? and How does one care for the self? First, what is this self, which is both subject and object of care? For the second time, Socrates invokes the Delphic inscription: one must know oneself. The first appearance of this principle referred to the recognition of Alcibiades' condition, the lack and the desire which define him. The first function of self-knowledge is to incite one to take care of oneself. Now the need to know oneself appears as a "formal or methodological" problem.[95] That is, one must know one's self insofar as one is the object of care.

The self is defined in a specific way in *Alcibiades*. By posing a series of questions to Alcibiades and forcing him to respond, Socrates leads him to a definition of the self as a soul, *psychē*. What is essential for Foucault is that the soul is not grasped as a substance, as a tripartite structure, as one's true nature imprisoned in the body, or as the eternal being which will separate itself after death and live on in another world. In order to grasp the soul, to make it appear as an object of care, Plato uses the term *khrēsis/khrēsthai*, or "use" (*se servir*). In *Alcibiades* knowledge of the self refers to the soul as *subject*, that is, the soul insofar as it "transcends" its surroundings, its body, all of its qualities and instruments by being the activity of "using" them. Foucault shows that the term *khrēsis* is rich in its extension.[96] It does not refer primarily to instrumental relations with the world, the body, or other people. It refers, rather, to the way one comports oneself with things, with oneself, and with others. For example, *khrēsis* when it refers to the relationship of human beings to the gods does not suggest that humans "use" the gods, but that they do what is appropriate, perform the proper acts according to the proper art which gives shape to this relationship, that they serve the gods.[97] With this notion of *khrēsis*, Plato points to the "singular and transcendent position of the subject" with respect to everything around it. The subject is not any of these things among which it finds itself, it is not even its own body, thoughts, or qualities; it stands in relation to them, it is a *comporting-itself-with, -through,* or *-by* them.[98] It is this self which, in the formula "take care of yourself," is both subject and object. The self-transformation of care of the self must modify one's manner, or style, of comporting oneself with oneself, with others, and with the world around one. But this self, as a subject which transcends its surroundings precisely through its involvement with them, is a subject defined by the activity of caring. The subject of *Alcibiades* is the subject of care. The care of the self is then an activity of taking care of the care which one is, which defines one's very being.

In this text Foucault discovers a problematic of the subject as transcendent agency, as a principle of action, as a principle of attending to, caring for, and controlling its environment. The term *khrēsis* refers to a problematic of special importance to Foucault. It is the central concept in his analysis of Greek practices of *aphrodesia* in *The Use of Pleasure.* But much earlier the notion of "use" (*se servir de* . . . ; *usage*), of the subject as modulation of engagement with the world, appears in Foucault's thesis on Kant's *Anthropology from a Pragmatic Point of View.* For Kant the pragmatic view takes up precisely the problem of what man has made of himself and what he ought to make of himself.[99] Are we heading in the direction of a Foucauldian notion of the subject as such when we approach this concept of *khrēsis?* It does seem that the conceptual problem indicated in his final lectures by the term *khrēsis* was a theme of Foucault's thought from its first expression to its last. The appearance of this notion in *The Hermeneutics of the Subject* adds another dimension to this theme. In his reading of *Alcibiades,* Foucault does not simply accent the soul-subject or soul-activity dimension of *khrēsis,* but he also draws our attention to its character as transcendence. The subject "appears" as transcendent, in the sense of being outside, beyond, or irreducible to its surroundings. It is able to take up concrete practices, and perhaps it is always only accessible by and through the activities it activates and the surroundings it inhabits, but it always "exceeds" them. One might say the transcendence of the subject is implicitly, or potentially, transgressive as well. The subject is in excess of its concrete dimensions. However, rather than attempt to spell out a theory of the transcendence of the subject, of the subject as such, Foucault leaves the problem open and leaves the subject alone in its irreducibility.

So far it has been determined that Alcibiades must take care of himself, he must attend to himself in the form of a "soul-subject," insofar as he is that which transcends his surroundings through the very movement of *comporting-himself-with* them. The next question to answer is, How does one take care of oneself as a subject of *khrēsis?* At this point, the principle, "know yourself," returns for a third time.[100] In *Alcibiades* the practice of care is defined as a practice of self-knowledge. In order to take care of one-self, to acquire the proper techniques of governing, one must practice a form of self-knowledge. The mode of knowing one must take up is a con-templation of the self, of the soul, through which one is able to grasp it in its being. Plato uses a metaphor to describe this act of contemplation: the metaphor of the eye and of vision. In order for one to contemplate, to *see* oneself, one needs a "mirror." The ideal mirror in which the eye can see itself is another eye. This is because it sees itself reflected in that particu-lar part of the other eye in which sight, the function which defines it as an eye, takes place: the pupil.[101] The eye sees itself in the "principle of vision." Similarly, the soul will only be able to know itself by seeing itself in an-other, in something with the same nature as itself. It must know itself through perceiving itself in a "double." What is this other to which it refers itself, which reveals to it its true nature? The soul must contemplate itself in the "divine being" because in the divine it will perceive its own nature, the pure activity of knowing. Self-knowledge is achieved through the con-templation of the divine being. In the divine one will discover knowledge, the foundation of the true and the false, the good and the bad, and the true art of governing.

At the end of the dialogue, the will of Alcibiades appears to be puri-fied, though Socrates, for good reason, remains anxious. Alcibiades takes his leave of Socrates, promising to care not for himself but for justice.[102] Foucault points out the fact that this resolution might appear, at first sight, a bit surprising. The whole dialogue has been an elaboration of a theory of care of the *self,* and here, at the climax, Alcibiades promises to take care and to occupy himself not with himself, but with *justice.* This apparent shift in the object and purpose of care is highly significant for Foucault. As he sees it, the meaning of this displacement is that through the con-templation of one's nature as it is reflected in the divine being, that is, through the proper care for oneself, one is naturally led to a concern for justice. Self-knowledge is the knowledge of what is just, what is the best government of oneself and others.[103] To take care of oneself is to occupy oneself with the proper government of one's soul—to establish the right and just relationship of oneself to oneself. Foucault reminds us that this notion of justice, for Plato, is a *psychological* as well as a political one. To know and be able to establish justice in the soul is the same thing as to know and be able to establish justice in the city.[104] Care of the self pro-duces a care for justice and therefore founds political life and action.

In *Alcibiades* care of the self is organized around contemplation of the divine being, through which one articulates an "ontology of the soul." It is through the knowledge of the true being of the soul, as *subject,* that one will be able to transform oneself and *become* a subject capable of true political life, of governing oneself as well as others. This practice of care must take place at a precise moment, its *kairos:* the moment when the individual, abandoned by those who designated themselves as his "lovers," that is, as his caretakers, is at the threshold of political life. The erotic relationship takes on the ethical function of occasioning the care of the self. Care of the self, in the form of contemplation, purifies the will which has been corrupted by the influence of the general opinion. This opinion was inscribed in Alcibiades' soul as his very mode of subjectivity, his very identity, through the practice of an inadequate, nonetho-poetic erotic relationship.

The authenticity of *Alcibiades* has been a source of debate.[105] Despite this problem, the text remains essential for Foucault's genealogy for a number of reasons about which he is quite explicit. First of all, it is the systematic outline of a theory of care of the self. In other words, the self as subject and object of care is defined; the techniques of caring are defined, the purpose of taking care of oneself is clearly articulated; and the results of care are indicated as well.[106] Second, in this text one can see the Socratic-Platonic shift of care toward self-knowledge. In the Socratic dialogues one finds references to earlier forms of spiritual practices—for example, we see in the *Symposium* Socrates' tests of endurance, his withdrawal of self from world, his imperviousness to pain and temptation, and so on—but care of the self is clearly recentered around the obligation to self-knowledge. Furthermore, self-knowledge requires the *parrhēsiastic* game initiated by Socrates.[107] Finally, the dialogue takes on a special weight genealogically because of the way it was appropriated by the Neoplatonists.[108] The *Alcibiades* was placed at the head of the Platonic oeuvre. Foucault argues that this reflects the centrality of philosophy as the spiritual practice of *parrhēsia*. In the genealogy of ethical subjectivity and care of the self, *Alcibiades* must take a central place.

Laches: Truth as Harmony

Socratic *parrhēsia* requires one "to give an account of oneself." In *Alcibiades* this means to discover the true nature of the soul. In *Laches* it is something different. One must provide an account of the way one lives and has lived—one must account for one's life (*bios*) and one's deeds (*erga*). As Foucault makes emphatically clear, this account of oneself is neither an autobiography of the events of one's life; an analysis of emotions, desires, thoughts, or fantasies; nor a confessional account and absolution of one's faults. It is neither interpretive nor juridical. Rather, the purpose of *parrhēsia* is to discover whether between the *logos* and the *bios* of the interlocutor there is "a harmonic relation."[109] The dialogue, for Foucault, is inscribed within the problematization of political *parrhēsia;* it responds to the questions of how to govern, who can govern, what makes someone capable of government. In *Alcibiades,* it was first necessary to show Alcibiades that he needed to take care of himself. In *Laches,* on the other hand, the dialogue opens with a recognition that the proper care of the self is necessary to prepare one to live well. However, the principal characters neither recognize the true master of care, nor do they know what care involves. Socrates will confront the other characters and transform the subject of the dialogue. Rather than pose the question of care in general terms, Socrates will challenge each of the other characters to give an account of the way he lives. At the end of the dialogue, the result of this confrontation is that the characters recognize Socrates as the master of care. He does not provide an answer to their questions, but rather, through his very manner of interrogating them, through his ethical *parrhēsia,* he shows what care of the self is and who has the capacity to care for others.

Foucault turns to the *Laches* dialogue as an example of Socratic *parrhēsia* for four reasons.[110] First of all, it exhibits three themes which, as we saw in the *Apology,* define Socrates' discourse: (a) the notion of *parrhēsia* is explicitly invoked and gives shape to the dialogue and definition to each of the characters involved; (b) Socrates' modality of *parrhēsia* is both characterized as and exhibits itself as a test and examination of the others; and (c) Socratic *parrhēsia* reveals itself as a practice of care of the self.

Second, Socrates confronts and tests individuals who exercise power in Athens—Nicias and Laches are important political and military figures. Socrates himself remains exterior to the field of political discourse, yet confronts the individuals who inhabit it in order to incite them to take up another mode of discourse that is necessary for the proper care of themselves.[111]

The third reason *Laches* is exemplary of Socratic *parrhēsia* is the role that courage plays in it. The topic of the dialogue, at least on the surface, is the true nature of courage. However, more important than this is the fact that courage, or the lack thereof, defines all of the principal interlocutors; it characterizes not only their past actions but also their willingness to accept the confrontation with Socrates. For Foucault the real purpose of the dialogue is not to provide a definition of courage but to respond to the question, In what way does the ethics of the truth require courage?[112] The problem of courage is not posed first and foremost in the "content" of the dialogue but in its form, in its procedure, in the manner of speaking that each participant employs and represents. What is at stake in the dialogue are the ethical and ascetic demands which access to the truth places on the subject; in other words, it is the question of spirituality. As Foucault has shown, this question is fundamental in Western thought. We usually think of spirituality in terms of rituals of purification, of renunciation of everyday concerns, denial of the body, overcoming desires, refuting the senses, and so on.[113] In *Laches*, on the other hand, the problem of the spirituality of truth is taken up in terms of courage. The spiritual condition of truth—or at least one essential condition—is the "will to truth." One cannot have access to the truth, to the truth about oneself or to the true life, without the courage for the truth. Access to the truth, in this dialogue, is not a question of "sacrifice but of combat."[114] The price of truth, the cost to the subject, is not measured in terms of the sacrifices one makes, of the rites of purification one performs, but in terms of the risk one runs.

The fourth and final reason for Foucault's choice of *Laches* as an example of Socratic *parrhēsia* is that it stands in contrast to *Alcibiades*. Both dialogues enact the principle of self-knowledge, in the form of an interrogation or examination of one's self, as a crucial practice of care. But the technique employed in the examination of one's self, and therefore the way the self appears as an object of knowledge and care, is quite different in the two dialogues. In *Alcibiades*, care of the self requires contemplation of the divine soul. It takes the form of an ontology of the soul. In *Laches*, on the other hand, care is not contemplation, but rather is an attempt to "give reason to life." One must give an account of what one has done and continues to do. The knowledge which care requires is not an ontology of the soul but instead amounts to a "test" of existence (*bios*), of one's manner of life. In *Laches* the interlocutors put their choice of a particular way of living into question in order to make sure that they choose well and live well. The test (*épreuve*) of Socratic *parrhēsia* reminds them of this task.[115]

The dramatic scene of *Laches* is rather complicated. There are several characters involved, but they can be divided into two sets of two characters each, in addition to Socrates. The first set is that of Lysimachus and Melesias—they have arranged the situation and initiated the conversation. The second set is that of Laches and Nicias—famous Athenian military and political figures—who have been brought together at the request of the first set in order to witness an exhibition by a renowned "martial arts" instructor.[116] The performance, in which the teacher gave a demonstration of his art, is over and the dialogue begins with Lysimachus and Melesias explaining the reason for all of this. Lysimachus and Melesias come from famous aristocratic families, and their fathers were well-known and important men in Athens.[117] But they themselves have achieved nothing. In order to overcome their shame about their lack of achievement they call upon their *parrhēsia*: they speak frankly, though what they have to say is embarrassing. They explain that the reason they have amounted to nothing is that their famous fathers neglected them. They were not properly cared for as children and therefore accomplished nothing as men. Their fathers were so occupied with the city, "with the concerns of others," that they failed to take care of their own children.[118] Lysimachus and Melesias do not want the same fate to befall their children, so they are seeking out the best education for them. Laches and Nicias also have children. But unlike Lysimachus and Melesias, Laches and Nicias are important and respected figures in the city. Lysimachus and Melesias have brought them to this exhibition because Laches and Nicias are successful, because they are experts in military affairs, because they are powerful politicians, and because they also have children for whom they must provide care. In other words, they are competent in the field of military training, they have good character, they are successful, and they have children, so they must know how to take care of them. Lysimachus and Melesias have brought them to this exhibition to get their advice.[119] They want to know if this professional teacher (the martial artist) is competent to take care of and educate their children.

There is another reason why Lysimachus and Melesias have solicited the advice of these two individuals. According to Lysimachus, Laches and Nicias are not "flatterers"; rather, they speak their minds:

> Some laugh at the very notion of consulting others, and when they are asked will not say what they think. They guess at the wishes of the person who asks them, and answer according to his, and not according to their own, opinion. But as we know that you are good judges, and will say exactly what you think, we have taken you into our counsels.[120]

The question of care of the self is situated within the problematization of *parrhēsia*. In order to succeed in life it is not enough to be born into an aristocratic family—one must take care of oneself. Neglecting oneself leads to a shameful life. But taking care of oneself requires finding a master—someone who is capable of serving as a guide to living. This is not an easy task—it implies a sort of Meno-like circularity: in order to recognize the true guide to living and the proper care of the self, one must already know how to take care of oneself. This knowledge is necessary to avoid flatterers and find a true *parrhēsiast*, someone who is serious, who is concerned about the question of care. One needs an advisor who will speak his mind, who will use *parrhēsia*. But not only must the advisor speak his mind, he must say what is true; in other words, not just anyone can use *parrhēsia* properly. This is evident in the fact that Lysimachus and Melesias use *parrhēsia* precisely to admit that they do not know how to take care of themselves or their children. Despite their impressive genealogy, they do not know the truth of what is best. They cannot, in this matter, use *parrhēsia* to say the truth, to take care of themselves or their children; they can only shamefully and frankly admit their ignorance and self-neglect. Therefore, the question is, Who is capable of using *parrhēsia* to speak the truth? Genealogy—a traditional foundation of true discourse—does not seem to lodge one's freely spoken words in the truth. For this reason they seek out the advice, the *parrhēsia,* of Laches and Nicias.

Laches and Nicias, then, will use *parrhēsia* to give their opinions about the teacher and his art. Their lives and actions, their ability to lead the city in war and in political life, appear as the foundation for their words. The notion of the ethical differentiation is at work here. Lysimachus and Melesias are willing to listen to, and be governed by, Laches and Nicias on the basis of an ethical differentiation. Their *ēthos* is what defines them as subjects capable of speaking the truth. Because they govern themselves well, as reflected in their actions and their reputations, and because they have been successful in military and political life, they can speak frankly. Their *ēthos* grounds their freely spoken opinions in the truth. At the same time, Laches and Nicias perceive themselves as subjects, as speakers of the truth, on the same structural condition, on the foundation of an ethical differentiation. They perceive themselves as subjects capable of truth because of the *ēthos* which defines them.

However, when they give their respective opinions on the matter, it turns out they are in complete disagreement. First Nicias speaks. Nicias keeps the company of Damon, a well-known Sophist, and is identified by Laches as a philosopher.[121] Nicias appreciates words, arguments, and making distinctions. He seems to think that the good is a matter of knowledge, perhaps is knowledge, and that this knowledge is transmitted through discourse, and especially through discourse with recognized, professional teachers. It is his opinion that the martial artist would improve the children of Lysimachus and Melesias. The martial artist is a professional, he is competent, he possess a *technē* which he knows how to pass on to a disciple. Laches, on the other hand, is a soldier, and essentially concerns himself with actions, not words. He is impatient with dialectic, with the "niceties" of arguments and of language, but is swept away by the beauty and truth of "fine deeds." He is less inclined to assent to a professional teacher, and more inclined to trust someone who can perform in the "real world." Laches, who trusts experience, saw with his own eyes this very same martial artist make a fool of himself in a real-life battle.[122] In other words, he is capable of making a fine display—a kind of theatrical representation of battle—but his art doesn't translate into real courage or skill in battle. To succeed one needs courage, not "art," and therefore care of the self should aim at forging an *ēthos* of courage. Laches believes that this teacher would harm rather than benefit the children of Lysimachus and Melesias.

The disagreement between Laches and Nicias reflects dramatically, and symbolically, a central problem in the dialogue. Nicias symbolizes words and Laches deeds; the two must be harmonized or there can be no truth. Although Socrates' presence has already been announced, it is at this point that he makes his entrance into the dialogue in order to settle the disagreement. Socrates will attempt to resolve the dissonance which has arisen in the dialogue, to harmonize the words and the deeds of the interlocutors. This harmony is necessary to solve the problems of recognizing who can use *parrhēsia* to articulate the truth and of distinguishing what grounds *parrhēsia* in truth. Foucault has shown so far that the dialogue undermines the traditional foundations for *parrhēsia*. Lysimachus and Melesias have an impressive genealogy, but their *parrhēsia* serves only to embarrass them. Nicias and Laches possess the kind of *ēthos* and reputation which should single them out as *parrhēsiasts*. They have forged exceptional lives and have successfully governed their city—when men like these speak frankly, one should expect to hear the truth. Yet when they give their honest opinions they are in complete disagreement. Since they have contradicted each other, one or both of them must be wrong. But how do we know whom to trust and what the truth is? The problem of recognizing the *parrhēsiast* was supposed to be resolved through the recognition of an ethical difference. Both Nicias and Laches possess the kind of *ēthos* which grants access to the truth—but at least one of them speaks falsely. Therefore, *ēthos*, at least as the characters of *Laches* understand it, does not grant access to the truth. Socrates will redirect the dialogue so that it no longer raises the question about the teacher before them, but rather raises questions about Laches and Nicias themselves, about the relationship they maintain between themselves and the truth. What Socrates reveals is that the dialogue about the care of the self is *already* a practice of care of the self. Asking and giving advice on the matter of taking care of oneself *is* an activity of taking care of oneself and others. The problem of the dialogue does not primarily deal with the quality of the teacher whom they discuss: it has to do with the qualifications of the characters themselves. What gives them the right and the capacity to care for others, to govern others, what technique of speaking do they employ to care for others? Socrates will show that the manner in which they address each other reveals both the way they already conceive of the practice of care and that they have neglected to take care of themselves; that they have neglected to define this practice and to establish it as the relationship to themselves and others. In other words, the dialogue is a reflection on, and a transformation of, the mode of being of the dialogue itself, which implies a transformation in the mode of being of the subjects who define themselves by the roles, duties, and privileges accorded to them in the dialogue.

Foucault brings to light Socrates' effect on the dialogue by drawing our attention to the way he transforms the "discursive procedures" which determine it. Before Socrates takes hold of the dialogue, the exchange between Laches and Nicias concerning the question of education unfolds "in a sort of *analogon* of the political scene, the *analogon* of an assembly."[123] Their discourse is based on a "political-juridical model."[124] In other words, their *parrhēsia* takes the form of political *parrhēsia:* each one asserts his opinion as truth in order to guide the others and the assembly/jury vote on which opinion is best. Since there is no agreement between the two, Socrates is asked to intervene and "to cast his vote."[125] The discursive setting is constituted on the model of the political assembly or tribunal.

Foucault's attention to this first shift of discursive procedure is significant given his suspicion of juridical-style critical discourse. If we pay attention to how Foucault characterizes this discourse and how he contrasts it with Socratic discourse, we can learn something both about his distrust of the former and his effort to develop something along the lines of the latter. The political-juridical model—a sort of normative model—attempts to take care of others, to govern them, by telling them what to do. It lays down the law. This form of discourse asserts that taking care of oneself—governing oneself—is fundamentally legislative; it is primarily a matter of giving and following laws and making decisions. In other words, Laches and Nicias have made political *parrhēsia* into the mode of being of ethical *parrhēsia.* In order to respond to the question of how to prepare individuals for political life, normative-juridical discourse has slipped into and defined the practice of care of the self. However, normative-juridical discourse presupposes an autonomous subject, a subject capable of giving laws and making decisions. Otherwise, the subject who is cared for by juridical discourse becomes little more than an obedient, law-abiding subject. In this case the foundation of a successful life, of an effective political life, would amount to doing what one is told. Therefore, one must already be an autonomous self-legislating subject and therefore be capable of care of the self. But then, one does not need to find a master to teach one. However, the dialogue shows that the individual must *become* capable of governing himself and others and that this requires a practice that is fundamentally different from juridical discourse. The foundation of normative-juridical discourse is the subject of care. The law must always be articulated and applied by *someone.*

Foucault makes this point in his 1983 course in an interpretation of the role of *parrhēsia* in Plato's *Laws.*[126] Even though the city as it appears in the *Laws* is perfectly constructed according to perfect laws, the role of the *parrhēsiast* remains necessary.[127] This is because the laws must always be spoken, interpreted, and mediated by an individual. There can be no law that establishes this mediation because such a law would also require mediation. In other words, the law and the discourse of law cannot be the foundation of the law; rather, there must be some other practice or discourse through which the laws are brought to life and made to play the proper role in the city. In other words, normative-juridical discourse presupposes what it is supposed to create: subjects who can govern themselves and others. In an aristocratic-authoritarian model, it presupposes one subject who gives the law and another who is subjected to the law. It presupposes subjects who are already determined and differentiated by their capacity for governing or caring for themselves and others. Such a discourse cannot form or produce the subjects it presupposes as its foundation. In a more democratic model, normative-juridical discourse presupposes subjects who together decide on the law through asserting their opinions and voting on which is best. But like the aristocratic model, it requires subjects who are capable of governing themselves and others as its foundation. The democratic practice of debate and decision cannot be the technique for the formation of the very subjects it presupposes in order to function democratically.

Both the democratic and aristocratic models are at work in the *Laches:* the ethical differentiation distinguishes who gives the law and who listens; the democratic model comes into play in order to decide which aristocratic opinion will serve as law. But by transposing normative discourse into the dialogue, the question of care of the self is deflected and the selves involved continue to neglect themselves. Therefore, the dialogue whose purpose is to help Lysimachus and Melesias take care of their children, whose purpose, in other words, is to care for and govern Lysimachus and Melesias, fails so long as it continues to be modeled on the juridical scene. It presupposes the subjects it is supposed to produce—subjects who care for themselves, who are capable of governing themselves and others.[128] Taking up the problem of care of the self in a normative-juridical style of discourse only serves to further the neglect of the self. By entering into the political scene and casting his vote, Socrates would not get them any closer to recognizing whether the teacher before them is suited to take care of Lysimachus' and Melesias' children because this act wouldn't get them any closer to taking care of themselves. Socrates, therefore, will not play the game of political *parrhēsia*. Foucault shows that Socrates instead changes the "procedure of the discussion," and displaces political *parrhēsia* as the modality of veridiction proper to the question of care of the self.[129] Philosophy, as care of the self and ethical *parrhēsia*, is not, for Socrates, a normative-juridical discourse; it is a preparatory work of forming subjects who are capable of caring for themselves and others. But if juridical-normative discourse, political *parrhēsia,* is not the proper mode of being of care, if it is not the discourse of government, then what is?

Socrates shifts the discursive procedure of the dialogue from that of political *parrhēsia* to that of *technē*.[130] The type of truth spoken in *technē* is not grounded in one's courage, one's family name, one's political experience, or one's character. It is a matter of the way one belongs to a tradition of learning and teaching. In political *parrhēsia* the speakers assert their respective opinions on the matter at hand. They attempt to persuade and take control of the assembly, which puts the matter to a vote and acts according to the will of the majority. Socrates suggests that the question of the best education is not a political decision but rather a technical one. It must be decided not by vote but by reference to the technician, the one who is competent to speak on such matters. In this case one must consult a "a technician with respect to the soul—*therapeuein*—care of the soul."[131] It *appears,* through this transformation, that according to Socrates, care, knowledge of how to take care of oneself and of others, knowledge of what is true in the domain of care, is a form of *technē*.

Socrates neither casts his vote, as if the dialogue and its interlocutors were a political assembly, nor does he assert his opinion, which would take its truth from his character, his experience, or his family name. Instead he tells the others that the best opinion on the matter will come from the individual who is "competent," who possesses knowledge, *technē*. Socrates suggests two criteria for determining the competence of someone on technical matters: the first is to discover one's link to the tradition of *technē* by identifying one's teachers in the art; the second is to determine if one has produced any "works" of one's own, that is, if one has used *technē* to care for and produce "good and noble" individuals.[132] These criteria serve to determine who is competent to speak the truth on a matter of *technē*. The modality of technical truth demands that the subject speaking the truth constitute himself through taking part in a tradition of learning and producing, of transmitting knowledge as *technē*.

After shifting the dialogue from a political model to a technical model, Socrates will introduce a second transformation in its mode of discourse. He does not ask about the competence of the teacher before them. Rather, he gives an account of his *own* competence in the art of care of the self. In other words, Socrates makes it explicit that the dialogue *itself* is a scene of care of the self. The characters must account for themselves, attend to and care about themselves, before they can answer any questions concerning the competence of the martial arts teacher. Socrates does not claim to possess the *technē* of caring for and curing the self. Instead, he admits that he has had no teachers because he is "too poor to give money to the Sophists, who are the only professors of moral improvement and [he] has never been able to discover the art" himself.[133] Therefore, Socrates is not a technician of care of the self, he has not constituted himself as a speaker of *technē*. Having admitted that he is not a technical expert, Socrates asks Laches and Nicias to give an account of themselves. He puts the question to them because they "are far wealthier . . . and may therefore have learned it from others, and they are older too, so that they have had more time to make the discovery."[134] Posing the question to Laches and Nicias reflects the way Socrates has transformed the procedure of the dialogue. No longer will each interlocutor simply assert his opinion as truth; instead each must "give an account" of his own competence, his *technē*, on this matter.[135] Foucault would seem to be placing himself alongside Heidegger here, arguing that Plato has superimposed the question of ethics (the question of the Being of beings) onto the model of *technē*. But Foucault is going to subvert this notion. He will show that the disclosure of the being of the subject in the dialogue is not based on the model of *technē*. Socrates introduces this model only in order to displace it.

The shift from political discourse to technical discourse leads to a second displacement: the question will no longer concern the teacher of martial arts but the competence of Socrates, Laches, and Nicias. Foucault goes on to show that this redirection of the question is not what it appears. A third discursive transformation is hidden in it. Despite the fact that Socrates explicitly gives an account of himself in terms of his technical competence and asks about the competence of Laches and Nicias, the actual style of the discourse which follows is not a modality of *technē*, and it does not presuppose that *technē* is the proper form of care of the self. The discursive procedure Socrates introduces is not *technē*, but rather a modality of *parrhēsia*. However, Socratic *parrhēsia* does not reenact the political scene by referring to, and grounding itself in, the political identities of the individuals and operating according to the normative-juridical model. The dialogue takes shape at this point as a practice of *parrhēsia* which is not simply grounded on a certain kind of *ēthos* that legitimates it, but rather is oriented toward that very foundation, attends to it, interrogates it, and cares for it.[136]

Though the third transformation in the dialogue is in a sense hidden, Nicias, because he knows Socrates, knows what is coming and he informs the others:

> You seem not to be aware that anyone who is close to Socrates and enters into conversation with him is liable to be drawn into an argument, and whatever subject he may start, he will be continually carried round and round by him, until at last he finds that he has to give an account both of his present and past life, and when he is once entangled, Socrates will not let him go until he has completely and thoroughly sifted him. Now I am used to his ways, and I know that he will certainly do as I say, and also

that I myself shall be the sufferer, for I am fond of his conversation, Lysimachus . . . I say for my part, I am quite willing to discourse with Socrates in his own manner.[137]

According to Foucault, this passage serves two functions in the dialogue. (a) It forms a pact between Socrates and the others: Nicias accepts the confrontation and examination, he submits himself to the *parrhēsia* of Socrates. (b) It offers a basic description of what Socratic *parrhēsia* is and what effects it produces in the listener. First, Foucault analyzes this text as a *parrhēsiastic* pact, the acceptance of a game. Nicias warns the others about the kind of discursive game they are entering, telling them that if they continue the dialogue along the lines Socrates has suggested, they will be made into victims; Nicias himself will be the "sufferer" of Socrates' *parrhēsia*.[138] But his warning is not an evasion or repudiation of Socratic *parrhēsia;* rather, Nicias makes it clear that he intends to let himself be "cross-examined" by Socrates.[139] He tells the others that he has regularly been Socrates' victim and, rather than resenting it, he enjoys it, claiming that it produces positive effects in him. Therefore Nicias agrees to be interrogated and examined by Socrates. Laches as well will submit, but as we shall see, for different reasons. This moment of the dialogue serves as the "*parrhēsiastic* pact" and, Foucault says, from this point on we witness "a good, entirely positive, *parrhēsiastic* game, where the courage of those who accept the *parrhēsia* of Socrates is going to respond to the courage of Socrates."[140]

Why does Nicias consider himself to be the "sufferer" of Socratic discourse? What is it about this discourse which causes pain and therefore requires courage to withstand? The second function served by this text answers these questions by indicating the nature of Socrates' style of discourse. The essence of Socrates' examination will be to force the "victim" to "give an account of himself . . . to explain himself [*donner raison de soi*]."[141] The question of technical competence ("give an account of your *competence*") is displaced by the question of the self ("give an account of *yourself*"). The confrontation with Socrates forces the interlocutor "to disclose the relation between himself and *logos,* and reason."[142] Socratic *parrhēsia* and care of the self, as it appears in *Laches,* is not a contemplation of the soul and of the divine being. Rather, in order to give an account of oneself, one must give an account of the "manner in which one lives."[143] That is, whereas the self is defined in *Alcibiades* as the soul-subject (*psychē*), it appears in *Laches* in the form of existence (*bios*). Philosophy is in this case a *test* (*épreuve*) of existence, a test through which the subject puts his very way of life into question, puts his *self* to the test of Socrates' interrogation. "It is this domain of existence . . . it is this which is going to constitute the field where the discourse, the *parrhēsia*, of Socrates is going to exercise itself."[144] Socrates interrogates the others, examines them, probing and prodding them to explain themselves. Socrates himself is the "touchstone" by which the others are able to test themselves.[145] Self-knowledge comes about in this test and interrogation: only by being put to the test of Socratic *parrhēsia* can one bring the status of one's own existence, one's *self*, into focus. But this test is also therefore a manner of taking care of oneself, of testing oneself, of seeing if one governs oneself properly and can withstand the Socratic interrogation. In other words, Socratic *parrhēsia* does not aim to *tell* the others what care is; to *tell* them who the master of care of the self is; to *tell* them what to do and how. Rather, it *is* care of the self. Within the *parrhēsiastic* scene each of the individuals involved attends to himself, makes himself into a question, a problem, an object not just of knowledge but of care. Furthermore, the confrontation with Socrates, which takes the form of an examination and interrogation, must be repeated throughout one's entire life.[146] One must be constantly put to the test of Socrates. Nicias states that the effect of an encounter with Socrates is that one begins to care intensely for oneself, one desires "to be learning so long as he lives."[147] The test of existence is not simply a preparation for life, it is a way of life.

Because taking care of oneself requires putting one's very being into question, entrance into the *parrhēsiastic* game requires courage. Socrates must show the courage to challenge the others, others who in this case are politically powerful. The others must have the courage to let themselves be examined by and measured against Socrates. They have to give an account of themselves, of who they are, in terms of how they live. They have to put this account to the test of Socrates' interrogation. In other words, they must have the courage to call their very identities, their very way of living, into question and put it to the test. Finally, they all must possess the courage to face the truth that arises from this test, to continue the interrogation, to follow it where it leads. Courage is the price of truth.

Foucault sees in this text "the emergence of life, of the mode of life, as being the object of Socratic *parrhēsia*."[148] In order to properly take care of oneself one must be tested and examined by Socrates. The object which one cares about when one cares for the self is *bios*, the mode or style of one's existence. One must examine one's mode of life, put it into words, and continue to do so throughout one's life. This form of *parrhēsia* is therefore radically different from political *parrhēsia*. Its procedure is not juridical; rather, it takes the form of an interrogation in which each one gives an account of his way of living. Its domain of truth has to do with action, but unlike political *parrhēsia* it does not tell others what to do. Instead it forces others to confront who they are, and the truth it reveals is whether they care for or neglect themselves. The practice of this form of discourse is already a central, if not the central, technique for taking care of oneself. In other words, there is no care without the courage to confront Socrates, to engage in the test of existence in a *parrhēsiastic* confrontation. Socratic *parrhēsia* forces the listener back upon himself, detaches him from the existence he leads, and forces him to reflect on the meanings which determine it. The purpose of Socratic *parrhēsia* is to forge in individuals the *ēthos* they need to live well. Through the courage of the truth, one is able to speak and hear the truth about *who one is*, and therefore begin to live the true life by caring for and governing oneself well.

Foucault points out that the dialogue must address a final lingering problem. What provides the foundation for Socrates' use of *parrhēsia*? We have seen so far that neither name, reputation, experience, character, nor technical competence ground one's *parrhēsia* in the truth. From what ground, then, does the *parrhēsia* of Socrates draw its truth? In other words, how do the others recognize Socrates as a *parrhēsiast*? In order to answer this question, Foucault turns to the portion of the text in which Laches assents to be interrogated by Socrates. In this passage Laches explains *why* it is he will let himself be interrogated by Socrates, *what* allows Socrates to use *parrhēsia* with him, and *how* the truth of that *parrhēsia* will manifest itself. For Laches what is essential is the "harmonic" relationship between one's life and one's words. The individual whose words and actions are in perfect harmony is "the true musician."[149] For Laches such a musician must tune his life and his language to the Dorian mode, the "true Hellenic mode," which as we know from the *Republic* is the musical mode of courage.[150] Laches is not an indiscriminate "lover of discourse." His ear is offended by any discourse that is not in tune with the life of the one who speaks it. The greater the dissonance between life and words, the greater the pain and hatred experienced by Laches. He will, however, let himself be examined by Socrates because he has experienced firsthand the virtue of Socrates, and states that "his deeds show that he is entitled to noble sentiments and complete freedom of speech [*parrhēsia*]."[151] As Laches sees it, Socrates' mode of existence, as evidenced in his past actions, serves to ground Socrates' *parrhēsia*.

Foucault says that Laches accepts the *parrhēsiastic* game with Socrates because of "this symphony, this harmony, between that which Socrates says, his manner of saying things, and his manner of living."[152] It seems, however, that we must hold off a bit on this observation. Laches accepts not because he has experienced the symphonic relation of life and words in Socrates' manner of being, but because he may hope for such an accord. At this point in the dialogue he only has experience of the deeds of Socrates. Based on this knowledge of Socrates' life he will attend to

Socrates' words, saying, "if [Socrates'] words accord [with his deeds], then I am of one mind with him."[153] The mode of existence which Socrates exhibited as a soldier evokes from Laches a will to listen. But Socrates' words must harmonize with these actions. We have already seen in the *parrhēsia* of Laches and Nicias that successful, courageous actions and political power do not ground one's words in truth. The truth of *parrhēsia*, as Laches suggests, is the effect, the "ontological characteristic," of the harmony between life and words, but what form this harmony takes and how it reveals itself is not evident.[154] Therefore, the problem remains: how does one's mode of existence translate itself through *parrhēsia* into a true *logos*? What style of discourse harmonizes with a virtuous way of life and therefore constitutes one as a subject speaking the truth, as an ethical *parrhēsiast*?

The questions with which Socrates interrogates the others concern the nature of courage. However, courage is the subject of the dialogue in more ways than one. Laches suggested that the art of the military teacher is useless without courage; that courage is what one needs to care about in order to live well. Nicias, Laches, and Socrates are all defined by their courage, either politically, militarily, or both. Furthermore, Foucault also showed that courage is the prerequisite for the truth of oneself because one must be able to withstand the barrage of Socrates' interrogation. Laches says that courage must be the harmonic unity of one's life and words, and this ontological harmony of courage grounds what one says and what one does in the truth. Finally, when the characters have agreed to participate in the Socratic examination, when they have agreed to put themselves to the test, it is precisely the question of the nature of courage they must answer. While both Nicias and Laches claim to live courageously—and are reputed for their courage—they cannot define what courage is. In other words, their discourse is not in tune with their way of living—they cannot say what they do and how they live. This fact calls into question the very meaning and style of their lives. How can they say that they live courageously if they cannot say what courage is? Of course, they both do say what courage is, they both define the virtue which gives form to their past actions. Yet each time one of them proposes a definition, he is roundly refuted by Socrates. The Socratic interrogation is therefore not an attempt to drag skeletons out of the closet or to judge people based upon what they have done; the examination of life is neither biographical, hermeneutic, nor narrative in style. In fact, Socrates' interrogation is much more radical, and this is why it requires courage: he calls into question the meaning individuals attribute to their lives. While Nicias and Laches take courage as the trait which gives their lives style and meaning, what in fact defines them is their inability to say what courage is even as they propose to live courageously. In this way there is no harmony between their words and their lives. The discord of word and life, which they exhibit in the dialogue, is therefore not simply the fact that they cannot define their way of living. Ontological discord resides in the fact that even though they cannot define their way of living, they still do so. They assert definitions, they desire and propose simple responses to the question, they continue to think that they know what courage is even though they cannot say what courage is. They continue to believe that they possess courage even when they have failed to define what that term means. For this reason, they cannot answer the original question posed to them by Lysimachus and Melesias. They cannot act as ethical *parrhēsiasts* because they do not possess the ontological harmony of discourse and existence which would ground their frankly spoken words in the truth.

What makes Socrates different? Just like Laches and Nicias, Socrates' mode of existence is defined by courage. And just like Laches and Nicias, Socrates never provides a definition of what courage actually is. Yet, at the end of the dialogue all agree that Socrates alone must be the master of their children, *as well as of themselves*.[155] The result of the dialogue is that the others all recognize Socrates as the true speaker of ethical *parrhēsia* and the master of care of the self. They are willing to submit themselves to be governed by him in order to learn how to take care of themselves. As Nicias had warned them, Socratic *parrhēsia* incites those who listen, those who accept to hear it and be victimized by it, to take up the practice of care. Therefore, through his *parrhēsia* Socrates somehow manifests the ontological harmony which grounds his words in the truth. However, this harmony cannot be found in the "content" of his speech. Just as the others, he does not say what courage is. But unlike the others, Socrates never claims to know what courage is. In other words, his style of nondefinition is quite different from the others'. Their style of discourse is to make bold assertions, whether they are true or not. They try to command and control the dialogue, to assert their power over others. The sense of their manner of speaking is that they think that freedom and duty are fulfilled in the assertion of power: that governing means controlling, ruling the others. This discursive style might seem courageous, but it is not the courage of the truth—it is not the kind of courage which leads to the truth. It is rather an attempt to dominate the situation, and therefore a neglect of the truth. Rather than take care of themselves or the others, rather than make the others capable of caring for and governing themselves, Laches and Nicias attempt to assert their power over them. This is not necessarily a conscious decision, nor is it reflected in the content of the words they speak; rather, it is manifest in the very being of their discourse. Socrates' style of discourse exhibits a different sense. Rather than make bold assertions in order to get the others to assent, he interrogates the truth of what they say. His discourse reflects his courage to recognize and admit that he does not possess the truth and that he will not neglect himself or the others by allowing a false opinion to dominate them. Therefore, even though Socrates does not define courage, the characteristic that supposedly gives meaning to his life, he exhibits the ontological harmony that courage gives to his life and his words. This harmony is not a correspondence between the content of his words and his past actions. Socrates does not define courage in his words or rely upon his past actions as the definition of courage. Rather, he manifests courage as a style that pervades his words and his actions, which is their meaning. This style of being is the ontological harmony of his life and his words. To detach his words or his actions from his way of being is to obscure their truth. In the confrontation with Socrates, the others come into contact not with disembodied words, or with a recitation of past deeds, but with his manner of being. Not only does this style manifest the ontological harmony of courage—even in its nondefinition of courage—it reveals the nature of ontological harmony as such. Laches searched for this harmony by trying to match the content of Socrates' words to his courageous deeds in the past. He defined harmony in terms of correspondence. Socrates' very way of being is *parrhēsiastic* in the sense that it reveals the truth of truth: that the truth of words and of actions is not to be sought in their correspondence to each other but in the ontological style which pervades and harmonizes them. As Socrates points out to Laches when their attempt to define courage runs aground, "We too must endure and persevere in the inquiry, and then courage will not laugh at our faintheartedness in searching for courage, which after all may frequently be endurance."[156] In order to answer the question, What is the truth of courage? one must have *le courage de la vérité*. Ethical *parrhēsia* is the courage of the truth, not in the frank assertion of one's opinion in the political scene, but rather in the perseverance in the problematization of one's self, in the mission of taking care of oneself and others. The courage of the truth is the ontological harmony of Socrates' discourse and life—a stylistic harmony. This style is the foundation of Socrates' actions and his words, it is their meaning, it is the truth reflected in his words and his actions. The truth of courage *is* the courage of the truth.[157]

Socrates' modality of *parrhēsia*, the investigation into the truth of assertions, which takes form as the confrontation and examination of souls, manifests a harmony between his mode of living and his mode of speaking. His words and his deeds are harmonized by the courage of the truth as it unfolds through the practice of care of the self. Socratic *parrhēsia* does not actualize itself and manifest its essential meaning in the opinion which it asserts. Therefore, it cannot be comprehended, "heard," in the same manner as political *parrhēsia* or *technē*. To hear *parrhēsia* one listens to the harmony between the mode of existence and the mode of discourse. The content of Socratic *parrhēsia* refers to and grounds itself in his *manner* of speaking, his actions ground themselves in his *manner* of living—it is this manner which pervades his life and his words and gives them meaning.[158] Socrates uses his *parrhēsia* to confront the other, whomever that may be, and force the other to give an account, to speak the truth of himself, in order to manifest the way reason gives shape to his life, as a style of living. Socrates' mode of existence is given its form and its definition by the freedom and courage to care for himself and the others, to maintain a constant vigilance over the mode of life they lead. His mission, the very form of his existence, is to care for the care the others take of themselves. Socrates' existence, the actions he performs, is a kind of language, a *logos,* just as his language is a kind of deed, *ergon.* His existence, *bios,* and his words, *logoi,* both say the same thing, the courage of the truth as a way of being, and in this way they constitute a perfect harmony. It is this harmony which grounds Socrates' words and life in the truth and lets him appear as a *parrhēsiast* to anyone willing to listen.

Before the interlocutors in this dialogue are able to say whether or not the Sophist is a good teacher for their children, they must themselves recognize what it means to take care of oneself. They must be able to put into words what defines a good life. In other words, they must take care of themselves before they can take care of others. Through Socrates' *parrhēsia* they realize that they cannot do this, they cannot give an account of their mode of life, or what constitutes a good, true life, or courage. However, it is through this test (and the failure of their discourse to attain truth on the question of how reason guides, or should guide, their lives) that a different truth comes to light. They fail to define the nature of courage and therefore they fail to exhibit an ontological harmony between their words and their modes of existence. That is, they fail if one looks to the "content" of their discourse, if one looks for a definition of courage. However, Socrates, while not providing a definition of courage, reveals through his *manner* of speaking, the mode of being of his discourse, an ontological harmony between his words and his life, and thereby reveals himself as the true "teacher," as the master of care of the self. It is his manner of speaking and living which defines Socrates as an ethical *parrhēsiast,* who is able to use discourse to lead the others to care about the choice, the reason, which gives shape to existence.

In the *Laches* dialogue, life (*bios*) takes shape as an object of veridiction. One begins to cultivate a form of attention, an anxiety with respect to the meaning that inhabits one's life and words—a meaning to be discovered not in some inner secret but in one's style of being. One begins to articulate those elements which define an ethical subjectivity, that is, the freedom and duty which are on the one hand the condition of the proper choice of existence, and on the other the effects which the proper choice brings into being. Socrates lays the foundation for a new relationship to the self by detaching the self from the regional "ontologies" where it appeared as the object of a pragmatic concern. The *self*, in the form of *bios*, comes into focus under the "gaze" of Socratic *parrhēsia*. It takes on a unity that is manifest as a mode of living traversed by reason and language, as a truth that must be put into words so that the one who bears that existence might take care of it and might govern it.

Conclusion: Ethical *Parrhēsia* and the Invention of the Self

For Foucault, the problematization of democracy was the horizon against which Socratic-Platonic thought appeared. The source of the crisis, as Plato and Socrates experienced it, was the absence of thought (care) about the self as a political and ethical subject. The neglect of the self was the basis of political turmoil and techniques of political manipulation such as rhetoric. As a response to this problem, Socrates and Plato initiated a new experience of the ethical, political subject. They redefined *parrhēsia*, the freedom to speak the truth, and reorganized the practice of *epimeleia heautou*. They invented a philosophical practice of working on the self, in large part through *parrhēsiastic* discourse, in order to fashion a subject who was ethically and politically responsible. This practice was a precise form of vigilance, a gaze directed toward the self understood as a soul-subject, and as a mode of existence. The care of the self aimed at the acquisition of the art of governing, an art of living a fully human, political, life. The soul-subject and the self as life are therefore defined pragmatically. It is necessary to care for oneself insofar as one is concerned with political life. However, the care of the self, the ethical *parrhēsia*, initiated by the thought of Socrates and Plato will take on an importance independent of the pragmatic framework from which they emerged. In the next two chapters, we will examine a number of ways that care of the self was appropriated by Hellenistic, Roman, and early Christian thought as the essence of philosophical, ethical life. Practices of caring for and knowing the soul, of examining it and speaking the truth about it, as well as practices of examining and testing one's mode of existence and speaking the truth about it, will proliferate and spread. The care of the self—its relationships, techniques, objects, and aims—will take on a variety of forms of freedom for the truth. These practices of the self serve as resistance to the domination harbored in self-neglect. However, we will see that the care of the self as an experience of freedom also comes to be appropriated as a field of control. The struggle for power, which was enacted in the political assembly, will come to be enacted in the relationships and techniques of caring for oneself and others. The soul and one's existence will become the new battlefields in the struggle for power, truth, and freedom.

3

The Poetics of the Subject

In the previous chapters I have attempted to explicate and develop Foucault's interpretation of Socrates and Plato. In this chapter I want to turn to his 1982 Collège course, *The Hermeneutics of the Subject*. In this course, Foucault excavates what he calls a "veritable golden age of care of the self" in Greece and Rome during the first two centuries A.D.[1] His study of care of the self and ethical *parrhēsia* in this period preceded his analysis of the Socratic moment. In 1982 Foucault had already conceived of care of the self, the ethics of self-fashioning, as a mode of resistance to political power.[2] However, he had not yet excavated the political origins of *parrhēsia* and therefore he had not yet seen that ethical *parrhēsia*—the *parrhēsiast* as spiritual director, *parrhēsia* as an examination of conscience or of life—had emerged from the problematization of democracy in Athens in the fifth and fourth centuries B.C. His initial discovery of *parrhēsia* was in the context of Stoic and Epicurean relationships of spiritual direction where he first analyzed it as just one among many distinctive features of Hellenistic and Roman philosophy.[3] As I have suggested, Foucault's original interest in an archaeology of care of the self and *parrhēsia* as spiritual direction was to destabilize the hermeneutics of the subject in terms of desire. The course title, *The Hermeneutics of the Subject*, is a bit misleading if one takes it to refer to the material addressed in the course. Foucault does not discuss hermeneutic practices in these lectures, except to mention them in occasional asides.[4] Rather, he analyzes the numerous forms of spiritual direction, none of which could be called hermeneutic, developed and practiced by Greek and Roman philosophers and their disciples. These practices were essentially etho-poetic.[5] They did not interpret the self, they fashioned the self; they did not approach the self as a text to be read but as a material to be formed. The discovery of care of the self as an etho-poetic practice transformed Foucault's understanding of his project and his understanding of philosophy in general. What I mean by this is that Foucault's initial project—a diagnosis of our present in terms of the hermeneutics of desire—led him to the discovery of non-hermeneutic practices of the self. These practices were not so much a means of subjecting (*assujetissement*) individuals to the interpretation of an expert (doctor, psychiatrist, psychoanalyst, priest) as they were ways of subjectivizing (*subjectivation*) individuals by guiding them in their own process of becoming capable of governing themselves and others.[6] The discovery of practices of subjectivation held out to Foucault the possibility of adding a new dimension to his work, what I have suggested is an etho-poetic dimension. To understand this, however, we have to take a close look at just what he discovered in Greece and Rome. That is the purpose of this chapter. However, to grasp the full significance of this etho-poetic possibility in Foucault's work we will then have to return to the diagnosis of our present, of ourselves, which he put forth in his studies of modern power and knowledge. That will be the task of part 2 of this book.

In 1983–84 Foucault examined the shift of *parrhēsia* from politics to ethics. This displacement, for Foucault, was a crucial event in the history of Western thought. It marked the "interference" of ethics and true discourse about the self; it linked the two together in a way that has been decisive for Western philosophy and Western culture.[7] By rereading Foucault's 1982 lectures in light of his realization about the political roots of *parrhēsia* and the way it became linked to care of the self, we gain a very different perspective on the place of the "golden age" of care of the self within the development of Foucault's thought and in the history of the subject. The "culture of the self" that Foucault discovers in Hellenistic and Roman philosophy unfolds in the space cleared by Socrates and Plato. The rise of this "culture of the self" shows that once the self is invested as a domain of truth and freedom, once it is defined as an area of resistance to and differentiation from the "general opinion," it develops into a goal to be achieved independent of politics. The establishment of the self as the goal of ethics had important consequences for Western experience, as well as for the development of Foucault's own thought. On the one hand, the "culture of the self" offers Foucault numerous tools for resisting political power and knowledge. On the other hand, focusing on the situation and development of this culture—between Socratic-Platonic care and Christian pastoral power—reveals the fragility and mutability of technologies of the self, of practices of freedom and subjectivation. The relationships and technologies developed in order to make individuals capable of governing themselves and resisting excesses of power were taken over as tools for submitting individuals to different and more profound forms of control. Modern power functions by producing individuals and subjecting them to the identities it fashions for them. The modern "political technology of the individual" absorbs the care of the self, the practice of speaking the truth about the self, making the dimension of subjectivity, which arose as a resistance to political control, the very site of political control. Foucault's genealogy of care of the self passes through the Hellenistic and Roman period because this period shows both the fertility of care of the self and reveals the danger of these practices. Conversely, by locating the distant origin of discipline and biopower in unfamiliar practices of the self, Foucault shows that the possibility of resistance resides within the very relationships of power and knowledge that constituted the danger of modernity.

The discovery of care of the self and ethical *parrhēsia* in ancient Greek, Hellenistic, and Roman philosophy also offered Foucault the opportunity to reflect upon the nature of his own discourse and his own status as an intellectual and a philosopher. First, it allowed him to add a new and irreducible dimension to his diagnosis of our present: that of the practices of subjectivity. Second, it suggested to him a new way of understanding the nature and the effect of philosophical discourse. The result of this transformation in his understanding of philosophical discourse in its very being opened up the possibility of supplementing his diagnostic work with etho-poetic work. Before moving on to Foucault's analysis of Hellenistic and Roman care of the self, I want to look at the twofold transformation in his understanding and practice of philosophy resulting from his experience of ancient philosophy.

First, Foucault's experience of ancient philosophy gave his diagnosis of the present a new line of development: the irreducible dimension of practices of subjectivity. The appearance of the subjective dimension in *The Use of Pleasure* and *The Care of the Self* in 1983 seems to signal a break from his earlier studies of power and knowledge. This is because Foucault's claims about the "death of man" and the supposed ubiquity of power had seemed to undermine any notion of subjectivity, freedom, or truth. But in his last two books he appears to contradict the supposedly deconstructive aim of his work by analyzing the practices by which individuals become subjects. What is more, he links the process of becoming a subject (becoming a free agent) to the process of gaining access to the truth. Despite the perceived dissonance between the early deconstructive Foucault and the late constructive Foucault, in numerous interviews from this period he claims that there is a fundamental unity to his intellectual project.[8] In his courses at the Collège from 1982 to 1984, this unity was a recurring theme. For instance, he saw his 1982 course within the framework of a resistance to political power.[9] He also stated that the purpose of the course was to analyze the relationship between modes of veridiction (the *dire-vrai*) and the government of oneself and others. He claimed that all of his earlier studies of madness, medicine, the human sciences, the prison, and sexuality were concerned with the same problem.[10] In 1983 and 1984 the relationship between his final studies and his earlier work on power and knowledge is made even more explicit.[11] In both of these courses he explains that the purpose of his excavation of political and ethical *parrhēsia* in ancient Greece was a way of identifying a zone of convergence where techniques of government, forms of true discourse, and practices of subjectivity merge with each other, respond to each other, or confront each other. In other words, what many too quickly perceived as a contradiction was instead a refinement. While it is true that Foucault's retrospective analyses of his own project are perhaps a little too neat (a fact which he was aware of), this does not mean that they are incorrect. It seems to me that by taking Foucault's accounts of the relationship between his early and late work seriously, we gain a fuller appreciation of the possibilities his project opens up.

Through his excavation of the problematization of democracy in Athens, Foucault was able to redefine philosophical discourse, in its diagnostic function, as a reflection on the interrelation of power, knowledge, and subjectivity. The malady that philosophy diagnoses is a certain "pathological" development in what Foucault had earlier named a *dispositif*.[12] While Foucault first adopted this term, in a more or less technical sense, to identify relationships of power and knowledge, his last lectures expand it to include a subjective dimension. Therefore, I take it to mean the more or less systematic deployment of (1) a system of relations and techniques of power, (2) forms of knowledge, and (3) modalities and practices of subjectivity. In the second lecture of his 1984 course, Foucault describes the crisis of Athenian democracy in precisely these terms. It is out of this crisis that the thought of Socrates and Plato emerges and with it, according to Foucault, the first full formulation of philosophical discourse as it will come to be understood in the West—a formulation of philosophy he attributes to Plato.[13] As Foucault sees it, what gives philosophy its impetus and its power is its living source in a problematization constituted along three "poles": "the pole of *alētheia* and of true-discourse; the pole of *politeia* and of government; finally, the pole which in the later Greek texts is called *ētho-poiesis*, the formation of *ēthos*."[14] These three dimensions constitute a kind of space within which an experience is able to take place. Therefore, they are both inseparable and irreducible. Philosophical discourse emerges from, and responds to, the three-dimensional space constituted by relations of power and knowledge and practices of subjectivity, three axes which are irreducible to each other but which are necessarily interrelated, which maintain themselves in a constant relationship of mutual dependence and support.

The "organic" relation to a problematic experiential field is the source of philosophical discourse. Because of its living source in a three-dimensional *dispositif*, philosophical discourse is able to develop along each of these three axes of experience. As Foucault sees it, the concern with all three poles of experience in their simultaneous independence and interrelation is what defines the full nature of the philosophical diagnosis of the present. Philosophy poses the question of truth, of politics, and of *ēthos*, but it distinguishes itself from scientific discourse (discourse about the real or the true), political discourse (discourse about relations of power), and ethics (discourse about morals) by examining the fundamental interaction between these three fields.[15] Starting from the question of truth, philosophy diagnoses the relation between "true-discourse"— scientific discourse—and, on the one hand, the practices of the self which give one access to the truth, which allow one to pronounce the truth, and on the other hand, the techniques of government which require this true-discourse, which give one both the liberty and the duty of speaking this particular discourse, and which establish a field of possible objects to be known.[16]

Likewise, philosophical diagnosis, as such, does not concern itself simply with the question of power, of the techniques, relations, objects, and objectives of power.[17] Or rather, it does not simply see these questions of power in terms of "politics"; the function of philosophy, as a diagnosis, is not to present a vision of the ideal political regime or to argue for a particular political policy. Rather, it explores the way that particular true-discourses found or justify relations of power and how such discourses articulate the technologies, relations, objects, and objectives of power. Furthermore, philosophical discourse attempts to show the links, or the ruptures, between power and practices of subjectivity. It raises the question of the "ethical difference" that gives one the right and the capacity to govern.

Finally, philosophy, according to Foucault, does not first and foremost attempt to define a morality, to set out rules for conduct, to instruct individuals in a particular ethic or moral code.[18] Rather, it articulates the relations (real or possible) between practices of subjectivity and, on the one hand, the truth to which these practices give one access and, on the other hand, the political structures within which these practices take place and the way in which these practices affirm or resist their political setting.

While this conception of philosophy might not characterize every text or thinker we identify as "philosophical," it clearly serves to characterize the thought of Foucault himself. Furthermore, it serves as a statement about the "source" of philosophy, its living energy, as well as a statement about its historical intelligibility as a concrete response to a concrete reality. Finally, it is a statement about the domain of inquiry, the nature of the "objects," which philosophy addresses. In other words, the "philosophical" emerges from that which, at a fundamental level, organizes an experience in these three dimensions. One can and must approach an experience from each of these different angles. For Foucault, these differing perspectives produce different kinds of questions concerning the relations between power, knowledge, and subjectivity. The variety of possible perspectives and questions can account for the "prismatic" effect of Foucault's own work.[19] Depending on what perspective one takes with respect to an experience, the various constitutive features of that experience appear in a different light. This suggests that the fragmentary nature of Foucault's thought as it appears in the various projects he pursued has more to do with its essentially philosophical character than with some internal incoherence or some radical rupture within that thought. One can always take each text or project as an independent reflection on a determinate question or field of problems. From this point of view, *The Order of Things* and *The Archaeology of Knowledge* are texts which study the historical shift in epistemic formations, the structures which define scientific objects, fields, and discourses. Similarly, one can take *Discipline and Punish* as a self-contained inquiry into the operation of certain relations of power, and so on. *The Use of Pleasure* can be read as a self-contained study of sexual morality and the genealogy of subjectivity. But it is in posing the problem of the relations between these different fields that we discover their philosophical import. Foucault was not content to analyze just one of these fields, and this is because of his essentially philosophical attitude. His analysis of philosophical discourse asks us to come to terms with his own works as the elements of a philosophical project. To do this requires us to seek out the links between these different projects. One must ask, for example, what relations exist between the epistemological formations analyzed in *The Order of Things* and the power relations taken up in *Discipline and Punish*. It is necessary to discover the relations between these particular epistemic formations and power arrangements, on the one hand, and the history of practices of the self in *The History of Sexuality* and Foucault's research in the 1980s, on the other. Through these questions one takes on the philosophical problem of the diagnosis of the present.

I would like to extend this methodological note just a bit further to include a moment in which Foucault's self-understanding as a philosopher is only slightly veiled. In 1984 he schematizes four basic "philosophical attitudes" which he thinks reflect the four basic modalities of veridiction: prophecy, sagacity, technology, and *parrhēsia*.[20] Each philosophical attitude is a way of thinking the interrelation of the three axes of experience. Here I will only look at the last of these, *parrhēsia*, because it is impossible not to hear it as a self-description on the part of Foucault. The *parrhēsiastic* attitude produces a thought "of the irreducibility of truth, of power, and of *ēthos*," but it is also "the impossibility of thinking the truth, power, and *ēthos* . . . without essential, fundamental relations to each other."[21] The *parrhēsiastic* attitude in philosophy results in a thought experiment which moves from one domain to the other to capture, if possible, their equi-primordiality. Philosophical *parrhēsia* attempts to articulate the complex unity of an experience along all three of its axes. This seems to me to express the essence of the Foucauldian diagnosis as well as any explicitly self-referential statement Foucault makes elsewhere. In addition, he links himself through this description to the *parrhēsiastic* tradition he analyzed at the Collège.

All of this so far has to do with the transformation of Foucault's diagnostic method brought about by his experience of ancient philosophy. What about the introduction of the etho-poetic dimension of his work? To grasp this we will have to follow his analyses of care of the self in the Hellenistic and Roman period. I have already attempted to show that in his lectures on Socrates and Plato, Foucault provides suggestions about how his philosophical *parrhēsia* induces what we might call a *conversion* of power. The technologies and relationships of modern power—for example, examination, vigilance, speaking the truth about oneself—are converted from their disciplinary contexts and functions and placed within the Socratic confrontation. Similarly, Plato's texts are converted from theoretical elaborations to *parrhēsiastic* events. However, the main purpose of Foucault's reading of Socrates and Plato was to show the event through which *parrhēsia* became an ethical, philosophical practice. While Socrates and Plato detach ethical *parrhēsia* from the political field, it is only in the Hellenistic and Roman texts that Foucault finds rigorously developed practices of care of the self and ethical *parrhēsia*. Therefore, in this chapter I intend to examine Foucault's analysis of this period in some detail.

The *Conversion* and *Salvation* of the Self

Foucault shows that there are a number of important characteristics that distinguish Hellenistic and Roman care of the self from Socratic-Platonic care as well as from Christian care of the self. The Hellenistic and Roman moment was, according to Foucault, marked by the development of what he called a "culture of the self."[22] Pierre Hadot, whose work on spiritual exercises in ancient philosophy was one of the main inspirations for Foucault's later work, takes exception to this formulation and suggests that it is misleading.[23] For Hadot, Foucault's conception of Hellenistic and Roman philosophy as a culture of the self is, as he puts it, "too centered on the 'self.'"[24] Hadot criticizes Foucault for being imprecise in his use of the term "self"; for ancient philosophers, it wasn't the self in general for which one cared, but the "best part of the self."[25] He also argues that Foucault's emphasis on taking "pleasure" in one's self as the goal of Hellenistic and

Roman philosophy obscures the important difference between "pleasure" and "joy" (*voluptas* and *gaudium; hedone* and *eupathia*) which plays a central role in Hellenistic and Roman ethics.[26] He worries that Foucault's version of care of the self, being "too purely aesthetic," heads in the direction of a "new form of dandyism for the 20th century."[27] Foucault's study of ancient philosophical practice is, according to this critique, both inaccurate *and* dangerous.[28] Hadot rightly believes that Foucault's idiosyncratic interpretation of ancient philosophy is rooted not in ignorance but in a choice: "His description of practices of the self . . . is not only a historical study, but it implicitly aims at offering contemporary man a model of life (what Foucault called 'aesthetics of existence')."[29] Hadot's objections to Foucault are based on his reading of *The Use of Pleasure, The Care of the Self,* and *Writing the Self.*[30] A close reading of Foucault's 1982 course, which puts forward a far more detailed interpretation of Hellenistic and Roman philosophy than do the published texts, offers some responses to these criticisms and some clarifications of Foucault's own position. In particular, it becomes overwhelmingly clear that Foucault's conception of the culture of the self in no way entails a detachment from relationships with, and responsibilities to, others—quite the contrary, in every form of care of the self Foucault analyzes, the relationship to others is a central component. Second, Foucault shows that care of the self in ancient philosophy does not mean disregard for the reality of the natural world and an obsessive attention to oneself, but rather involves both sophisticated engagement with and knowledge about the world. Finally, concerning the political and ethical choice that motivates Foucault's particular interpretation of the care of the self, one has to see his studies within the context of his analysis of contemporary forms of power and knowledge. Given Foucault's persistent political and intellectual effort to identify and resist excesses of power, and the dangerous implications of discourse and power, which control individuals by constructing their very identities, his insistence on the care of the self is anything but arbitrary or aesthetic in any simplistic and narcissistic sense of the term.

What is the "culture of the self" as Foucault sees it? First of all, Foucault is hesitant to use the term "culture."[31] In this context, he uses it in a technical sense and defines its meaning in the following way. Culture, according to Foucault's particular definition, requires four conditions: (1) a systematization and hierarchy of values; (2) these values are posited as universal but are only accessible to a privileged few; (3) the access to these values requires highly regulated and precise conduct, it requires effort and sacrifice; and (4) these regulated and difficult activities have to be able to be taught, validated, elaborated—that is, they have to be constituted as a "field of knowledge."[32] The self, in Hellenistic and Roman culture, organized a culture in this strict sense of the term. The culture of the self is therefore not simply an undefined, generalized narcissism.

The particular definition of the value of the self, the kinds of labor and sacrifice required to attain this value, and the forms of knowledge implicated in this process varied from one school or thinker to the next. But at the general level, a number of characteristics defined it more or less universally. Hellenistic and Roman philosophy in general, according to Foucault, was marked by a unique understanding of the ultimate value of the "salvation of the self" and its correlative notion of the "conversion to one's self." The self, the care of the self understood as the salvation of, and conversion to, one's self, was the goal of ethical life in this period. This goal was posited as the universal task of humankind—every individual was seen to be capable of salvation. However, in practice, the care of the self was limited to a select number of individuals who had the luxury to occupy themselves with it. This required not only a certain amount of leisure and wealth, but also the involvement in a group or a relationship devoted to the task of care of the self.[33] In this section, I will examine some of the general characteristics of Hellenistic-Roman care of the self. In subsequent sections, I will turn to more particular dimensions of this experience.

Foucault's analysis of the general dimensions of the culture of the self focuses on several themes. The first thing to notice is that positing the care of the self as an end in itself rather than as a preparation for political life differentiates Hellenistic and Roman philosophy from Socratic-Platonic philosophy in several important ways. Foucault claims that the temporality of care of the self will change. The specifically Platonic model thematizes care as a response to a failure of pedagogy and erotics, and to a political need.[34] The moment of action, the moment where care was absolutely necessary, was defined as the threshold between adolescence and adulthood—at the point where one is expected to become a subject-agent in the political life of the city. Because the institutions of the city were not capable of preparing individuals to be political agents, care of the self filled this role. In this way, according to Foucault, care of the self functioned on a pedagogical model. It made the individual aware of his ignorance and provoked him to take care of himself, that is, to know himself and to discover in this knowledge of himself the technology of government necessary to be a responsible political agent. However, with the transformation of care into the end rather than a means to some other end, this structure is necessarily abandoned. Care of the self in the Hellenistic and Roman model is more "critical" than pedagogical. Foucault makes this difference clear in a number of ways. First of all, the moment of *parrhēsia* and care of the self—the *kairos*—is no longer located at the threshold of political subjectivity, "manhood." Rather, these activities take place throughout one's life. Second, care of the self will become less associated with the model of pedagogy and more closely linked to a medical model. Where care is linked to the transition from childhood to adulthood, its function is essentially one of "formation," of education, of conversion away from an inadequate or incomplete upbringing. Furthermore, it leads the individual to the acquisition of the arts of life, and of governing. The care of the self is necessary in order to acquire the proper political art—the proper technology of political existence. One cares for oneself in order to be able to care for the city. Third, the primary target of Socratic-Platonic care is ignorance. Care is necessary, as we have seen, because of the neglect and forgetfulness of the self. In Hellenistic and Roman philosophy, on the other hand, care becomes a self-critique. "The practice of the self imposes itself on a foundation of errors, bad habits, deformation, and well-ingrained dependencies that it will have to shake off . . . In this practice of ourselves, it is necessary to work in order to expel and expurgate, to master, to free oneself and deliver oneself from the evil which is interior to us."[35] The self inherently tends toward error, falsehood, and vice, and therefore care of the self is a necessary and constant corrective. More and more care plays the role of a self-critique. Through care one is able to achieve the truth of oneself, to become who one truly is, by rejecting what one has made oneself into. But in recovering this true self, one recovers something which one never was. The self is always already "occupied with something" when it begins to care for itself; it is always already other than itself.[36] That is why "learning the virtues means unlearning the vices."[37] Care of the self is a desubjectification. One unlearns what one has learned, or one unbecomes what one has become. One strives to overcome custom, culture, and education in order to achieve nature, what one really is as opposed to what one has been made into by cultural forms—such as the family, religion, the market, and so on.[38] But one also overcomes "nature" in order to achieve nature. The self, from the very beginning as a little child, is already deforming itself. The self, if it doesn't take care of itself, tends naturally away from its own truth. In other words, in becoming oneself and returning to one's true self, one becomes someone one never was.

The care of the self will become less like a form of education and more like a form of medicine.[39] The philosopher uses the truth to heal the diseases of the soul.[40] The relation between the philosopher and the other is analogous to that between the doctor and the patient. The central concept in the philosophical care of the self is that of *pathos.* Hellenistic and Roman philosophers "describe the evolution of a passion as the evolution of a disease."[41] The passion is the "irrational movement" of the soul—*pertubatio, affectus.* The condition develops from a passion, through a series of intermediary states, finally resulting in a chronic condition: vice.[42] The practice of the self is intrinsically understood to be a medical activity— *therapeuein*—which has the goal of responding to the condition of vice, of mastering the irrational passions which have taken over the life and defined the mode of being of the subject.[43] Philosophy, care of the self, and the practices of the self are essentially therapeutic. The philosophical communities were, in a sense, medical places. Foucault notes that Epictetus considered his school "as a hospital of the soul."[44]

What is the condition that the medicalized relationship and practice of care must cure? In order to provide an exemplary formulation of the experience of the deformed subject, Foucault draws on Seneca's description of *stultitia*. Seneca describes *stultitia* as a "sickness," a state of being or a condition in which one is constantly pushed and pulled from one thing to another. Seneca compares it to being in a river and carried along helplessly. In order to exit from this condition one needs help—someone has to extend a hand and pull one out of the water.[45] In other words, one cannot cure oneself of *stultitia;* rather, one needs the aid of another. Foucault calls this cure, again drawing on Seneca, an exit (*emergere, sortir*). The practice of care of the self is an exit from the present, from sickness. This is the same formulation that Foucault attributes to Kant in his attempt to describe the essence of the Enlightenment.[46] Care of the self is essentially an exit—from ignorance, from malformation, from immaturity, and perhaps for Foucault from normalizing practices, discourses, and relationships.

> When one has not taken care of oneself, one is in a state of *stultitia. Stultitia* is therefore the other pole with respect to the practice of the self. The business of practices of the self—the primary matter, if you like— is *stultitia,* and its objective is to exit from it [*d'en sortir*]. On the other hand, what is *stultitia*? The *stultus* [the patient who suffers the condition of *stultitia*] is the one who has not taken care of himself.[47]

If we take Foucault's ethical categories as they are articulated in the introduction to *The Use of Pleasure,* then we can say that the passions are the ethical substance—the subject defined as a problematic material to be worked upon—and *stultitia* is the disease of the passions.[48]

Who is the *stultus*? His first characteristic is that he is open to and determined by the "representations" coming to him from the outside world. He is under the influence of external sources of ideas. He is compelled, dragged down the river, by the representations entering his mind from the outside world. Therefore, *stultitia* is a disease that affects one's relationship to the outside, it affects one's way of being in the physical—spatial— world. These representations are a mix of external forces and internal forces. His "passions, desires, ambition, habits of thought, illusions" control his thought from within just as much as the representations of things coming to him from the external world. These representations remain unexamined: the *stultus* does not know what they represent.[49] Because the *stultus* receives representations from the outside and pressure from the inside, leaving himself open to their pervasive influence, he lacks the power of *discriminatio*—the power to discern, to examine, to discriminate and distinguish the various contents of representations and the influence of passion, desire, ambition, and imagination. He is dispersed among the representations coming from the outside and the concoction they create when mixed with the various forces determining him from within. He is pushed and pulled in different directions, toward different goals. Foucault describes a second characteristic of the *stultus*. Not only is he controlled by various forces and dispersed among them, he is dispersed in time. *Stultitia* is also therefore a temporal condition, a disease of one's basic temporality. The *stultus* has no memory, and therefore no connection to permanence—no ability to apply himself to the work of remembering the things which he needs to know. He does not keep his objective firmly in mind and therefore has no connection to the future. He lets his life "pass away" and is led in various directions during the flow of time. He changes his style of life with each passing moment without attempting to introduce unity into it.[50] "The consequence—consequence and principle—of this opening to representations which come from the external world and of this dispersion in time, is that the individual, the *stultus,* is not able to will as he should."[51] *Stultitia* is a disease which disables the *will* of the individual, it affects the subject qua agent. The exit from *stultitia* frees the will and in this way is the constitution of an agency where previously there had been dispersion, multiplicity, passivity.

In other words, in the Hellenistic-Roman model, the will is not originally free, but must be constituted, put into place. The will must be liberated from *stultitia*. The free will, the subject as an agent, is not determined by internal forces or by representations from the outside. Furthermore, this free will is an "absolute" will.[52] It wills one thing only and it wills it constantly. In the condition of *stultitia,* the will is divided and dispersed—it wills against itself. The subject liberated from *stultitia* has an active and permanent will. The free will has its proper object, the only object which one can will, according to Foucault's reading of Seneca, in a way completely independent of passions and desires, of representations coming from the outside, and with a permanent activity: one's *self.* The will, the true will, is the will that wills itself. The condition of *stultitia* is a disease of the will that does not will its own freedom: "In *stultitia* there is a disconnect, non-connection, a non-belonging of the will to itself which is at once its most obvious effect and its most profound root."[53] The free will wills freedom.

The proper form of the will—the will that wills itself—is impossible in *stultitia,* the absence of will. Therefore, what is required is the intervention of someone else who is able to guide one in the "constitution of oneself" such that the resulting self can serve to "polarize" the will.[54] The nature of this intervention is not teaching or education in the sense of transmitting knowledge from one individual to the other. Rather, the form of education is care of the self, the art of forming a self worthy of the will. The goal is not the development of knowledge. Instead, the other carries out "a type of operation which bears upon the mode of being of the subject herself."[55] The intervention of the other has the purpose of transforming the being of the subject who suffers *stultitia.*

The person who is capable of curing the *stultus,* of guiding him to himself, of helping him to constitute a self which serves to unify, absolutize, and permanently activate the will, is the philosopher.[56] The philosopher, in the Hellenistic and Roman period, defines himself as the master of the arts of living, and in particular as the master of the art of care of the self. This care of the self appears as an art of governing—it guides the other to the point where the other becomes capable of taking care of herself: the right, the capacity, the duty, the privilege, and the art of governing others are founded upon the proper government of oneself. The master of care of the self, as an art of self-government, is the master of government *in general* because the foundation for governing others is the proper government of oneself. Foucault also distinguishes rhetoric as an art of governing from philosophy as an art of caring for the self. "Rhetoric is the inventory and analysis of the means by which one is able to act upon others through discourse."[57] Rhetoric is a technology of domination; it aims to determine the actions of the other. Philosophy, on the other hand, is a way of allowing others to become capable of caring for and governing themselves: "It is the ensemble of principles and practices that one can have at her disposition, or put at the disposition of others, for taking the proper care of one's self or others."[58] Philosophy, as a medical care of the other, attempts to give her the capacity to care for herself, to become a self she can will freely, to help her exit from the condition of *stultitia.*

Care of the self in the Hellenistic and Roman *dispositif* is, according to Foucault, comprehended as a form of "salvation" and of "conversion." To care for oneself is to save and convert oneself.[59] Foucault shows that these two terms have meanings independent of their religious significance, and in particular of the sense which they take in the context of Christianity. What is salvation in the philosophical sense as opposed to the religious sense? According to Foucault, it is a result of our Christian legacy that we tend to think of salvation in terms of an event by which one passes from one state or place to another. Salvation is conceived in binary terms and as a form of passage between these terms: one moves from this world to the next, from sinfulness to purity, from death and mortality to life and immortality.[60] But the philosophical notion of salvation as Foucault develops it through his reading of Hellenistic and Roman philosophy is not grasped as an event, as a passage,[61] or in binary terms.[62]

Foucault shows that salvation, as a philosophical concept, refers to a permanent *activity* rather than to an *event:* "Salvation is therefore a permanent activity of the subject on himself which is compensated in a certain relationship of the subject to himself, when he has become impermeable to exterior troubles and when he finds in himself a satisfaction which does not need anything other than himself . . . in salvation in Hellenistic and Roman philosophy the self is the agent, the object, the instrument, and the finality of salvation."[63] Salvation is the activity of maintaining oneself, protecting oneself, guarding against danger, being alert to trouble; one is saved when one is well prepared for life. "The one who saves himself is the one who is in a state of alert, in a state of resistance, in a state of sovereignty and mastery of himself which permits him to repulse attacks and assaults."[64] It is significant that Foucault defines salvation in these terms. Hellenistic and Roman salvation is the production of a subject of resistance. While the danger confronted by ancient philosophers was problematized in terms of *stultitia* (for example) rather than relationships of power and knowledge, Foucault is able to grasp the practice of philosophical salvation as resistance. The notions of attentiveness, of resistance, of continuous activity inform Foucault's ethic of the self as a resistance to political power and to the self as an effect of this power. Furthermore, saving oneself, philosophical salvation, is not the passage from one state to another, but the effort one makes to resist power. Salvation, in the Hellenistic and Roman schema, is immanent in the world rather than transcendence from it. Foucault's ethic of the self, care of the self as a resistance to normalization, is an immanent salvation which does not posit the necessity of a passage to an ideal world but rather the transformation of one's self within the world. In other words, this suggests that in Foucault's reading of ancient practices of "salvation" we should be attentive to the ways these practices might also function as modern arts of resistance to normalization, discipline, and biopolitics.

As with salvation, Foucault takes up the notion of conversion in a nonreligious sense. He argues that Hellenistic and Roman philosophers practiced a form of care understood entirely as salvation and conversion—the salvation of and the conversion to the self represent the goal of care of the self. The purpose and nature of salvation and conversion is to establish the proper relationship to oneself—one of freedom, vigilance, mastery, and pleasure. This relationship is not simply a static coexistence of two terms but is first and foremost an activity; one protects oneself, equips oneself with the tools one needs to live well, maintains oneself, defends oneself, and so on. It is also, in addition to being a relationship defined by activity and effort, an attitude of self-respect, honor; a state of self-mastery, self-possession; and a pleasure or delight in oneself.[65] Foucault's discussion of the theme of conversion in Hellenistic and Roman philosophy aims not only to grasp it positively in its essential characteristics but also negatively in its differentiation from both Platonic and Christian conversion. His understanding of conversion as a spiritual exercise began with his reading of Hadot, who contrasted the Platonic and Christian experiences: *epistrophe* and *metanoia,* respectively.[66] The Platonic notion of conversion (*epistrophe*) speaks of an "awakening" in which one is "illuminated" by the light of the truth which takes the form of (self-) knowledge and recollection; it is a return to one's self in the form of self-knowledge.[67] Christian conversion (*metanoia*), on the other hand, is understood in terms of death and resurrection, of radical rupture with oneself, of transcending oneself and being reborn.[68] The term *metanoia* in Greek has the sense both of conversion and of repentance. Christian conversion therefore involves repenting for guilt, renunciation of oneself insofar as one is guilty. Within the framework of Hellenistic and Roman care of the self and conversion, the practices of the self are not modes of repentance, of guilt or renunciation. Rather, care of the self was what protected one from living in a way that would necessitate repentance.[69] Neither the Platonic model of illumination through recollection nor the Christian model of transcendence through repentance and rupture fit with the Hellenistic and Roman experience of conversion.

In order to take this experience up positively, Foucault examines its two basic aspects: the conversion of one's gaze (*regard*) "away" from others and "toward" oneself, and the conversion of one's attention "away" from knowledge of nature and "toward" knowledge of oneself.[70] I use quotation marks here because while the language of the conversion to oneself suggests a movement of disengagement from, of turning away from, other people and the external world and a corresponding movement of turning within, Foucault's analysis shows that the actual activity of conversion is neither disengagement from an exterior nor a turn inward.

First of all, let's look at Foucault's discussion of the conversion of one's gaze away from others and toward oneself. Foucault argues that this conversion is not to be understood according to the Platonic form of self-examination—for example, the ontology of the soul described in *Alcibiades* or the examination of life in *Laches*. To turn away from others and toward oneself does not result in self-examination or self-knowledge. It is also not a Christian hermeneutics. Hellenistic and Roman practices of the self do not attend to the interior life of the individual—the movement of thought, desire, imagination, and so on—and do not attempt to interpret the meaning of one's inner experience or actions. The "self" toward whom one converts one's gaze is not to be found within. Furthermore, the conversion does not in fact turn one away from others or from the external world. The language of the conversion can be misleading given our tendency to think in hermeneutic terms. To see this we have to understand what it is one is turning away from as well as what it is one is turning toward. Foucault takes an example from Plutarch.[71] The gaze that one has to convert is a gaze which is curious about, and agitated by, the secrets and the faults of others. One has to convert one's "pleasure in knowing the faults that they commit."[72] Therefore, turning away from others and not regarding them has a particular sense. To what does one convert one's gaze? Plutarch suggests the study of nature, history, or by way of a retreat, the countryside.[73] In other words, converting one's gaze toward oneself does not mean turning inward, becoming obsessed with oneself rather than concerned about others. Instead, it means converting the desire to watch others at their worst into a desire to study nature and history. Foucault shows that this conversion is effected through the application of various anticuriosity exercises—we will explore a variety of Hellenistic and Roman technologies of the self in the sections that follow.[74] Converting one's gaze from the others and to oneself results in a curiosity about the world, and the application of certain exercises are what bring this conversion about. But in what sense is this new curiosity about history and nature a conversion to oneself? When applied properly, these exercises save one from distractions and convert one's gaze to one's objective: one's self. One becomes free from a pleasure which depends upon the failures of others. This new regard directs one toward one's goal of pleasure in oneself by detaching one from the faults of others. "If it is necessary to detach oneself from the malicious and malevolent gaze towards the other, it is so that one can concentrate on oneself, on the straight path that one must follow and maintain while heading towards one's goal."[75] One's gaze, one's manner of seeing the world, must become "teleological."[76]

The self one gazes upon is not within but is outside—in the world. It appears as a goal and a "trajectory." For Hellenistic and Roman philosophers, care of the self required an "athletic concentration." To clarify this notion of trajectory, Foucault uses a classic "Zen" example: the concentration of the archer. The archer must focus on the "distance" between himself and the target. In care of the self, one must focus on the distance between one's current condition and the target—one's self as a full and complete subject. The self discloses itself, then, not only in its present form but also as the goal to be attained and the distance to be covered.[77] In order to be present with oneself, one must perceive oneself in the very distance which separates one from who one truly is, teleologically. The nonbeing of the self—the distance of oneself from oneself—is what becomes evident through this other way of looking. The conversion of one's gaze toward one's self is not therefore a conversion so much of the "objects" toward which one looks—one does not avoid the external world and the others in order to focus on oneself. Rather, it is a conversion of the "modality" of one's gaze. The point is to change the way one sees the world, such that the tension between one's self as material and as goal becomes evident, and so that one is able to perceive in the external world, and in one's relationships to others, the trajectory toward the target. One has to look in a way that contributes to the therapy of the self, the freedom of the will to will itself, to exit from the condition of *stultitia*. In the following sections I will look more closely at Foucault's discussion of the techniques for bringing about this conversion and the particular modes and types of relationships to others that this conversion implies.

The other aspect of the conversion of the gaze is the conversion of one's knowledge of the natural world. The point of the conversion of knowledge is to give up "useless" knowledge and concern oneself with "useful" knowledge. However, the conversion here is the same as that of the transformation of one's attention toward others. Through a reading of Seneca, Foucault shows that the purpose of the conversion to oneself is not to disengage one from external reality and to become obsessed with oneself. One continues to gaze out upon the same objects—the gods, the natural world, other human beings. What changes is the manner of knowing these things.[78] The kind of knowledge which is useless is knowledge of "causes." It is not necessary to know what causes things to happen or to be the way they are. The discovery of causes is nothing more than a pleasant pastime—it cannot be considered an urgent task for the constitution of the subject. The pursuit of causal knowledge is fine for a subject who has already established, and knows how to maintain, the proper rapport with himself—but for someone striving to achieve freedom, such knowledge can only be a diversion. Therefore, one must convert one's knowledge to oneself. But again, this does not result in self-examination or self-interpretation. Rather, the conversion results in a different modality of knowing the natural world. Foucault identifies this modality according to three characteristics. First, it is a "relational" knowledge.[79] What this means is that one needs to know not what the causes of nature are, but rather the relationship between the natural world and one's self—grasped as material and teleology. For example, rather than trying to learn what causes death, one needs to know the relationship between death and the realization of the truth of oneself, the accomplishment of oneself as a subject. The second characteristic of this mode of knowledge—what Foucault calls later the spiritual modality of knowledge—is that the principles of nature are essentially prescriptive. To know the truth about the world, to learn the truth about the external world, is to transform one's way of being and acting. To grasp the truth of the world in terms of one's place in the world, in terms of the relationship of external reality to one's process of becoming a subject, transforms one's way of being and doing. The conversion to oneself therefore converts knowledge of the world into knowledge of principles for living. The third characteristic is the "return effect" of the truth on the subject. To know the truth about the world is to complete oneself, to solidify oneself, to see clearly one's path toward the goal of freedom. Knowledge of the world equips one—that is, saves one—to fight off the distractions and diversions from freedom. Foucault's focus on the modality of knowledge shows that the way in which we look at nature, the way in which we constitute the world as an object of knowledge, has an effect on the way in which we constitute ourselves as subjects.

Foucault's interpretation of the Hellenistic and Roman model of philosophical care of the self is in constant reference to Christian hermeneutics of the self. However, we can also see it with constant reference to the contemporary problem of disciplinary, normalizing forms of biopower. These modes of power constitute us and our world through a particular kind of objectifying gaze; they constitute us as subjects who look out at the world and who look within ourselves through the lens of disciplinary techniques. The care of the self, as a conversion, suggests the possibility of converting our gaze toward ourselves; that is, converting our way of seeing the world, ourselves, and others as objects of power and knowledge. It offers the possibility of salvation—not as the event of passage from one state to another, but as the activity of vigilance, as the acquisition of the tools necessary to remain free from excesses of power. The conversion of the gaze is a conversion from a disciplinary and objectifying mode of knowing to an etho-poetic mode of knowing.[80]

In the following sections I will go through some of Foucault's analyses of the particular forms that care of the self as salvation and conversion, as etho-poesis, took in the Hellenistic and Roman period. I intend these to function as examples of what Foucault meant by the care of the self and the arts of living. I also intend to look at the implications of his analyses for the diagnosis and etho-poetics of the present. In other words, I want to pose the question: what can we learn from these analyses about the relationship between techniques of power, forms of knowledge, and practices of subjectivity?

Care of the Self as a Relationship to the Other

Contrary to the criticisms often leveled against Foucault for valorizing an aestheticized, narcissistic attention to the self, his study of Hellenistic and Roman etho-poesis places a heavy accent on the fact that care of the self implied all sorts of relationships to others. Foucault addresses this aspect of care of the self from two different points of view. First, when one takes care of oneself, an essential dimension of the self that requires attention is the relationship one maintains with others. In the Hellenistic-Roman model, the goal of ethical life is to establish the right relationship to one's self. But this relationship to one's self transforms and is transformed by one's relationships to others; it does not dissolve these relationships but intensifies them by giving them a fundamental ethical—etho-poetic—dimension. This model is different from the Socratic-Platonic model. For Socrates and Plato, one must establish the proper relationship to oneself *so that* one can have the proper relationship to others: one must save one's self so that one can save others. And the salvation of others, the care of the city, is the fulfillment of one's self. Therefore, the relationship to one's self is mediated by and finalized in one's relationship with others in the form of the salvation of the city.[81] For the Hellenistic model, however, one does not save oneself so that one can then save the others; the salvation of others, the salvation of the city, is not the ethical goal of life and the practices of the self. Rather, one's relationships contribute to the care of the self; in order to establish the right relationship to one's self and in order to maintain that relationship, one must take up the right relationship to others. The relationship to the other is absorbed by the care of the self. In other words, care of the self does not dissolve the relationship to others. In fact, having the proper relationship to others is an indispensable and irreducible aspect of the salvation of one's self.

The second perspective Foucault brings to bear on this dimension of care of the self has to do with the practice of *parrhēsia*. As we know, *parrhēsia* is an ethical practice—it is a relationship to the other which serves the purpose of converting and saving the other. In the Hellenistic model *parrhēsia* is the discourse of spiritual direction. The activity of *parrhēsia* is therefore essentially a way of being with others. The Hellenistic model of philosophy develops various forms of *parrhēsia;* philosophy is understood not simply as a practice of care of the self, but to be a philosopher, as opposed to someone who uses philosophy to take care of himself, is to be a *parrhēsiast*, to be a spiritual guide. The devotion to, the development of the capacity for, *parrhēsia* is what distinguishes an individual as a philosopher—a master of the art of spiritual direction. This does not necessarily mean that *parrhēsia* was conceived of as the goal of life; rather, it was part of one's proper relationship to oneself, as a philosopher, to take up a *parrhēsiastic* relationship to others. *Parrhēsia* is also fundamental because in the Hellenistic model one cannot save oneself—the relationship to a master, a *parrhēsiast*, is absolutely necessary in order to take care of oneself: "The master is a catalyst in the reform of the individual and in the formation of the individual as a subject."[82] The other—the *parrhēsiast*—is the mediator of the relationship of oneself to oneself. The philosopher, defined as a *parrhēsiast*, must intervene in the relationship that nature, culture, and self-neglect have formed between oneself and oneself. *Parrhēsia* resists what one has become through one's upbringing; this resistance is necessary in order to become a subject. "When it is a matter of transforming a bad routine [*mauvais habitudes*], when it is a matter of transforming the *hexis*, the manner of being of the individual, when it is a matter of correcting one's self, then *a fortiori* one will need a master."[83]

What are the different kinds of relationships to the other implied by care of the self and *parrhēsia*? In his 1982 course Foucault makes a distinction between Hellenistic philosophy, which is basically oriented by the community, the school; and Roman philosophy, which tends toward the private relationship between friends or relatives.[84] However, in 1983 Foucault groups these relationships into a different set of categories and associates each kind of relationship with a particular form of Hellenistic philosophy, admitting that this is "only a general schema."[85] The three categories of relationship and their corresponding modes of philosophy are community life, practiced for the most part by Epicureans; public life, practiced by the Cynics; and private relationships, practiced generally by the Stoics.[86] The point is not so much to link a social relationship to a philosophical school as to show both the variety of possible philosophical forms and the overarching experience of the subject and of philosophy which motivates them. What is important for Foucault has to do with (a) the general necessity for, and the great variety of, these relationships, and (b) the possibilities they represent for the present. Therefore, it seems to me that the discrepancy between his two ways of organizing the material is insignificant philosophically. In the following I will examine Foucault's discussion of Epicurean and especially Stoic philosophical lives, relationships, and techniques. For reasons that will become clear, I will deal with Foucault's analysis of Cynic philosophy separately. I will look at three aspects of Foucault's sketch of the relationship to the other in care of the self. First, there are the institutions that this relationship takes place in; that is, the forms of the community, the school, and the private relationship and the way these are defined as spaces exterior to, within, or in opposition to the social-political world at large. Second, there are noninstitutional relationships to the other which care of the self implies. In other words, how is the other constituted as an ethical concern when care of the self is the goal of life? Third, there is the role of *parrhēsia* as an ethical relationship to the other in the Hellenistic and Roman model. In the following I will move back and forth among these three different aspects of the relationship to the other in the ethics of the self as I outline Foucault's discussion of Epicurean and Stoic philosophy.

Foucault uses the Epicurean schools as privileged examples of the *community* model of care of the self. These schools were self-contained communities organized around the principle of spiritual guidance and the hierarchy of spiritual guides. One's position in the hierarchy, in principle, was linked to one's progress in the work of self-transformation and self-mastery—self-mastery was the foundation for serving as a master and a guide to others.[87] These were places of spiritual formation, communities which fulfilled the necessary place of the relationship to another in one's accomplishment of oneself. Foucault refers to Philodemus, Peri Parrhēsias, who insists on the necessity of following a spiritual guide in the care of the self.[88] This relationship between director and disciple requires "an intense affective relationship, a relationship of friendship."[89] Effective spiritual direction also requires an "ethic of speaking [*parole*]."[90] This is *parrhēsia*, "the openness of heart . . . necessary for the two partners not to hide any of their thoughts from each other and to speak frankly."[91] *Parrhēsia* as a virtue and a "kairotic" technique manifests itself in a variety of relationships between individuals in the Epicurean community: in the range of modes of teaching and of "confessing" which take place there. Foucault points out three different forms of producing the truth, and of self-disclosure which the community aims at: there is the "authoritarian" lecture technique in which the master tells the others the truth; there are private relationships between a master and disciple in which the master is the spiritual guide leading the other to a conversion of self; and finally there is the practice of group confession, which is the "salvation by one of another"[92] and which is a practice of symmetrical *parrhēsia* in which each individual has the duty of taking on the role of speaker.

Foucault's discussion of Epicurean physiology (*physiologia*)—the science of physics—provides us with an idea of the difference between, on the one hand, the spiritual formation one receives in the community and, on the other hand, cultural norms at large. Epicurus criticizes *paideia* and replaces it with the study of nature, of physics, which he calls physiology.[93] *Paideia* is the cultural formation, the liberal art, of a "free man [*homme libre*]."[94] According to Epicurus, *paideia*, "education," is brought about through a certain art of the *phonē*—of the word understood in its material, sonic element. Foucault understands this critique to mean that teachers of *paideia* do not concern themselves with reason—*logos,* words in their significant dimension—but rather they attempt to produce physical, irrational responses in their students. In other words, they use "special effects" that divert and please the senses while inhibiting the formation of subjectivity. This kind of education indoctrinates the student into a culture of external dependence—one is initiated in the life devoted to pleasing the crowd. The critique of *paideia* and of the teachers who are essentially wordsmiths rather than philosophers continues the Socratic-Platonic critique of rhetoric and the Sophists. The product of *paideia* is a man who feels free when he receives the adulation of the crowd, and his education in word play—learning how to make good speeches—gives him the means to get the attention he needs. Physiology, the study of nature, on the other hand, forms individuals who "are independent and who pride themselves on what is really their own."[95] Rather than indoctrinating individuals into external dependence, into the need for admiration, physiology "equips" an individual "to resist all the movements and solicitations coming from the outside world."[96] In effect, by studying nature, as we have seen, one takes care of oneself because through this study one acquires the knowledge one needs to be free. The study of nature is an exercise of the self, a technique by which one becomes a "free subject [*sujet libre*], a subject who is going to find in himself the possibility and the resources of unalterable delight [*volupté*] and permanent tranquility."[97] The free subject possesses the equipment (*parasekeuē*) necessary to resist the influence of culture—*paideia*—and the desire for admiration.

Foucault's definition of the Epicurean form of education is interesting for a couple of reasons. First of all, he sets the Epicurean school in opposition to culture—the formation of a "free man." The cultural practice of education is in fact a means of constraining the individual by constituting his sense of self and his vision of the good life in terms of a particular cultural idea of "man." Second, insofar as Epicurean physiology resists this "deformation" of the individual, this confinement of the individual within a particular vision of "man," and forms a "subject" by equipping the individual to fight off the influences of culture, it is a kind of "death of man." The "free subject" who is produced through the exercise of the self in the study of nature stands in opposition to the "free man" who is produced through cultural rhetoric. Finally, Foucault shows that the technique for teaching physiology—that is, for the formation of a free subject—is none other than *parrhēsia.*[98] Openness, frankness, and courage to say what will not win the admiration of the crowd are the qualities required for the formation of a free subject.

Foucault points out that in the Epicurean groups the practice of *parrhēsia,* as the philosophical relationship of care for the other, is understood not only as a "virtue, or personal attitude, but also as a *technē.*"[99] *Parrhēsia* as a virtue is evident in Socrates' practice of dialogue and his concern for the ontological foundation of discourse, *logos,* in a mode of life, *bios.*[100] But with the Epicureans, the notion of *technē* is taken up in a more systematic way. *Parrhēsia* is compared to the arts of medicine and politics.[101] The comparison of philosophy or of philosophical *parrhēsia* to these arts runs throughout the Hellenistic experience. The two features of *parrhēsia* which make the analogy possible are (1) the fact that *parrhēsia* is a "kairotic" or "clinical technique," that it concerns itself not merely with general principles but with particular, singular circumstances; and (2) that it requires one individual to make a decision and the other or others to obey; it is a decisive technique of governing.[102] *Parrhēsia* is a technology, a practical knowledge, a decisive art, possessed by the philosopher, the master of the care of the self, and it is a mode of conducting, governing, caring for the other. The philosopher must know how and when to intervene in the life of the disciple in order to bring about the desired results. In other words, it is not simply a matter of saying the truth: *parrhēsia* is a *technē* because one must know precisely how to use discourse in order to free the other, to have an effect on the other; the truth has to be said at the right moment and in the right way or it is useless.

Foucault contrasts the Epicurean school with an example of the Stoic school, that of Epictetus. While the Epicureans lived together in a closed community, the Stoics did not. Their institution appears to have been based on meetings or gatherings. In other words, the Stoic school was just that, a kind of classroom setting, with students of different levels and with different goals coming and going. The students could be finishing off an education started elsewhere, or preparing themselves for a life of politics, or they could be in preparation to become philosophers themselves. The latter students, and their preparation, formed what Foucault calls a kind of "*école normale* for philosophers."[103] This professional formation aimed primarily at training individuals in the art of caring for others. The skill needed for the philosophical care of others was argument, because care often takes the form of a kind of intellectual combat. This combat is a struggle to force individuals to give up false opinions which are the source of unhappiness and vice. Vice is in fact already a kind of internal struggle, a contradiction, in which an individual does what he thinks is good—that is, useful. But he has a mistaken idea of what is useful, which does not lead to his own happiness, but rather contributes to his own suffering. The philosopher is able to confront such an individual and "show that, in fact, he did what he didn't want to do, and he didn't do what he wanted."[104] The art of discourse, then, is the art of showing the other who he really is, what he really wishes for, and that he has contradicted himself in his actions. The philosopher is

> *protreptikos* and *elegktikos*. These are two technical terms. *Protreptikos:* the one who is capable of giving a *protreptic* teaching, that is, a teaching which can turn the soul [*esprit*] in the right direction. On the other hand . . . [the philosopher] . . . is *elegktikos:* he is good in the art of discussion, in the intellectual debate through which one separates truth from error, refuting error and substituting for it a true proposition.[105]

Discourse is an art of conversion, of pointing the soul of the other in the right direction so that it can see the truth. If the philosopher cannot realign the soul of his interlocutor, it is not the fault of the interlocutor. The fault in such a situation lies with the philosopher who has not mastered his art. The philosopher is therefore defined precisely in and by his rapport with the other.

Whether it is in the form of the closed community or the school, care of the self defined a particular space, and an institution, outside of the everyday world and in important ways in opposition to the de-formation brought about by culture. This was a space devoted to the care of the self: individuals learned from masters how to take care of themselves, or they trained to eventually become masters in order to take care of others.

Having outlined two forms of Hellenistic communities, Foucault takes up the question of the Roman model. The institutional form of care in this model is that of the "personal advisor."[106] The role of the philosopher in the Roman model was to be an advisor in the art of living—a director of conscience.[107] The philosopher advised on particular matters such as political decisions, offered theoretical arguments for or against certain courses of actions, and provided guidance on the practice of living. Philosophers, in the Roman model, became a part of the society: "One is going to find them involved everywhere in the political life and the great debates, the great conflicts . . . which are going to mark the middle of the first century."[108] The practice of philosophy, as an art of spiritual direction, is an important part of everyday life in Roman culture. It is not restricted to a community or a school set apart from the everyday world and defined in opposition to or at least exterior to society. Rather than being a scholastic discipline practiced in a community isolated to some degree from the social-political world, philosophical care of the self is integrated into the very activities of this world.

Foucault's analysis shows an ambivalence in this generalization and incorporation of philosophy into the everyday. While on the one hand philosophical practice is removed from the schools and from the well-regulated modes of control of those institutions, and while it becomes more particular and more suited to advising and caring for individuals in concrete political and ethical situations, it simultaneously *loses its critical distance*, its ability to critique from a position that is removed from, and *other than*, the norm. "Therefore, to the extent that one sees the figure of the philosopher develop, to the extent that one sees the importance of the figure of the philosopher grow in stature, one also sees that it loses, more and more, its singular, irreducible function exterior to the quotidian, exterior to day-to-day life, to political life."[109] Taking care of oneself and living a life connected to the truth is less and less something set apart from the norms of the social and political world. Rather, it invests the activities of the everyday world, transforming them from within. Though Foucault does not explicitly make the connection, it seems plausible that the way Roman philosophers define the "condition" to be treated by the "clinician" in the Roman practice of philosophy reflects its new place as a part of the social-cultural world. Rather than conceiving of itself as a cure of, or opposition to, *paideia*, a new focus will be "self-delusion" and "self-love." The *parrhēsiast* is necessary for one's salvation because one always remains blind to the truth about oneself. Foucault refers to Plutarch and to Galen to show that "self-love" (*philautia*) is the source of error, of unhappiness, and of injustice, which one cannot overcome, or even *see*, without the presence, and the words, of the other.[110] Because of self-love one is not capable of carrying out the critical work on oneself necessary to exit from slavery to oneself without the frank words of someone else. Foucault points out the importance of this experience of the subject for Christian ethics. According to Foucault, the Stoic critique of self-love was transformed in the practice of Christian asceticism into a renunciation of the self, of one's own subjectivity (the preference of one's own will over the will of God). This renunciation was considered necessary to achieve the steadiness of a permanent contemplation of God and was achieved, in part, through confessional practices with the aid and guidance of the pastor.[111]

The Roman de-professionalization of philosophy resulted in a couple of important problems. First, when the philosopher is not clearly defined institutionally, how does one recognize a philosopher? The philosopher is not defined by his singularity but rather lives a life pretty much like that of anyone else. In other words, the problem of recognizing who is able to use *parrhēsia*—this time in order to act as a spiritual guide rather than as a political leader—is reactivated through the "privatization" of care. The private relationship can take various possible forms: the *parrhēsiast* is sometimes in the position of a friend (according to Plutarch, Seneca, and Marcus Aurelius and Fronton, for example), sometimes in the position of a stranger (according to Galen), and sometimes in the position of a professional "advisor." Plutarch, for example, attempted to respond to the problem by providing two criteria for recognizing a *parrhēsiast:* (1) the true *parrhēsiast* exhibits the ontological harmony of *bios* and *logos* which figured prominently in the *Laches* dialogue;[112] and (2) the true *parrhēsiast* is marked by "the permanence, the stability, and the steadiness . . . regarding his choices, his opinions and his thoughts."[113] The one who knows the truth about himself, who has mastered himself and has achieved tranquility of mind, will exhibit a constant and steady harmony between his words and his deeds. Such a person is not deluded about himself because of self-love, nor is he given to flattery, to deceitfulness with others, but is willing and able to speak the truth. This individual is the true *parrhēsiast,* and is for Plutarch the true friend.[114] In other words, *parrhēsia* is the form of friendship, it is the duty of the true friend, and friendship is the condition of *parrhēsia.*

The second problem brought about through the integration of philosophy and culture has to do with the extension of relations of power.[115] This is not to say that communities and schools are free from relationships of power—in fact, they are defined in large part by such relations— rather, the infusion of ordinary relationships with practices of care of the self opens up a new conduit for the "control of the individual by others."[116] Despite the fact that this development creates new problems, it remains a rich source of philosophical inspiration for Foucault. In fact, from 1982 on, Seneca and Marcus Aurelius—two nonprofessional philosophers— will hold a special place in Foucault's understanding of care of the self as a relationship to the other, as a form of knowledge, and as an *askēsis.*

The integration of philosophy into the social world is cast as an opposition to a radical form of philosophical *parrhēsia.* Philosophy as a socially regulated and instituted practice is a kind of "anticynicism."[117] Cynicism represents the extreme form of the philosophical critique of culture: it is a total rejection of culture. Foucault spends much of his 1984 course at the Collège presenting his view of the Cynic—both as a figure of ethical *parrhēsia* and in relation to other philosophical schools. It seems to me that Foucault wanted to develop the opposition between Cynicism and more socially integrated forms of care of the self and *parrhēsia* because he saw this rift as fundamental in the history of practices of the self. All of these forms of philosophy represent ways of integrating modes of veridiction, relations of power, and practices of the self. Perhaps, however, it is precisely the effort to differentiate themselves that resulted in the movement toward social-cultural integration on the one hand and total rejection of culture on the other. It is also important to note in these examples the proliferation of relationships of care, of governmentality, outside the political, religious, and socially codified institutions of Greco-Roman culture, as well as the conversion of these institutions toward the goal of care of the self. In order to take care of oneself, in order to save oneself and accomplish oneself, a whole field of supplemental relationships arose. One needed a true friend, a true advisor, a spiritual guide or a community of spiritual comrades in order to accomplish the ethical formation of oneself because one needed to be saved by the true words, the *parrhēsia,* which the other speaks.

So far, I have covered some important elements of Foucault's discussion of Hellenistic and Roman institutions of spiritual direction and care of the self. However, even outside of the relationship of spiritual direction, care of the self implies ethical relationships to the other. This is clear in Foucault's treatment of the Epicurean theory and practice of friendship, and the Stoic notion of the world community.[118] Foucault takes up this aspect of Hellenistic and Roman philosophy in order to show that the prioritization of "care of the self" does not result in cutting off one's duties and relationships to others. Rather, when the activities of life are subordinated to the care of the self, those activities take on a different ethical significance.

First, let us examine Epicurean care of the self and the relationship to the other. In order to give us an idea of the way care of the self implicates a fundamental ethical link to the other, Foucault takes up the Epicurean discussion of friendship. For Epicurus, friendship is good because it is *useful* and because it is desirable in and of itself.[119] As we saw, the notion of utility is an important concept in the care of the self. The term is not reducible to our sense of "utility." Foucault showed that the word— *khrēsis*—really refers to the way one is involved with something. To use something in this sense means to be properly involved with it, to treat it properly and to gain from it what one ought as well as to give to it what is proper. Friendship begins in utility of a very basic kind—one's relationships with others begin in situations where one needs them to accomplish one's tasks—"it inscribes itself in the regime of social exchanges and services which links men together."[120] But these relationships are pleasurable and become enjoyable and desirable in and of themselves. This does not mean for Epicurus that they are no longer useful—they must maintain their utility as part of their pleasure and desirability. The combination of pleasure and utility constitutes friendship as one of the most important elements of the good life and happiness.[121] This happiness for Epicurus results from a state of certitude in one's independence, one's freedom from pain and from fear: "The knowledge of the fact that we are surrounded by friends and that these friends will have with respect to us an attitude of reciprocity which will respond to the friendship that we feel for them is what constitutes for us one of the guarantees of happiness."[122] The real existence and aid of friends, the mutual usefulness of friends, allows us to be free of fear—we know we can count on our friends and they know that they can count on us. Certainty in friendship is in this way part of happiness understood as freedom from pain and fear. Friendship is understood within care of the self: one has friends, one is a friend, and one performs the activities of friendships insofar as one strives to save oneself, to establish and maintain the proper relationship to oneself (*ataraxie*, freedom).[123] A good friend is precisely the one who takes care of himself, who is concerned about himself. Through this concern he knows the importance of friendship in his own life and knows how to be a friend. Furthermore, he knows the importance of taking care of his friends; the care of the other in Epicurean friendship is therefore inseparable from the care of the self, but it in no way dissolves one's relationships to others. It simply displaces the teleology of these relationships; they are no longer perceived as the end to be attained, but rather are a means to an end. One has friends because one cares for oneself; one is capable of friendship to the extent that one cares for oneself.

Foucault presents the theory of Epictetus as a representative of the Stoic implication of care of the self and care of the other. According to Epictetus, the cosmic order is grounded upon care of the self: when each thing seeks its own good, it contributes to the good of the things around it. To take care of oneself is implicitly to take care of others, not out of selflessness, or out of a deliberate decision to do so, but because the good of each thing and each person is linked.[124] Within this order, human beings are distinct because while other things are governed by natural determinations, humans are responsible for taking care of themselves.[125] In other words, while animals instinctively seek what they need, without practicing a deliberate exercise on themselves and turning their gaze toward themselves, human beings can only begin to live as they should, and take care of themselves, through turning their attention to themselves (which, as we have seen, in no way implies a flight from the external world). According to Epictetus, an individual takes care of others, shows them love and looks out for them, by taking care of herself. Individuals belong to a "community" in this fundamental sense—that each one taking care of herself aids the others in doing the same, and in this way each one participates in the care of all the others.[126]

Askēsis: The Subjectivation of Truth

The care of the self, in Hellenistic and Roman philosophy, is essentially a practice through which one becomes a subject. It is composed of processes of "incorporating" truth, of forming oneself as the truth one hears, speaks, writes, and practices. It is a process of becoming the truth. Care of the self is therefore an *askēsis*, an exercise through which one becomes a subject. *Askēsis* is, as Foucault puts it, the transformation of *logos* into *ēthos:* "*Askēsis* makes of the truth [*dire-vrai*] a mode of being of the subject."[127] Foucault distinguishes this experience of the subject from a modern experience. For modernity, the relationship between the subject and knowledge is objectivity. That is to say, the problem is to try to produce an objective knowledge of the subject. For antiquity, the problem is to develop practices of transformation through which the subject constitutes itself as the truth. In other words, one does not try to objectify the subject in discourse, but rather to produce discourse (knowledge) that has a transformative effect on the subject. Furthermore, for modernity the ethical problem is to submit the subject to the law. For antiquity, on the other hand, the ethical problem is not primarily that of making the subject submit to the law, but that of constituting the subject in her very being—not just so that she will do what she ought, but more essentially so that she will be as she ought and as "she wants to be."[128] This ontological dimension of *askēsis* has to do with producing the subject as a certain kind of relationship between the individual and herself. The task of ancient philosophy was the "formation of a certain relationship of the self to itself that is full, accomplished [*achevé*], complete, self-sufficient, and that is likely to produce the transfiguration of the self that is the happiness [*le bonheur*] one takes in oneself."[129]

Not only does the notion of *askēsis* separate care of the self from the modern experience of the subject, it also differentiates ancient philosophical practices from Christian ascetics. Foucault considers Christian practices to be focused on hermeneutics—that is, the objectification of the self in discourse through confessional practices—and on renunciation or sacrifice of one's self. *Askēsis* as care of the self is not renunciatory but rather productive; it adds something to the self, and this addition is precisely what transforms the individual into a subject. In order to produce and maintain the proper and full relationship to oneself one needs to incorporate, in a material way, the truth into one's very being. This truth is what will protect the individual from the dangers she might confront in life, the challenges that might disturb the proper and full relationship of self to itself. This "equipment" (*paraskeuē*) is discursive in nature, but its mode of being is unique. The main function of *askēsis* as a process of incorporating the truth is that of implanting in the individual true discourse, true statements, the *logoi*. The *logoi* must be present "in the muscles and nerves" of the individual.[130] To call this practice a memorization technique is to understate the case. One does not merely collect knowledge and store it away; rather, one makes knowledge—discourse, *logos*—active as one's very mode of perception of the world, of others, and of oneself; it becomes one's corporeal relation to things—the body itself becomes a philosophical corpus, a philosophical oeuvre. The body is a thinking body, a body-subject, not simply a biological process. The *logoi* must be able to function *as* the subject of action; when one confronts the world it is the *logoi* which "automatically" structure that world, lay it out before the individual both in terms of its reality and in terms of its value. The subject that responds to the world is the subject constituted through the incorporation of true discourses, principles. The resulting subject is constituted by the truths, the statements, which it has incorporated and which function as what Foucault calls a kind of "discourse-action."

Foucault never puts it this way, but it is as though the practice of philosophy in this sense is the active fabrication of a conscience. This philosophical subjectivity would not function as a "bad conscience"—punishing the individual for guilt—but rather as an active one—a mode of disclosing the world as the place where one lives and acts, a mode of responding to that world. The manner of being of *logos* as a subject, as a future-looking conscience, is described by various metaphors: discourse must be a pilot/navigator who guides us through the dangers of life, or a guardian who provides security, or a fortress within which we can take refuge, or again as a "therapy" for the wounds inflicted on us.[131] Foucault describes this active mode of being in another way, still drawing on the formulations used by Hellenistic and Roman philosophers: "This *logos*, in order to play this role of security, in order to effectively be this good pilot, or this fortress, or this remedy, must be 'ready-to-hand': *prokheiron*, which the Latins translate as *ad manum.*"[132]

In order to develop the notion of *askēsis* as an exercise of incorporating true discourses and thereby constituting the individual as a subject, Foucault in his 1982 Collège lectures focuses on three particular domains of exercise: listening, reading and writing, and speaking. Hellenistic and Roman philosophers developed exercises and technologies in order to transform each of these activities into an *askēsis*. In other words, in order to take care of oneself, it is not enough to listen to philosophy lessons, to read and write arguments and propositions, or to speak the truth—one must do each of these things in a precise way. Furthermore, in addition to the transformation of listening, reading, writing, and speaking into ascetic practices, Foucault shows in other lectures and articles that Hellenistic and Roman philosophers developed technologies to turn everyday activities such as eating, walking, preparing for sleep, and so on, into spiritual exercises. I will examine a few of the many examples Foucault gives so that we can get an idea of what it means to constitute ordinary activities as spiritual exercises.

Foucault identifies two broad forms of *askēsis,* which nonetheless leave room for and perhaps necessitate various intermediary types. First there are meditative practices—*mēlētē,* a term that has the same root as the word *epimēleia*—some of which are solitary activities while others are social (*parrhēsiastic*); and second there are the *gymnasia,* exercises which unfold in the "real world."[133] Meditation is an exercise of thought isolated from the "real world," from the actual social-political or natural world. It is an "exercise of the subject putting herself, by thinking, in a fictive situation where she tests [*s'éprouve*] herself."[134] In a meditation the subject is transformed, put to the test, and is, in a sense, at the mercy of the thoughts that she thinks. We will see this in the examples below, but also later in Foucault's interpretation of the *Meditations* of Descartes. "Descartes doesn't think at all about what things could be doubted in the world . . . Descartes puts himself in the situation of the subject who doubts everything."[135] That is, Descartes's procedure is not to consider the status of his thoughts or the objects they represent, but rather to think in such a way that he becomes a subject who doubts. In addition to meditative exercises—fictive situations—there are also the *gymnazein.* In these exercises one confronts the world itself or the things themselves.[136] The subject puts herself in real situations, but these situations function as tests or serve to alter the subject who experiences them. Some of these practices are forms of examination of conscience, of spiritual direction, while others are practices of physical endurance or abstinence. The techniques developed by Hellenistic and Roman thinkers will be appropriated and transformed in various ways by Christian ascetics and will become essential elements, albeit in altered forms, in the institutions of the pastorate. Furthermore, these developments, as historically remote as they are, provide the specific techniques that, after many transformations and reappropriations, will be deployed as biodisciplinary processes of normalization.

In order to illustrate the process of subjectivation, I will look at a few of the many practices of *askēsis* Foucault analyzed. For example, Foucault provided a detailed description of the art of listening. Because *askēsis* is the "subjectivization of true discourse"—that is, one constitutes oneself as a subject through the appropriation of the *logoi* as principles of action and as ways of "seeing" the world—the "first form" of *askēsis* is the exercise by which true discourse enters into the individual.[137] However, listening, the auditory sense as such, is ambivalent because of its extreme passivity. On the one hand, hearing is the most "logical" sense because it is what allows for the reception of *logos:* "hearing is the only sense by which one can learn virtue . . . because virtue cannot be disassociated from *logos.*"[138] On the other hand, the body is most passive with respect to its power of hearing. We are materially at the mercy of sound in a way that we are not with vision or taste, for instance. Second, sound has a more powerful hold on our "soul" than do the other senses—music and flattery are the proof of this.[139] However, this is also what makes listening so important in philosophical care of the self; philosophy as an etho-poetic activity has a powerful tool at its disposal—discourse. Discourse, because of the passivity of the sense of hearing, is able to work on the listening subject, to induce virtue, to draw out the undeveloped elements or "seeds" of virtue that exist in every rational being.[140] But, in order to do this, the student (patient, disciple) must listen, and listen in such a way that she will be able to hear the truth in what is said. That is, improper listening can inhibit the work of discourse and can contribute to the deformation of the subject. Therefore, one needs to develop a practice of listening.[141]

The first element of the "art" of listening is silence.[142] In order to take care of oneself, in order to allow the *logoi* to enter into one's "soul" and fashion one's subjectivity, it is necessary that one be quiet. Constant chatter, speaking when one does not know the truth, when one has not taken care of oneself, inhibits care and blocks the appropriation of the truth, the conversion of "*alētheia* into *ēthos*."[143] The disciple must remain silent—if not constantly for a certain period, as in the Pythagorean schools, then at least during lessons or encounters with the master. Furthermore, silence, the restriction of speech to what is necessary and beneficial, is a practice one must continue throughout one's life. Foucault insists that Hellenistic spiritual exercise is therefore different from Christian asceticism. The obligation to speak, to confess, is a fundamental part of Christian spirituality. For Christianity the subject must be expressed and objectified in discourse, whereas for Hellenistic philosophy the subject must be constituted through the appropriation of true discourse.

In addition to the work of silence, there is a "physical attitude" proper to the art of listening.[144] This embodiment of proper listening has two aspects: first, it is necessary to maintain the posture conducive to listening, which allows one to attend to the truth of what is said; and second, there is the "semiotics" of the body, which indicates both to the listener and to the speaker that one is following and grasping what is said. In order to focus one's attention on the truth being spoken, one must practice "immobility." The stillness of the body is, at least for Hellenistic and Roman thought, linked to the mastery of oneself and to the direction of one's entire self to what is being said. The agitated body is linked to the condition of *stultitia*.[145] To work at listening means to resist the disturbances of the soul manifested in the agitated body. In addition to the control of the body, it is necessary that one inscribe in the body a whole series of signs and gestures that allow the master to know that the disciple is following the lesson, concentrating on what is said, and comprehending it. The way one holds one's head, or nods, the expression on the face, the position of the hands, all serve as signs. A good listener puts the body to use "to guide the rhythm of the speaker, to guide the rhythm of the discourse and the explications of the one who is speaking."[146] One is not listening if one's body is not properly involved in the activity both as a mode of attention and self-mastery and as a means of engaging and even guiding the master's discourse. The body is not simply an added feature, a medium through which sounds pass into the brain; the body is the listening subject, and therefore the practice of embodiment is essential. Furthermore, the good listener is one who is focused not just on the words or on the master, but on the truth being expressed. The good listener has a "will" to hear the truth.[147] The body and the actions of the listener are the material existence of this will. Silence, immobility, and gesture must all convey to the master that the individual is interested in taking care of herself; to practice these "arts" is already to take care of oneself.

Finally, the activity of listening involves the proper mode of attending to the meaning of the discourse heard. In order to listen, one must attend to the "meaning" of the words—not just to the words themselves.[148] How does one hear the "meaning" of philosophical discourse? What kind of "meaning" does philosophical discourse convey? Listening philosophically "is a matter of taking a proposition, an affirmation, a statement, and little by little arriving, by meditating on it, at transforming it bit by bit into a precept of action, a rule not only for conducting oneself but for living in a certain general manner."[149] In other words, to listen to the meaning of philosophical discourse is to grasp it in its relationship to one's manner of living and one's relationship to oneself. To listen in this way involves two things. First, one has to pay attention to the meaning of the statement. The meaning of the statement is not its reference to other statements or to things so much as its truth as a principle for living and as a manner of seeing life and the world in general. Second, the listener has to take in each statement and allow it to "etch itself in the soul." This requires that in listening to and absorbing the discourse one "examines oneself" in order to see how this statement adds to oneself, transforms one's way of living and seeing the world. Listening requires that the soul "se surveiller elle-même."[150] In this technique or art of listening, one must remain vigilant with respect to oneself. As we saw in Foucault's interpretation of Socratic care and *parrhēsia,* making oneself visible to oneself is essential to care. And yet there are innumerable ways of self-visualization. Foucault's proliferation of ways of seeing, of making oneself visible, perhaps serves a tactical purpose in his struggle against the panoptic operation of modern power. Perhaps one way that care of the self can provide relief from this operation is through the conversion of it, and the multiplication of the processes through which we become visible (or invisible) to ourselves and others. That is to say, the normalizing effects of disciplinary panopticism might be diffused through the proliferation of countervisibilities, alternative modes of making selves visible, processes that manifest nondisciplinary selves and counterknowledges.

In addition to the arts of hearing, there are numerous solitary meditative practices. These are various modes of vigilance over one's thoughts and feelings, modes of attentiveness to oneself and attempts to give an account of oneself for oneself. There are also practices of meditation that are not self-examination but rather self-tests, thought experiments through which one learns how one stands with respect to the truth, whether one has attained self-mastery and has become the full and complete subject of one's thoughts and actions. I will mention only a few of the many examples of these practices that fill the lectures Foucault gave in the 1980s.

First, an example of the examination of conscience Foucault finds in Seneca. This is the nightly review of the events of the preceding day.[151] In this exercise, Seneca reminds himself of the activities which took place that day, the things he did and the errors he made. The purpose of this exercise, according to Foucault, is not essentially juridical: Seneca is not first of all interested in passing judgment on himself and punishing himself. He does not explore his actions and thoughts to seek their inner source and meaning, he does not judge them according to their intrinsic value and then dole out penance for himself. He does not cleanse himself of his sins. Rather, Foucault shows that the activity is modeled on an administrative practice—one draws up the balance sheet and checks the books. The key is to identify errors, to see where and how he went wrong and to remind himself to act differently next time. The exercise is essentially futural; it is a technique of intensifying the hold that the truth, the rational principle of action, has on him. It is a way of more thoroughly subjectivizing the truth, of becoming truth. The truth should operate in, through, and by him; it should be his immediate attunement to the world and everything in it. This activity of remembering the past, thinking about it, writing it down or telling others about it, comparing it to rules, will be taken up by Christian ascetics and transformed into a far more juridical exercise. And we shall see that rather than being a practice of subjectivization, it will become a hermeneutical work, an exploration, a mining activity, through which one digs deeper into the darkness of the soul to find a truth already there—the self.

Another meditative practice is found in Epictetus. Here the work of self-examination is likened to the work of a "night watchman" or to that of a "money changer."[152] Epictetus uses these two analogies to show the nature of the examination of conscience. The task of this work is to examine each thought, each representation or image, which passes through the mind in order to determine whether it is acceptable or not, whether it is "authentic or counterfeit."[153] Foucault thinks that both of these analogies, and the techniques which they indicate, are significant for the role which they play in Christian as well as in psychoanalytic experiences of the self. Of course, the notion of the night watchman, of the doorkeeper, resonates with the Freudian concept of the censor watching the door to consciousness. However, while in Epictetus the doorman is the very work of the conscious subject watching over himself, for Freud this censor operates below the threshold of consciousness and is what makes that conscious ego possible to begin with. The money changer is an important analogy for self-examination in Christian ascetic practices such as those recommended by Cassian.[154] For Cassian, one examines each thought to see if it is "authentic" or "counterfeit," that is, if its origin and destination are God or the Devil. Those that come from and lead back to the Devil must be rejected. The practice Epictetus recommends is different. What one seeks to know, to authenticate, and to accept or deny is the relationship of the thought, as a representation of the exterior world, to the will. One must only concern oneself with those things that are within the provenance of the will, those things which "depend on" and are controlled by the individual. Epictetus proposes various exercises for performing this examination, or this test (*épreuve*). For example, there is the "walking test." In this exercise one takes a walk through the streets of the city, and for everything that one sees one asks oneself if it is something within the control of one's will or not; if it is something whose existence is controllable by the will, then it takes on a value, good or bad, and is an object of concern. Another practice is to respond to a series of questions posed by someone else who asks if something pertains to one's ethical life or not. For example, "So-and-so's son is dead. Answer, 'That lies outside the sphere of the moral purpose, it is not an evil' . . . [His father] has borne up under it manfully. 'That lies within the sphere of moral purpose, it is a good.'"[155] Death is something which lies outside deliberate determination, but the way in which one comports oneself with respect to death is a matter under the sway of the will.

An example of Stoic spiritual direction and the examination of conscience comes from Seneca's *On Tranquility of Mind*.[156] The passage Foucault refers to concerns Seneca's letter to a friend, Serenus, who is striving to achieve the state of tranquility (the steadiness of mind which one experiences as joy, *jouissance*, as self-possession and pleasure) through his practice of Stoic philosophy.[157] Serenus is not progressing as he wishes and therefore describes his condition to Seneca in order to receive his advice. Essentially, he lives a life that conforms to Stoic principles, yet his mind is unsteady. Foucault shows both in what way this letter is a kind of confession, and how opposed it is to confession in either the Christian or the modern, psychoanalytic sense.

Foucault divides the aspects of life which appear in Serenus's self-disclosure into three categories: private wealth and luxury, political power, and public honor. These domains are important because they represent "the three types of activity possible for a free man."[158] Now in each of these domains Serenus's pleasures are, for the most part, "correct": he takes pleasure in a simple, not a luxurious, life at home, he is not full of ambition, he prefers political service over the accumulation of power, and he is restrained in his use of language to influence others.[159] Yet in each domain of free life, though he is pleased by the proper things and within the proper limits, he experiences temptation by more excessive pleasures of luxury, ambition, power, and rhetoric. That is, the pleasure which the thought of these things raises for him is a source of anxiety and is an indication that his mind is not "stable." In other words, though he is on the way, and though he lives a restrained life and is pleased by it, he has not become the truth—he has not attained the *ēthos* of perfect self-mastery and tranquility which is his goal. Temptation, anticipatory pleasure, and the anguish over his weakness are "indications," signs, that there is something else, another voice, other than the truth, speaking through him at the very level of his will and yet beyond his control. The spiritual direction he seeks from Seneca is meant to accomplish the subjectivization of the truth that is not yet complete. "For [Serenus] it is a question of his own state and of adding something to the knowledge of the moral precepts. This addition to what is already known is a force, the force which would be able to transform pure knowledge and simple consciousness into a real way of living."[160] The purpose of this "confession" is to show Seneca his state, not to attempt to interpret the deep sources of his pleasures—pleasure here is not concupiscence; nor is his anxiety treated as a kind of neurosis which has a psychological, pathological origin to be worked out. The treatment for Serenus's spiritual "malaise" is for Seneca to give force to the truth which Serenus already "knows."[161] "And that is what Seneca tries to do when he uses a set of persuasive arguments, demonstrations, examples . . . Seneca has to give a place to truth as a force."[162]

This form of *parrhēsia*, which requires that Serenus open up his heart to Seneca, is an *askēsis*, it is a "kind of practical training or exercise."[163] It does not move toward interpretation, toward hermeneutics; nor does it move toward renunciations or purification. It is not a matter of identifying faults, passing judgment, or meting out punishment. It moves rather toward a more intensive "incorporation" of the truth as a force, as the very unity of will and knowledge in Serenus, that is, as the very form and being of his subjectivity. The force which truth requires is not a "coercion coming from elsewhere."[164] There is not a supplemental determination of the will which forces one to conform to the truth which one knows; rather, the truth *is* force.

There are other practices of *mēlētē* and *gymnasia,* such as the *premeditatio mallorum.* This form of meditation consists of imagining various possible evils that can or will necessarily befall one, such as death, in order to eliminate any false fears or opinions concerning them. One learns to accept the truth of one's finitude, and one learns that these are all only illusory evils and that the only true evil, as Socrates claimed, is to commit injustice.[165] There are exercises of self-denial: for example, sitting down to a sumptuous meal, after having engaged in strenuous exercise, only to exchange that meal for the slaves' food.[166]

In these practices, just as in the practices of Seneca, the purpose is to form and solidify one's *ēthos,* one's subjectivity. The guiding thread of all these practices is what Foucault calls the "gnomic self"—that experience in which the truth of the self "is something which is before the individual as a point of attraction, a kind of magnetic force which attracts him toward a goal."[167] Foucault refers to the ancient experience of the *gnomē,* the etho-poetic language of truth spoken by the sage. The *gnomē* "were very short, very imperative, and so deeply illuminated by the poetical light that it was impossible to forget them and to avoid their power."[168] This is the conversion to the self, the salvation of the self which occurs through the *askēsis* by which "*alētheia* becomes *ēthos.*"[169]

Foucault's excavation reveals the intensification of the function of *parrhēsia* and the multiplication of relationships and techniques of care of the self. Furthermore, his analysis reveals that a shift has taken place in the moral teleology of *epimeleia.*[170] As a result of this constant attention to the self, to life (*bios*), the social-political world which one inhabits comes to be experienced as the place where one tests and examines oneself. The relationship between *epimēleia heauton* and *technē tou biou* is in this way reversed. For Socrates and Plato, the care of the self culminates in a just, happy, and true political life; one saves oneself *in order* to fulfill one's freedom in the political sphere by governing and saving the others, and by saving and preserving the polis; one's ownmost project and destiny is unified with the project of the *polis.*[171] Through the practice of *epimēleia heauton* one discovers the proper *technē tou biou* and one acquires the self-mastery to be able to apply this *technē* in order to govern others. In Hellenistic and Roman thought, on the other hand, the care and salvation of oneself is the *telos.* Political life is not abandoned, but it is absorbed within this originally supplementary, external work on the self. *Bios* and the technologies one applies to *bios,* culminate in a subjectivation of the truth and finally in the inner joy or fullness which one attains and maintains through them.

The *technē tou biou* come to be the ensemble of techniques which allow one to transform the external world, the natural world, and the social-political world into the place where one forms, tests, and reaffirms one's *rapport à soi*. Care remains a social practice and the relationship of *parrhēsia* as a relationship of care for the other remains essential. However, *parrhēsia* will eventually become, through this intensification of relationships to oneself—of vigilance, of testing, of exercise, of an inner openness of oneself with oneself—a duty to remain true to oneself, to articulate that truth, to cultivate it, to produce it in one's thoughts, practices, and life, as well as in one's speech with others.[172] The practices of care of the self become a more constant part of life even as they become more varied; they become essential elements in the relationship to the other, the spiritual guide, the *parrhēsiast;* and they become permanent elements of one's relationship to oneself.

This new form of self-consciousness, this new mode of subjectivity, is the "aesthetics of the self."[173] Of course, it should be clear that this "aesthetization" of the self is not at all unethical or antiethical. Rather, it is a fundamental experience of ethical subjectivation—of attaining an *ethos* through *poiesis*. The subject, the ethical subject, is a work of art, of *ēthopoiesis*.[174]

Knowledge of the World as Spiritual Exercise

Philosophy, in the Hellenistic and Roman model, is founded on the necessity of "conversion to one's self."[175] However, Foucault shows that this conversion to oneself does not imply self-obsession. To take care of oneself is not a matter of turning away from the "outside" world to explore and express one's "inner" truth. The self of care here is not yet conceived in terms of "inwardness," as an interior substance to be cultivated. Rather, in this schema the conversion to the self requires the practice of precise modes of knowledge of the natural world. To this end, Hellenistic and Roman philosophers developed elaborate theories of nature and of the universe. Foucault discusses these theories and their ethical purpose in his 1982 Collège course. What is important for us to see in these theories is that the spiritual modality of the subject—subjectivity as the product of spiritual work, conversion, and salvation—brings along with itself a spiritualized knowledge of the world. Converting one's gaze toward oneself means turning one's attention to nature and studying it in a particular way. To know nature, to think about the universe, is to engage in a spiritual exercise that contributes to the subjectivation process.[176] Through the contemplation of nature the individual becomes a subject. Knowing nature, for Hellenistic thinkers, is not the accumulation of propositions about natural objects, it is not the experience of a field of objects independent of the subject who perceives and judges them. To know the world is to grasp the true meaning, the true value, of things and of oneself.

Foucault identifies four characteristics of this spiritual modalization of knowledge: (1) the subject must displace herself, take up an alternative perspective from her habitual way of seeing in order for things to appear in their reality; (2) this alternative perspective makes things appear in their truth and in their value simultaneously; (3) one perceives the truth of oneself through this true perception of things; and (4) this truth reveals to the subject the nature of her freedom, the possibility of happiness and of the perfection of her potentialities.[177] What this means is that the conversion to the self and knowledge of the world are not mutually exclusive in Hellenistic philosophy. The conversion to one's self, focusing one's attention on oneself, does not require turning away from the outside world. Rather, it will entail knowing the truth about the natural world; it is intrinsically an ethical and spiritual task. One does not renounce knowledge of the world, because in fact knowledge of the world is one essential way of transforming oneself. In other words, the conversion to the self is not a turn "inward" but a conversion toward the truth to be seen, through reason, "outside," in the natural world.

Foucault's interpretation of the relationship between the conversion of one's gaze toward oneself and the exercise of thinking about nature in Hellenistic philosophy is carried out with constant reference to his understanding of Christian hermeneutical practices of the self.[178] His emphasis on the direction of attention toward an "exterior" world rather than toward an "interior" truth is an attempt to detach himself from a particular relationship to himself as an inner truth. However, this interpretation also reflects Foucault's new way of conceiving the nature of philosophical thought as a resistance to the operation of discipline and normalization. One of the essential dimensions of our present, as Foucault has diagnosed it, is the fact that knowledge is conceived as an act of looking at objects and forming judgments about them. Furthermore, one of the central objects of knowledge is the human subject. In other words, when we turn our gaze toward ourselves we make ourselves into objects of knowledge, just as when we turn our gaze to nature we take a disinterested and objective relationship toward it. In part 2 of this book I will try to show how Foucault links these two features of our objectifying gaze. Right now I want to note that his interpretation of Hellenistic physics, as an exercise in the formation of a subject, as a conversion to oneself, offers an alternative mode of "self-knowledge" to the objectivizing gaze of modern normalizing knowledges. In the Hellenistic model of care of the self, one neither objectifies oneself in discourse, nor does one experience knowledge as the accumulation of observations about natural objects that can be grasped through and exhausted by the simple act of looking. To convert one's gaze toward oneself means to examine the world in which one lives. For Foucault, this meant to grasp it along those axes where our relationship to ourselves is formed: power, knowledge, and subjectivity. By looking at and thinking about the world, one does not, according to the Hellenistic model, simply accumulate knowledge; rather, one displaces and transforms one's being qua subject. This is the etho-poetic dimension of thinking. Foucault proposes a way of thinking which displaces the self such as it is constituted in discourse as an object of knowledge and control. Foucault's conversion to the self directs his gaze outward toward the world in which our experience of the self is constituted.

Foucault provides examples of this spiritualized modality of knowledge drawn from the works of Seneca and Marcus Aurelius. However, in Epicurean thought as well, it is evident that the theoretical knowledge of the universe was an entirely ethical project: knowing the truth is simultaneously detaching oneself from the fears and desires which are produced in one by false opinions.[179] For the Epicureans, the study of nature leads one to an experience of freedom and peace: one is free from the fear of death, free in the knowledge that moral life is possible and joyful. Knowledge of things, of the world is a spiritual practice insofar as it transforms the self.[180]

Foucault's reading of Seneca presents a detailed characterization of a way that the study of nature is, or can be, both a process of desubjection (a detachment from oneself) and a process of subjectivation (the formation of oneself as a free subject). Foucault draws on letters Seneca wrote to introduce and explain the purpose of the *Natural Questions*—a text on physics Seneca was sending to his disciple, Lucilius.[181] Seneca wrote these letters late in his life and explains that at his age, with time running out, it's especially necessary to take care of oneself, to be occupied with oneself. For Seneca, and Foucault suggests more generally in the Hellenistic and Roman model, old age was the ideal point in life.[182] Old age is the point where one's life reaches its term, where one's life is accomplished—therefore one strives to arrive at old age ready to die, that is, having achieved a full life. But old age also has a sort of symbolic meaning: to be "old" is to be free from the passions, and therefore a master of oneself. To be old, to achieve the ideal point of old age, also means to be able to look back at one's life with pleasure—therefore, freedom from passion, and simultaneously pleasure in one's self. Furthermore, old age is not just a point one arrives at late in life; it is a goal to be achieved. Therefore, it is necessary to work, to practice old age. In fact, old age, in a real sense, is this work, which puts one in a certain relationship to oneself—a relationship of mastery, pleasure, and freedom. Old age is a practice. This means that it is a mode of subjectivity one strives to attain, and this mode of subjectivity is produced and maintained by techniques of the self. Seneca is old, but this doesn't mean his task is complete; rather, it means that he has less time to prepare himself, to become old in the ideal sense: to free himself from the passions, to master himself and to achieve the state of tranquility, of pleasure in himself. Time is essential in this practice: time is both that which passes away, and it is the existential significance of old age. It is the material flow of one's life and it is the promise of an ideal "moment" to be attained and perpetuated. The point is to readjust the flow of time so that it corresponds with the ideal that one wishes to achieve; not a moment in the future, but a way of existing that is maintained through practices of subjective transformation.

Foucault suggests that the letter, which serves as an introduction to a book on physics, seems rather paradoxical. Seneca is asserting the importance of taking care of himself, keeping his eye on himself. Yet at the same time he is suggesting that what is of utmost importance is to study the elements of nature—the stars, the sky, air, and water. In what way could the study of nature—of the external natural world—be compatible with the injunction to turn one's gaze toward one's self? Foucault argues that the purpose of the study of nature, and of the care of the self, is to achieve freedom.[183] For Seneca, freedom is not a civic right but a "natural right"; therefore, it is by regarding nature that one will see the nature of freedom. Furthermore, Foucault shows that one is struggling to free oneself from a particular kind of slavery. One is always, inevitably, enslaved to oneself: "We always start from this point."[184] In other words, the goal is to care for oneself, to accomplish one's self; it is necessary to get free of oneself, and this work of getting free is perpetually recommencing from the same starting point. The enslavement of oneself to oneself has a particular form for Seneca. One is caught up in a system of obligations and debts. First of all, there is a tendency (in the self, in nature, in culture) toward a state of "busyness," of overcommitment—business, family, and politics are the examples Foucault lists. This system of obligations, which tends toward too much, is the "traditional active life."[185] That is to say, the domain which for the Greeks was the goal of care of the self (the ideal was to acquire and master the proper arts of living precisely such an active life) is here a form of slavery. The other aspect of slavery to oneself is linked to the first. Because one is so obligated and overly busy with tasks and errands, one feels compelled to reward oneself. The busier one is the more one requires compensation in the form of riches, recognition, glory, physical pleasure, or comfort. To get free of oneself is to get free of this relationship to oneself in which one is caught up in a system of external obligation to others and internal indebtedness to oneself. Turning one's gaze toward oneself, taking care of oneself, means exiting from this type of relationship, and for Seneca, the study of nature is a powerful technique for accomplishing this.

The study of nature, as Foucault illustrates, is the second part of a two-part course of study necessary to prepare oneself for life. The first part of this program is the study of *man:* the "liberal arts," the "common arts," which teach one what to do and how to conduct oneself in day-to-day life. But this education is incomplete by itself. It needs to be fulfilled in a higher form of study: the study of nature, of the sky, of the gods. While the study of man allows one to do the right things on a daily basis and to know how to behave in the various situations of the everyday world, the study of nature "wrenches us up from the depths."[186] This second course of study does not, like the first, teach us rules of conduct. It does not impart knowledge, it is "not a form of knowledge at all."[187] Rather than the accumulation of knowledge, the study of nature "consists of a real movement of the subject and a real movement of the soul which raises itself above the world and wrenches itself free of darkness."[188] The first form of study results in the accumulation of pragmatic knowledge—it tells one how to behave. The second, however, is not a form of knowledge. Rather, it is an exercise whereby one gets free from the very self who is tied to the world of obligations and indebtedness and who learns how to negotiate that world.

The study of nature and the gods establishes a relationship of distance with respect to oneself; it establishes what Foucault describes as a maximum "tension" in the relationship of the self to itself. To study nature in this way means to break away from one's ordinary perception of the world from within it, as an active participant at the center of it. One strives to attain a point of view above the world looking down on it—a godlike point of view: *vue plongeante.* Foucault differentiates this movement from a Platonic passage from the visible to the intellectual realm: for Seneca there is only one reality, the world in which we live. The spiritual exercise of studying nature does not lead one to perceive some other reality, but is a movement by which one achieves within the world a different perspective on the world. From this new perspective one sees the same world in which one lives but sees it in its truth. This is the same perspective from which god sees the world, and the movement by which one ascends to this position reveals the "cofunctioning" of human and divine reason. In other words, in seeing the world from above, one experiences that one's own reason is in a sense the same as that of god, that we are subjects of the reason which governs the universe. But in seeing the world in its truth, we also "see ourselves in the world"—we grasp the "smallness and the artificial character of everything which appeared to us, before we were freed, of being the good."[189] The study of nature is the displacement of one's self in one's very being as a subject: one discloses the world from a new perspective in which the world is revealed as a whole, and is therefore revealed entirely differently from the way it appears to a subject defined by the system of obligation/indebtedness. The *vue plongeante* reveals the smallness of the individual and causes one to hold in "contempt all the false splendors brought about by men."[190] To see the world, and ourselves in the world, is to see the true nature of things, but also to see the true value of things. We see that we are "caught up with false values and false commerce . . . [we] . . . take the measure of what we are on the earth."[191] One appears for oneself in one's truth—as a "point in space and a point in time."[192]

Therefore, on the one hand, one is this insignificant point surrounded by other insignificant points in a vast universe. At the same time, one participates in the divine reason, which orders and governs the universe, in the sense that one grasps the world in its order and totality from above. The self in its truth is revealed through this displacement of perspective, not by making itself into an object of knowledge. It is not through objectification of the self, or through the hermeneutics of the inner truth of one's self, that one knows one's self, but through the liberating movement by which one ascends to a perspective of the whole that one becomes aware of one's self both as a point in nature and as a rational subject. The self is not something to be deciphered but to be "placed," to be seen in its place in the whole: "Interiority is obviously not the problem. The only problem which poses itself is at once to situate oneself right where one is and to accept the system of rationality which inserted one's self in this particular point in the world."[193] Therefore, one establishes with respect to oneself a relationship of tension: one is both a point in the world and a rational subject gazing down on oneself from above. As a point, one is an insignificant element playing a determined role within a much larger reality. As a rational subject, one ascends above this point, grasps it in its reality, and frees oneself from the false values and pressures that one imposes on oneself out of a misperception of oneself and one's surroundings. To turn one's gaze toward nature in this sense, to ascend to the point from which one is able to grasp the truth, the "secrets" of nature, is to attain the virtue of the soul.[194] Through this movement one becomes a master of oneself. As a point in space and time, one is under the control of the laws ordained by divine reason. However, through the ascent to the perspective of divine reason one liberates oneself from this determination and situates oneself in the position of the reason which governs all; one sees that this is the same reason which defines one's self as a subject.

Foucault sees in Seneca a theoretical practice that allows one to escape the limited perspective of one's habitual address to the world (the self as obligation/debt): one ascends to a global perspective from which the truth of each thing, its proper place and value within the whole, become evident. One learns that human existence is "localized" (*ponctuelle*): it is a singular and momentary point within a system, a larger reality, of which it is an insignificant part.[195] Therefore, the conversion to self is not a rupture with the world, one does not pass beyond the world striving to exit from it. It is, rather, a conversion to the *truth,* to the true nature of things and the realization that one is within the world, one has a place, a fixed moment where one's existence unfolds and within which it is possible. This nature, this world, is governed by divine reason and universal laws. The act of knowing is an act through which one sees that one is a situated element in nature, but is also open to universal reason. Seneca does not find truth in another world, such as the Platonic world of ideas or the Christian afterlife, but through a spiritual modulation of the knowledge of this world. The conversion to self is accompanied by the development of a theory of the universe, of the laws which govern it, which is at the same time a spiritual practice through which one overcomes the errors of the general opinion, the fears and desires which that opinion forms and which are the source of falsehood, injustice, and unhappiness.

Foucault also provides an extensive exposé of the general form of knowledge as a spiritual exercise in Marcus Aurelius.[196] He announces this practice as being the "symmetrical inverse" of the Senecan practice. While Seneca describes for us the ascending movement of a view looking downward from above, Marcus Aurelius practices something more like an excruciatingly detailed and rigorous burrowing into the heart of things. Foucault calls this the *vue infinitésimale* in order to distinguish it from Seneca's *vue plongeante.*[197] Though these practices are marked by different techniques for producing knowledge, and therefore result in quite different pictures of reality, they both represent the fact that the study of nature was an element of the care of one's self.

As a point of departure, Foucault takes up a passage in the *Meditations* where Marcus Aurelius recommends a certain exercise, a certain practice of thinking, which has the result of "enlarging the soul."[198] The soul, enlarged by this exercise, is "independent" of external determinations, of illusions which stir the passions and provoke violent emotions and thereby enslave the subject. In other words, the exercise frees the subject from the power of objects as they appear to him and results in "tranquility," in a true perception of reality, in a "sovereign indifference" to things, and in an "adequation to divine reason."[199] The exercise is composed of two general practices. Marcus Aurelius writes: "Always define and describe the object which presents itself to the mind [*l'esprit*] by way of an image."[200] For every "representation" by which an object presents itself to the mind, one must attempt to *define* and *describe* the object itself so represented. To "define" has two senses in this case: to trace the border, to establish the true "shape" or dimensions of the thing, that is, to perceive it as it really is; and to establish the correct value of the thing, to see it in its true worth, to set its price.[201] The activity of definition has then a sense of providing an adequate definition of the object and of establishing its true value. Description, on the other hand, presents in detail the "intuitive contents of the form and elements of things."[202] The "flux of representations," according to Foucault, "must be taken under surveillance and must serve as the pretext, the occasion, and the object of a labor of definition and description."[203] The purpose is to cut through the "images" that "present themselves to the mind" in order to determine their "objective content."[204] One's attention is turned upon one's own thoughts, the flow of thought, of images and representations: it is a matter of self-surveillance. In other words, the theme of *vigilance* returns yet again in Foucault's account of Marcus Aurelius. Once again it is an attitude and an art of attending to one's self, grasped as the flux of representations. But this vigilance is set over and against a "world" which is understood in terms of its tendency to induce negligence. Marcus Aurelius watches over himself in order to produce himself as sovereign master of his representations, rather than as subjected to them. I will come back to this below. I will also return to the importance of Foucault's characterization of this "self-examination" as one that cuts through images and representations to arrive at the objects that give rise to them. This marks an important distinction between the Stoic practice and the Christian practices which will be derived from it.

Grasping the representation and distilling its objectivity from it involves two meditative operations.[205] The first, which Foucault calls an "eidetic meditation," is the process of stripping the object down to its essence, seeing it "nude," without any additional and misleading superfluous elements mixed in. The object seen as a whole, in its nakedness and isolation, is the "essence." In other words, spiritual knowledge is a kind of phenomenology. This characterization of the meditation as "eidetic" shows Foucault's debt to Husserl as well as the way he transforms phenomenology from a theoretical into a spiritual activity. Marcus Aurelius practices a "return to the things themselves" in order to return to himself. However, at the same time, in an inseparable counterpart to the eidetic meditation, there is the work of "naming," of "speaking." The first activity is one of "contemplation"; it is a theoretical activity insofar as it involves looking, discerning, and disclosing. The second aspect of this process is, however, an exercise of "speaking."[206] The point is not just to look at the essence of the thing, but also to speak the name of the thing and to say the name of each part, each constitutive moment of the whole, the essence. To discern the object is at the same time to name it; isolating its parts in their connective relationships requires naming these parts. "Speaking to oneself [*Se dire à soi-même*] . . . this means not only knowing [*connaître*], recollecting the name of the thing and its different elements, but it is necessary to say it to oneself in oneself [*en soi-même*], to say it to oneself for oneself [*pour soi-même*]."[207] In other words, Marcus Aurelius does not just instruct one to "think about it," but rather, it is necessary "to say": "It is necessary to see and to say."[208] Seeing and saying cut through the image and go directly to the naked essence of the thing. It is as though one cannot manifest the essence of the object, which presents itself to the mind by way of representations, without a word to draw it out of hiding and into the light. The interweaving of seeing and saying is a theme that Foucault had isolated and explored from his earliest works, particularly *The Birth of the Clinic* and *The Order of Things*. The knot formed between "words and things," between "seeing and saying," is the core problem of these texts, the point at which a field of objects and subjects becomes possible.[209] Speaking of the attempt to grasp the structure which made clinical medicine a social reality in the late eighteenth century, Foucault writes: "We must place ourselves, and remain once and for all, at the level of the fundamental *spatialization* and *verbalization* of the pathological, where the loquacious gaze with which the doctor observes the poisonous heart of things is born and communes with itself."[210] It seems that Foucault, in his Collège lectures, remains at that level where space—the field of the visible—and language are inalienable. But whereas in *The Birth of the Clinic* the goal was to grasp an event at the level of structure—"one had to read the deep structures of visibility in which field and gaze are bound together by *codes of knowledge*"—here Foucault is isolating an art developed precisely to intervene in that field.[211] Foucault did not isolate the practices of the self through which doctors in the eighteenth century formed themselves as knowing subjects. Rather he analyzed the codes, the structures which manifest this event of transformation in which the subject was caught up and with which he went along: "New objects were to present themselves to the medical gaze in the sense that, and at the same time as, the knowing subject reorganizes himself, changes himself, and begins to function in a new way."[212] In 1982 Foucault again takes up the "knowing subject," the "living subject," in an event of transformation—a work of conversion—but here he has allowed the dimension of subjectivity to come to center stage. In the exercises of defining and describing, seeing and saying, the interwoven text of words and things is the material upon which Marcus Aurelius works in order to "reorganize himself" and to "function in a new way."

The practice of definition is also, at the same time, a practice of valuation. The purpose, again, is to liberate the subject, to make her independent of the power that her representations of objects have over her. By working on these representations, by cutting through them in order to achieve the objectivity of the object, their power is dispelled. Working over the representations that present themselves to the mind is a way of testing them.[213] The term Marcus Aurelius uses for this test is *elegkhein*—in other words, the Socratic test (*elenchus*) is reinvented by Marcus Aurelius. Instead of testing one's soul, or one's way of life, through the confrontation with the other, one confronts and "accuses" or "refutes" the thing that presents itself through mental representations. The test determines "what utility (*khreia*) this object has for what universe, for what *kosmos*."[214] Marcus Aurelius strives to know and to grasp the value the thing has for "man" insofar as he is a "citizen of the world." In other words, there are various "worlds" that the individual inhabits. But insofar as the individual is a subject, free and independent, the individual exists in the world that encompasses all of these other "particular" worlds. It is in terms of the universal, the *kosmos*, that all of these other worlds have their particular value. Therefore, insofar as "man" is a subject who lives in the universal, he must learn to see each thing in its true value and not confuse it with a particular value it may appear to have when it is not grasped in its objectivity.

The accusation of the thing, its refutation by way of confrontation (*elenchus*), takes on a number of forms. Foucault gives three examples of these spiritual exercises: "First, the exercises of decomposition of the object in time; second, the exercises of decomposition of the object in its constituent elements; third, the exercises of reductive and disqualifying description."[215] These different types of exercises free the subject from the power of the flux of representations. If one does not attempt to master this flux—not so much to determine the flux as to see through it to the truth of objects given by it—one is mastered by it. For instance, music and dance are given through a flow of representations. The power of music and dance to evoke passions, to overwhelm us with feeling and with the experience of beauty, is to be found precisely in the flow of representations, the seemingly fluid and uninterruptible continuity of sound and motion. Left in this state of flux, these representations are too powerful for the individual to resist and to master. Therefore, the subject must practice an exercise of decomposing the apparent temporal continuity of music and dance—the flux of representations—in order to grasp the object in its truth, in its objectivity. Perceiving the music or the dance in their objectivity will devalue them, since their power and beauty are intrinsically given to them through the flow. Foucault shows that for Marcus Aurelius, the only truth, the only thing that exists, is the present moment. If the subject grasps the present moment in its pure presence, then the subject grasps the truth and frees herself from the false power of the flux. Each momentary note, each present sound, which composes the piece of music, when grasped in its pure presence, disconnected from what preceded it and from what will follow it, is absolutely valueless—it has no power over the emotions or the passions and therefore over the subject who perceives it. It is the attachment to what is no longer or is not yet—the past and the future—that gives the present its power over the subject and makes the object appear as something it is not. But what truly is, the present moment, is devoid of attractiveness, of meaning; it is pure presence, discontinuous and dispersed.[216] One might say that the Stoic practice of decomposing the flow of representations in time is a technique of a metaphysics of presence. The object as a present-at-hand thing—a sound or a movement—is not a static, permanent, and meaningful thing, but rather a fleeting nonbeing, disconnected from all other presence, from all other present moments. That which is present at hand, that which exists in a sort of permanent present, is the subject herself. To lose oneself in the flow of representations is to be pulled along with the dispersion and nonbeing of the flow of representations in time. The subject in its truth is an eternal presence, whereas the object in its truth is a fleeting and discontinuous present moment. Foucault shows that this practice is a deliberate technique of mastering the flow of representations. In other words, it is not a theoretical metaphysics of the present; it is a spiritual technique by which the object in its objectivity is constituted, just as the subject in its subjectivity constitutes itself. The metaphysics of presence is practiced by Marcus Aurelius as an attempt to constitute the individual as a subject who is free, independent, and self-possessed. Foucault shows that this practice of "presencing" determines the relationship between the subject and his own body as well. He describes a breathing exercise in which the subject concentrates on his breath, focusing on the difference of each breath taken in and the dispersal of the breath as it is exhaled. This results in a realization of the discontinuity of the living body, its constant self-differentiation and its dispersal. What remains present is the subject insofar as the subject concentrates on each fleeting and disconnected instant. Only the constant presence of the subject allows for continuity, but continuity is not the reality of the object, only of the onlooking subject.[217]

Just as Foucault shows that the temporal decomposition of the flow of representations causes the subject to "despise" the object given by those representations, he shows that the exercise of "material decomposition" has the same effect.[218] Marcus Aurelius describes a practice of reducing the object that appears before us to its pure materiality. In other words, rather than seeing a nice steak, one would see the flesh of a dead cow; rather than seeing a stylish sweater, one would see the sheared-off fur of a sheep. Furthermore, rather than seeing one's body as a natural form, one would see it as a package of fluids, flesh, and bones. Through this materialist reduction the objects lose their attractiveness, which is built on an illusionary abstraction from their material truth. The form and beauty these objects take on does not belong to them but is given to them through the constituting power of the flux of representations. But the only thing that gives this flow its identity is the subject herself insofar as she is "reason."[219] In other words, reason itself is beautiful, has a form and an identity; the object, in its temporal and material reality, is pure discontinuity and dispersal, void of meaningful content.

A final type of exercise is the "reductive description" of the object of our representations.[220] Here the task is to detach the subject from an object whose power comes from a partial representation—a partial representation hides the ugly truth of the object. For example, the rich and powerful attract us and capture our imagination because they appear through partial representations. In order to overcome the attraction they have one must practice describing them in their mundane and distasteful reality: one must picture the powerful man "when he eats, when he sleeps, when he has intercourse, when he goes to the bathroom."[221] The description of this individual in his entirety reveals the falsehood of the partial representation of him.

The conversion to the self in Marcus Aurelius requires an elaborate attention to the world, a rigorous attempt to see things in their objectivity and to assign to things their true values. The exercises of temporal decomposition, material decomposition, and reductive description are ways of dispelling the power that the flow of representations has over the subject—they free the subject to know herself and see that it is her rational nature that provides identity and continuity to the world, that the objects represented are totally discontinuous, isolated instances, bits of material and nothing more.

Foucault contrasts these spiritual modes of knowing, of meditating on the nature of things, of searching one's thoughts in order to understand the truth, with both Christian practices and the "intellectual method" of Descartes.[222] The Christian ascetic will not concern himself with the *objectivity* of the idea but rather with its *origin* and its *being*. In this way Christian practices are hermeneutic rather than analytic. The representation is examined to discover the meaning interior to it, whether its source is good or bad, whether it allows one to contemplate God or whether it secretly attaches one to oneself, to the flesh.[223] That is, the idea is not taken up in its possible relation to an object in the world, but rather in its being as a representation, as an element of thought present in the subject and in its relation to the soul. Marcus Aurelius, on the other hand, is concerned with the truth of the object that the representation shows us. The point is to consider the representation in its objectivity and to know the object represented in its truth, in its proper relationship and place within the cosmos, what its function is there and how it is attached to our own happiness and truth. Furthermore, the exercise of objectivity displaces and modifies the subject; the subject is, in a sense, first brought about through this exercise because his freedom is its effect. Thus the Stoic is concerned with the objectivity, the exteriority of the thought, and the constitution of the subject in his truth and freedom, whereas the Christian is concerned with the very being of the representation and its interiority rather than its objectivity.[224]

The "intellectual method" that Descartes practices requires one to deliberately determine the movement of thought according to a law established by the subject who thinks. Frédéric Gros suggests that we refer to the discussion of Cartesian "order" in *The Order of Things* in order to understand what Foucault means by this.[225] The intellectual method described there requires first a unit of measurement in order to differentiate and compare representations and second a rule for determining the relationship, or order, which connects elements together in an object. By applying the units for comparing and measuring representations and the order that regulates the relationship between representations, one will accept representations as true or correct only when each representation fits perfectly into the proper movement as this is defined analytically.[226] The purpose of measuring and regulating the flux of representations is not to disengage the subject and to decompose the object, but rather to reconfigure the representations, which in themselves appear in a disorderly way but which represent an object whose form and unity, whose order, can be discerned through the method. The representations are rearranged according to the terms of comparison applied to them by the subject and in order to grasp the object given by them in its reality. Marcus Aurelius, on the other hand, is interested in examining the flux of representations just as it presents itself in order to discover behind it the reality—the discontinuity, dispersal, and meaninglessness—of the objects it represents. It is not a matter of applying a method that allows one to redistribute the elements into the proper order, but to open oneself up to the nature of the objects which show themselves, and hide themselves, in and behind our images of them. This is the difference between spiritual exercise and scientific method. It seems to me that this distinction allows us to perceive two separate but related movements in Descartes's *Meditations:* the First and Second Meditations are a practice of spiritual purification and catharsis; the Third through Sixth Meditations are the deployment of a method which is revealed through that purification and grounded in the subject found there. Foucault shows that to understand the *Meditations* one must see that it is precisely the spiritual experience of the subject and truth which Descartes is attempting to displace in order to found philosophy as a scientific discourse grounded in evidence and method alone.[227]

4

The Cynic and the True Life

In the preceding chapter we saw various forms of philosophical activity and philosophical life that created a space alongside the general political and social practices of life in the Hellenistic-Roman world. Philosophy as an activity inhabited a part of the day, determined certain relationships, and introduced various practices into the everyday existence of an individual. The philosopher was someone who used *parrhēsia* to care for these individuals. The foundation of philosophical *parrhēsia* is the care of the self, the conversion and salvation of the self that results in an art of living, an art for transforming the world into the testing ground for one's self-relation. Because the philosopher had mastered the art of care of the self, he was capable of governing others and caring for them up to the point at which they were able to govern and care for themselves. In this experience of philosophy, the domain of *bios*, of social-political life and action, was essentially a testing ground—it was traversed by techniques, by an *askēsis*, through which the individual cultivated and preserved his self-mastery and tranquility. One might describe this philosophical work, these relationships of governmentality, and this testing process as an "outside within" or an area "alongside" the norm because they constituted a way of living the *same* life, in the *same* world as the others, but of living that life and inhabiting that world *otherwise*, by maintaining a very *different* relationship to oneself. However, there was another significant philosophical development which took its cue from the Socratic-Platonic event and which bridged the gap between that event and the formation of the Christian pastorate: Cynicism. Cynicism was different from other philosophical practices in a number of ways (and they all differ from each other in various ways), but primarily in the fact that it constituted itself as a radical rejection of the social-political world. For the Cynic, it is not just that this world is full of error and false opinion, but that it is essentially false, that the social-political world is necessarily opposed to the truth. Therefore, the Cynic practices a form of *bios* that is true to nature, a natural life completely other than *conventional* forms of life. For the Cynic, reason (*logos*) emerges from the natural passions, desires, instincts, and needs of the body, and it leads one back to nature as the source and destination of individual life. The Cynic takes up the true, natural life through a particular experience of the body. The body is confined and falsified by social customs and values. Therefore the body—the space it inhabits, the time it moves through—must be stripped of every aspect of falsehood, rhetoric. In other words, rhetoric is not just artificially ornamental language; it is the artificial falsification of life through the addition of unnecessary adornments. Bodily, existential rhetoric is constituted by culture, society, custom. The true life, then, is an "outside," an *other* which does not inhabit the world of everydayness but remains outside of it as a permanent challenge to it. The bodily presence of the Cynic is a physical, material affront to the society it resists. Furthermore, the Cynic unites in the most radical way *parrhēsia* and the true life. The Cynic recognizes himself and is recognized by the others as the *parrhēsiast* par excellence.

In this chapter I will summarize some elements of Foucault's consideration of Cynicism, particularly the Cynic variation on the themes of care of the self, the true life (*alēthēs bios*), *parrhēsia,* and otherness.[1] The figure of the Cynic and the practices of care that define his existence play a central role in the history of the subject for a number of reasons. First, it is the Cynic who pushes to its limits the practice of the true life and the otherness of the *bios philosophicos* as the true life. Cynic *parrhēsia* is a mission to proclaim the truth, to manifest the truth in word, in deed, and in the very body of the Cynic, which appears as the "scandal of the truth."[2] The radicality of this project and the philosophical-spiritual reaction against it is an important part of the historical process through which philosophy will be despiritualized and will become, rather than a way of life, a theoretical, scholastic discipline. In other words, Foucault thinks that the radicality of Cynicism as a *parrhēsiastic* form of life generated a critique not only from the general society and the political establishment, but also from the less radical philosophical institutions and movements. This rupture internal to the practice of philosophy is an early form of the split to come between philosophy as a form of knowledge and philosophy as a form of life. Furthermore, it scandalized philosophy as a practice of an other life. A second reason for the importance of Cynicism is that many of its spiritual practices and styles of life were appropriated by the early Christian ascetics. But, as in philosophical circles, this resulted in rifts within the spiritual community. Foucault claims that the formation of the pastorate, of rigorous practices of spiritual direction in communities and in personal relationships, were attempts to get control of the radical and scandalous practices of asceticism. The philosophical-spiritual critique of Cynicism played a decisive role in the formation of Christian care of the self, subjectivity, and power. And third, though Cynicism resulted in an exteriorization of the *bios philosophicos* from the theoretical practice of philosophy, the Cynics, Cynical *parrhēsia,* and the experience of philosophy as a way of life will linger in our cultural memory and our culture practices.[3] According to some of his most careful readers, Foucault himself was powerfully attracted to the Cynic model of philosophical life and discourse. In other words, we should pay particular attention to the way Foucault characterizes the Cynic's form of life because it reflects a central strain both in the historical ontology of ourselves and in the self-realization of Foucault as a philosopher.[4]

The True Life

The Greek word *alētheia,* "truth," as Foucault shows, resonates in four different keys.[5] First of all, *alētheia* means unhidden, revealed. The truth is, in this sense, that which is transparent to vision or intellect. Second, *alētheia* means pure, unmixed, or singular, as opposed to impure, intermixed, or multiple. Third, *alētheia* means law-abiding. The truth, in this case, is that which follows the straight path of the law and has the unswerving character of rectitude. Finally, *alētheia* means self-sovereign. The true, in this sense, is that which is immutable, incorruptible, self-sovereign, and reigns above all else.

Foucault shows that *alētheia* is not merely a matter of words and thoughts, but is a possible modalization of life. He shows that this is apparent in the work of Plato.[6] In fact, one of the essential domains in which the true is experienced is that of *erōs,* of love.[7] The notion of the *alēthēs erōs* is central in the thought of Plato, and it includes and exhibits all four variations of the truth: true love does not hide itself, it is not deceitful, but rather is completely open toward the beloved. It is also pure; its motives are not mixed with any thought of personal gain or utility. Third, true love is lawful in the sense that it follows the necessary course; it proceeds in the pursuit of the beloved by following the rational and natural order that determines the path love must follow. Finally, true love is immutable; it is not altered by outside events or external considerations. Of course, the notion of true love is the culminating point of *The Use of Pleasure.* There Foucault shows how Plato has Socrates argue for an "ontological" love—a love determined by its progress from the particular to the universal, from appearance to Being, to the Truth. That is, the true love is the love of Truth. Therefore, this notion of *alēthēs erōs* in both Plato and in Christianity, and in our own culture, "will be the effort par excellence of the true life."[8] The privileged example of *erōs* shows that *alētheia* is not limited to a quality of judgments or a relationship between thought and being, but is a fundamental aspect of living.

The Cynic Transvaluation of the Value of the True Life

According to Foucault, Cynicism is fundamentally a practice of *parrhē-sia*—it links in a profound way the notion of the true mode of existence to the capacity, the right, and the duty to speak the truth. The Cynics explored the possibility of living the true life in a most rigorous and persistent way. The way they did this, as Foucault understands it, was to perform a series of experiments by which they displaced the central philosophical principles, the most widely diffused and accepted principles of reason, from the "element of *logos*" to that of *bios*.[9] In other words, the Cynics deployed reason in their very lives, actions, and bodies to produce a truth that cannot be reduced to the dimension of language. The displacement of truth from *logos* to *bios* was guided by the two central principles of Cynicism. First, the Cynic principle par excellence is "change the value of the money."[10] This injunction has many possible meanings, but primary among them is the sense that laws and customs (*nomoi*) are counterfeit and must be changed into the authentic laws of nature. Therefore, the Cynic rejects custom and lives according to reason understood in a specific sense as nature. In order to live a life of reason, the Cynics dramatize the *logoi*, the truth as it is *spoken* by the philosophers. The result is that the Cynic lives a life according to truth, he lives the true life and in so doing "makes the other lives, the life of the others, appear to be nothing other than counterfeit money, money with no value."[11] The second defining principle of Cynicism is the association with the dog (*kunikos*) from which the Cynic receives his name. The Cynic life is the life of the dog.[12] Foucault outlines four ways in which the life of the Cynic is a dog's life. First, the dog is shameless, living publicly, not hiding any dimension of its natural, bodily life. The dog has no respect for custom, does not hide its true nature out of shame, and is incapable of deception, of concealing its true nature and identity from anyone. Second, the dog is independent and indifferent, "it has no other needs than those it could satisfy immediately."[13] The dog does not need or want anything it is incapable of attaining. Therefore, the dog's instincts and needs remain pure, undiluted by external influences. Third, the dog is *diakritikos:* the dog barks. In other words, it confronts its enemies directly and noisily, and it is able to recognize and point out the good and the bad, "its masters and its enemies."[14] Finally, the dog sacrifices itself to save its master, the dog protects its master. The Cynic's life is like the life of the guard dog, sacrificing itself for the good of the others.[15] These four characteristics map onto the four aspects of *alētheia:* unhidden = shamelessness; pure = indifferent to outside temptations; lawful = recognition and articulation of good and bad; sovereign = protection of the others. Foucault's analysis shows how these four characteristics of the Cynic's dog-life take form through the dramatization of the *logoi*, of reason. In so doing the Cynic "changes the value of the money." The conventions of the city are shown to be false, as are the lives lived by the others, and finally the meaning and truth of philosophical discourse itself, Reason as merely *logos*, is called into question.

Shame and Shamelessness

The true life as a life that hides nothing is a common theme in ancient thought. Foucault suggests that the predominant way of thinking such a life, and of living such a life, is in terms of avoiding "shameful" acts. One does not commit any act which is "dishonest, reprehensible, which could result in reproaches from others and make those who commit [the act] ashamed."[16] In other words, the unhidden life is one which does not *need* to conceal itself; nothing about it need be hidden from view because one doesn't do anything shameful. Such a life avoids contact with shameful things: actions, words, thoughts, feelings, and desires that cannot bear the light of day. Any aspect of life, any act or thought or feeling which could cause shame is denied, avoided. To illustrate this idea of the unhidden, Foucault shows that it appears in several foundational texts. For example, in Plato's dialogues on the theme of eros—in *Phaedrus* and *Symposium*— the true lover avoids all shameful action because he does not want to appear in a bad light before his beloved.[17] As another example, Foucault refers to Seneca, where he finds the idea that the true life is the one lived as if "one were under the watch of another, of the others in general, but especially and preferably under the eye, the gaze, the control of the friend."[18] The technique of letter writing plays a key function in this practice of the true life. Writing letters in which one recounts daily activities, thoughts, and feelings allows one to be under the constant surveillance of one's correspondent and thereby forces one to avoid doing, thinking, or feeling anything one would be ashamed to write.[19] In Epictetus, on the other hand, one is always under the supervision of the "inner watch of the divinity which inhabits us."[20] Because of this constant surveillance from within, from the daimon which lives in the soul in the form of the *logos,* one avoids shameful behavior.[21]

    The true life as it appears in these formulations maintains the value of shame and the avoidance of shameful actions. One masters oneself by avoiding any type of action which would make one ashamed of oneself and which would be considered improper by others: by one's beloved, by one's friend, or by the god, the daimon, which protects us. The Cynic will also place a high value on the unhiddenness of the true life, but the Cynic practice of unhiddenness will operate a "transvaluation" of this notion. This is carried out through the "dramatization of this principle, a dramatization of this principle in life and by life itself."[22] The Platonic and Stoic practice of living a nondeceptive life by never acting shamefully is replaced by a life, the corporeal life, the physical life, of the Cynic as absolutely public. Through the unhidden life of the philosophers, "the habits of modesty" are internalized and the bodily life of the individual, bodily life itself as the source of the truth, is closed off in favor of aesthetic, social, or rational norms.[23] In other words, the philosophic, or societal, form of living an unhidden life means denying the truth of the body and its desires. It means establishing false divisions between what is seeable and what cannot be seen, what is acceptable and what cannot be accepted. Therefore, rather than living a life that is perfectly exposed to view, the philosophers hide the truth of their own bodies and desires, avoiding that in themselves which reason, detached from nature (the body), tells them is shameful. The division of space into public and private is a way of instituting this contradiction; the private exists as precisely that which is shameful, which cannot be brought into the open space and clarity of the public. By contrast, the Cynic lives a life of shamelessness in which the customs of the social world and the words of the philosophers are cast aside as false. According to the Cynic, these norms and the division of public and private space introduces into the natural truth of life an artificial principle of concealment, of deceit and hiddenness. The body, the private, is hidden behind the walls of the house. Arbitrary barriers are erected in order to hide away the truth of the body, its physical reality. The Cynic practice of the true life requires rejecting this arbitrary concealment, and it refutes the philosophers who speak of the true life as unhidden but who live a life which conceals itself and therefore contradicts itself. This dramatization therefore shocks the public space by introducing the other, the excluded, nature and reason. Furthermore, it scandalizes philosophy by embodying and living corporeally a principle that is commonly spoken and thought. It shows that the truth of reason is other than that which appears in philosophical discourse and that these sayings produce a radically other form of life. The true life as the embodiment of reason is necessarily other than the life lived according to custom. In this way the value of the money, both the customs as well as the meaning of the words of the philosophers, is changed.

The Poverty of the True Life

The second determination of the true life is its purity. Something is true if it is unmixed with external or outside realities. The pure is nothing other than itself. The application of this sense of truth to the practice of life leads philosophers to an *askēsis* of poverty. One purifies one's soul and one's body by releasing them, to varying degrees, from material possessions and from dependence on these things. More radically, it means purifying one's desires. Desire attached to material possessions is impure, it leads desire away from its pure truth. A life of poverty detaches desire from the body and the material world, and it represents the refusal of temptation and dependence on material possessions.[24] Therefore the *bios philosophicos*, the true, pure, and independent life of reason, is a life of poverty. In his discussion of the philosophical practice of poverty, Foucault distinguishes three different modalities of this exercise. These are Socratic, Stoic, and Cynic poverty. Socratic poverty is a sort of "negative" practice of poverty; Stoic poverty is what Foucault calls "virtual" poverty; and Cynic poverty is active, real, and infinite poverty.

First, Socratic or negative poverty. Socratic poverty is a consequence of his care of the self. Because he cares for the truth, and because he cares for the condition of his soul and the souls of his fellow citizens, he disregards the pursuit of wealth in order to devote himself to the truth. In the *Apology*, Socrates explains that his care for himself and the other Athenians "has kept [him] too busy to do much either in politics or in [his] own affairs. In fact, [his] service to God [Apollo] has reduced [him] to extreme poverty."[25] The philosophical life occupies one's time and attention to such a degree that the result is poverty. But conversely, the care for wealth, occupying one's self with political power or material gain, results in neglect of one's soul. Socrates makes this clear when he asks the jury rhetorically: "Are you not ashamed that you give your attention to acquiring as much money as possible, and similarly with your reputation and honor, and give no attention or thought to truth and understanding and the perfection of your soul?"[26] Care is a zero-sum game: one can spend it on the soul or on wealth. If one devotes oneself to the soul one will, to that extent, neglect wealth. The poverty of the Socratic life of philosophy is evident in the *Symposium* as well, where Socrates' appearance and hygienic practices are described as less than perfect or regular.[27] Furthermore, the dialogue describes Eros, who is a philosopher and a mythical reflection of Socrates himself, as born of poverty.[28] In other words, the philosophical life is a life of Eros and Eros is inseparable from poverty, from lack. The poverty of Socratic philosophy is a necessary consequence of the direction of one's care toward the truth and away from material concerns. The true life, the examined life, the life devoted to care of the self, is a life of material lack.

Foucault refers to Seneca in order to illustrate the Stoic practice of poverty.[29] For Seneca, care of the self results in an attitude of indifference with respect to wealth. Foucault calls this Stoic practice of truth "virtual poverty" as opposed to actual poverty.[30] In order to attain this attitude, Seneca recommends exercises by which one experiences, for short periods, the life of a truly poor person. He writes to Lucilius: "Set aside now and then a number of days during which you will be content with the plainest of food, and very little of it, and with rough coarse clothing, and will ask yourself, 'is this what I used to dread?'"[31] Seneca stressed that this exercise needed to be a "genuine trial and not an amusement."[32] However, the goal was to achieve a certain attitude, not to actually become poor: "I am not, mind you, against your possessing [riches], but I want to ensure that you possess them without tremors; and this you will only achieve in one way, by convincing yourself that you can live a happy life without them, and by always regarding them as being on the point of vanishing."[33] For this reason he urges Lucilius to "start cultivating a relationship with poverty."[34] In other words, one practices periodic poverty in order to form a certain relationship to oneself, a relation unmediated by the desire for and dependence on material wealth. A full and true self-relation is purified of this dependence. The consequence of Seneca's practice of poverty is a form of "independence," a particular mode of self-mastery in which one does not remain attached to material objects, but rather takes joy in (the best part of) oneself. Furthermore, insofar as one practices the proper form of life and attains the proper self-mastery, one is capable of acting as a spiritual guide—helping govern others in their attempt to take care of themselves.

The Cynics also practiced the *bios philosophicos* as a life of poverty, of indifference to material wealth, but they did so in a radical way. Cynic poverty is "real, it is active, it is indefinite."[35] It is *real* because it is neither the "negative" poverty of Socrates, in which one simply neglects the pursuit of wealth; nor is it the "virtual poverty" of Seneca, where one periodically lives like a poor person in order to establish the proper, true, and pure relationship to oneself. Cynic poverty is real: it is an actual physical and material poverty and not virtual. It is *active* in that the Cynic does not just allow his fortune to dwindle away or remain fixed without growing but renounces what he has; he gives it away or throws it away. Foucault says that "Cynic poverty must be an operation which one performs on oneself in order to obtain the positive results of courage, of resistance, and of endurance."[36] It is both a gesture of rejection and an act of strength and self-appropriation. Poverty itself is a goal to be attained which brings tangible benefits to the one who practices it. Finally, "Cynic poverty is infinite."[37] The Cynic continues to search out and eliminate the ways in which he remains dependent on material possession and therefore remains impure. This life of poverty is an unending task in which one strives for a more and more complete renunciation of possessions and the desire for material possession.

Through this total displacement of truth from the domain of *logos* to the domain of life, and from the inactivity of a negative and in a sense passive poverty to an active and real poverty, the Cynic makes the true life appear as a radically *other* life. Foucault shows that there are a number of important "side effects" that accompany this displacement and this dramatization of the truth.[38] What results is that the Cynic *bios philosophicos,* the life according to the principle of reason, affirms the values of "ugliness, dependence, and humiliation."[39] These three things directly and flagrantly contradict values central to the Greek and Roman worlds: beauty, independence, and honor. The Cynic affirmation of the true life gives meaning to the ugliness and the uncleanliness of poverty; to the dependence on the charity of others which defines the life of the poor who must beg to survive; and finally and most radically to the active pursuit of humiliation which takes on the meaning of a test and an exercise through which one becomes stronger and a more complete master of oneself (and paradoxically of the situation around one). Beauty, independence, and honor were values essential not only to the cultural world at large but also to the philosophical life of ancient civilization. The *bios philosophicos* of Socrates and the tradition which follows him does not reject these cultural values, but rather replaces them with the true, philosophically purified version of them: spiritual beauty replaces physical beauty; self-mastery replaces domination of others as the true form of independence; and honor as a life according to reason and justice replaces honor as mere reputation. The philosopher reaffirms these values by playing on the difference between appearance and reality, knowledge and opinion. The Cynic, however, through the practice of an actual, active, and infinite poverty replaces these values altogether. Through the practice of poverty, the truth, as purity and independence, which *appears* to support the values of beauty, independence, and honor, instead turns out to undermine them. The truth, in the form of purity lived as the life of poverty, replaces beauty, independence, and honor with new values: ugliness, mendicancy, and dishonor. Once again, the truth of reason culminates in a life which is radically other.

True Life and Law

Lawfulness, the possibility of knowing and abiding by the law, is a definitive characteristic of human being. The true life is a life lived according to the law. The question for the philosopher who strives to live truly is to know which laws are true and to comprehend the source of these laws— human reason, divine revelation, nature, custom. The Cynics respond to this question by asserting that nature is the source of the true laws.[40] Nature, for the Cynics, is radically opposed to all conventional laws, all laws established by human communities. Furthermore, while the philosophers tend to associate nature with reason as one discovers it written in the soul, through contemplation of the divine, or through rational argument or inquiry, the Cynic defines nature as animality, as the corporeal, embodied, and "instinctual" source of action and desire. Law is to be sought in the animal nature of human beings rather than in the *logos* in the soul. Therefore, Cynic lawfulness is the absolute reversal of conventional and of philosophical lawfulness. According to the latter, "It is by distinguishing itself from animality that the human being manifested and affirmed its humanity. Animality was always more or less a point of repulsion in the constitution of man [*l'homme*] as a reasonable and humane being."[41] For the Cynic, on the other hand, the animal has a positive meaning—it is the source of the law and it is the truth of human being. However, the life of the animal is not immediately open to human beings because we are absorbed within a culture. Therefore, "animality is not a *given*, animality is a *task*."[42] Animal truth and natural law are, on the one hand, the given nature of human beings insofar as we are born into a bodily life. But insofar as we are born into a social world of convention and culture, animal truth and the laws of the body present themselves as a goal to the individual, a task to be accomplished, and the true life presents itself as a challenge to the cultural life of human beings.[43]

True Life as Sovereign

Sovereignty is the final form of the true life—it is the life led by one who has mastered himself and is, therefore, master of the others. Foucault shows that sovereignty expresses itself in two characteristics. First, it is *jouissance* in the sense of self-possession, the total enclosure of the self within its own power; and in the sense of self-pleasure, the joy of being which accompanies and completes perfect self-mastery.[44] The second expression of sovereignty is that it maintains a necessary relationship to the other.[45] The relationship to the other is the obligatory beneficence of the one who has achieved perfect self-mastery and perfect mastery of those around him. Absolute self-possession and self-joy obligate the individual, through a kind of "supplemental" movement, to take care of the other.[46] The *bios philosophicos* takes up this theme in various ways. For example, Foucault refers to the Platonic theory of the philosopher as sovereign. This theory has two different aspects. On the one hand, the philosopher is *like* the king in that the philosopher "is capable of establishing in his soul and in relation to himself a type of hierarchy and a type of power, which is of the same order, which has the same form, which has the same structure as the power exercised in a monarchy by the monarch."[47] In other words, the philosopher is king by way of a structural analogy with political power and order. The second aspect of the Platonic theory is that the philosopher *would* be king in the ideal city even though he is without power in the actual city. In each case it is clear, according to Foucault's analysis, that the Platonic philosopher is not *actually* sovereign but is so either by way of analogy or of idealization.

The Cynic, however, will proclaim himself the *actual* sovereign.[48] The *bios philosophicos* will present itself as the true sovereign, opposing itself to the "actual" political sense of sovereignty, and to the "virtual" sense of philosophical sovereignty.

Of course, *actual* political sovereignty experiences itself and is recognized by others through its domination, its power to conquer and control, its glory and wealth. It is recognized by the external display of power and virtue. The philosophical experience of sovereignty argues that the virtues are the true definition of the king and are the source of true power and glory—the king's appearance, the kingly act, kingly might, are only actual insofar as they originate in the kingly *ēthos;* the sovereign soul is the spiritual source of the external display. These two kinds of kingship reflect each other: the philosophical sovereign is a sort of spiritual mirror of the political sovereign. The Cynic, on the other hand, by actualizing the principle of sovereignty will produce himself as the "antiking." His kingship will express itself not in might, in outward brilliance, in power over others, in conquest. The Cynic as "antiking" is illustrated vividly in Dio Chrysostom's account of the confrontation of Diogenes the Cynic and Alexander the Great.[49] As the story goes, it is Alexander who recognizes and approaches Diogenes, not the other way around—Alexander himself has a suspicion that it is the Cynic who is the true king and who lives the true life. In their confrontation Diogenes antagonizes, refutes, and mocks Alexander for being an illegitimate ruler, not a king by nature; cowardly, ignorant, and weak.[50] Furthermore, the very possessions and qualities that Alexander believes express and verify his sovereignty, for Diogenes, confirm Alexander's lack of true sovereignty. Alexander is dependent on his weapons, his wealth, his army, a mythology about his divine birth, and so on, in order to accomplish the many tasks he sets for himself. Because of this his life is entirely circumscribed by his reliance on others and on external, material goods. Furthermore, the tasks he sets himself are intrinsically false; he is consumed by superfluous (unnecessary) desires for conquest, wealth, and reputation among men. In all these ways Alexander deepens his enslavement to material goods, to other men, and to the desires that rule his soul. Diogenes, on the other hand, has purified and mastered his soul, his desires, and therefore he is absolute master of himself and of his world. He relies on absolutely no external aid, he needs no other man but is completely independent and indifferent. His perfect virtue, the perfect truth of his soul and his life, links him much more closely to the gods, to Zeus, then does the mythic story of Alexander's divine birth. Finally, Alexander, like any "political" king, lives in the constant fear that his fortune, his glory, and his possessions could be lost or captured, whereas the Cynic king can never be deposed but rather has attained a permanent sovereignty over himself, over the vices which are the true enemies of human beings, and therefore lives without fear and in perfect contentment.[51] That is, because his mastery of self is complete, he is the master of every situation.

The Cynic is the true and actual king who lives the true life. But, as is to be expected, the true life comes to pass as radically other than either the political sovereign or the sovereign as it appears in the *logoi* of the philosophers. The Cynic, the true king, "is a king of sorrows [*le roi de misère*]."[52] The true king, the true life as sovereign, is totally unrecognizable because it is the life of shamelessness, of poverty, of humiliation, of the constant test of oneself through humiliation and sacrifice. But the sovereign life, the true life, as one of sacrifice has the special signification of a mission to save others. The king must lead the others to the truth, must save and protect them. In this way, the fourth category of truth explicitly links the life of the Cynic to the practice of care of the others. If the Cynic life is essentially a practice of care of the self, of transforming one's subjectivity through *askēsis* in order to have access to the true life, then it is the sovereignty of this life which opens it up to the other. The Cynic king takes care of the other. This care is missionary insofar as the Cynic sacrifices himself in order to save the other; it is "medical" insofar as the other must be saved from a condition in which his soul is sick, is impure, is contaminated and must be cured.[53] And it is a struggle, a combat, insofar as the Cynic must go to war with the forces of injustice and of subjugation that enslave human beings.[54] The Cynic goes to war "against his desires, his appetites, and his passions . . . but it is also a battle, a battle against customs, against conventions, against institutions, against the laws, against an entire state of humanity; it is a struggle against the vices, but these vices are not simply those of the individual, these are the vices which affect the entire human race."[55] For the Cynic, society along with all of its laws, its social and religious forms, and the kinds of individuals it requires, is linked to the vices of the human soul and its body. Therefore, the Cynic struggles not merely to save an individual but to save the human race from the falsehood that afflicts it and that has its concrete form in and as the social-political world.[56] He struggles, he lives a life that is other and that is true, not merely for himself, but because he must change the world and save the others. Cynic self-sacrifice, the misery of the Cynic life, is linked to the falsehood of the everyday world and to the need to purge it, to bring about a different world in which true life is possible for the entire human race.[57]

The Cynic life in this way is at once banal and scandalous because it absorbs the principles of the philosophers, the principles of reason, and lives according to them. But in so doing it "transvalues" them, creating the dog-life of shamelessness, of indifference to custom, of poverty with its corresponding ugliness, dependence, and humiliation, and finally of the missionary link to others, the inversion of sovereign *jouissance* into the self-sacrificing care for the salvation of the human race as a whole.

Cynicism and Self-Knowledge

As Foucault sees it, an essential part of being a Cynic is self-knowledge. But this knowledge takes the form not of introspection, or dialogue. Rather, in order to recognize oneself as a Cynic it is necessary to *test* oneself. One must know one's nature, if one is made for the life of the philosopher. One must learn if one is able to live without shame, without the safety of a private world, a home, to retreat to for comfort and protection. One must learn if one is able to live the life of "errancy," of poverty, the purity of which connects one to the earth and to the gods.[58] And one must know if one is able to speak out against the faults, both those of individuals and those of society as a whole. One must test one's potentials, capacities, talents, strengths, weaknesses, endurance, and so on. This testing process is, as Epictetus put it, not simply one of "privation."[59] But rather "there is an acceptance of violence, the acceptance of blows, of injustice to which the others submit one . . . for the Cynic they are an exercise. And this exercise has the value of training."[60] The Cynic discovers his truth through the test (*épreuve*) of violence, the violence done against him by others; through the humiliation he must endure. Through the pain his choice produces in him the Cynic learns who he is.

The True Life, Self-Knowledge, and *Parrhēsia*

What is the mission the Cynic is made for and called to? "It appears as a sort of universal watchfulness."[61] The Cynic must watch over the others, must take care of the others by caring for the care they take of themselves.[62] The Cynic in this way recovers the Socratic duty and practices that Foucault, citing Epictetus, describes as the "very function of *politeia* understood in the true sense of the term."[63] The Cynic speaks to all in order to take care of all, and this is the true political work and life.

For Foucault, the philosophical life of the Cynic is not merely the true life, but it is the life devoted to speaking the truth, making the truth of life evident to the others. The Cynic manifests the truth through his actions, his life, his very body, and through his words.[64] The body of the Cynic must be the pure expression of the truth, of the true life, and therefore it must eliminate any bodily "rhetoric," any ornamentation or artifice which attempts to seduce, to persuade, or to deceive the other about the true nature, the truth of the body and of life.[65] The Cynic also produces the truth by practicing a constant *vigilance* over others. The Cynic practices a particular occupation of the public spaces of the city. He maintains himself in constant and complete visibility before the others and at the same time watches over them. This maximization of mutual visibility is not entirely symmetrical, of course, because the others always have recourse to their private space and the others are not devoted to the duty or practiced in the art of self-disclosure. Furthermore, the Cynic is merely *seen* by the others, they come across him and discover him there waiting and watching; while the Cynic, on the other hand, actively *observes* "what they do, how they live their lives, what they care [*soin*] about, and what they neglect contrary to their duty."[66] Epictetus compares the Cynic to a "general who inspects the troops, who reviews them, who watches over [*surveille*] them, and who punishes those who disturb the discipline."[67] As we saw in Foucault's analysis of Socratic *parrhēsia* and care of the self, both examination and vigilance are powerful tools for battling self-neglect and for confronting the political forces of the "general opinion" and rhetoric. The Cynics practice a form of vigilance and examination quite different from that of Socrates. While the Socratic examination was mediated by the statement of the oracle, the Cynic examination is more immediate;

the examination takes place at a more physical level, the opposition of bodies rather than of souls and statements. Socratic vigilance takes place in private conversations where he is able to examine the condition of the other's soul; Cynic vigilance takes place at the intersection of gazes, and the occupation of spaces. The life of the Cynic culminates in this way of being with others, this way of producing the truth, this way of caring for and vigilantly watching over the care that the others take of themselves.

What's more, the Cynic practice of *parrhēsia* is necessarily the practice of a *bios* that is absolutely other. For Foucault, the otherness of the Cynic's life is not accidental but essential to the truthfulness of it. "There can only be true life as living-otherwise, and *it is from the point of view* of this other life that one is going to make the ordinary life of ordinary people appear to be precisely as *other than the truth*."[68] The connection between the true life and the other life was also essential to the Socratic practice of truth. This theme of otherness runs throughout Foucault's analyses of spiritual exercises and care of the self. But it is the Cynics and the early Christians who push the otherness of the truth to the extreme. Is Foucault suggesting that otherness as such is ingredient to the truth of the true life? This may in fact be the case. Given Foucault's understanding of power as confining and conforming—in Athens power functioned as "nondifferentiation," and this was precisely what eliminated truth from the assembly—such a view would make sense. Power, in the sense of the normal, the nondifferentiated, establishes itself through the exclusion of what is different, other, abnormal. Therefore, in a sense, the *other* of power is the truth upon which power is grounded. In fact, the other toward which Foucault's work gestures is more likely something other than either term in the binary relation of normal and abnormal. Rather, it would be other than the *dispositif* that establishes itself by differentiating normal from abnormal. Insofar as this differentiation grounds itself as natural, as human nature itself, the otherness of the truth would more likely be something unnatural or antihumanistic.

The Critique of the Cynics

In his 1982 course, Foucault showed that as philosophy became more incorporated into everyday life it tended to lose its ability to critique the normal, the general opinion, and the inherent injustices, hypocrisies, and deficiencies of society.[69] The critical power, and the truthfulness of the philosophical life and of philosophical discourse come from their anteriority, their otherness. Philosophy as the true life was linked to practices, relationships, and modes of speaking that interrupted the norm. But Foucault also showed that the domestication of the philosopher did not occur without being made the object of criticism. This critique came both from within the social world on the part of the Sophists and the teachers of rhetoric and from other philosophers who saw the dangers of this development. The Cynics represent the philosophical mission of critique and of otherness in a radical form, as Foucault has shown us. Therefore, in a way, the Cynic is the true philosopher in the fullest sense. Both James Miller and Thomas Flynn have suggested that Foucault as an intellectual and a political activist perhaps saw himself in the Cynics more than in the other ancient thinkers he analyzed.[70] Indeed, Foucault certainly saw something of himself in the Cynic style, the "scandal of truth," even if he refused ultimately to privilege Cynic care and *parrhēsia* over other forms.[71] In any case, the place of the Cynic in Foucault's genealogy of philosophy is important. Certainly, the Cynic practice of "changing the value of the money," as Foucault analyzed it, seems a lot like Foucault's style of subverting modern rationality: asylums create mental illness, prisons fabricate criminals, repression produces sexuality, and so on. Foucault's philosophical vigilance might also be said to be Cynical in the fact that he used his body as "an instrument to measure the intolerable character of the present, an instrument of struggle for confrontation [*pour faire face*], an instrument of investigation, an instrument of thought."[72] But the Cynic was for Foucault more than a mirror, or a model, for his own activity. The Cynic represents the other pole of philosophical activity with respect to the more socialized practice of the later Stoics, for example. On one hand, the critique of the socialization and pacification of philosophy is embodied literally in the Cynic. On the other hand, the Cynics, as one might imagine, were themselves the object of bitter attacks.[73] However, the Cynics were viewed in an ambivalent way. There were the "good" Cynics and the "bad" Cynics.[74] In other words, Foucault shows that the philosophical and cultural discourse about the Cynics has not simply tried to reject Cynicism and Cynic *parrhēsia,* but also to tame it and appropriate it. The good Cynics are those who are not too disturbing, not too critical, who, in fact, pretty much resemble everyone else. The bad Cynics, on the other hand, are too radical in their critique of cultural norms or principles of reason. Anticynicism casts the "bad" Cynic in terms of a narcissistic "affirmation of '*moi*.'"[75] It is certainly not without irony that Foucault makes this observation, given that he himself was often characterized in just such terms and thus was something of a "bad" Cynic. Foucault shows that this ambivalent attitude toward Cynicism is an almost continuous part of Western history. Despite the critique, Cynicism persists in Western culture. In the present, Foucault thinks that modern art is the "vehicle" of

Cynicism.[76] In other words, Cynicism, as the otherness of the true life, continues to be part of our experience of subjectivity. It persists both in a modern critical discourse that condemns the narcissism of the "bad" Cynics (Foucault, contemporary art) and in the appropriation of the notion of the true life in the form of the "good" Cynic whose critique of society and culture is based on sound and recognizable reasons.[77] If this ambivalence toward Cynicism is a more or less permanent part of the Western experience of the subject and truth, what does this reveal about ourselves? What does it reveal about the Western experience of subjectivity? And what does it reveal about the Western practice of philosophy, perhaps especially the modern, institutional, academic version? At the very least, we can say, tautologically, it represents ambivalence! The notion of the otherness of the true life haunts our experience of the relationship between the subject and the truth. Even as we establish well-disciplined institutions for the normalization of philosophy and philosophical truth, our discourses, practices, and history point to an irreducible otherness ingredient to the true life. Despite our institutions, somehow philosophical truth continues to be seen as irreducible to a theoretical or methodological truth; it continues to be thought of, however vaguely, as a way of living and a way of speaking.

Cynic *Askēsis* and *Parrhēsia* in the Christian World

In his 1984 course at the Collège, Foucault gives a *very* provisional account of the movement of ethical *parrhēsia* and care of the self from the ancient, pre-Christian world into the world of the first Christians.[78] He argues that early Christian asceticism was in important respects a practice of Cynicism, even if it was different in its ultimate aims. The Christian ascetic renounced the conventions of culture as untrue and strived to return to a life of natural, even animal simplicity.[79] Like the Cynic, the Christian ascetic worked on the body. The body of the ascetic was "the visible theater of the truth" of Christianity.[80] The practices of radical poverty, of mission, of vigilance, all resembled practices employed by the Cynic not only to manifest the truth, but also to become the truth. The ascetic, like the Cynic, according to Foucault, manifested the truth in her very being, in her body and life, as well as in her words. However, the purpose of Christian asceticism was not essentially to achieve a transformation of *this* world but rather to achieve salvation in the form of a passage to the *next* world: "Christianity tied together the theme of an 'other-life' as 'true life' and the idea of access to an 'other-world' as access to the truth."[81] Another essential difference between the Cynic and the Christian ascetic is that for the Christian, as Foucault sees it, access to the true world required a condition of permanent and total obedience.[82] By combining Cynic asceticism, salvation in the other world, and the principle of obedience in this world, Christian asceticism created a new mode of subjectivity, a new relationship to the other and to truth. Foucault examines the ways this difficult arrangement manifested itself in the Christian experience of *parrhēsia*. Though his comments are provisional and brief, and therefore ought not to be taken as a final statement about his view of the history itself, they do afford us another opportunity to see how he understands the relationship between power and truth as *parrhēsia*. This tenuous relationship is reflected in the ambivalence concerning Cynicism and *parrhēsia* noted above, which is continued in early Christianity. The fact that *parrhēsia* is both embraced and rejected reflects something about its critical and difficult nature. Foucault points to a rupture between *parrhēsiastic* Christianity and anti-*parrhēsia*. But the critique of *parrhēsia* does not result in its complete destruction. Instead it leads to an attempt to control *parrhēsia* by appropriating it. In other words, it seems as though *parrhēsia* is somehow necessary but dangerous; it is threatening, especially to established norms, but at the same time too essential and irrepressible to eliminate outright.

Both in pre-Christian Judeo-Hellenic texts and in early Christian and New Testament texts, Foucault discovers a number of different uses of the term *parrhēsia*—all of which have a positive connotation. First of all, in pre-Christian Judeo-Hellenic texts, *parrhēsia* is the courage to say the truth out of a sense of justice. This courage and its discourse of truth are made possible by "purity of heart" and nobility of the soul.[83] Another sense of the term *parrhēsia* is the "transparency of the soul . . . [the] openness of the heart" which defines the proper relationship to God.[84] *Parrhēsiastic* openness is possible, again, because of the purity of one's soul. It is the complete disclosure of oneself before the gaze of God. This self-disclosure is experienced as an ascending movement by which one approaches God. Furthermore, *parrhēsia* is the "*jouissance* that the soul can experience when it has contact with God."[85] *Parrhēsiastic* openness to God is joy, delight. In the pre-Christian Judeo-Hellenistic world, *parrhēsia* is also used to designate a characteristic of God Himself: "It is the very being of God *in his manifestation* which is called *parrhēsia*."[86]

In the early Christian world and in the New Testament texts, on the other hand, Foucault finds that the term *parrhēsia* no longer refers to God but is, rather, always a quality and an activity of human beings. It has two significations. First, it refers to the characteristic confidence every human being or every Christian must have in God; it is therefore not a verbal activity but an attitude, a state of mind, an openness of one's heart to God and a "confidence" in God.[87] Christian confidence in the love of God makes it possible for the Christian to "enter into relation" with God through the activity of prayer.[88] What kind of rapport is this? What makes this confidence possible, or what is the nature of this confidence? The Christian experiences *parrhēsia* when in his prayer he expresses "nothing other than what God wants."[89] In other words, *parrhēsia* is linked to *obedience* to God's will—one relinquishes one's will and identifies oneself with the will of God. In this period, *parrhēsia* was also experienced as the "courageous attitude of the one who preaches the gospel."[90] *Parrhēsia* was the virtue that allowed one to confront injustice and error; it was the virtue that the act of truth required.

Finally, Foucault looked at the ascetic tradition of the first centuries A.D. In these texts Foucault found alongside the continuing valorization of *parrhēsia* the development of a new critique of it.[91] First, the positive meaning of *parrhēsia* continued. For example, it referred to the quality of the individual who speaks courageously, who is willing to maintain and proclaim his faith despite the danger he faces. In this sense the martyr was the ultimate *parrhēsiast*.[92] The *parrhēsia* of the martyr, the courage of risking one's life for the truth one knows, was grounded in one's relationship to God, in one's confidence in God's love.[93] The courage of truth was founded on a faith and confidence in God. *Parrhēsia*, therefore, was the act of critique and of defiance in the name of truth, and it was the *ēthos*, the attitude of absolute confidence in God's love that such an act required. Furthermore, through the work of self-examination, by which one is able to interpret the obscure and impure thoughts and feelings of the soul, one strives to perceive there the original purity and the original condition of man in paradise.[94] Through this hermeneutic work one is able to recover the lost relationship to God, the *parrhēsia*, the open and direct vis-à-vis with God which was the original state of man.[95] In man's primitive and natural state, his state before the fall, his relationship to God was one of frank openness. *Parrhēsia* was linked to a hermeneutics of the self, of the soul, and it is the natural, though lost, condition of the human heart.

Along with this positive experience of *parrhēsia*, a critical discourse began to challenge its value and effects. First, according to Foucault's reading, *parrhēsia*, as immediate openness to God, as confidence in one's rapport with God, in one's salvation and joy, and as the courageous act of speaking the truth, was at odds with the principle of obedience so important in the Christian experience of the self and the institutions which revolve around that experience.[96] Second, *parrhēsia* is an embrace of the self through the confidence the self has in God, the confidence in the salvation God promises. However, in Foucault's view, this confidence was counter to the fear and trembling before God and the rule of silence: "*Parrhēsia* is going . . . to appear as a sort of arrogance and presumption."[97] *Parrhēsia* came to be experienced as a neglect of self rather than as a care for the self. One had to remain a "stranger" to the world and to oneself.[98] Foucault's reading shows that *parrhēsia* came to be considered a vice, self-love. One had to detach oneself from oneself and hold oneself under a suspicious regard. This critique, from the fourth and especially the fifth and sixth centuries A.D., takes place as Christian asceticism, individual asceticism, becomes regulated and institutionalized in monastic practices: "You see these structures develop, you see the theme of a relation to God which can only be mediated by obedience."[99] The institutionalization of the spiritual master and the relationship of confession, so central to the pastorate, mediates the relationship of the self to itself and of the self to God. In this pastoral experience of the self, one cannot attain salvation without submitting to a spiritual director, a hermeneut who can interpret the inner life of the individual, the inner life that the individual cannot understand by himself because he is too attached to himself.[100] Without the constant presence of the spiritual director one cannot attain the proper relationship to oneself, the proper distance from oneself, nor can one attain the proper relationship to God.

But the relationship to others was also dangerous. Therefore, one had to maintain a certain distance from them. *Familiarity* with others, with one's director, with one's monastic brothers, was called *parrhēsia*, and it was dubious because through it one was given over to the unexamined impulses and thoughts in one's heart. In monastic life, familiarity was experienced as a constant danger with the power to interrupt the spiritual progress of the community. Furthermore, *parrhēsia* was experienced in an almost corporeal way—the body, the familiarity with one's own body, the proximity of other bodies, the sounds of the voice, were all seen as attachments to the world, to the self, and to others, which inhibited the proper renunciation of self and embrace of God.[101] Foucault suggests that this deep suspicion with respect to oneself, to one's nature and one's body, represents a transformation of philosophical attention to the self. In Christian asceticism, suspicion and anxiety about the self led not to self-formation but rather to self-renunciation and a rupture with oneself. Beginning with Socrates, the primary difficulty to be overcome was the "general opinion." The failure of *erōs* and of *paideia* resulted in false opinions passed around and generally accepted. With the Hellenistic extension of care of the self to cover life as a whole, this critique of opinion became more of a medical-style critique of the diseases (*stultitia*) intrinsic to and definitive of selves as such. This medical form of care allowed the suspicion of nature and of the body to take on new urgency. Yet the philosophical response to this danger was the practice of care through which the individual *remade* herself. The Christian care of the self responded to the danger of the body and its passions in a different way, created new techniques and new forms of therapy for the soul.

Foucault claims that the Christian critique of *parrhēsia* was a fundamental catalyst in the formation of the pastorate. On the one hand, the confessional scene and the relationship of spiritual direction arose as well-regulated and institutionalized forms of speaking the truth and in this way allowed a certain facsimile of *parrhēsia* to continue in a highly controlled and contained setting. In other words, *parrhēsia* was not eliminated so much as transformed, contained, and put to use as a technique within a new form of spiritual practice. On the other hand, the more radical *parrhēsiastic* form of Christian asceticism was absorbed in Christian mysticism, the tradition in which the individual, because of the purity of his soul and his confidence in God's love, is able to achieve some form of immediate contact with God.[102] Therefore, Foucault can say that the critique of *parrhēsia* was central in the formation of Christian subjectivity. The pastoral practice of spiritual exercises arose through a critical appropriation and control of *parrhēsia;* and mysticism as a counterpractice, which resisted incorporation into the pastorate, took over the uncontainable, critical openness of *parrhēsia*. Therefore, "it is around this [critique of *parrhēsia*] finally that all the pastoral institutions of Christianity were developed; and the long persistence, the difficult persistence of the mystic and of the mystical experience in Christianity is nothing other than the survival . . . of the *parrhēsiastic* pole of confidence in God which has subsisted in Christianity."[103]

The formation of the Christian pastorate through the critique of *parrhēsia* established a new ensemble of relationships of the subject to herself, to the truth, and to the other. However, Foucault claimed that after the formation of pastoral power, knowledge, and subjectivity, the "problem of the relations between knowledge of the truth and the truth of the self, this problem will no longer be able to take the form, in some way full and complete, of an 'other-existence,' which would be at once the existence of truth [or true existence, *existence de vérité*] and the existence susceptible of knowing the truth about itself."[104] How are we to take this claim? On the one hand, Foucault is clearly making a statement about the historical nature of the relation between the subject and the truth. But the claim is in fact broader. Foucault says, in effect, that the "full and complete" form of the problem of the relation between the subject and the truth is experienced in the framework of "spirituality." Should we read Foucault to be indicating something about his understanding of the very nature of subjectivity? In fact, I think that this is exactly what he was doing, not only in the above statement, but in his entire reinterpretation of ancient philosophy. At the very least, it is clear that, according to Foucault, for a certain historical moment, self-knowledge was only accessible through the ethical fashioning of subjectivity. In order to know the truth of oneself one had to live a true life, and to attain the true life required transformation, it required living otherwise. Foucault shows that Western culture took on a different relationship to the other in the course of its history. Other forms of life, and the spiritual meaning of the other life as the true life, were forcefully excluded from the social world and lost their meaning in the domain of thought as a spiritual task. The other was confined and controlled in order to constitute a field of the same.[105]

Conclusion: The Birth of Pastoral Power

In the preceding sections we have seen the way the early Christians adopted the practices of *parrhēsia* and Cynicism, which were then submitted to critique and exclusion. The practice of Cynicism, the true life as animality, the sovereign life as self-sacrifice, the courage to say the truth and the confidence that one is justified by God, are first embraced and then rejected. The Cynic tradition of *parrhēsia* continued, though pushed to the margins of Christianity, in the form of mysticism. In its place, other techniques of spiritual conversion developed by Hellenistic and Roman philosophers—for example, Stoic and Epicurean techniques—were adopted and transformed in order to operate within the framework of Christianity. This new experience involved different relationships between the subject and truth, new relationships to oneself, and new relationships to others, in particular to the spiritual guide or master. This new ensemble absorbed the spiritual dimension of thought and opened a rift between spirituality and philosophy. The notion of the *bios philosophicos* as the essence of philosophy, the practice of the true life as the goal and the work of the philosopher, began to fade into the background and philosophy eventually became a purely theoretical activity. Life, as a material to be formed and a task to be accomplished, was taken up within the practices of Christianity. The practice of care of the self shifted into the framework of Christian spirituality along with the arts it took over from the ancient world and transformed to meet new demands. The critique of Cynic *parrhēsia*, and the institutionalization of relationships of spiritual direction, were the beginning of what Foucault calls "pastoral power."

In addition to the displacement of *parrhēsia* into relationships of pastoral power, there were modifications of the subject as an "ethical substance" to be fashioned. This new subject-substance is not the soul-activity cared for in *Alcibiades,* or the *bios* which appears in *Laches.* It is also not the *ētho-poietic* self of the Hellenistic and Roman schools or the *alēthēs bios* of the Cynic. In the monastic practices, where this experience emerges, one is not primarily concerned with actions, with a plurality of social relations, responsibilities, and temptations—the monastic world is a disciplinary world in which actions are thoroughly controlled.[106] One must be vigilant over "an area anterior to actions, of course, anterior to will also, anterior even to the desires . . . The monk has to examine a material which the Greek fathers call (almost always pejoratively) the *logismoi,* that is in Latin, *cogitationes,* the nearly imperceptible movements of the thoughts, the permanent mobility of the soul."[107] *Thoughts* or rather *thought itself* is the object of anxiety. In early Christianity the self is reimagined as an ethical problem in terms of "thoughts." But thought, in this sense, exists prior to and independently of the deliberate control of the individual. Foucault himself throughout his explorations sought to grasp this mysterious dimension in its very being. From his early literary meditations on Bataille, Blanchot, Roussel, Rousseau, Jules Verne, Flaubert, and others, to his excavations of epistemic and discursive formations, and finally to his analyses of problematizations, he constantly tried not only to understand thought but also to immerse himself in it, to be carried along with it.[108] The problematization of thought as such—which perhaps first appears in these early monastic experiences—seems to lie behind Foucault's analyses of language, the flesh, the dream, the heterotopia, the outside, fiction, the imagination, and so on. In an essay originally intended to preface *The Use of Pleasure,* Foucault made one of his final attempts to define this level of reality.[109] Thought, in his technical sense of the term, exists at the level at which an experience of the truth is constituted:

> By "thought," I mean what establishes, in a variety of possible forms, the play of true and false, and consequently constitutes the human being as a knowing subject [*sujet de connaissance*]; in other words, it is the basis for accepting or refusing rules, and constitutes human beings as social and juridical subjects; it is what establishes the relation with oneself and with others, and constitutes the human being as ethical subject.[110]

This is not to say that it is purely formal. That thought is experienced in terms of the flesh, the dream, fiction, and so on clearly indicates that the being of thought is thicker than mere words. I have already indicated the importance of the notion of thought for Foucault. Here we must concern ourselves with the historical emergence of thought as an ethical substance and as a source of anxiety—that is, with the problematization of thought as such.

How did thought reveal itself within the practice of Christian *askēsis* and care of the self? What form of attention did the monk bring to this area? He was not concerned to examine the relationship between the *logismoi* and objects in the external world—it is not insofar as thought refers to an outside reality that it is troubling. Rather, the very nature and quality of its interiority and its being are at stake.[111] The purpose of the examination of conscience is that

> one must verify the quality of one's thoughts, one must know if they really bear the effigy of God; that is to say, if they really permit us to contemplate him, if their surface brilliance does not hide the impurity of a bad thought. What is their origin? Do they come from God, or from the workshop of the demon? Finally, even if they are of good quality and origin, have they not been whittled away and rusted by evil sentiments?[112]

The monk is anxious about the origin and meaning of his own interior life. Does his own interior world lead him away from God? Are his very thoughts, his very feelings produced by an evil force? Thoughts themselves are constituted as "subjective data which have to be interpreted, which have to be scrutinized, in their roots and in their origins."[113] One must look into the dark depths of the heart out of which representations flow. The form this vigilance takes is confessional; one examines one's thoughts by confessing them to the master who is in a position to interpret their true meaning. The techniques of the self formulated and practiced by early Christianity are techniques of interiorization; they elaborate an ethical subject who attends to herself in order to unlock the inner truth and being of her thoughts.[114] It is this experience of the subject as an inner world of thought, revealed through confession, which Foucault indicates in the expression, "the hermeneutics of the subject." This is the formation of the hermeneutic subject.

The confession functions as an act of truth in a peculiar way. The very act of confessing is a proof, a test, a verification. The confessional situation itself indicates which thoughts are good and which are bad—those which are difficult to confess are bad: "If one seeks to hide one's thoughts, if even quite simply one hesitates to tell one's thoughts, that is the proof that those thoughts are not good . . . Verbalization constitutes a way of sorting out thoughts which present themselves."[115] Foucault also discovers this truth-effect of confession in the ethical importance of techniques for writing down one's thoughts and one's actions: "The fact of obliging oneself to write plays the role of a companion by giving rise to the fear of disapproval and to shame."[116] The very act of writing introduces the possibility of the other, of the other to whose gaze one's inner life is exposed—the act of writing constitutes an otherness with respect to oneself through which one renounces the shameful elements of oneself.[117] Verbalization is a constant process which must continue to probe deeper into the thoughts residing below the surface of consciousness in order to bring to light "the deep movement of thought."[118] Furthermore, the act of confession is an act of self-sacrifice. Thought, the substance which constitutes the reality of the ethical subject, leads one away from God by attaching itself to the individual and attaching the individual to himself—the shame and difficulty one experiences in confession comes from the attachment of oneself to the thoughts one thinks.[119] "The centrality of the confession of sins in Christianity finds an explanation here. The verbalization of the confession of sins is institutionalized as a discursive truth-game, which is a sacrifice of the subject."[120]

Here the problematization of *parrhēsia* and care of the self has clearly set out on a new path. New games of truth, new relations of power and government, new practices of the self have arisen. A whole new *dispositif* of power, knowledge, and subjectivity begins to take shape. The domains of *psychē* and *bios,* which came into view as fields of truth, as objects of etho-poetic work, are now set within the framework of pastoral power. Prior to the formation of Christian institutions of care and power, philosophical spiritual direction led to a contemplation of the true nature of the soul or to the *épreuve* of one's style of life. The techniques, context, and teleology of care of the self and ethical *parrhēsia* varied and underwent many transformations. However, through all of this the relationship of the subject to the truth remained a spiritual one. One required *askēsis,* self-modification, in order to access the truth and be saved by it. In the practice of care of the self, the link to the spiritual guide was necessary in order to convert and to save the individual. However, with the formation of pastoral power this link became obligatory, permanent, a matter of authority and obedience; and spiritual direction deployed, in this new framework, a practice of confession and hermeneutics that resulted in a permanent and necessary renunciation of oneself, of one's subjectivity. This new complex laid the remote historical foundation for, and is in a sense the first move in the direction of, modern disciplinary power and modern bio-power. Techniques of individuation, of a surveillance which particularizes, of the formation of a subjectivity which experiences its freedom in the discovery of and production of its inner truth, all these eventually became elements of the modern *dispositif* of power, knowledge, and subjectivity.

Part 2

Care of the Self and *Parrhēsia* in the Age of Reason

In part 1 we followed Foucault's genealogy of philosophical *parrhēsia* and care of the self in the ancient world. In part 2, I want to show how this genealogy transforms our understanding of Foucault's earlier work on relations of power and knowledge. The isolation of the historical problematization of *parrhēsia* allows us to rethink the meaning of those earlier projects. While Foucault's return to Greece was structured by the problematization of power and knowledge developed in his major works of the 1960s and 1970s, it is clear that what he experienced there had "return effects" on him, transforming his original problem and giving him a new understanding of it, a new angle of attack. Our task is to see how modern philosophy came to be understood as a completely cognitive or discursive practice and how care of the self, ethical *parrhēsia,* and spiritual transformation fade into the background. In order to do this, we must examine what Foucault calls the "Cartesian moment." This is the event of thought that displaced the etho-poetic dimension of philosophy. After this event, philosophy ceased to be a form of *askēsis* or spiritual exercise. Furthermore, we must examine the problematization that forms the horizon against which this event unfolds. This horizon was constituted by the techniques of the self, relations of government, and modes of veridiction developed by ancient philosophers in order to resist political power. Once these practices and relations were separated from the problematization that called for them, they came to be imposed as "natural" and "necessary." As such they provided the prereflective, thoughtless, limits within which individuals constituted themselves as subjects. At the same time, however, they became the conditions of new forms of resistance, new technologies and practices of the self, new modes of veridiction and relations of power.

In order to trace the relations between philosophical *parrhēsia, dispositifs* of power, and forms of knowledge, and in order to see how Foucault's new understanding of practices of subjectivity enriches and transforms his earlier studies, I intend to focus on his interpretations of Descartes and Kant. Just as in part 1, where I imported Foucault's earlier concepts of power and knowledge in order to elucidate the nature of his later project, in part 2 I make use of his later insights into care of the self to elucidate the earlier work. I do this not without justification from the texts themselves. First of all, Foucault makes frequent references to both Descartes and Kant in his lecture courses in the 1980s. He gives each of them a fundamental place in his genealogy of philosophy as a practice of the self and ethical *parrhēsia*. Second, both of these figures play important roles in his earlier major works, and thus they serve as unifying themes. In particular, Foucault's interpretation of Descartes, which appeared in 1972, anticipates the studies of philosophy he will take on during the 1980s. Third, one cannot overstate the importance of Foucault's relationship to Kant. His *thèse complémentaire* was a translation of Kant's *Anthropology from a Pragmatic Point of View*, with a substantial and revealing introductory essay. *The Order of Things* continues the engagement with the thought of Kant initiated in the *thèse*. In addition, Foucault frequently referred to Kant's essay "What Is Enlightenment?" as the text where philosophy was first defined as a diagnosis of the present in its singularity. In fact, his 1983 course at the Collège begins with an analysis of this same essay in which he argues that Kant attempted to provide an Enlightenment definition of the philosopher as *parrhēsiast*. Therefore, there are good textual reasons for focusing on Descartes and Kant. Furthermore, philosophically, Foucault names the major modern event in the genealogy of care of the self and ethical *parrhēsia* the "Cartesian moment" and locates Kant within that moment as, in a sense, its pinnacle.[1] These two thinkers are situated at the two hinges that Foucault returned to with such frequency in his analyses of power and knowledge. Descartes resides at the moment of the rise of the classical episteme of order, and Kant at the point of the emergence of the problem of "man," the formation of the disciplines, and the beginning of the project of normalization. If we reread Foucault's earlier engagement with the thought of these two philosophers from the perspective of care of the self and ethical *parrhēsia*, we will gain further insight into the dynamic relationship between practices of the self—as forms of resistance—and relationships of power and knowledge. This will also give us a better appreciation of how Foucault fashioned his own identity as a philosopher and of the ethical and political meaning of his final lectures on ancient philosophy.

Foucault's Cartesian Meditations

Foucault's encounter with the thought of Descartes spans the length of his intellectual career, from his first major work, *History of Madness*, to his last lecture courses on "care of the self." The dialogue Foucault maintains with Descartes is perhaps easy to overlook because there are only two published works in which Foucault provides an extended interpretation of Descartes's text: the appendix to *History of Madness*, and part 1 of *The Order of Things*.[1] However, given our new appreciation of Foucault's notion of philosophy as care of the self and as ethical *parrhēsia*, we are in a position to rethink his earlier interpretation of Descartes. In his courses from 1982 to 1984, Foucault places Descartes at a turning point in the genealogy of philosophy: his name is used to mark an event in the history of thought, the Cartesian moment. My intention in this chapter and in the two which follow it is to bring the genealogy of philosophy together with the analysis of order—a notion which identifies both a *dispositif* of power and an epistemic formation—that Foucault presents in *History of Madness* and *The Order of Things*.[2] Doing so will reveal to us an important interaction between practices of the self, relations of power, and forms of knowledge. But there is another important reason for carrying out such a reading. By reinserting Descartes within the history of spirituality and the ascetic relationship between the subject and truth, Foucault loosens the disciplinary grip which philosophy has on Descartes's text. By reimagining it Foucault frees it to have new effects on us as readers and thinkers. And consequently, this loosens the grip of discipline on us as readers, offering us a new experience of the agency and power of the text and of ourselves as subjects capable of being transformed by the very practice of thinking.

Madness, Reason, and Care of the Self

In the first chapter of the *History of Madness*, Foucault details the strange dialectic that determines the thought of the fifteenth and sixteenth centuries.[3] He shows that in the cultural imagination of late fifteenth-century Europe madness replaces death as the great source of dread. Both death and madness are signs of the "nothingness" which hovers over existence. However, while death lies in wait just at the edge of existence and is the nothingness toward which we all move, madness, embodied in the skeletal grin of the madman, reveals that existence itself is only a thin veil over an essential nothingness: the ordinary everyday world along with all the meanings that permeate it are illusions to which we cling out of the madness of not being mad.

Two different paths of thought are opened up in response to this new dread of madness. The first is expressed primarily in the visual imagination of the age, the paintings that depict the senseless, animal rage of madness and that reveal the "tragic madness of the world."[4] Along this path one descends into the dark night of untruth which engulfs the reassuring world of truth and daylight. The second possibility is explored in the literary works of the moralists. Here madness is seen not in terms of metaphysics, but rather within a moral framework. The moralists develop what Foucault calls a "critical consciousness of man."[5] The madman does not prefigure the violent destruction of truth and the fundamental untruth of things. Instead, madness is a purely human phenomenon: madness is error, and in particular it is a moral error. Within this framework, the center holds and the cosmos retains its essential perfection. However, human reason is too flawed in its fallen state to grasp the ultimate meanings or truths of the universe. Because of this, reason is always open to error.

This second way prevailed in the sixteenth century. It made possible a constant dialogue of reason and madness—two elements which cannot exist without each other, each sounding out the other and each discovering itself in its opposite. The moral task of the thinker was to check the vanity, the self-love, which causes one to think that he can attain knowledge and certainty about things. Such an error, a moral fault, leads one to accept illusions as reality, to take oneself as something one is not—namely as a sort of god, a perfect being who is able to attain absolute knowledge.[6] Madness is complicit with this moral error, and is both cause and effect: the madness of self-love, of mistaking one's true nature, and the madness which results, the ensuing illusions and absurdities. But because reason leads us to accept as true what is uncertain, perhaps false, we are all, in a sense, mad. Wisdom is the result of accepting the limits of reason and its essential errors. This way of thinking takes on its particular character with the help of Christian metaphysics.[7] The transcendence of God and his reason dazzles that of human beings. Our task is to practice an ethics of humility. Madness plays its role, then, in the progress of wisdom and the ascetics of humility. Madness and the madman are the constant reminders of human frailty and vanity. Madness even holds within itself a power of conversion: it is perhaps a necessary step along the way, the error that reveals the truth. Therefore, even though the madman does not issue from the other world and signal its approach or presence, he remains important, a reminder of the human condition, its limits and moral exigencies. Reason itself is always unreason; it can never become self-sufficient, certain. Madness is "tamed" but not conquered. The confrontation continues. In such a world, wisdom is an ethic, hard won and always precarious; reason, on the other hand, remains encircled by its own unreason.

This scene is altered in the seventeenth century. Reason and unreason become clearly defined and divided. Reason becomes sure of itself and puts unreason in its proper place: "The development of Cartesian doubt seems to bear witness that for the 17th century the danger [of madness] finds itself dispelled and that madness is placed out of the domain of belonging [appartenance] where the subject retains its rights to the truth: this domain which is, for classical thought, reason itself."[8] What we have is a new experience of subjectivity and its "right to truth." The subject takes place in, and belongs to, the field of reason which is defined by its fundamental difference from unreason. The subject discovers himself in this field of reason, and here he retains the right to truth. The subject who resolves to maintain himself within the limits of reason speaks with certainty. "While man [l'homme] might always be mad, thought, as an exercise of the sovereignty of a subject who sets himself to the work of grasping the true, cannot be nonsense."[9] "Man" can always fall prey to madness. In other words, the individual who succumbs to madness is de facto cut off from the experience of subjectivity and the right to truth. But reason itself, thought defined as reason, is in itself certain and true. Reason alone, "the exercise of the sovereignty of a subject," has the right to truth. This sovereign, rational subject has the right to govern and care for "man" because he alone has the right to truth, and truth is what rightfully governs and cares for "man."

Descartes's text is one manifestation of a new experience which displaced both the "tragic madness of the world" and the "critical consciousness of man." Foucault sees in the Meditations the outline of a new practice of subjectivity that is no longer threatened from within by its intrinsic limit and madness. Limit, error, and fault are extrinsic to reason. Unreason is not internal to and complicit with reason. In the following, our task is to show how and why Descartes fashions this new figure of truth as well as to understand precisely what this figure represents and what its implications are. In the next section I will analyze Foucault's essay "My Body, This Paper, This Fire," to show how it is that Descartes fashions a new subjectivity.[10] Then it will be necessary to show the practices of subjectivity, relations of power, and discursive formations against which Descartes struggles. In other words, in order to understand Descartes's thought, we must see it as a form of resistance to a *dispositif* of power, knowledge, and subjectivity.

Foucault characterized this event of thought in a number of different ways. As early as 1962, he identified it enigmatically as the "moment at which the great confrontation between reason and unreason ceased to be waged in the dimension of freedom, and in which reason ceased to be for man an ethic and became a nature."[11] The reference to the confrontation between reason and unreason is understandable in terms of his study of madness in the classical age. The great confinement is the event which takes place at this moment, which removes this confrontation from the "dimension of freedom" and sets up a controlled space in which reason, in the guise of science, can master its opposite, unreason. What is particularly interesting in this striking statement is Foucault's understanding of reason as an *ethic*. It is only in his later work, in particular his 1982 Collège course, that he explains the way that reason as such is an ethic, the way that thinking in the dimension of freedom is intrinsically ethical.[12] In these lectures he names this moment, this event, the "Cartesian moment." And it is here in fact that the fascinating and elusive claim of the earlier work—the claim that reason at this moment ceases to be an ethic—is made concrete. Foucault explains that the Cartesian moment is the event by which "care of the self" (*epimēleia heauton*) is finally displaced by the imperative to "know oneself" (*gnōthi seauton*).[13] The relationship between the subject and the truth is fundamentally altered, as is the relationship of the self to itself. Access to the truth will no longer be grounded upon *askēsis*, an etho-poetic task by which one transforms one's being; rather, it will be grounded in the nature of the subject prior to and independent of any *askēsis*. In other words, reason as an ethic is the experience of the ascetic ground of the relationship between the subject and truth.

In his 1983 course at the Collège, Foucault adds another layer to his understanding of this event and this moment.[14] He describes it as the pivotal point where modern philosophy reemerges as the practice of ethical *parrhēsia*. For a long time, the function of care of the self and ethical *parrhēsia* had belonged to the pastorate and had been invested in the figure of the pastor. The right of *parrhēsia*, the duty and the privilege of ethical truth-telling, of critique, of governing individuals, had been claimed by the church. In the sixteenth and seventeenth centuries philosophy begins to redefine this activity as its own proper function. Foucault identifies Descartes as playing an essential role in this process. This is because Descartes redefines philosophical *parrhēsia* in a way which allows him to detach it from pastoral power. The mode of care and ethical *parrhēsia* invented by Descartes was linked to the rise of a new form of knowledge and a new mode of power.

What is the connection between the simultaneous return of philosophical *parrhēsia* and the process whereby the relationship between the subject and truth is removed from the ethical dimension of freedom? In the following chapter I will show that for Foucault, Descartes's project is a response not only to the epistemological problems raised by the discoveries of the new sciences, but also to the struggles over the care for, and government of, individuals, life, the soul, and thought itself. Descartes will be able to reclaim the right of truth by removing philosophical care and *parrhēsia* from the ascetic, spiritual, dimension and founding it on a new relationship between the subject and the truth. This movement is captured in the famous text from part 6 of the *Discourse on Method:*

> It is possible to arrive at knowledge that is very useful in life and that in place of the speculative philosophy taught in the Schools, one can find a practical one, by which . . . we could . . . make ourselves, as it were, masters and possessors of nature. This is desirable not only for the invention of an infinity of devices that would enable us to enjoy without pain the fruits of the earth and all the goods one finds in it, but also principally for the maintenance of health, which unquestionably is the first good and the foundation of all the other goods in this life; for even the mind depends so greatly upon the body that, were it possible to find some means to make men generally more wise and competent than they have been up until now, I believe that one should look to medicine to find this means.[15]

Foucault, like many others, takes this passage to be essential to understanding the Cartesian project.[16] We can see in it a rejection of the "scholastic" practice of speculative philosophy—one which is useless because it lacks a sound method and foundation. Furthermore, the search for truth, the practice of philosophy, is here inscribed within the history of care and government: philosophy is a way of using the truth to correct, heal, and govern individuals and nature itself. This control takes place at the level of the body in the form of medicine and has the goal of health. Many of the familiar aspects of care as a practice of the self, an exercise, and a way of life are apparent here, yet they are transformed in their meaning. To the notion of mastery of the self is added the new idea of a mastery of nature. Medicine as care of the self will place a new emphasis on the health of the body as its primary target, rather than the health of the soul, and this will include placing an accent on the way medical intervention at the level of the body can produce positive effects at the level of the soul. It is a medical ethic, but one founded on scientific, "useful" principles rather than speculative "scholastic" principles. In ancient practices of the self, the body was an area of exercises and tests through which the soul could be sounded out and transformed. But it was not conceived of as an object that could be manipulated at the level of its organic functioning to transform the subject who inhabits it. In other words, ancient medical ethics perceived the body as a subject, while Cartesian medical ethics will displace this approach—without being able to eradicate it—in order to take up the body as an object.[17]

What makes Foucault's account of this movement unique is that for him Descartes's text, in particular the *Meditations,* bears within it traces of the ascetic foundation of the relationship between the subject and truth. The *Meditations* cannot be reduced to the modern form of this relationship and therefore it can serve, if properly experienced, as a resistance to the relationships of power and knowledge which link themselves to this text and the event which it signals. Second, while Descartes is often vilified as the one who subjected nature and the body to the cruelty of a heartless instrumental rationality, Foucault reminds us that the movement of Cartesian thought was fundamentally one of freedom and resistance. In other words, Descartes did not simply enslave the body to the horrors of reason, a body which would have been natural and free before he caught it in his net. Rather, the body, and in a sense, nature, were already caught within the grip of a different form of reason and control, a different set of technologies of the self. In what follows I will outline these technologies in some detail. They will include a particular deployment of political power and its counterpart, pastoral power; a determinate epistemic formation; and various sets of practices of the self. Descartes attempted to liberate individuals from relations of power—political and in particular pastoral relations—that lacked a solid foundation in truth and therefore served to inhibit the freedom and health of the body and the development of true knowledge of the world. He attempted to free us by placing us under the proper authority and figure of government: reason defined in terms of method and evidence. To do so, however, meant for Descartes attacking directly the foundation upon which these relations of control were founded. Foucault reveals that this foundation was deeply ingrained in Descartes's very subjectivity; it was not a matter of discrediting the senses (which are not inherently deceptive), nor was it a matter of refuting a certain false opinion about the starting point of knowledge. In order to displace this illegitimate foundation of relations of control Descartes had to alter his very way of being-in-the-world, the very form of his subjectivity. For this reason, it is through *askēsis,* and not simply through argumentation, that Descartes displaces the pastoral claim to practices of subjectivity and discovers a new foundation for, and form of, philosophical *parrhēsia.*

Cartesian Meditation

Let's begin with a brief reminder of the nature of Descartes's task in the *Meditations* even though this is familiar territory. The stated purpose of the *Meditations on First Philosophy* is to demonstrate the existence of God and the distinction between the soul and the body. This is, after all, the subtitle of the *Meditations*. This task is necessary because it will provide Descartes with the solid foundation upon which his method of reasoning can stand and from which he will be able to develop absolutely certain, scientific, mathematical knowledge of the world. As Descartes tells us, the *Meditations* were provoked by the fact that he had for so long accepted certain opinions as true that turned out to be false. Not only this, he had allowed these false ideas to serve as principles upon which he had based many other opinions.[18] The extent and the depth of his errors force Descartes to admit that he lacks any sure criteria for distinguishing true beliefs from false ones. Therefore, he writes, "I realized that once in my life I had to raze everything to the ground and begin again from the original foundations, if I wanted to establish anything firm and lasting in the sciences."[19] Descartes is no longer sure that in his very being as a thinking, reasoning subject he has access to the truth and that he can ever be certain that what he thinks or believes is really true.[20] The *Meditations* will attempt to resolve this uncertainty and to discover what access (if any) the subject has to the truth, and how and when it can be sure of itself in its claims to truth. In other words, the matter dealt with in the text is the relationship between the subject and the truth. Foucault will claim that Descartes's *Meditations,* rather than being simply an inquiry into this relation between subjectivity and truth, and rather than being an argument about this relation, is an *askēsis,* an "exercise," whereby the subject is led to self-knowledge and through this self-knowledge is able to perceive the mode of its access to the truth. What's more, this self-knowledge also results in clearly perceiving the nature of those objects we can know and the form of knowledge we can have of them. In this way self-knowledge becomes the real foundation for philosophy (both metaphysics and ethics): *epimēleia heautou* is displaced by *gnōthi seauton.*

To resolve his problem, Descartes employs a methodical doubt. In order to discover a solid foundation, one which is certain, he must refuse to accept any idea as true that he can doubt for any reason: that which can be doubted is, by definition, not certain. Furthermore, rather than examine each idea in itself, he will "attack straightaway those principles which supported everything ... [he] ... once believed."[21] The fundamental principle which lay at the basis of everything which Descartes had taken "as most true" was sense-perception. The senses seem to allow us to come into contact with objects in the world, that is, with things other than our-selves. Not only that, they seem to show us things in the world as they really are. "However," Descartes writes, "I have noticed that the senses are some-times deceptive; and it is a mark of prudence never to place our complete trust in those who have deceived us."[22] The task is clear: the senses have deceived us, therefore, it is prudent, wise, and reasonable not to trust that which deceives. The goal of the *Meditations* will be to "withdraw the mind from the senses as well as from all prejudices" and to "meditate seriously" in order to establish once and for all what kind of access the subject has to the truth.[23]

How is it that Descartes disengages himself from his uncritical re-liance on sense perception? Foucault argues that he does so through *askēsis*, through a transformation of himself qua subject in the practice of a meditation.[24] In order to disentangle himself from the confusions, mis-direction, and disorder which have defined his life and his thought for so long, Descartes must ground knowledge on some certain foundation, a true and certain knowledge of himself. But to know himself requires a spiritual exercise, a meditational practice. There is a long debate about the nature of the *Meditations* and whether they are meant to be read as a "spiritual exercise."[25] There are several aspects of the *Meditations* which indicate that they are in some way a kind of exercise. Obviously, there is the very title, *Meditations*. Furthermore, several of the meditations open or close by invoking themes drawn from the "genre" of manuals of spiri-tual direction.[26] In particular, there are the frequent references to the pas-sage of time and to Descartes's spatial situation as he engages in the medi-tation. For example, Descartes refers to the right moment for meditating, the right phase in his life. Descartes claims that systematic doubt is some-thing that anyone who pursues the truth must practice once in his life.[27] He says that he waited until he had reached a "mature enough age" and that "he put the project off" but that he did not want to miss "the time still left for carrying it out."[28] In other words, the doubt is a necessary moment in life—one which the individual must go through but which he must practice at the right time. Furthermore, it is possible to miss the opportu-nity. At the end of the Second Meditation, Descartes indicates that he is "pausing" in order to "meditate for some time on this new knowledge I have gained, so as to fix it more deeply in memory."[29] At the end of the Fourth Meditation, he writes that "I should like to pause here and spend some time in the contemplation of God . . . the supreme happiness of the next life consists solely in the contemplation of the divine majesty, so ex-perience tells us that this same contemplation, albeit much less perfect, enables us to know the greatest joy of which we are capable in this life."[30] At the beginning of the Second, Third, and Fourth Meditations, Descartes refers to the passage of time during his exercises in terms of days. Moreover, this passage of time is linked to the formation of a habit which allows him to more and more easily withdraw his mind from the senses, something which was nearly impossible to do at the beginning of the meditations.[31] The duration of the *Meditations,* the use of and experience of time, and the effects of the passage of time are all ingredients in the work of meditation. This is not the case in an argument where time is perceived as inessential, or even an obstruction. In addition to time, Descartes refers to his spatial situation frequently, and it is clear that being in the right kind of space, in the right place, is also essential to the successful meditation. The right place allows for withdrawal into solitude in order to meditate on the ideas to which he is led. In other words, there are several clear indications in the text which suggest that proper understanding is linked to an exercise involving the meticulous arrangement of space and time and the proper disposition of the body and mind. These features of the *Meditations* are not mentioned as external details but as intrinsic elements of the meditational exercise.

Having pointed out some of the many traces of the tradition of spiritual exercises in the *Meditations,* I will return to Foucault's interpretation of the First Meditation. It will be necessary, however, to point out the context within which Foucault first presents this reading of the *Meditations.* In this way we will be able to see the very specific problem Foucault addresses in the 1972 text the *Meditations* and the way his response to this problem indicates a more comprehensive understanding of the text and its overall intelligibility as an event in the history of thought.

In the *History of Madness* Foucault writes: "The doubt of Descartes dispels the charms of the senses, crosses the landscape of the dream, always guided by the light of true things; but it banishes madness in the name of the one who doubts, and who is no more likely to be unreasonable than he is not to be thinking or not to be."[32] Foucault shows (more by way of a sketch of an argument than an actual argument) that Descartes, in the *Meditations,* performs the intellectual act of expelling unreason from the kingdom of reason, anticipating the massive social-political act of confining the poor, the mad, and the disorderly to come some fifteen years later. Descartes is said to be "excluding" madness because for Descartes, quite unlike the Skeptical tradition, the possibility that one is mad, even when one takes oneself to be reasoning clearly, is ruled out.[33] The possibility of madness does not play a role in Cartesian doubt because one cannot be doubting—that is, reasoning, thinking—and be mad. The very essence of madness is the incapacity of doubting. Thought, or reason, is in this way saved from the illusions of unreason, of disorderly thinking, just as the social world is saved from the dangers of all those who do not adapt themselves to the social, political, moral, and economic order which was beginning to take shape at the time. In 1963, just two years after the publication of the *History of Madness,* Jacques Derrida, Foucault's one-time student, famously deconstructed the project by way of a critical reading of Foucault's interpretation of Descartes.[34] Derrida's argument is that Descartes, far from excluding madness, places it at the very center of the doubt, as the defining moment of the cogito. For Derrida, Descartes's *apparent* dismissal of the possibility that he might be mad and therefore should doubt his senses is really an objection raised by a "nonphilosopher" who is not ready to accept so radical a hypothesis. But Descartes, through the possibility that he is dreaming, reintroduces madness into his doubt, and then again to the most radical degree, in the hypothesis of the "evil genius."[35] In 1972, when Gallimard republished the *History of Madness,* it included as an appendix Foucault's response to Derrida, an essay titled "My Body, This Paper, This Fire." Leaving aside the argument with Derrida, Foucault's essay is remarkable in its own right for the interpretation of Descartes it puts forward and for what it reveals about Foucault's project as a whole. It is in this essay that Foucault first proposes that Descartes's *Meditations* must be read not merely as an argument proceeding according to logical reasoning, but also, and especially at certain points of its progression, as an "exercise," as a kind of *askēsis,* a work or practice.[36]

Because Foucault's interpretation of Descartes is articulated as a response to the critique made by Derrida, it takes as its point of departure one very precise problem, Descartes's alleged exclusion of madness. However, the overall development of the text is much more comprehensive, and in fact seems to be more concerned with putting forward a reading of the *Meditations* and even a certain *technology* of reading philosophical texts. By way of the dispute with Derrida, Foucault answers two questions: (1) Why is it that Descartes refuses madness as a reason to doubt the senses—this is the specific question which arises first from the *History of Madness,* and then Derrida's critique? and (2) More generally, why is it necessary for Descartes to consider first the possibility that he is mad and then to take up the possibility that he is dreaming, and even assume that this is the case? This second, broader problem is what underlies the narrower first one and is what structures the essay as a whole. So while ostensibly Foucault is responding to Derrida's criticism, he is, more important, arguing for a particular way of approaching the text as a whole.

Foucault's interpretation of Descartes in the *History of Madness* and in "My Body, This Paper, This Fire" focuses on the First Meditation. In particular, Foucault is interested in the passages where Descartes, in order to discover whether or not it is possible to doubt the senses with respect to things which are "vivid and near," as opposed to those things which are "small and distant," invokes the example of "madmen" and that of the dream-state. As we have already pointed out, the task of the meditation is to withdraw the mind from the senses. Prudence, reason, tell Descartes, according to a "practical syllogism,"[37] that he must do so: "I ought to be wary of something that has deceived me once. My senses, through which I have received the truest and surest things I possess, have deceived me, and more than once. I ought therefore no longer trust them."[38] Yet against his better judgment, he cannot bring himself to doubt them. "There are many other matters concerning which one simply cannot doubt, even though they are derived from the very same senses: for example, that I am sitting here next to the fire."[39] It is at this moment that he suggests first the possibility that he "liken [him]self to the insane" and then considers whether he might actually be dreaming it all. Madness is quickly dismissed as a valid reason for doubting. Descartes writes, "But these people are mad, and I would appear no less mad, were I to take their behavior as an example for myself."[40] Foucault insists on the precise meanings of the terms Descartes uses in this passage: *amentes, demens.*[41] These terms "are in the first place juridical . . . [they] designate a whole category of people incapable of certain religious, civil, and judicial acts. The *dementes* do not have total possession of their rights when it comes to speaking, promising, pledging, signing, starting a legal action, etc."[42] What is indicated here is that for Descartes, if one were to designate oneself mad, then one would simultaneously forfeit one's right both to meditate systematically and to convey to the reader the progress and discoveries of the meditation. The meditation, then, must be performed by a kind of "juridical subject" which has the right to control and judge what takes place in and through that meditation. Such is not the case for the skeptical tradition (Foucault has in mind here thinkers such as Erasmus and Montaigne).[43] In the epistemological space inhabited by the skeptics, madness is always a distinct possibility and therefore a good reason to doubt. This is because it is possible that one is mad even when one meditates. Far from disqualifying the meditating subject, madness is experienced as a possible path to, voice of, or element of speaking the truth—madness counts as one of the possible prices one might have to pay for access to the truth. Descartes initiates a very different kind of meditation by dismissing madness without ever really considering the possibility that he, even as he meditates, and perhaps especially when he meditates, might be mad.

Having dispatched madness, Descartes makes the observation that he is "a man who is accustomed to sleeping at night, and experiencing in . . . [his] . . . dreams the very same things, or now and then even less plausible ones, as these insane people do when they are awake."[44] Descartes will take the case of the dream-state as a valid reason to doubt even perceptions which appear to be most certain, those of the "vivid and near." This is because it is always possible that he is asleep, even as he performs the meditation. He writes, "How often does my evening slumber persuade me of such ordinary things as these: that I am here, clothed in my dressing gown, seated next to the fireplace—when in fact I am lying undressed in bed!"[45] All of the evidence which the senses provide—vividness, clarity, self-awareness, the sense of belonging to an environment, deliberateness—all of these things exist in the dream-state in the same way they do for someone who is awake. Therefore, "there are no definitive signs by which to distinguish being awake from being asleep."[46] In other words, it is possible that he is asleep and even these vivid sensations are false. Why is it that Descartes rules out madness and accepts dreaming as a valid reason to doubt the senses? This is the problem that Foucault handles in "My Body, This Paper, This Fire." However, there is another more fundamental question which determines the essay and to which it responds: Why is it that Descartes cannot doubt the senses in certain matters even though he has "just established a completely binding syllogism" that tells him that the reasonable thing is to do just that? "What, then, is this obstacle that opposes our doubting 'entirely,' 'wholly,' 'completely' (rationally?) given that we've just performed a rationally unassailable piece of reasoning?"[47] It is the series of questions arising around Descartes's "cannot" with respect to what he "ought" to do that determines Foucault's reading of the *Meditations*. The way that Foucault answers these questions will show us how Descartes arrives at a new experience of subjectivity not simply by arguing for one, but through an alternative practice or technology of the self.

Foucault writes, "We must keep in mind the very title of 'meditations.'"[48] This is a claim which he repeats in 1982 when he explains more precisely what he means: "Keep in mind . . . that this idea of meditation, not as a game the subject plays with its thoughts, but as the game which thought plays with the subject, is, at bottom, exactly what Descartes was doing in the *Meditations*, and it is precisely the meaning which he gives to 'meditation.'"[49] A meditation, as an *askēsis*, is a way of thinking in which the thoughts the subject thinks displace the subject who thinks them. Foucault claims that the *Meditations* are composed of two different kinds of procedure: they follow both a "demonstrative order" and an "ascetic" order.[50] On the one hand, the text unfolds as an argument composed of a series of propositions linked together according to rules of inference, deduction, and demonstration. On the other hand, and especially at certain moments, it is a set of "exercises" which are to be performed. The reference to the dream-state is one of those moments that are essentially "ascetic" rather than demonstrative. At this moment, as Foucault sees it, the text does not simply put forward another proposition in an argument, but rather attempts to use thought to displace the subject, to transform its mode of being. The dream-hypothesis "is an exercise by which the subject puts itself, by its thoughts, in a certain situation. Displacement of the subject with respect to what it is by the effect of thought."[51]

Why does it make sense to read the reference to the dream-state as part of an *askēsis,* or an exercise, rather than as part of an argument? Foucault argues that if we read the text solely as an argument, then we can see no good reason why it is necessary to pause over the questions of madness and dreaming. According to reason, according to the logic of prudence— the practical syllogism which renders the imperative: doubt!—Descartes has a *reason* to doubt, he *must* doubt, yet he cannot. Why not? Because he runs up against a certain "resistance" to this doubt: those "other matters" that are too real, or "vivid and near," which simply *are* to such a degree that one cannot doubt that they are. It is not enough to understand that one ought to doubt these things because reason tells one to do so. One has to *make* oneself doubt them. In other words, doubt requires work. Making oneself doubt something which appears indubitable calls for some kind of technique or device. It is within this ascetic problematic that the device of dreaming is chosen while that of madness is dismissed. Again, why not madness? According to the demonstrative order, the case of the dream is equivalent to that of madness. Foucault writes: "In their power to make uncertain, dreams are not outdone by madness; and none of the demonstrative force of madness is lost by dreams when I need to convince myself of all that I must call into doubt."[52] Therefore, if the task is to seek out reasons to doubt, then dreams and madness are on an equal footing. They equally imply the derangement of the senses. However, while dreams and madness are equivalent with respect to their potential to undermine sense experience, Descartes dismisses the case of madness as not effectively challenging his certainty in the senses. Dreams, on the other hand, while being no more intrinsically disruptive of sense experience, are an acceptable source of doubt. The reason for this, according to Foucault, is to be found not in the demonstrative order of the meditation but rather in its ascetic order. Foucault writes that the "advantage of dreams is . . . [that] . . . they are frequent, they happen often; my memories of them are recent, it is not difficult to have access to these vivid memories which they leave. In short, this is a *practical* advantage when it is no longer a question of demonstrating, but of performing an exercise, and calling up a memory, a thought, a state, in the very movement of meditation."[53] The real difference between the example of madness and that of dreams, according to Foucault, is to be found in a certain pragmatics—the dream is more useful as a technique for producing doubt. It is so because of its *"accessibility* as an *exercise."*[54]

Descartes introduces the dream-hypothesis not as a demonstrative proposition but as a device, or a technique, for the transformation of the mode of being of the subject who meditates. The very mode of being of the subject is manipulated by the thoughts that the subject thinks. Why is it a matter of the subject's mode of being when what appears to be at stake is whether or not Descartes can doubt certain "matters," or things, given by the senses? Let's return to Foucault's reflection on that particular point in the text. Foucault states that the dream allows the doubt to continue though it has run into a certain resistance: the perception of the immediate and actual world, what Foucault calls the "vivid and the near." What is important is that the resistance to doubt is not, in fact, any particular object, or even class of objects. It is not even the body as a particular sense object which is too "vivid and near" to really doubt. What offers resistance is, rather, "an area defined as 'the vivid and the near' (in opposition to all those 'distant' and 'weak' things which I can *place* in doubt without difficulty): I am here, wearing a dressing gown, sitting beside the fire—in short, the whole system of actuality which characterizes this moment of my meditation."[55] The subject who doubts, here and now, can place these other things in doubt; but what resists doubt is the actuality, the "precise instant," the present, or presence of myself, here and now, with myself—wearing these things, sitting here by the fire. How can I place my own actual presence with and for myself into doubt? "Clearly, it is not certain things that in themselves (by their nature, their universality, their intelligibility) resist doubt, but rather that which characterizes the actuality of the meditating subject (the place of his meditation, the gesture he is in the process of making, the sensations that strike him)."[56] It is the immediacy of the subject which cannot be doubted—the actuality, the precise instant in its singularity, that resists the demands of reason. Descartes's actual "being-in-the-world," his existence, his presence to the world and to himself, is the ground of his reason, despite what prudence tells him. "If he really doubted all this system of actuality, would he still be rational? Would he not precisely be renouncing all these guarantees of rational meditation which he gave himself in choosing . . . the moment of the undertaking (quite late in life, but not too late: the moment that must not be allowed to slip past has come), its conditions (peace and quiet, with no cares to form distractions), its place (a peaceful retreat)."[57] This actuality is the decisive moment, it is when and where doubt must take place, and it is just this moment and the whole "system" which defines it, which makes it what it is, that cannot be placed in doubt. However, doubt can only continue if the subject's mode of presence to itself, its mode of appearing within this "system of actuality," can be somehow disentangled from the doubting subject itself. It is the very systematicity of the "system of actuality" that is the source of error, uncertainty, and confusion. It is this system that must be reconfigured in order to provide a new foundation for certain knowledge. But this system is not simply a matter of method, a set of opinions or ideas. It is the *dispositif* that structures Descartes in his very being as a knowing subject and structures a field of objects to be known. This system constitutes his relation to himself, his world, and others. The doubt must allow the subject to disclose itself in a new way, as something whose very mode of self-disclosure is distinct from the "system" of its "actual" being-in-the-world; or rather, the subject's very mode of being-in-the-world—the system that structures the subject as a mode of being-in-the-world—must be altered.[58]

The device of the dream-hypothesis produces this doubt because of its accessibility as a possible and perhaps actual condition of the subject. The dream is present in the meditation not simply as a proposition: it is a virtual state of the meditating subject. The example of the dream "modifies the subject."[59] "The meditating subject is put to sleep by way of artifice . . . and on this basis the meditation will be able to develop anew."[60] The very act of meditating on the nature of dreaming and its likeness to being awake causes Descartes, causes the meditating subject, to become "quite dizzy, and this dizziness nearly convinces . . . [him] . . . that . . . [he is] . . . asleep."[61] The obstacle to doubt, one's existential grounding in the immediate present, is overcome by the power of the dream.

Not only does the meditating subject's mode of being change, but the possibility of meditating remains. To assume that one is, or might be, mad would be to give up one's right to speak the truth.[62] However, if one is dreaming, one is not disqualified as a subject with the right to speak, and the capability of speaking, the truth. Just the opposite, in fact. Given this newly produced state, new propositions and new developments become possible. For example, only on the basis of the radical doubt of the senses and even of mathematics will the experience of evidence, of certainty, of clarity and distinctness, the nature of the cogito, and so on become clear to Descartes. The reason it is possible for the dream to succeed in displacing the subject while leaving open the possibility for the practice of meditation and an experience of the truth becomes clear when we see the difference between the function of dreams and that of madness. To see this difference we must turn to what Foucault writes concerning another one of the "ascetic" moments of the *Meditations*. Foucault writes that the function of the "great deceiver" is exactly the same as that of the dream: "It could even be said that he [the evil genius] is the contrary of madness: since in madness *I believe* that an illusory purple covers my nudity and my poverty, while the hypothesis of the evil genius permits *me not to believe* that my body and hands exist."[63] The important distinction is that madness binds one to a concrete representation which is taken as a reality, but which in fact is not real. Descartes's hypothesis does just the opposite in releasing him from assent to any and all representations. As Foucault puts it, Descartes's underlying resolution is to say, "I shall take great care not to receive any falsity into my belief," while "the madman receives all falsities."[64] In other words, the madman accepts a false image as real, his representations transport him out of his surrounding world and into an imaginary one. The meditating subject, however, denies the reality of all images. It is clear that this is also a fundamental difference between the dream hypothesis and that of the madman—dreams cause a current and actual reality to fall into doubt, while the madman is certain of a "reality" which does not exist. Madness/unreason is a release from will toward image, while reason, on the other hand, is a release from image toward will. In other words, madness disengages the will of the subject, thus subjecting the individual to the flow of representations. Reason, on the other hand, disengages the individual from the flow of representations and constitutes her as a subject who wills the truth. The movement in the first direction is that of confinement on an ontological level; one releases oneself from one's own being as a subject, becoming, in effect, an object of the representations given to one. On the other hand, the movement away from the image will be that of freedom and of the true experience of subjectivity, the freedom of truth. Therefore, on a purely abstract and merely discursive level one can say, "I might be mad, therefore I should doubt that what I see and feel is really there." However, one cannot really think that thought because it is a contradiction: to be mad is to lack the will to separate oneself from the illusionary world one inhabits in order to doubt it. To assume that one is mad and therefore should doubt is to assume that one is not mad, it is to act as if one is not mad, but rather as if one is in control of one's own thoughts. To assume that one is dreaming, on the other hand, is not contradictory in this way—one is able to maintain control of one's thoughts, and one's will, to withhold assent—to determine oneself rather than to be determined by the power of the images before one. In other words, one cannot *be* mad and *be* meditating.

The *Meditations* lead to a particular mode of being, that of certainty: "Through what is said in meditation, the subject passes from darkness to light, from impurity to purity, from the constraint of passions to detachment, from uncertainty and disordered movements to the serenity of wisdom, and so on."[65] And they do so by altering the subject's mode of being— its presence to itself and to its world. Through this exercise the subject is displaced with respect to its own actuality. Through the practice of meditation the subject will "become accustomed to withdrawing" itself from its existential and perceptual grounding in the environing world.[66] "In short, meditation implies a mobile subject modifiable through the effect of the discursive events that take place."[67] The meditation does not produce knowledge so much as a new mode of being of the subject itself. The subject discloses the world and itself in an utterly new light.

In the *Meditations*, the subject begins in a state of uncertainty because it is bound to and dependent on its senses. It is too tightly woven to the perceptible world, and especially to the "vivid and the near," to a whole "system of actuality." The First Meditation is meant to disengage the subject from the perceptual world. The first major obstacle in the path of the meditation is the difficulty of really doubting one's immediate presence to the world, and thus "the impossibility of constituting oneself as a universally doubting subject."[68] According to the premises established by Descartes, logically it is enough that the senses have fooled him in the past to consider them untrustworthy. But in effect, he cannot bring himself to give them up so easily. Resistance to doubt does not take place at the level of the demonstrative order of the meditation—at this level, doubt is not a problem. But to actually constitute oneself as doubting, as doubting the senses themselves, is difficult because of their "existential density," so to speak. Meditating on the dream-state and its likeness to wakefulness is an exercise the subject performs and through which the state of the subject is altered. Meditating on madness has no such effect. Therefore, in order to understand why Descartes considers these questions about madmen and dreaming, it is necessary to take into account the ascetic character of the *Meditations*. They must be read, at least in part, as an exercise of thought through which the subject displaces itself, transforming its mode of being, that is, its mode of disclosing itself and its world.

Descartes and the Ascetic Tradition of Philosophy

So far we have seen *how* Descartes arrives at a certain experience of the subject and its relation to the truth; that is, how he arrives at a certain experience of thought. He does so through a work on himself, through the *practice* of meditation, an *askēsis* by which he purifies his mind, allowing it to experience certainty, evidence, and the true nature of itself. Foucault suggests that the ascetic aspect of the *Meditations* is obscured by the very tradition that it inaugurates. This is because Descartes's ascetic work is fundamentally different in its consequences from previous ascetics of thought. In an interview conducted by Hubert Dreyfus and Paul Rabinow in 1983, Foucault, echoing his 1972 essay, reminds us of how we are supposed to read Descartes's *Meditations:* "We must not forget that Descartes wrote 'meditations'—and meditations are a practice of the self." In this interview, however, Foucault links the *Meditations* not to the struggle over madness and reason, but to another history altogether:

> The extraordinary thing in Descartes' texts is that he succeeded in substituting a subject as founder of practices of knowledge, for a subject constituted through practices of the self . . . In Western culture up to the sixteenth century, asceticism and access to the truth are always more or less obscurely linked. Descartes, I think, broke with this when he said "To accede to truth, it suffices that I be any subject which can see what is evident." Evidence is substituted for *ascesis* at the point where the relationship to the self intersects the relationship to others [*parrhēsia,* care, government] and the world [knowledge, truth] . . . After Descartes we have a non-ascetic subject of knowledge. This change makes possible the institutionalization of modern science.[69]

As we have already seen, in his lectures at the Collège de France from 1982 to 1984, Foucault shows that Western culture has developed two different forms of the relation between the subject and the truth: "spirituality" and "knowledge."[70] Ancient philosophy was fundamentally a mode of spirituality. According to Foucault, a historical break allowed the "knowledge" model to displace spirituality as the structure of philosophical truth. The historical event of this displacement is what Foucault in 1982 names the "Cartesian moment."[71] In the *Meditations* we experience the coming to pass of this event. In other words, the *Meditations* are part of that event by which the subject is detached from spiritual practice as the ground of its access to the truth. As result of this event, access to the truth no longer requires ascetic self-transformation; rather, it requires employing the proper method of reasoning. According to this new way of thinking, this new mode of *perceiving* oneself as a thinking being and of *perceiving* the world as a something to be known, self-transformation no longer *appears* to be necessary in order for one to have access to the truth. A new system of actuality is set up.

Descartes's *Meditations* form, in a sense, one of the hinges between these two experiences of the subject and the truth. As such, the *Meditations* lie simultaneously within and outside of this ascetic tradition of subjectivity and truth. They are within it insofar as they are a "practice of the self," an ascetic transformation of oneself through which one will become a subject capable of knowing the truth. They are outside of this tradition because the kind of subject revealed through meditation no longer requires *askēsis.* The cogito is a mode of subjectivity that does not appear to be linked to any particular way of living. Truth for the cogito is grounded in "evidence," not in an *ēthos* produced through *askēsis;* one arrives at knowledge by following the proper method of thought, not by living the proper kind of life. Finally, the truth that the cogito discovers does not take the form of salvation, of fulfillment. Instead of truth, what one acquires is knowledge, an accumulation of true statements about reality. Knowing does not lead to the saving experience of truth/being; rather, it is the infinite accumulation of knowledge about things/beings. This way of being, which we take for granted and to which we belong, this way of being which to us is rational and perhaps self-evident, was for Descartes a project and one which demanded a mighty effort. And what seems so *natural* to us is in fact a distinct style, a historical system, of thinking and being, a particular subjectivization or *ēthos*. In other words, our experience of the cogito/subject and the modern form of the relationship between the subject and the truth which dissociates the cogito from any particular mode of living, is in fact grounded in a particular mode of thinking and of living.[72] It is this legacy of the *Meditations,* and more generally of the "Cartesian moment," that obscures the ascetic dimension of the project.[73]

Conclusion

Returning to Foucault's 1972 text on Descartes's *Meditations,* and reading it within the framework of care of the self, allows us to see clearly that the cogito is not a substance but a technology of the self. The *Meditations* are a set of spiritual exercises in the sense that they aim to modify the being of the subject in order to give that subject access to the truth. This work on the self is what freed Descartes from a certain "system of actuality" which prevented him from having access to the truth.[74] But if we read the *Meditations* as spiritual exercises, shouldn't they, in fact, produce some kind of modification in our own way of being subjects, in our way of disclosing the world and gaining access to the truth? I would suggest that this is precisely the point at which Foucault wants us to arrive. Such an experience of the *Meditations* is meant to destabilize our position as subjects, as masters and possessors of a text which we submit to our controlled activity of reading. From our modern, Cartesian subject-position, the text is simply another object, an inert entity in the external world from which our mind extracts meanings through a kind of surgical operation. The text in this sense is a kind of corpse: an extended body which has an order and a structure, an articulation that reason actively surveys. In other words, our position, our mode of disclosing the text, is that of the cogito—it is a technology which lays out the body of the text and operates on it, but which is not implicated in the text itself. To take the text as an object, inert and lifeless, a container of concepts hidden within the words written on the page, concepts which the activity of a subject—a reader— must render visible though his operation of logical incision, is to presuppose a certain Cartesian relationship between a subject and an object. However, to take up this text as a spiritual exercise, to engage it as a set of games of thought, brings about a transformation. The text as a game of thought repositions us, displaces its reader. To read Descartes's text as an *askēsis* is to allow the agency of the text to function. The text, independent of the author's various possible intentions, desires, or strategies, demands a certain kind of reader to subject to its operation. To allow the text to reveal itself in this way is to allow it to operate, to subject the reader to a certain activity. It is to allow the text to do its work. This work is that of thinking—through the activity of reading the subject is "displaced by the thoughts that it thinks."

The *Meditations* are structured to transpose the subject who engages in them into the position of the cogito. The reader would have entered into them in order to take on the position of the cogito—she would not have started from that position. This is what the title, *Meditations,* demands of the reader: a subject who finds in the text a series of exercises for realizing a new way of disclosing and being-in-the-world. However, it is this position from which we enter into them. We arrive at the *Meditations* as Cartesian subjects—we see the text as an object to be controlled. And yet, precisely because they are a set of techniques that move the reader from a precogito subject-position into the position of the cogito, the *Meditations* contain within them that starting point. Therefore, approaching the *Meditations* as spiritual exercises produces the opposite effect in a modern, Cartesian reader as it would have produced in a premodern reader. Recovering the ascetic dimension of the *Meditations* serves therefore to destabilize the cogito—without destroying it—by giving it back its foundation: the practices of the self which bring it into being.

The Prince and the Pastor: Figures of Power, Care, and *Parrhēsia*

> The passage from spiritual exercise to intellectual method is very clearly evident in Descartes. And I think that one cannot comprehend the meticulousness with which he defines his intellectual method if one does not have a clear idea of what his target is negatively, precisely these methods of spiritual exercise that were being practiced at the same time in Christianity, and which derived from the spiritual exercises of antiquity, particularly Stoicism.[1]

It is clear that for both the early and the late Foucault, Descartes's *Meditations* are at least in part a spiritual practice, a form of *askēsis*. This links them to an ancient tradition, but they are at the same time a break with this tradition. Now we must examine the problematization that led Descartes to break with this tradition. In order to do this we must see how Foucault inserts the *Meditations* into a broader historical context. This means grasping, in its basic structure, the "system of actuality," in other words, the *dispositif*, which both calls for doubt and yet resists doubt in the *Meditations*.[2] In this chapter I will sketch the system of actuality or the *dispositif* from which Descartes's *Meditations* detach themselves and free themselves, and in the following chapter I will turn to the system/*dispositif* that arises through the Cartesian moment.

The Art of Government as Resistance to Political Power

As Foucault has shown, the practice of philosophy in the ancient world did not stop with the transformation of one's *own* way of being.[3] The philosopher also had the duty of taking up the role of guide to others. The philosopher was the one who, because of the very life he lived, was capable of taking care of others. Philosophy realized itself in a relationship to others constituted as a practice of care. The philosopher practiced a way of life and developed an *ēthos* which gave him access to the truth. This came with the duty of speaking the truth to others and in so doing getting them to change their lives and save themselves as well. This way of being and speaking was the philosophical, ethical form of *parrhēsia*. It represented the philosophical appropriation of a political activity, the democratic act par excellence, of speaking before the assembly in order to govern the city. In part 1 we saw, through Foucault's genealogy, how care of the self and ethical *parrhēsia* migrated from the Greeks to the Hellenistic and Roman thinkers and finally to the earliest Christians. These first Christians appropriated practices of care and ethical veridiction which had been developed by the Epicureans, Cynics, and Stoics, and set them to work within new contexts.[4] Now we must continue this genealogy in order to establish the dramatic scene in which the "Cartesian moment" unfolds.

This *parrhēsiastic* dimension of philosophy, according to Foucault, was largely taken over by the church and eventually invested in the figure of the pastor. The activity of speaking the truth to others in order to take care of and save them was transferred to the Christian practice of spiritual direction and confession. As early as 1975, Foucault showed that what he took to be significant and novel about the church was the peculiar modality of power it developed and deployed. From the mid-1970s to the early 1980s, Foucault analyzed what he called "pastoral power." In this work, he revealed the manner by which the church establishes and institutes certain individuals in a particular position of authority. These individuals "can, by their religious quality, serve others not as princes, magistrates, prophets, fortune-tellers, benefactors, educationalists, and so on, but as pastors."[5] The pastor, then, is the legacy of the ancient spiritual master, the master of *epimēleia heauton,* the one who is able to care for the care which the others take of themselves. The institution of the pastor is in fact an institutionalization of a precise modality of power—a modality of *governing* individual souls. It is a form of power grounded upon the ascetic experience of subjectivity and truth, and it watches over the lives and the souls of individuals. The pastor's access to the truth and his capacity and obligation to take care of others is grounded upon his way of life and the condition of his soul—that is, upon who he is. It is his very being as a subject—a mode of being inseparable from a detailed care of the self and a particular style of existence—which allows the pastor to take care of others, to serve them as shepherd. His hold on the conduct of individuals is his ability to know and to say the truth about who they are and to use that truth in order to save them. The figure of the pastor lives at that intersection of care of the self and *government* of others, the intersection that was a constant concern for ancient philosophy.

Foucault explains that political reason did not develop or reflect on a properly political art of governing until the sixteenth century.[6] Rather, the rationality of sovereignty remained completely external to the question of government which was the domain of the pastor. While Aquinas's theory of kingship is an exception to this mutual exclusivity of sovereignty and government in the Middle Ages, it does not develop a specifically political art of governing. Aquinas assimilates political reason into a continuum of different relations of pastoral power that are analogous to each other, rather than isolating a specific, irreducible art of political government. For Aquinas, the king's relation to his subjects is analogous to God's relation to the universe and the father's relation to the family.[7] In general, therefore, prior to the sixteenth century government was not thought of as a political art or institution. It meant, broadly, "conducting," leading, or guiding and it could refer to a variety of spheres in which someone had to take care of something by watching over it and guiding it: for example, the father governs the household, his children, his wife; the shepherd governs, guides, conducts the flock; and finally, with the Christians, the pastor, the shepherd of souls, governs, cares for, guides the faithful and in so doing leads them to salvation. This notion of "shepherding" had nothing to do with how political power was wielded or how it conceived of its own activity, purpose, or rationality. Despite the fact that ancient texts in various traditions (Hebrew, Egyptian, and Greek, for example) employ the metaphor of the shepherd to identify the prince, Foucault shows that the articulation and application of political rationality were not, in a precise sense, modes of government.[8] Therefore, two separate regimes and rationalities of power were deployed in the Western world, a political regime and a pastoral regime, which coexisted in a fragile, uneasy situation.[9] Each of these regimes established an ensemble of technologies for forming the subject who exercised power—whether that subject was the prince or the pastor. What's more, both of these forms of power maintained "tactical" relationships to an epistemic formation which was displaced during the sixteenth and seventeenth centuries by the rise of the classical episteme. During this period, the tension between political power and pastoral power erupted, resulting in a massive diffusion of the problem of governmentality throughout society—it is this struggle over governmentality that Foucault takes to be the meaning of the Reformation and Counter-Reformation.[10] The following analysis will show how Foucault conceived these two regimes of power, the nature of their links to a determinate epistemic form, and the kinds of subjects they required. The goal of such an analysis is to grasp the system of actuality from which Descartes struggled to exit even as it self-destructed, and to see the formation of a new system in which the Cartesian cogito will eventually come to play a privileged role.

First, I must provide a very general and schematic outline of a few characteristics that seemed to define the rationality of political power in the era just before the rise of the classical age; that is, in the late Middle Ages and Renaissance up until the sixteenth and seventeenth centuries. As we shall see, for Foucault it is pastoral power, and the techniques of government and of the self developed by it, that came to occupy such a decisive place in our society. However, it was only able to do so through a conflict with the regime of political power, and out of this conflict emerged a new form of governmentality. If political power prior to this event was not a form of government, then what precisely was it? In other words, what form did the rationality of power take, what made power effective and reasonable rather than arbitrary and foolish? This is neither a question of actual political practices, nor is it a matter of pure theoretical or speculative reason. Rather, it is a question of the way ruling was conceived, the way its purpose, tactics, legitimacy, and forms were articulated and deployed. Resolving this will help us appreciate just what Foucault had in mind when he isolated the notion of governmentality as a unique mode of power. The model of, or figure of, political power that defines the late Middle Ages is that of sovereignty and its central personage, the king or prince. Foucault's analysis, to put it simply (and really, too simply), elucidates the structure of this form of political reason by grasping it from three different angles. First of all, political sovereignty establishes a determinate relationship between the prince and the subject. Second, it requires an ensemble of technologies of the self through which the prince, as a mode of subjectivity capable of ruling, comes into view. And third, political rationality solidifies itself on the basis of a certain interpretation of the world that makes the role, purpose, and practice of the prince comprehensible and legitimate. That is, political power has a tactical link to an epistemic formation.

First, what is the relationship between the prince and his subjects in political power as it was conceived and exercised until the sixteenth and seventeenth centuries? In a word, this relationship was mediated by the law—political sovereignty is primarily juridical.[11] Political power was not conceived of in terms of *conducting* or guiding—it was a matter of *lawgiving*. The prince ruled the land—his territory—and those who lived on it by making and establishing law and justice and by using his forces to maintain law and justice.[12] The art of the prince, the virtue of the prince, had to do with his ability to establish and maintain justice and peace—that is, lawfulness. The ruler was not in a "pastoral" relation with his subjects. The relationship between the prince and the subject was based on an abstract juridical notion of the sovereign and of the juridical subject; the prince makes and keeps the laws, the subject abides by the laws or is punished. In other words, the individual who is submitted to the political power of the prince is anonymous.[13] And the real penetration of power into the life, thoughts, and desires of individuals was minute or nonexistent. Rather, the prince was concerned with the "common good."

Second, what is the relationship the prince must take to himself? In other words, what are the practices of the self through which the subject who rules fashions his identity? The prince, the subject who must exercise political authority, must acquire the *virtue* and the *wisdom* to be able to rule effectively. He must know the end to be attained and the means to attain that end. We saw in part 1 that Socratic-Platonic *parrhēsia* was an attempt to care for the care that the potential ruler takes of himself. He must acquire virtue, wisdom, and the knowledge of justice, he must be able to perceive the good, in order to rule the city and choose what is best for the city, thus unifying the many in the pursuit of the good. The art of the ruler is to know and to apply the universal good that will safeguard the city. In order to carry out this function, the prince must himself become just. That is, he must become philosophical; he must acquire the virtue to see the whole, and he must know how to apply the law in his city. We can contrast this practice of the self with the Machiavellian practice. The art of the prince, according to Machiavelli, requires being able to know and do what will preserve his own power over his subjects. However, the relationship to the self is still conceived of in terms of virtue; the prince must form the proper character, the proper mode of subjectivity to rule. For Machiavelli, just as for the Platonic tradition, the prince's capacity to rule is grounded in his identity, his virtue. It is the very being of the prince which grounds his political power, and his being is cultivated through the practices of the self which result in virtue. Machiavelli, with a different end in sight, takes on the same relationship to the prince that Plato does in his ill-fated adventure in Syracuse: they both serve as instructors in virtue.

Finally, what link does the political regime establish to knowledge, to an epistemic formation? Here Foucault's reference to the Christian tradition, as it appears in the privileged example of Aquinas, provides the clearest example: "The King's government of his kingdom must imitate God's government of nature or again, the soul's government of the body. The king must found cities just as God created the world, just as the soul gives form to the body."[14] Politics is the art whereby humans create a political state which mirrors God's creation of the world as ruled by his will. Aquinas grasps political ruling in a "cosmological-theological continuum" in which the art and activity of the king are understood through a series of analogies and resemblances.[15] The intelligibility of the world as such is that it is created and governed by God. The relation God takes to this world is pastoral: "The world is submitted to an economy of salvation, which is to say that it was made so that man should achieve his salvation."[16] In order to govern this world toward its proper end, God intervenes in it: "He obligated entities to manifest his will by signs, wonders, marvels, monstrosities which were menaces of punishment, promises of salvation, marks of election."[17] The world, then, is itself intelligible in terms of government and as such it is constituted as a system of signs to be interpreted in order to properly achieve salvation. "The world is a book, an open book in which one could discover the truth, or rather, in which the truth, the truths taught themselves, and they taught themselves essentially in the form of a reciprocal reference of one to the other, that is to say by resemblance and analogy."[18] The rationalization of political power is structured by the episteme of the Renaissance: the epistemic structure of analogies, resemblances, and signs that Foucault excavated in the first chapter of *The Order of Things*.[19] The prince in his activity of lawmaking resembles God, and it is this resemblance which legitimates his rule. The virtue of the prince will be to form human laws, which are a reflection in the world made by men of the natural and eternal laws in the universe made by God. In other words, the practices of the self, which fashion the subjectivity of the prince, fashion him in the likeness of God. The practices of the self will form in the prince a virtuous character, which means they will give him access to the truth he needs to rule properly.

In sum, ruling in the late Middle Ages and Renaissance has to do, first, with a juridical model, with the centrality of justice and the law—whether that means establishing the common good, that which is universal, that which preserves the city or which sets the conditions for salvation, or whether that means making laws which will control the subjects and preserve the power of the prince. Second, the prince is defined in terms of his identity, his way of being—that is, his virtue. Therefore, the prince has to form a certain character because his rule is grounded on his virtue. Finally, the political regime is linked to an epistemic form that structures and legitimates it. In the Platonic and Christian traditions, virtue defines the being of the ruler and makes him a mirror of the good or of God, and therefore links him to the truth that he needs to form good laws. Wisdom or prudence means recognizing "transcendental rules, a cosmological order, or a philosophical-moral ideal."[20] The prince will have to acquire a certain kind of *ēthos* which conforms to a series of analogies: god-king, father-family, head-body. His formation must give him the *ēthos*, the wisdom to establish a human law and justice that resemble the divine law and justice that governs the universe.

The rationality of *government*—the "art of governing souls"—developed by the church is something altogether different from political reason prior to the sixteenth and seventeenth centuries.[21] This pastoral art of government was developed not as an art of political power, but rather in that extrapolitical space defined by Socrates and Plato and developed throughout the Hellenistic and Roman periods. The art of government was taken up and formed by Christian thinkers who modified and developed Greek and Roman relations of spiritual direction into a rich and complex technique for the "government of souls," which is what Foucault calls *pastoral power*. It is through their appropriation of techniques, relations, and types of subjectivity from the ancient tradition of *epimēleia* that they will begin to forge a new experience of subjectivity linked to new ends and technologies of the self.

First of all, pastoral power is "a form of power whose ultimate aim is to assure individual salvation in the next world."[22] That is, an individual submits to the authority of the pastor in order to save himself, in order to be led to his own salvation, a salvation which lies not in this world but in the next. Out of concern for one's soul, out of and as the very form of care for oneself, one allows oneself to be guided by the pastor. Second, "pastoral power is not merely a form of power which commands; it must also be prepared to sacrifice itself for the life and salvation of the flock. Therefore, it is different from royal power, which demands a sacrifice from its subjects to save the throne."[23] The pastor's raison d'être is the salvation of the others—the pastor therefore does not wield power in order to maintain his own authority, or to accumulate goods for himself. Rather, the pastor's only purpose is the salvation of those for whom he is responsible. In other words, care, not the law, mediates the relationship between the pastor and each individual soul in his flock. Furthermore, the *telos* is neither perfection of the city, nor making laws that set the conditions for individual salvation, nor finally preserving one's power. It is the salvation of the individual soul of each member of the flock.

The relation of the pastor to each individual is, therefore, essential to this form of power. The pastorate is an individualizing power.[24] Sovereign power, the prince, is interested in the individual only as the abstract subject of the law; apart from that, the sovereign has no interest in, or knowledge of, the individual's thoughts, feelings, or way of life. The individual comes to the attention of the sovereign primarily through violation of the law. This is because the real concern of the sovereign is to maintain his own power and justice, the law, the common good. Pastoral power, however, is essentially concerned about each individual under its supervision and is concerned about that individual all of the time. Therefore, "this form of power cannot be exercised without knowing the inside of people's minds, without exploring their souls, without making them reveal their innermost secrets. It implies a knowledge of the conscience and an ability to direct it."[25] Pastoral power does not simply attend to the salvation of individual souls. It does so through the accumulation of a detailed knowledge of each individual. To this end it develops and puts to use a powerful technology, the confession, which requires the individual to express all of his thoughts, feelings, and deeds to the pastor who, in turn, has the power to interpret this data, to use it in order to instruct the individual and to guide him to his salvation. Pastoral care, or government, extends over the life as a whole of the individual—in order to govern the soul to its own salvation, the pastor must take into account the life of the individual. In this sense, life itself—both interior life as well as the life of the body—is the *object* of pastoral power, even if the salvation of souls is the *objective*. The authority of the pastor, the government of souls, the practice of an individualizing knowledge, are legitimated by the teleology of salvation in the next world. We can say that as opposed to political reason which uses the law to control abstract juridical subjects, the pastor uses precise knowledge of concrete individuals' lives, thoughts, and desires in order to help them attain personal salvation.

Pastoral power, like its Greek, Hellenistic, and Roman predecessors, involves a personal relationship between the pastor and the individual. The pastor is able to save the individual based on the knowledge he develops about that individual: about what the individual thinks and feels, says and does, desires and needs, about how the individual lives and should live. What gives the pastor access to the truth that will save the individual is his very being: who he is, the life he lives, the virtues he has, the purity of his intentions, his ordination, and the interpretive technique he utilizes. The pastor is a particular kind of subjectivity. It is his identity, his mode of life, which gives the pastor the right to speak truth as power. To borrow Foucault's later terminology, the pastor is a particular modality of veridiction. In other words, the pastor is a particular way of constituting a subject who has access to the truth, who has a certain experience of language, and who speaks to and about a particular domain of truth. The pastor is a modulation of *parrhēsia* because he speaks ethical truth, discloses *ēthos*—yet *parrhēsia* here is grounded upon purity rather than courage. The pastoral practice of ethical truth arises not as a simple appropriation of *parrhēsia*. Rather, as Foucault suggested in his sketch of early Christian *askēsis*, pastoral government was a reaction against *parrhēsia* in the form of Cynicism and mysticism. The institution of the pastorate is a way of controlling the open confrontation of *parrhēsia*. It does not control it by suppressing it, but rather by taking it over and transforming it. On the one hand, it seems to me that in Foucault's genealogy the pastor is an unlikely heir to the Socratic practice of ethical *parrhēsia*. On the other, it is this modality of subjectivity that the Cartesian cogito displaces, reclaiming for philosophy, construed on the model of mathematical science, the right to tell others the truth and to govern their lives, their thoughts/psyches, and their very bodies.

In what follows, I shall provide a sketch of the development of this art of governing souls, as Foucault understands it. I will draw on a lecture Foucault gave during his 1975 Collège course to show the formation of the pastor as a particular modality of veridiction. This lecture offers a brief genealogy of the technology of confession. In it Foucault shows how the practice takes shape and how it gives rise to the particular subjectivity of the pastor as well as to that of the confessing subject. Finally in this lecture, and in those that follow it, Foucault shows how a particular domain of knowledge is articulated as a corollary to this technology: the flesh. This genealogy traces the way individual living beings, the ordinary inhabitants of the land, who, as individuals, had long remained below the threshold of political knowledge, were formed into objects of knowledge and government, highly visible objects with discreet, distinct, unique, knowable qualities. The individual became apparent as someone to be attended to in every aspect of her life, mind, and body. Individuals were led to take care of themselves through vigilant self-attention and confession; that is, they had to express a self. Furthermore, in the confession the individual was led to acknowledge the truth about herself, a truth which can only be discerned, and revealed to her, by the pastor. Finally, one cares for one's self by transforming one's soul and one's life through practices of purification, penance. In this way the individual satisfies that need to be led to her own salvation. The individual, under the gaze of the pastor, becomes available as a spiritual being whose salvation depends upon the constant care she takes of herself because she inhabits a dangerous body and world.

But Foucault's genealogy reveals at the same time the *fragility* of this relationship of power. It shows that pastoral power was never a fixed, stable, and completed structure but rather a movement, an effort to establish such a static system: "If the pastorate was not instituted as an effective, practical government of men during the Middle Ages, it has been a permanent concern and a stake in constant struggles. There was across the entire period of the Middle Ages a yearning to arrange pastoral relations among men."[26] Pastoral power, for a long time, remained an activity that very few people actually participated in.[27] There were a number of reasons for this. For example, it was limited by the fact that "the pastorate of souls is an especially urban experience, difficult to reconcile with the poor and extensive rural economy at the beginning of the Middle Ages . . . [and] the pastorate is a complicated technique that demands a certain level of culture, not only on the part of the pastor but also among his flock."[28]

Furthermore, this fundamentally sophisticated activity was also a fundamentally controversial one, since it represented the attempt to govern individuals in the way they think, desire, and live. Therefore, it was *agonistic* by nature. First of all, pastoral power remained exterior to, and in tension with, political power—operating according to a different rationality of power and care. Second, the attempt to institute "pastoral relations among men" generated internal forms of resistance, struggles over what form this power should take, who should exercise it, what limits ought to be set on it. The question is then, How did this mode of subjectivity emerge from the exclusive world in which it was born? In order for government to spread into society on a large scale, the social world itself had to be transformed and the technology and rationality of government had to be modified. For Foucault it was precisely its agonistic energy that propelled pastoral power to transform itself, to migrate and to take on new forms and roles within society.

The art of government and theories about governing began to escape the pastorate and enter into society at large in the sixteenth century. This is reflected in the whole series of questions around the notion of governing which were being raised at that time:

> One has, for example, the question of the government of oneself, that ritualization of the problem of personal conduct characteristic of the sixteenth century Stoic revival. There is the problem too of the government of souls and lives, the entire theme of Catholic and Protestant pastoral doctrine. There is government of children and the great problematic of pedagogy that emerges and develops during the sixteenth century. And, perhaps, only as the last of these questions to be taken up, there is the government of the state by the prince.[29]

The problem of the art of government began to be disseminated throughout society. For Foucault this is a reflection of the agonism through which the pastorate deployed itself. Foucault claims in his 1978 course that Christianity and its particular practices of power and care arise as "counterconducts."[30] This means that they are posed as modes of being-with-others and of being-with-oneself which run counter to established—*normal*—forms of conduct, values, and modes of life in a society. There is an inherent tension between Christian practices of the self and social (economic) and political (juridical) practices. Christian spirituality struggles against social and political definitions of ethical subjectivity in order to establish a practice of life that serves the spiritual care of the soul. Christian practices are, therefore, in many cases either explicitly or implicitly critical of society. They involve different practices of living and different techniques of self-knowledge and self-transformation. This is another way that they show themselves to be the descendants of philosophical *parrhēsia:* they take part in the struggle to live the true life over and against the ordinary and false life.

The point is that the pastorate was a *dispositif* whose deployment was always interrupted, resisted, rethought, and redeployed in new ways. As a result, it was composed of fragments of practices and plans. The constant problematization of governmentality made possible a translation of spiritual techniques of governing *souls* into political techniques of governing a *population.*[31] The great conflicts that arose in the sixteenth and seventeenth centuries around the problem of the government of life do not lead to a rejection of government, but to alternative models of governing. The "yearning to arrange pastoral relations" remains: the thought of the individual as an object of government, as needing government in the most intimate details of her existence, defines our own subjectivity. The individual and the pastor, the two terms of the pastoral relationship of power and knowledge, live on in our modern forms of care/government: analyst-analysand, doctor-patient, teacher-student, counselor-patient, and so on.[32] This form continues to determine our thought, particularly insofar as it shapes the relation we maintain to ourselves as hidden texts to be interpreted, as hermeneutic subjects.[33] That is to say, the struggle to critique and to resist the deployment of the pastorate did not eliminate the pastoral relationship—far from it: "We have since become a singularly confessing society. The confession has spread its effects far and wide . . . Western man has become a confessing animal."[34] It is within this series of struggles over the question of government—of conduct and care—and over the question of the practices of subjectivity that Descartes inscribes his voice.

In order to see how these struggles contributed to the development of pastoral theories, I will look at Foucault's genealogy of the pastoral technique of confession, a pivotal technique in the agonistic history of pastoral power. This genealogy will focus primarily on the way that the church attempted to develop and deploy this technology, as a central component of its pastoral function, in response to the challenges from within the spiritual community. The care for the conduct of the mind and the body is what is at stake in the confession. The pastor/confessor is the subject who is the master of care of the self and of the true government of souls. Therefore, insofar as Descartes posits a new sovereign subject who has the "right to truth" as care and as ethical *parrhēsia,* it is the pastor, as a mode of subjectivity, whom he displaces.

The Hermeneutics of the Self: Fragment
of a Genealogy of the Confession

The earliest forms of penance in the Christian West were not connected to "obligatory confession."[35] Penance was a condition which one entered with the approval of the bishop. One could take on the status of a penitent only once, and it involved a total and difficult transformation of one's life in order to absolve the guilt of one's sin or sins. Thus, penance in this form was reserved for very serious offenses and required self-mortification and exclusion from many aspects of the social and religious life of the community.[36] The confession of sin does not play an important role in this ritual. Foucault points out that what was required was nothing more than telling the bishop "in general, the reasons and justifications" for one's request to become penitent.[37] Sins were cleansed by ritual mortification, by taking on and fulfilling the function of penance, and finally through being reintroduced into the religious community. This form of penance "is not nominal but dramatic."[38] It requires a public display in which one's truth as a sinner is made manifest before the community. This dramatic practice is closer to Cynic practices of the self than those of the Stoic: "What was private for the Stoics was public for the Christians."[39] This form of penance, like the Cynic practices of *parrhēsia* and the *bios philosophicos*, attempted to establish the public space as the theater of individual conversion and salvation. Of course, in the monasteries and in the practice of asceticism, Christianity was already engaged in a very different appropriation of practices of care, which more closely modeled on the techniques practiced by the Stoics and the Epicureans.[40]

In the sixth century a new form of penance comes to exist alongside the old one. This new practice is based on an "essentially secular, judicial, and penal model."[41] In this new model one would confess a sin and the priest would decide upon an act of penance called a "satisfaction." In other words, one begins to practice a system of "tariffs": one begins to develop knowledge of the different sins and the "satisfactions" which correspond to them.[42] The confession plays a necessary role here, though a secondary and rudimentary one. Before, penance was a status that one entered once and for all; it took on a ritualized form that was independent of the particular sin or sins which it absolved. It was the drama of absolution that took priority, not the narrative of individual fault. However, in the new practice of penance there is a strict relationship between the sin and the penance, and therefore an act of confession is necessary. Furthermore, one confessed and did penance for each individual sin and in the way specific to that sin:

In effect, starting from the moment where it is necessary, after each sin, after each grave sin in any case, to give a certain satisfaction, and starting from the moment where the tariff of this satisfaction is indicated, prescribed, and imposed upon you by the priest, the enunciation of the sin, after each sin, becomes indispensable. What's more, so that the priest can apply the right penitence, the right satisfaction, so that he can properly distinguish between the sins which are serious and those which are not, it is not only necessary to tell the sin, but it is necessary to recount it, giving the circumstances, explaining how one committed it. It is in this way that, little by little, across this penitence, the origin of which is clearly judicial and secular, this little core, still very limited and without any efficacy other than utility, the core of the confession [l'aveu], begins to take shape.[43]

The confession is necessary because the priest must be able to administer the proper satisfaction in order to heal the patient suffering the effects of sin. The medical metaphor becomes explicit in this era.[44] The confession is a necessary part of penance because the priest, like a doctor, can only cure the penitent if he knows precisely the nature of the sin, the condition of the patient. But it is with this new role of the confession that the practice of penance will transform itself once again. The act of confession itself will be recognized as a kind of satisfaction. This is because the act of confession, the act of recounting to another the details of one's sins, is intrinsically painful. One experiences the pain of humiliation, and this pain is enough to absolve one of guilt.[45] If it is constituted in such a way as to humiliate the individual who confesses, confession itself will be a form of penance. This ritual of penance is, therefore, no longer essentially a juridical practice, nor even a medicinal practice. This is because it is not necessary to link particular sins to particular satisfactions; recounting the sin is the satisfaction.

An important consequence of this transformation of the practice of penance will be that one no longer needs to confess to a priest in order to absolve the sin. The central roles of the church, of the bishop, of the priest in the original forms of penance are bypassed.[46] If absolution comes merely from the act of confession and the pain of humiliation which it provokes, then one does not require the special knowledge of the priest to prescribe the proper satisfaction, nor does one need the approval of the bishop for spiritual reintegration into the community: "To the degree that the mechanism of remission of sins is restricted to the avowal, the power of the priest, and even more so, the power of the bishop, finds itself dissolved."[47] Across the ninth, tenth, and eleventh centuries, the practice of lay confession weakens the pastoral control of the religious life of the individual. Around the practice of confession a struggle for power over the spiritual being of the individual will take place. The pastorate reasserted itself in this struggle by deploying new confessional relations and practices. In the confessional relationship the pastor will appear in a rigorously defined way as a particular modality of veridiction, as the speaker of ethical truth. Likewise, the corresponding object of pastoral care and government, the individual, will come into being as an object of knowledge to be interpreted by the pastor, to be governed by the pastor whose particular mode of being gives him access to truth and the power to save.

Perhaps the first systematic effort toward the articulation and deployment of a specifically pastoral form (or institution) of power, outside of the institution of the monastery, is the appearance in the thirteenth century of the "obligation of regular confession, in a fashion more or less yearly for the layman, and monthly or even weekly for the cleric."[48] Confession is deployed as a mode of power over the flock, a mode of care/government: it is necessary for each individual to confess to a priest in order to attain salvation. The individual, as a being searching for spiritual salvation, must give herself over to the pastor who will care for her. The new obligation to confess to the priest differs from previous forms of penance in important ways. First of all, the practice of confessing one's sins is abstracted from the particularity of the sin itself. Before, one would make a confession of each grave sin: the act of confession was tightly linked to the particular sin. In its new form, confession is meant to be a regular practice. And, with the exception of serious sins which required immediate confession, the sins would in a sense accumulate and be stored—in the conscience, memory, guilt—in order to be confessed and cleansed on a periodic basis.[49] Abstracting the practice of confession from the particularity of the moment allows it to spread across the life of the individual as a whole and in a sense unify it as a spiritual project. Thus what one envisions is not simply a series of actions and events, but rather a "self," a unified project, and later a particular individuality or personality or style which defines the tendencies, temptations, and weaknesses of that individual. The individual is obligated to confess every sin he committed since his previous confession—Foucault calls this the totalization and the exhaustivity of the confession.[50] Confession reaches into every corner of the individual's existence. Exhaustivity is required because the individual is not capable of deciding for herself what constitutes a mortal or a venial sin. Therefore, everything must be recounted to the priest—including all of the details which affect the status of the sin and the satisfaction required to cleanse it.

Other innovations further alter the confessional relationship and constitute the nature of the power deployed in that relationship. In order to ensure that confession covers the totality of the individual's spiritual career, the regular confession will be accompanied by periodic confessions where one recounts the history of one's entire life.[51] The individual must turn herself into a narrative of sin and redemption and must periodically retell her story to the priest. Furthermore, the continuity, totality, and exhaustivity is ensured by the requirement that one always confess to the same priest; thus, in a sense there will be two authors to compose and to confirm the story.[52] Finally, the priest will play a far more active role in the composition of the narrative. No longer will he simply perform the calculus of satisfactions: "The priest himself controls what the faithful say: he is going to push him, he is going to interrogate him, he is going to sharpen the confession [*l'aveu*], by a whole technique of examining the conscience."[53]

Pastoral power is asserted in this practice in several different ways. As we have already seen, the individual is committed to the practice of total, regular, and exhaustive confession to the same priest, who becomes an important coauthor of the narrative of sin that the confession has become. The confession becomes a kind of "interrogation" which is more and more minutely codified in order to be comprehensive.[54] Furthermore, the system of "tariffs," the codification of the relationship between a particular sin and a particular satisfaction, is modified. It will be the priest, based on his understanding of the penitent and her sins, who will decide what the penance shall be. In other words, there will be no strict code used to administer satisfactions, and the confession itself will no longer be considered a satisfaction.[55] The role of the priest is solidified by both of these developments. The priest alone is capable of deciding upon the necessary act of penance. The priest alone has the "power of the keys."[56] "There is penance only if there is confession, but there can only be confession if the confession is made to a priest . . . From now on, one could say that the power of the priest is anchored, and definitively anchored, interior to the procedure of the avowal."[57]

One is required to speak, to tell the truth about what one has done and thought. One's story is guided by the interrogation of the priest who holds the key to salvation. This story is filtered through the pastor's knowledge in order to be converted into the proper satisfactions, acts of penance. Through the struggle over the spiritual being of the individual, this form of penance, which began as a kind of juridical practice, was transformed into the basic structure of Christian confession as it would be practiced henceforth. The juridical model is only one element of a far more complex practice whose tactics, means, forms, and purposes are unique.

It is in the sixteenth century that the proliferation of confessional manuals will begin. This development corresponds with the movement that Foucault identifies as the recovery of the philosophical problem of care of the self.[58] This is the period of the Reformation, an event which Foucault describes as being more essentially a struggle over the problem of governmentality than over doctrine.[59] The question spreading through Western culture is, as Foucault sees it, How to be governed? and How not to be governed?[60] The question of government begins to be separated from its religious and spiritual element and will slowly be taken up as a political problem, a question of the government of the "people."[61] The appearance of these manuals for the practice of confession represents, in a sense, an offensive in the battle over the government of individual lives and the attempt to define the true form of care of the self. So far we have seen how the practice of confession becomes the "anchor" for the institution of pastoral power. Now Foucault turns to the techniques of confession detailed in the practical manuals appearing at the time. He uses these manuals to reveal how the pastor as a particular modality of subjectivity comes into focus and how the being of the individual who must confess is constituted.

This period of the sixteenth century, the period of the various reforms and counterreforms, the religious wars and the Renaissance, is what Foucault calls "a phase of Christianization in-depth" of Western civilization.[62] "Christianization" does not mean that culture becomes more religious, but rather that government—its techniques, its subjectivities, its objects and objectives—becomes a fundamental problem throughout society. The intensification of government will take place within the church, but it will also become a political problem (I will examine this in the following chapter), and between these two problems of governing individual lives there will be a struggle for control. In other words, what takes place is that "Christian frameworks tighten their hold on individual existence."[63] This means, first of all, that "the whole of life, of action, of the thoughts of an individual must be able to pass through the filter of the avowal."[64] The entire range of experience of the individual must be translated into the language of the confession, "if not, of course, as sin, at least as an element which is pertinent for an examination, for which the confession from now calls."[65] Second, within this deployment the power of the confessor, the pastor, is going to increase itself. The role of the pastor will become not simply confessor, but also a figure of "governmentality."[66] Finally, it means that Christian frameworks will spread throughout society in a secularized variation.[67]

At the center of this technology of power is the pastor, the subject who bears this power. The pastor is a peculiar modality of subjectivity. It is his very mode of being that allows him to save the others. It is his very identity, the identity he has in part by nature, in part through ordination, in part through self-fashioning, that gives him the power to save. In other words, the subjectivity of the pastor is linked to his mode of life, and it is this particular form of subjectivity linked to a way of life, which gives the pastor the capacity for ethical truth-telling.

Therefore, the question is, Who is the confessor? Foucault points out that the confessor must have certain qualities and capacities. He must have "le caractère sacerdotal."[68] That is, the individual must receive authorization from the bishop. Only someone who has the institutional authority can speak ethical truth in the confession. It is only before this particular individual that one will be able to speak in such a way that one's confession will lead to absolution. Furthermore, the confessor must possess "le zèle."[69] This zeal is "a certain 'amour' or 'désir.' "[70] In other words, the confessor must be erotic, but his erotic character is that of a spiritual Eros.[71] The conversion of eros from "concupiscence" to "good will" is therefore another condition of possibility of the veridical power of the confessor. The confessor must care for the "interests of others."[72] The centrality of eros as a force of spiritual transformation and transcendence has been a fundamental aspect of Western spirituality at least since Plato. The confessor must care for the care that the others take of themselves. His capacity to take care of their care is to be found in his very identity, his mode of subjectivity gives him access to the truth: the truth of the self as an object of care.

The confessor must also be free of sin. In other words, the confessor must take care to manage his own actions and thoughts, to practice a constant vigilance over, and purification of, his soul. If the confessor is given to sin, then he remains open to the dangers that the practice of confession presents.[73] The confessional situation is compared to the relation between the doctor and the patient in which the doctor, while treating the patient, is exposed to the diseases of the patient. The confessor, in order to remain impervious to the contagiousness of sin, must keep himself free from temptation and must keep his actions and his thoughts free of sin: "It is necessary, finally, that the priest who performs confession has a religious horror of venial sins . . . Venial sins, in effect, blind the spirit, they attach to the flesh."[74] Even minor sins are dangerous because they transform the mode of being of the confessor. They open him up to the temptations posed by the confessional scene.

All of these qualities are necessary aspects of the confessor's identity and way of life. Ethical truth-telling calls for a peculiar mode of subjectivity, one whose access to truth is not a theoretical matter but is rather achieved through the practice of a specific form of life. Finally, the pastor, the confessor, must have knowledge. This knowledge takes three main forms: (a) it is juridical: the pastor must know the laws and the penalties for infractions; (b) it is medicinal: the pastor is like a doctor who must be able to recognize the condition of the patient, understand the nature of his illness, its causes and its cures, and be able to apply the proper remedies; and (c) it is practical: the pastor's knowledge is that of a guide. The role of the pastor is no longer simply to match a sin to its proper satisfaction. "From now on, a whole series of supplementary conditions are added to these simple requirements, which qualify the priest as a person intervening, not simply by sacrament, but rather in the general operation of examination, of analysis, of correction, and of the guide of the penitent."[75] The priest must be able to offer the individual advice on how to live, how to avoid sin, how to keep his soul pure. Taken altogether, the priest's virtues culminate in that of prudence. "Prudence is the art, which the confessor must possess, of adjusting this science, this zeal, this holiness to the particular circumstances."[76] He must be able to recognize what is truly individual about each individual so that he can tailor his knowledge appropriately. The practice of confession must take into account the individuality of the person to be saved. The confessor must be able to intervene in just the right way so that his knowledge will be effective in transforming the individual. This means knowing how to speak to and guide each unique individual. The confessor is going to possess a technology of individualization: of making individuals appear in their uniqueness. Through the confession, and through the technology of the confessor, individuals will come to care about that in them which is truly individual, they will begin to attend to it, to see it as the ultimate ethical substance, and will be led to focus their attention and their activity around the *telos* of salvation.

The pastor/confessor is a special mode of subjectivity which is required to govern individual souls and to provide for their salvation. The nature, virtue, knowledge, and institutional authority of the confessor combine to give him access to the truth of the individual through the practice of confession. This practice is a mode of interrogation and self-disclosure, it is a technology through which the individual, in her truth, in her identity, is produced as discourse and as the object of knowledge—the confession, and the technique of the confessor, is a technology which allows the individual to translate her entire existence into words. The result is a knowledge of oneself which allows the pastor/confessor to prescribe penance in the simultaneous forms of punishment for sin, as remedy for spiritual sickness, and as preventative care to alter the individual's life, to produce good habits, to transform the individual's way of thinking and living in order to avoid future infractions and spiritual diseases. Finally, all of this through the confessor's virtue of prudence is tailored exactly to the particularity of the individual and is applied in the way most likely to effect a transformation in the particular, idiosyncratic individual.

Foucault's genealogy of the pastor—and of the correlative to the pastor, the individual who becomes available and intelligible through the grid of confessional technologies—continues with an overview of the precise deployment of this technology. How does the confession take place? What kinds of technologies are developed to care for and govern individual souls? How is the confessional scene articulated? Again, Foucault reminds us that these technologies are rarely deployed in the systematic and complete forms that they take on in the technical manuals that describe them. They never reach the population as a whole, or even a majority. In the most developed form they existed only in the seminaries and in the *collèges*.[77] While it is true that the confessional technologies described in these manuals represent an ideal form of total pastoral government of the individual (at least insofar as this is possible outside a complete pastoral space such as a monastery, seminary or *collège*), they are not presented or experienced as ideals. Rather they are instructions, manuals for setting up an ensemble of practices and places devoted to the spiritual care for, and government of, souls. These manuals produce actual transformations in the lived world of the spiritual community. Foucault points to the invention of the confessional box as the architectural crystallization of this technology.[78] Thus one might say that the confessional box is the material realization, the architectural embodiment, of the technology of the confession. It holds the same relation to that technology, to that deployment of power, subjectivity, and knowledge as the Panopticon holds with respect to surveillance and disciplinary power. However, it will only be through the secularization of this mode of power in the form of the "police" that these technologies will be able to spread through society at large.[79]

The procedure of confession is meticulously organized from beginning to end. All of the senses are deployed in order to read off of the movements, the expressions, the sound of the voice, what the inner state of the confessing subject really is: "In order to support the sacramental power of the keys, the priest's empirical powers of the eye, of looking, of the ear, and of listening are formed."[80] Every aspect of the confessional situation is ordered and directed toward the goal of complete and effective knowledge of the individual, as well as the complete and effective communication of that knowledge back to the individual in the form of penance and guidance.[81] From the way the individual is greeted to the way she is dismissed, every detail is part of the deployment of the pastoral government of the individual. For example, the greeting must signify to the individual that the priest is open to the individual and cares about her, that the confession is neither a chore, nor even something indifferent to the priest, but is something the confessor is serious about and glad to perform. The confessor must show that the individual has his complete attention. Furthermore, "there is an entire economy of pain and pleasure: the pain of the penitent who does not like coming to confess his faults, the consolation that he experiences in seeing that the confessor, to whom he comes, experiences, of course, the pain of hearing his sins, but consoles himself of this pain which he is given by assuring, through the confession, the healing of the penitent's soul."[82]

The confessor must be able to read in the penitent the signs of contrition. The proper government of the individual is only possible if the individual is truly sorry. Therefore the confessor must be able to recognize this contrition, to know when it is sincere. Furthermore, the actual progress of the confessional interrogation is systematically arranged in order to produce a complete knowledge of the individual. The confession is a practice of the "examination of conscience."[83] The conscience of the individual is, in effect, constituted in a particular way by these technologies of examination. The individual is constituted as an object of knowledge, as the correlative of the confessional technology through which this object is made to appear and brought together as a conceptual unity. Foucault provides a sample of the confessional procedure for drawing out and isolating various aspects of one's existence in order to constitute them as the truth of the individual as a spiritual being:

> First, revisit the important stages of existence; second, follow the different states that one has known: unmarried, married, the offices one has occupied; retrace, next, the different fortunes and misfortunes that one has had; enumerate and examine the different countries, places, and homes that one has frequented. It will be necessary to interrogate the penitent on his other confessions. Then interrogate in the following order, first the list of "commandments of God"; then the "commandments of the Church" . . .[84]

This procedure continues until one has covered all of the various domains in which it is possible for one to err and one has constructed a comprehensive account of the individual's sins. Finally, given this precise individual knowledge, the priest is able to prescribe penance. And as we have pointed out, this prescription is at once penal, medicinal, and correctional. It is not enough simply to state the penance. Because of its correctional, futural function, "it will be necessary that the penitent accept the punishment, and not only accept it, but that he recognize its usefulness, even its necessity."[85]

The individual, through the matrix of the confessional technology, is constituted as a particular kind of subject. This subject is at once an object of pastoral care and knowledge, and the subject of her own narrative. She must tell what she does and thinks, and she must comprehend the prescription of the pastor. Pastoral power can only function through the subject's deployment of that advice in her own life. The individual subjectivizes herself by accepting the instruction of the pastor, thus freeing herself from sin and guilt and making salvation possible. The practice of confession as it is developed here "introduces the entire life of individuals into the procedure, less of absolution than of general examination."[86] This process of subjectivation extends outside the confessional box. The new practices of spiritual direction which have arisen out of the transformations of the practice of confession will not restrict themselves to the confessional, but will inform the relationship between the pastor and the subjects whom he directs. "In the most Christianized areas, also the most urban, in the seminaries and equally, up to a point, in the colleges, one is going to find the rule of confession, the rule, or in any case, the strong recommendation of the direction of conscience."[87] This "strong recommendation" of spiritual direction is an extension of the process of subjectivation by which pastoral government enters into the life of the individual, produces that life in discourse, and intensifies and perpetuates one's attentiveness to oneself. The individual is led to be in a state of constant self-awareness as a being whose spiritual career is at stake in every detail of his existence. In particular, this practice of direction is focused on the *interior* life of the individual: that area which is not yet sin but is the field in which sin originates—the dimension which first appeared in the monastic practices and which was defined as the *logismoi,* "thought." "It is necessary, therefore, to treat with the director that which has to do with the person and the interior: *les petites peines d'esprits,* the temptations and the bad habits, the repugnance to the good, even the most common faults, along with the sources from which they arise and the means which it would be necessary to employ to correct them."[88] The pastor is the expert in matters of the spirit, in questions of how to conduct one's life in order to live truly, in order to fulfill one's spiritual task of salvation. The individual must constitute his own life around the project of spiritual salvation. This process of subjectivation—the process whereby the individual becomes the subject of his own salvation and becomes subject to the power of the spiritual guide—requires that he speak, that he tell everything about himself to the pastor.

In the face of challenges to the authority of the church and in order to reclaim the practice of confession and penance for the church, the practice of confession itself was completely transformed. It became much more than a form of penance. Rather, it was the anchor point of a detailed technology of subjectivation, a technology grounded in the very identity of the pastor. Whereas early forms of confession had an *intrinsically* redemptive quality—the pain of humiliation absolved guilt—the new practice is only effective if it is practiced by the pastor. This is because only the pastor has the power and the virtue to be able to perform the proper interrogation and to see the proper way to effect penance. Furthermore, only the pastor has the expertise to advise the individual on how to transform his life, his thoughts, and his feelings so as to avoid sin in the future. Spiritual health, spiritual freedom, require a constant "discursive filter, within which all comportment, all conduct, all relations with others, all thoughts, all the passions . . . must be filtered."[89]

The articulation and deployment of these technologies of spiritual government in society does not take place without resistance. In particular, Foucault claims that the various Reformation movements were essentially a struggle over the problem of governmentality. As Foucault sees it, the Reformation both resisted the deployment of pastoral power in the institutions of the church and searched for alternative practices of care of the soul, governmentality, and processes of subjectivation. According to Foucault's genealogy of confessional practices, the pastorate comes to have its particular form as a result of the struggles to define techniques of the self and relationships of government. In his 1978 course Foucault sketches some of the various types of counterconducts that resisted pastoral power. For example, throughout the Middle Ages practices such as *asceticism,* the singular and solitary work of the self on itself; the formation of spiritual *communities* independent of the pastorate; *mysticism,* the direct experience of God unmediated by the guidance of the pastor; all of these took shape as modes of spiritual subjectivation which opposed pastoral technologies.[90] As another example:

> In the same epoch where this immense practice of confession-
> examination of conscience is formed as the perpetual discursive filter
> of existence, for example, in the milieu of English Puritans, one sees the
> appearance of a procedure for permanent autobiography, where each
> one tells the story of his own life, to himself and to the others, to the
> group, to the members of the same community, so that they can detect
> there the signs of divine "election."[91]

These styles of thinking and living functioned as modes of counterconduct, countersubjectivizations, which defied pastoral power.[92] But they resist the pastorate not so much by a refusal of the imperative to confess; rather, they form new modes of confessing, different relationships and techniques for expressing one's self in order to learn the truth and to be absolved of that truth. "With the rise of Protestantism, the Counter-

Reformation, eighteenth century pedagogy, and nineteenth century medicine, [the confession] gradually lost its ritualistic and exclusive localization; it spread; it has been employed in a whole series of relationships: children and parents, patients and psychiatrists, delinquents and experts."[93] The genealogy of the confession reflects the ways in which the pastorate transforms itself and reconceives itself in order to respond to those resistances and to tighten its grasp on the soul of the individual. In other words, the agonistic dimension of this history was not an obstacle to the formation of confession, but rather played a productive role in it. As this power relation became more and more demanding, the forms and number of resistances proliferated and extended further into culture. That is, these struggles had the consequence of extending the problem of government beyond the confines of the church.

Foucault argues that the underlying theme of the cultural reforms, revolutions, and transformations of the sixteenth and seventeenth centuries is the problem of governmentality.[94] The attempt to establish relationships of government "explodes" at this time and extends far beyond the religious or spiritual situation where it had resided for so long. The question of government comes to play an essential role in political rationality from this point forward. The political problem comes to be seen as a question of government, the government of the *population* and of individual bodies. Government also becomes a philosophical problem at this point. Foucault claims in his 1983 Collège course that the sixteenth century sees philosophy reclaim the role of ethical, critical *parrhēsia* from the church. It is in this light that we understand the Cartesian project. Descartes provides a manual for the proper conduct of the mind, as well as a practice of self-transformation through which one wins access to the truth. Furthermore, the truth he discovers is "practical." It is a truth that can be used to organize and govern life itself. Finally, Descartes provides us with an understanding of the nature of the object that manifests itself to this new mode of perception.

The Incarnation of Thought:
The Constitution of the Body as "Flesh"

Foucault's genealogy of the confessional subject—both the subject who governs this practice and the individual who is subjectivized by it—moves to an analysis of the way in which the body itself comes to be invested by pastoral concern. This happens around the confessional interrogation of infractions against the sixth commandment. Up until the Council of Trent

(1545–63), the object of concern was the "the relational aspect of sexuality."[95] The danger lay in one's relationships with others, the temptation these relationships presented, and the thoughts and actions they elicited. But in the new practice of confession "it is the body itself of the penitent, it is its gestures, its meanings, its pleasures, its thoughts, its desires, the intensity and the nature of its experience of itself, it is this which is going to be, now, at the very heart of the interrogation around the sixth commandment."[96] The body itself will appear as the field of objectivity which must be translated into discourse. "The new examination is going to be a meticulous tour of the body, a sort of anatomy of delight."[97] This new technology produces a body which is traversed by pleasure and desire, which moves spontaneously and lies at the source of feelings, ideas, passions, and so on. In other words, the area of primary concern and danger is not so much the relationships one maintains with others, but the relationship which one has with respect to the body now experienced as the "flesh."[98] It is not so much what one says or does that matters, and it is not even the way one desires others. It is the body itself which is the real source of sin and which must be dealt with in the confession. The body comes to be seen as a kind of pleasure machine: "Concupiscence begins with a certain emotion in the body, a purely mechanical emotion which is produced by Satan."[99] Of course, as we know, Descartes, and modern philosophy in general, will develop this notion of the body-machine in a thoroughly despiritualized sense by positing an absolute dualism of intellectual substance and extended substance. The Cartesian body-machine will be driven by natural laws, physical determinations, not by the strategies of a malevolent will or spirit. Within the *dispositif* of confession, however, sensuality arises from another mechanics of the body, a mechanism controlled, at least in part and at times, by an evil will. That is, the body is invested with an evil force, and thus the individual must struggle against this body-machine whose sensuality is produced as a trap to lead one astray. Foucault shows that the late confessional manuals describe this mechanics in minute detail, revealing how emotions lead to passions and to physiological transformations, and how this development derails the power of judgment. The mind becomes entranced by the body. The flesh itself "awakens the power of rationality to the pleasures which it puts itself to examining . . . This calculation of pleasure can provoke a new pleasure, that is, the pleasure of thought itself."[100] For this reason, "the operation of the examination bears now on this body of pleasure and desire which constitutes from now on the veritable partner of the operation and the sacrament of penance."[101] The flesh is the incarnation of thought. In a concrete way, the *logismoi*—the ethical material that disturbed the ascetic's contemplation of God—become a corporeal substance. The flesh must be made to confess, to speak, through or behind the words of the confessing subject. The flesh is the subject who confesses and the object of the technology of confession.

This technology hardly resembles the practice of confession that takes place throughout the Christian world.[102] However, these technologies are deployed in the constitution of the "confessors themselves."[103] In other words, this technology of subjectivation is a practice of the self, a practice of veridiction and a work on the self through which the confessor himself is produced: "There is an entire didactic of penitence . . . It is in the seminaries (the institutions which had been imposed, at the same time, invented, defined and instituted, by the Council of Trent, and which were like the *écoles normales* of the clergy) that this practice of penitence, such as I have explicated it, was developed."[104] The seminary is the site of this technology, yet it is not the only place organized around this process of subjectivization:

> The subtle technology of the confession was not practiced en masse,
> but it was also not a pure dream, a pure utopia. It effectively formed the
> elite. It suffices to see the massive fashion by which all of the treatises,
> for example on the passions, which were published during the seven-
> teenth and eighteenth centuries, had borrowed from the landscape of
> the Christian pastorate, in order to understand finally that the extreme
> majority of the elite of the seventeenth and eighteenth centuries had a
> profound knowledge of the concepts, notions, methods of analysis, grids
> of examination, proper to the confessions.[105]

The technology of confession-examination, and the forms of subjectivity and individuality which are its correlates, have a concrete existence and are the foundation of these institutions. This form of governmentality structures these places. The individual is isolated as an object of discourse, power, and care. The individual takes care of herself by giving herself over to the government of the pastor. The body itself is the primary area of danger that must be transcribed into a careful knowledge and kept under vigilant watch in order to be controlled. The soul is in this way freed from sin and given over to the true life.

Conclusion

Through this government of souls the life, thoughts, feelings, actions, and body of the individual become a domain under the control of the pastor.

In order to care for the soul of the individual, the pastor and the individual have to take up a determinate relationship with respect to that whole domain. Of course, as has been pointed out, this relationship and the technology that defines it could not penetrate very deeply into society. However, the life-world, the everyday lives of individuals, bodies, and souls, to the extent that it was possible to transform these into the object of systematic forms of power and knowledge, were invested by spiritual meaning and direction, knowledge and power. This is the world described by Foucault in the opening chapters of the *History of Madness* and *The Order of Things*. It is a world composed of things that bear sacred meanings and of lives lived according to spiritual order. Each thing had some significance which could be read in its very appearance, "the theater of life or the mirror of nature."[106] It is a world whose meaning and purpose can be read from its very appearance if one possesses the right hermeneutical key: "To know must therefore be to interpret: to find a way from the visible mark to that which is being said by it and which, without the mark, would lie like unspoken speech, dormant within things."[107] The *actual,* what is, what appears all around, is a *system* of analogies, resemblances, and signs. The way that things signified was through some visible mark of resemblance: one could see the analogy, the obscure yet in some way visible resemblance between things.[108] In his 1978 Collège lectures, Foucault explicitly argues that the sixteenth-century system of knowledge functions as a correlative of power relations, and its structure is analogous to those relations. The very structure of the knowable world was a kind of power: the natural world was governed according to pastoral power, a world whose underlying meaning was God's design and the salvation of "man."[109] It was within this spiritualized world that ruling had its meaning and its rationality as a worldly reflection of God's rule of the universe. This epistemic arrangement served as a support to two independent forms of power and government, that of the prince and that of the pastor. Each figure maintained a tactical relationship to this structure, which legitimated his role as lawgiver or as master of care and speaker of ethical truth. In the seventeenth century, this experience of the natural world and life was displaced by another one. *Hermeneutics* was replaced by *analysis*.[110]

> In the sixteenth century, resemblance was linked to a system of signs; and it was the interpretation of those signs that opened up the field of concrete knowledge. From the seventeenth century, resemblance was pushed out to the boundaries of knowledge, towards the humblest and basest of its frontiers. There, it links up with imagination, with doubtful repetitions, with misty analogies.[111]

The interpretation of the visible marks on things in order to understand their sacred truth will give way to an analysis of their composition, to a classification and arrangement of these things into a "rational" order, that is, an order imposed upon them (in their natural disorder and chaos) by reason through the acts of a "sovereign subject." With the rise of this new episteme, the old formation of power relations, which founded themselves in the old episteme, gave way to new ones.

This event in thought underlies the dissemination of the problem of government starting in the sixteenth century. The government of life, of the *population*, is going to become a problem of political power. However, the political government of life will not understand itself in terms of a spiritualized world within which government aims at the salvation of souls. Government will have a new end: the well-being of life. Salvation takes on a completely "worldly" meaning: health, productivity, economy. "Health (*santé*) replaces salvation (*salut*)."[112] In the next chapter, I will sketch Foucault's account of the political art of governing and its rationality. The rise of this new art of governing will require a new kind of subject who has the right, duty, and capacity to govern individuals. A new care of the self becomes necessary in order to give the subject access to "a clear and steady knowledge of everything that is useful for life."[113] According to Foucault, this event provides the historical intelligibility of the Cartesian project. Descartes's practice of care makes possible the mode of subjectivity that will have the right to use the truth to govern life. In other words, the *Meditations* are an exercise through which Descartes detaches himself from a certain *dispositif*. He frees himself from confinement in the disorder of analogies and signs, from trying to achieve knowledge by interpreting the visible marks on things. He will free knowledge, and nature, from confinement in that system of thinking. And he will free himself to establish rules for the proper conduct (government) of one's thoughts, one's life, and one's body through medicine. The hermeneutic relationship of power, knowledge, and subjectivity would be redeployed in a new form. The new confessor would not be formed as a spiritual guide but rather as a doctor—the master of a scientific discourse rather than a religious one. The flesh is transformed into an organic, biological force, a set of drives, instincts, and energies. And the purpose of the confession will no longer be spiritual salvation, absolution of sin, renunciation of the evil force that inhabits one's flesh. Rather, the aim will be to discover, express, and liberate the inner truth of one's self.

7

Rage for Order: The Advent of Biopower

In this chapter I want to focus on the formation of a new system of actuality. In order to grasp the historical intelligibility of Descartes's project, we must see it not just in terms of its resistance to the Renaissance and pastoral *dispositif* of power, knowledge, and subjectivity. We must also set it in the context of the organization of the classical *dispositif.* This means that Descartes's project not only bears the traces of the spiritual relation between the subject and truth but is also structured according to the modern model of "knowledge" (*connaissance*). This model establishes a new relation between the subject and the truth and is linked to new forms of power and knowledge. In other words, our task now is to see how the Cartesian resistance to pastoral and Renaissance power and knowledge is not just negative but positive. It develops new practices of philosophical subjectivity and new relations of power and knowledge. Therefore, we must see how pastoral power is both transformed into and displaced by political governmentality and biopolitics, and we must see the place philosophy establishes for itself in this new *dispositif.*

A New Political Rationality

For a long time the problem of the formation and education of the prince was handled in terms of virtue, whether reflection on the problem was Greek, Roman, Christian, or Machiavellian:

> Throughout the Middle Ages and classical Antiquity, we find a multitude
> of treatises presented as "advice to the prince," concerning his proper
> conduct, the exercise of power, the means of securing the acceptance
> and respect of his subjects, the love of God and obedience to him, the
> application of divine law to the cities of men, and so on.[1]

Toward the end of the sixteenth century and through the seventeenth and eighteenth centuries, a whole new genre of political manuals appears that no longer fits into the category of "advice to the prince," the handbooks on the art of living, the formation of virtue, or the accumulation of power. The new modes of thinking about the formation of the prince that manifest themselves in the modification of the guidebooks reflect a transformation in political reason. Rather than taking on the problem of the ruler's *ēthos*, his virtues, these books deal with the problem of the political art of governing. Political government is not an art modeled on juridical theories of law and justice. Rather, it is an art, a technology, which for the first time takes up the conduct of living beings as the object and objective of political power. This is the migration of the problem of government out of the pastorate and into the specifically political dimension. This new political art will therefore begin to overlap with the practice of pastoral power, penetrating into what was for a long time the jurisdiction of the pastorate. It will do so, at first, by targeting the body, both the individual body (through the disciplines) and the social body (through biopolitics).[2]

The new genre of political manuals represents the appearance of a new way of seeing and arranging individuals as objects of political power and knowledge. In its first articulated forms, this new mode of power and knowledge was called raison d'état, and it represents an early attempt to develop what Foucault will understand as biopolitics or biopower.[3] Foucault turns to several texts from the period to show the first articulation and the early development of this form of rationality. When it first appears, the raison d'état is something "scandalous" because it argues that political power becomes rational only on the condition that it "observes the nature of what is governed, that is, the state itself."[4] The scandal is that political power is not modeled on God's rule of the world, it does not ground itself in juridical categories of justice and law. It is not structured according to the Renaissance episteme of resemblance. Rather, it must know and serve the ends which are natural to the object governed, *the state*. The state appears as "a kind of natural object . . . an order of things," and therefore what is required is a "certain specific knowledge . . . concrete, precise, and measured knowledge as to the state's strength . . . political arithmetic."[5] The order of things that is the state is what Foucault describes as

> men in their relations, their links, their imbrication with those things that are wealth, resources, means of subsistence, the territory with its specific qualities, climate, irrigation, fertility and so on; men in their relation to those other things that are customs, habits, ways of acting and thinking, and so on; and finally men in their relation to those still other things that might be accidents and misfortunes such as famine, epidemics, death and so on.[6]

Knowledge of the state—the appearance of the *state itself* as an object of experience—resulted from the analysis which breaks things down into elements, classifies them, synthesizes them according to the relations they maintain with each other, and is able to arrange and order them in the most appropriate, orderly way. Political government is a new way of seeing, a new way of spreading out the world before it as a domain of objects to be understood and controlled. The epistemic order in which things were constituted in their very being as signs to be interpreted has given way to a new ontology in which the being of the thing, as an object, is grasped through an analysis of its internal composition and its relationship to other things insofar as together they represent parts of a larger whole.[7] The purpose of government is to *take care* of these things through ordering and arranging them: "Government is the right disposition of things."[8] Political power must manage all of those things of which the state is composed. These "things," as we have just seen, are processes and relations, they have functions and needs, or they are resources; they have potentials that are natural to them. Furthermore, this state is a complex synthesis composed of a plurality of things, each of which has its own "appropriate" end. Rational government attends to these innate functions, "disposing them" to the ends which are fitting and appropriate to them.[9] The purpose of government, what it *cares* to bring about, is the strength and the health of the state understood as the composition of living things in their relations to each other. Therefore, to govern well requires understanding these living relations and how to make them as healthy and productive as possible: "The finality of government resides in the things it manages and in the pursuit of the perfection and intensification of the processes it directs."[10] Law and justice are not the concern of the raison d'état. It is instead a matter of tactics, of knowing how to manage the things it governs so that those things flourish. However, it is clear that flourishing here is directed toward life as function and process, as a natural productivity, and also as that which can get sick, injured, and die, which can be used productively or wasted. It is through the rational, deliberate management and manipulation of these processes that individuals and the state will flourish.

The art of political government is the art of managing the processes of life on the scale of the state. It is the art of "economy." The notion of the economy, of the management of the life processes which are the essence of the state, allows for the introduction of the model of the household into political thinking. "Economy" in its ancient and medieval meaning is of course the art of managing the household; it is the *technē* of "the correct way of managing individuals, goods, and wealth within the family . . . and making the family fortunes prosper."[11] The household is defined by the management of life: taking care of food, health, reproduction, wealth, all of those things which are necessary for living. Economy is concerned with what the Greeks identified as *zoē*, life itself, in the sense of natural, organic, biological function.[12] This domain, being attached as it is to necessity and life as a natural and unreflective process, was considered to be below the threshold of political life, *bios*, life in the fullest sense, for ancient philosophy. With the development of political government, however, what was once a means to the end of living politically and thereby in a fully human way now begins to become the end, the purpose, the *telos* of politics. Political life, *bios*, is organized to serve the proper management of *zoē*. The central problem of the political art of government is "how to introduce this meticulous attention of the father toward his family into the management of the state."[13]

In the first formulations of the art of government in the form of the raison d'état, the household served as the *model* for political governing. "To govern a state will mean, therefore, to apply economy, to set up an economy at the level of the entire state, which means exercising toward its inhabitants, and the wealth and behavior of each and all, a form of surveillance and control as attentive as that of the head of a family over his household and his goods."[14] This model had to be discarded as this new political rationality became more sophisticated. The problem with the raison d'état was that it continued to focus on the theme of sovereignty and that of the state. In order for the art of government to advance as an effective technology of power, it needed to articulate the object of its management. It was necessary to discover that the specific nature of its object, the *population*, is not at all like a family and therefore it cannot be managed, governed, or understood in the same way.[15] Political science showed that the "population involves a range of intrinsic, aggregate effects, phenomena that are irreducible to those of the family, such as epidemics, endemic levels of mortality, ascending spirals of labor and wealth; finally it shows that, through its shifts, customs, activities, and so on, population has specific economic effects."[16] Economy shifts from being a *technē*, a mode of thinking and acting, to being a substance, an independent reality that must be properly managed.[17] As an element within *the economy*, the family will no longer serve as a model but will become an instrument of government. It is at the level of the family that government can bring about its effects in the population: the family serves as an instrument that makes knowledge and control of a population possible, that allows for parents to observe and control children, doctors to observe and control families, and so on.[18] Bodies and desires as productive forces will find themselves deployed, managed, and developed within the governmentalized family.

By the end of the eighteenth century this results in a new medical perception of politics.[19] Modernity develops technologies for knowing and controlling not just individuals but entire populations; it is this concern with the population that Foucault calls "biopolitics" or "biopower," a term he used at least as early as 1974.[20] While discipline works on individual bodies, the object of biopolitical control and fashioning is "man-as-species."[21] Biopolitics deals, therefore, with "a set of process such as the ratio of births to deaths, the rate of reproduction, the fertility of a population, and so on."[22] The object and the objective of biopolitics is life in a biological sense. The social body is therefore conceived not metaphorically but literally as a body—it is an organic, biological form. As such it is given to illness—endemics and epidemics—conceived of as "phenomena affecting a population."[23] Government as biopolitics, then, is to a considerable extent a medical practice dealing with the social body, with man-as-species. The formation of a political practice that conceives its objective to be the biological health of a population results in the "development of a medicine whose main function will now be public hygiene, with institutions to coordinate medical care, centralize power, and normalize knowledge. And which also takes the form of campaigns to teach hygiene and to medicalize the population."[24] Political government cannot restrict itself to purely juridical, legislative, economic, or even ethical problems: politics is intrinsically a medical activity dealing with the biological existence of the population. The goal of this medical activity is a happy, healthy, productive, and regulated social body. Foucault shows that the rise of biopolitics is "the emergence of the health and physical well-being of the population in general as one of the essential objectives of political power."[25] Power diagnoses the illnesses threatening the social body and attempts to outline and institute cures for them.

With the rise of this new form of political rationality, the old formation of the prince is no longer adequate. Political power will require a new subjectivation, a new type of sovereign subject who can govern effectively according to this new rationality. It is not according to virtue, wisdom, and justice that one governs, but rather through a detailed "political arithmetic." The philosopher-king, the virtuous lawgiver, and even the Machiavellian "realist" are not competent managers of life as a natural process and therefore cannot govern an economy. Their mode of subjectivity is attached to the law, and they rule over abstract juridical subjects. To fashion one's subjectivity in this way not only does not give one the right or the capacity to govern life; it can inhibit such government. The form of the law, of justice, or of power, the conception of a political subject as an abstract legal category, is often at odds with the form of economy and the conception of the individual as a living being whose health, productivity, and way of life are the elements that compose the state.

The art of politics is no longer founded upon the virtue of the prince, but rather on the competent method of the economist and the doctor. At the end of the eighteenth century, as biopolitical rationality and institutions are beginning to deploy themselves, Foucault claims that two political and ethical myths take shape.[26] First, medicine is invested with the powers of healing that were once possessed by the clergy. Second, the dream of a disease-free society is established as a political goal.

The first myth implies the formation of a nearly perfect secular doubling of the church—along with its political-ethical logic—in the institutions of medicine. "Having become a public, disinterested, supervised activity, medicine could improve indefinitely; in the alleviation of physical misery, it would be a sort of lay carbon copy [of the church]. To the army of priests watching over the salvation of souls would correspond that of the doctors who concern themselves with the health of bodies."[27]

The second myth—of a perfectly healthy society—in a way follows from the first. Doctors were going to be the means by which the perfect society would be constructed through the elimination of physical and spiritual suffering and disorder. However, this requires not just curing individuals—it means curing societies. The social body is conceived very concretely as a medical body, and doctors are the ones who can heal. They have the task of outlining a politics of health. "The first task of the doctor is therefore political: the struggle against disease must begin with a war against bad government."[28] The good government of everyday life is necessary to rid society of disease. Bad governments allow the conditions of social sickness to linger and fester. Society in this way can begin to be grasped in terms of biological and medical normalcy. Medicine takes on the role of defining and bringing about "normal" activities, normal patterns of living—eating, sleeping, working, exercising, recreating, reproducing, and so on—that produce and maintain healthy individuals and societies.[29] The lives of healthy, productive individuals do not need to be made into the objects of biopolitical intervention—but the lives of those who are unproductive, individuals whose poverty can be linked to disorderly patterns of life, do need to be either regulated or contained. In other words, insofar as biopolitics must establish a healthy, sanitary social body, it will have to deal primarily with the trouble spots, the unsanitary, unproductive, and unhealthy. It can do this using medical practices of therapy—that is, improving and healing the diseased part—or surgery—isolating and removing that part.

The political art of government will deploy a particular technology in order to carry out its functions. This technology is called the "police." Foucault uses the term in its original technical sense. The police are all of those institutions and activities which are used systematically to organize and manage the state, to set up an economy by which the state as living things, goods, health, life processes, and so on is able to function. Within this political rationality, individuals are essential elements of the strength and health of the state. Therefore individuals—what they desire, what they do, how they live, and so on—are the objects of government, and the police will be the technology by which individuals are governed: "life is the object of the police."[30] The police will be the real technology of governing. The police do not essentially perform a juridical function, but rather an administrative one; the "police see to living."[31] They ensure that the conditions are right for individuals to be healthy, productive, and happy because the "happiness of individuals is a requirement for the survival and development of the state."[32] Political government targets *living,* the lives of individuals, their health, the condition in which they live, and in so doing it encroaches upon the territory which was once that of pastoral power and the church.[33] The government of life will become not simply a spiritual and religious problem, but a political one.

The deployment of the political art of government through the technology of the police is the meaning of that major event described by Foucault in the *History of Madness:* the establishment of the Hôpital Général and the "great confinement." Rereading the first part of the *History of Madness* will show how life as a result of this act is despiritualized, is removed from the control of spiritual direction, given a new meaning, and taken up by a new form of government. The classical *dispositif* is imposed upon the world through an act of force, just as the subject must impose this *dispositif* on or even *as* itself, through an act of force, an *askēsis*. While this force, especially in the form of self-fashioning, is an act of freedom (freeing one's self from falsehood, confinement, domination, confusion) and a movement of salvation, it will achieve its freedom and salvation from one confinement by confining itself in a new way. Everyday life and individuals will appear in a new light and under a new form of government. In other words, the first major police intervention will be to establish the world in which the police function according to the rationality of political government. That is, if the political government projects before itself a space ordered according to the function of life, the police are the technology which imposes this projection on the world and makes *real* space conform to that projected onto it.

The act of confinement is a redefinition of space and a new claim of politics on life. Social space, that landscape constituted not so much by buildings and streets as by living beings and the variety of actual and possible modes of life available to them, was through this act leveled in order to create a "vacant plain" so that later some "engineer" could come along and lay out in its place a "well-ordered" city.[34] Given this new object (bios/life/$zoē$) to be cared for, a problem arises: who has the capacity, the technique, the knowledge and therefore the right to govern individual life, and life itself? Who is able to speak the truth, to be truthful, in order to take care of life itself? What is the nature of the subject who has access to the truth which will save—not save the soul for the next world, but save life, the body, in this one? This is the problematization which motivates the Cartesian moment.

The Confinement

The coming to power of a new system of actuality did not take place primarily through argument, reasoning, discourse, but rather through an act of force. Through this act, the "great confinement," one system of actuality was overcome by another. The old order was displaced by the classical *dispositif* of power, knowledge, and subjectivity:

> Internment, this massive fact, the signs of which one finds all across 17th-century Europe, is a "police" matter. Police, in the precise sense which one gave the word in the classical period, that is to say, the ensemble of measures which made work at once possible and necessary for all those who would not be able to survive without it . . .[35]

The confinement of all those who do not or cannot work and support themselves is the *occupation,* on the part of political power, of a social landscape which had previously understood itself and structured itself according to a division between the prince and his political regime of law and the pastoral government of souls. The confinement is the deployment, through the police, of the art of government: social facts, people, buildings, space, time, and natural things will be seen in terms of political economy, rather than through the prism of the premodern, "pastoral" interpretation of the world. The operation of the "police" is to rearrange the social space and its inhabitants. It will eliminate the barriers to work and make sure that all those who cannot work are not left on their own where they could pose a threat to order. What made confinement "necessary . . . is an imperative to work."[36] The obligation to work will be a practical exigency, but more fundamentally it will be a moral obligation—a social duty, a personal ethic, and a spiritual necessity. The priority of work reflects the new form of political reason that manages an economy. The state is an essentially economic entity and the population is essentially a workforce. But work will have moral and spiritual meanings that blend with medical and biological meanings: working is mentally and physically healthy, idleness is mentally and physically unhealthy.

On the inside, the houses of confinement will strive to control their inhabitants, to reshape the lives they live by introducing order through supervision and discipline, by transforming the attitudes as well as the behaviors of individuals, by taking over their conscience: "In every one of these houses, one led a nearly monastic life, scanned by readings, services, prayers, meditations."[37] The life of those who are confined is structured in order to transform them into the kind of individuals who are able to inhabit a world newly transformed into an ordered space. However, the world from which these individuals are excluded does not exist *before* the act that removes them and confines them. It is only by removing the disorderly that a social order can be established. Certain types of life, certain acts, modes of thought, certain types of individuals must be excluded so that other types of life may be lived without interruption or interference. A world begins to take shape through the act of exclusion and confinement. Furthermore, only in the "house of confinement" will one in fact fully realize such an ordered world and will one be able to conceive of thoroughly ordered, supervised, and structured lives and minds.

"It was necessary that, silently and over the course of many years, without a doubt, a social sensibility common to European culture was formed and that it suddenly reached its threshold of manifestation in the second half of the 17th century."[38] The act of confinement is the clearest manifestation of the rise of this new mode of perception, a new experience which is able to organize life, space, individuals, and things against a horizon of "order." This mode of perception

> organized in a complex unity a new sensibility with respect to misery and the duties of assistance, new forms of reaction to the economic problems of unemployment, idleness, a new ethic of work, and a new dream of a city where moral obligation overlapped with civil law, under the authoritarian form of constraint.[39]

Prior to the seventeenth century, the government of human existence was a religious-spiritual concern. Human concerns were assigned meanings within the spiritualized perception of things. The day-to-day needs of living beings (*bios, zoē, oeconomia*), the facts of daily existence, were grasped as objects of care, of government, of power, within the pastoral modality of subjectivity and truth. The church and the pastor were the institutions of this mode of care and this mode of perception. However, the seventeenth-century confinement of the poor and the disorderly reflects a new mode of perception, a new technique of "caring" for human life.

The practice of internment outlines a new reaction to the miserable, a new pathos—more generally, a different relation of human beings to that which might be inhuman in their existence. The destitute, the miserable, the man who could not respond to his own existence assumed, over the course of the 17th century, an appearance which the Middle Ages would not have recognized.[40]

Within the medieval Christian deployment of power, knowledge, and subjectivity, poverty was intelligible in terms of human fallenness and redemption, in terms of the suffering of Christ and the sacred truth of the human place in creation. This is clear in Foucault's treatment of the change in the meanings assigned to "poverty" and "charity." The confinement displaces the old meanings of poverty and the act of charity and substitutes for them new ones. In the *dispositif* of the Middle Ages the poor have an "absolute meaning": in their poverty they are especially close to God. As a result, charity receives its value from the poor themselves.[41] This means that one does not provide charity as a means to improve the social situation of an individual or a community. The act is a sacred duty and an end in itself. And the poor are not simply "unemployed" or "unemployable" but are intrinsically sacred because of their poverty. The Reformation alters these meanings and represents the rise of a modern *dispositif*. The attempt to assign new meanings to these facets of human experience, over and against the meanings assigned to those things by the medieval church, is a sign of the struggle over the spiritual subjectivity of individuals. It is part of the problematization of pastoral relations of power and knowledge. Within this new system the poor have no special significance or proximity to God—they reveal God's design no more than do the rich. Instead, each figure—the poor and the rich—testifies to God's will in its own way. For this new experience, wealth reveals God's generosity as poverty reveals his anger. The religious-spiritual significance of charity in such an order can no longer come from its caring for the poor. Rather it comes from the faith which is at the root of such works. Those who do not or cannot work are especially bad, because work is the condition of fallen humanity. And while work cannot save, not even the work of charity, it is still necessary because it has "the value of an indication and of evidence of faith."[42] What this new religious experience does, almost paradoxically, is desacralize the world by moralizing it. The sacred meanings of poverty and charity are displaced by the moralization of work and laziness. Religion becomes, rather than a force of spiritual transformation in order to gain access to the truth, a primarily moralizing force.

The effect of this attitude is the desacralization and *instrumentalization* of acts of charity, of taking care of the poor.[43] First, there is a moral imperative to work: work is necessary because it is the outward sign of faith. As fallen beings we are destined to labor. To refuse to work is to refuse one's fallen status. Furthermore, God has destined us to work, and though it is only his grace and mercy that saves us, not laboring is an affront to God. To avoid work is to expect life and nourishment to be offered to one without earning it. Second, this shift in religion, from an experience of the sacred to an experience of the moral, allows poverty to appear within a new perception of human existence:

> An experience of pity was born which no longer spoke of a glorification of destitution, nor of a common salvation of Poverty and of Charity, but rather talked about humanity only in terms of its duties with respect to society and found in the miserable both the effect of disorder and an obstacle to order. It did not act, therefore, to exalt misery in the gesture that cared for it, but simply to suppress it. Addressed to Poverty as such, Charity is also only disorder.[44]

Poverty and charity are now seen against the horizon of social order rather than against a horizon of fallenness and salvation. The poor do not hold a special place on earth, and the act of charity does not lead one to salvation. Rather, poverty is a social problem. The poor are the effect of social disorder, and their presence in the world creates even more disorder while obstructing the path back to an ordered and efficient society. Furthermore, charity in its pure and spiritual form is itself simply disorder because it does not strive for the abolition of poverty as such. It is not a technique for the production of social order, it is not a means to an end; rather, it is an end in itself. Within the new horizon of social order, poverty must be eliminated and "charity," in order to be rational, must be instrumental in this effort.

> From now on, misery is no longer taken up in a dialect of humiliation and of glory; but in a certain relation of disorder to order which confines it in guilt. That which already, since Luther and Calvin, bore the marks of a divine punishment, is going to become in the world of socialized charity, complaisance with respect to oneself and a fault against the proper functioning of the state. It slips from a religious experience that sanctified it, to a moral conception that condemns it.[45]

The link between poverty and God's anger will linger in the secularized mode of charity as a moral attitude: poverty will be seen as self-indulgence and laziness, as a crime against society. In other words, the secularization and instrumentalization of charity is a movement by which poverty is desacralized and simultaneously made into an object of moral condemnation: it is perceived as a social problem. This is the mode of perception that supports the formation of the Hôpital Général. Foucault cites the original edict of 1656 which identifies "begging and idleness as the sources of all disorder."[46] The houses of confinement will be places of work and punishment with the goal of forming the kind of moral beings who *want* to live in an ordered state, who recognize their duty to contribute to that order, and who have the habits and skills necessary to do so. Poverty arises from a certain relationship to oneself—indulgence. It is this *rapport à soi* which must be transformed through work on the self. Foucault shows that while the pastorate resists the movement of secularization, it too is slowly brought within the functioning of this new form of government. The moralizing attitude creeps into its perception of poverty, and instrumental rationality displaces the spiritual foundation of charity.[47] The pastorate too will come to experience its acts of care within this horizon of instrumentality and social order.

For Foucault, what is original in the practice of internment is that it does not simply "exclude or chase away" the poor, the disorderly, or the unfortunate. It is not merely a negative technique.[48] Confinement actually means much more than eliminating individuals from the social world. It is positive in the sense that it is a mode of "taking care" of the poor: "The unemployed person is no longer chased away or punished; one takes charge of him, at the expense of the nation, but at the cost of his individual liberty. Between him and society, an implicit system of obligations is established: he has the right to be nourished, but he must accept the physical and moral constraint of internment."[49] A new social contract is established, by force on the one hand, and submission on the other. This practice will make possible the complete control, both "physical and moral," of the individual. Within the walls of the Hôpital, an artificial world will be constructed with the purpose of transforming individuals: it will punish them for their guilt; it will protect them from temptation, from themselves, that is; it will force them to do penance and to reform; it will order their lives and their souls, giving them the moral attitudes, the practical skills, and the habits to become responsible members of the social world outside. In other words, the houses will be ordered toward the exertion of a constant pastoral-type power over the lives of those confined there. The aim of this government is *salvation:* the disordered individuals, those who could not conform themselves to social order, will be *converted*, saved, to go into that other world; not, of course, heaven, but that other world outside the walls of the Hôpital. The house of internment will take on its particular dimensions as a unique form of space and time through the deployment of a number of tactics and techniques which all aim at producing a certain mode of life (*bios*) and a certain moral consciousness (*psychē*). The individual will be cared for in the sense that his life will be preserved, ordered, and "improved," and in the sense that his heart will be made to conform to the moral obligations of work that integrate the individual with himself, with his society, and with his God.

This other world where the poor will be placed is the deployment of an ensemble of technologies of the self: "It will have to be not only the aspect of forced labor, but rather of a moral institution charged with punishing and correcting a certain moral 'bankruptcy' . . . And at bottom, it is in this context that the obligation to work takes on its meaning: at once ethical exercise and moral guarantee. It will have the value of *askēsis*, as punishment, as sign of certain attitude of the heart."[50] Work in the houses of confinement takes on the meaning of a practice of the self. It is a mode of being governed and of governing oneself; an ascetic practice by which one acquires the proper habits, skills, and attitudes for life; the sign that one has acquired these; and finally, it is the life one is destined to live as a fallen being. But this rigor, this ethical-ascetic, is one which takes place in the "other world" established *within* the state or social body. The house of confinement will in fact be the ultimate utopia of the new political art of government. Only here will moral order and social order be united in a perfect harmony. Only here will individuals' bodies, lives, and hearts be completely ruled by the moral imperatives of working. In other words, the state conceived according to the raison d'état was made real in that "other world" which it created and enclosed in a perfectly ordered space. "For the first time, one establishes institutions of morality where moral obligation and civil law unite themselves in an astonishing synthesis."[51] Political power has transformed itself into governmentality. It has extended itself into the domain of individual lives, the domain formerly occupied by the pastorate with its relations of power, its spiritual meanings and techniques. In taking up the problem of life, politics has become a technique of governing, of caring for, individuals. Political power and pastoral power, which had been strictly divided, begin to merge. The extension of political government takes place, then, through the deployment of

> a police whose order would be entirely transparent to the principles of religion, and a religion whose exigencies would be satisfied, without restriction, in the rules of the police and the constraints with which it can arm itself . . . In this sense, the "confinement" hides both a metaphysics of the city and a politics of religion . . . The house of confinement in the classical age was the densest figure of this police which conceived of itself as the civil equivalent of religion for the construction of a perfect city.[52]

The meaning of confinement is to be found in this new mode of perception that sees everything against the horizon of order: it is the forceful seizure of life by raison d'état through the technology of the police. Foucault argues that one must not understand confinement anachronistically. It is tempting to assume that all of those who were locked up were recognized at the time as "asocial."[53] According to this prejudice, anyone who was unable or unwilling to conform to the social order of economy, morality, family, hygiene, and so on would have been perceived as a threat to public order, safety, and sanitation; they would have represented a threat to the structure of the family; they would have been seen as a threat to morality and religion. Such a view suggests that these types of individuals would have always been perceived as "asocial"—as not belonging, out of place. But Foucault shows that this is not the case: the antisocial individual, the "alienated" individual, "this character was brought to life in the very gesture of segregation."[54] These different individuals—or rather, the particular modes of living, of being, of thinking and speaking—were not, before the act of confinement, perceived in a unitary fashion as "antisocial" or "asocial." Rather, these modes of subjectivity, and the individuals who lived/inhabited them, were distinct, and perhaps necessary, landmarks on the social landscape. The confinement itself "did not isolate misunderstood strangers, too long hiding behind custom; it created them, altering familiar faces on the social landscape, in order to make them into bizarre figures that no one would any longer recognize."[55] These modes of living were familiar and comprehensible. They had distinct and necessary metaphysical or social meanings. The madman was not someone who lacked the ability to function in society, but rather one who had a clear and recognized meaning in society. His face, however strange, comic, or terrifying, was meant to be seen regularly. His meaning was that of the intrinsic finitude and *errancy* of human reason, if not the essential untruth and madness of the world. The impoverished body of the beggar was not only a common phenomenon; it was a religious-spiritual opportunity. The presence of the poor was the presence of God and the occasion for the sacramental act of charity. It is only *after* the confinement of thought within biopolitical reason that such individuals can appear as asocial because the particular society to which they do not belong was brought into being *by and through* the act that excluded them. Mad, homeless, impoverished, or poor bodies can appear as a disruption and a problem only on the basis of a prior act through which they are defined as such.

Foucault asks therefore not "what pathological or criminal category" these different asocial types "really" belong to. The problem is rather to figure out "what experience classical human beings made of themselves at the moment when certain of their most familiar profiles began to lose their familiarity and their resemblance to that which [human beings] recognized as their own image."[56] It is not that the (kinds of) individuals locked up would have been long recognized as asocial, as misfits. Instead, they become misfits because of a transformation in the relationship which human existence takes up with respect to itself in the seventeenth century. The act of confinement imposes on the world this new relation of the self to itself, of the subject to the truth. This is the creation of world in which these individuals do not fit. "In a word, one could say that this gesture was the creator of alienation."[57] Through this act, human existence is separated from a number of experiences of itself and of its world which had been familiar to it. These modes of suffering and loss, these different ways of inhabiting the body, of seeing and speaking, of experiencing finitude, nonbeing, and the fragility of human life become confined and controlled. At the same time, the space outside is locked out from these modes of being. Those on the outside will become unfamiliar to themselves insofar as they are locked *out of* the experience of these others who reveal a multitude of unexpected variations on the theme of being human. Such modes of existence cannot therefore be perceived as valid modes of access to particular truths or values—they are intrinsically distortions of or deviations from the normal, they are inessential, untrue, and inconvenient. Not only are these others removed from the social world, but their very confinement serves to fix the rest of the community firmly in its proper and normal places. The presence of the Hôpital Général will serve as a mode of control—the constant threat that transgression leads to confinement. Being locked out of the Hôpital means being confined in a space that is ordered and normal. Those on the inside become unfamiliar and unacceptable. There is a place for them, but not one in the ordinary everyday world. This barrier is what alienates them from the ordinary and from the socially accepted. Just as those on the outside will no longer be familiar with the language and the gestures of the confined, those on the inside will no longer be familiar with that of the free.

The alienation brought about by the confinement is one which, in creating a world defined by order, turns those who do not conform to order into objects without a voice or a meaning to express. The thought that these individuals might have a valuable contribution to make, might be meaningful, or might in any way be more than a deviation from a social, moral, or medical normalcy is displaced by the idea that the poor are essentially a problem. Furthermore, thought becomes alienated from itself in terms of *askēsis*. Reason will no longer be linked to *askēsis;* the right to govern belongs to reason defined in terms of method and evidence rather than in terms of virtue, *ēthos*. While those who cross the line into unreason will be submitted to a series of practices to bring them to their senses, this is no longer an experience for which access to the truth is fundamentally ethical. The recovery of one's senses will become a medical problem, not an ethical problem. Access to the truth is rather the *natural* right of a subject, and the mad only represent the unfortunate loss of that power.

A new political and ethical rationality, a new relation between the subject and truth, a new relation between the subject and itself, was formed in which the individual as a living being became the object of political management. In other words, the old system was displaced by an administrative power over individuals and over life itself, over "man" as a living being. From this point on, what will make power rational will be its ability to govern and to produce, to cultivate, to know and improve life. It will do this by forming precise knowledge of living beings, and of populations. It will also put to use various techniques to control these individuals and populations. Political reason will appropriate the model of the family to understand itself and its activity of governing. It will concern itself with the management of life, birth, desire, the satisfaction of need, the production of health and happiness—in short, the problems of *oeconomia*. Its purpose and its form will be "economy." That is, it will strive to make the population, and each individual in it, orderly, efficient, happy, productive. This *system* begins to *actualize* itself on a grand scale through the great confinement, the deployment of the technology of the police, the exclusion of the disorderly, and the definition of a social order through this act of exclusion.

Conclusion

In the last three chapters I have tried to knit together Foucault's analyses of power and knowledge with his genealogy of care of the self and ethical *parrhēsia*. I wanted to see the relationship between Descartes—as a figure of the *parrhēsiast*—and the formation of a new epistemological and political system. As early as 1972 Foucault had read the *Meditations* as spiritual exercises. This reading takes on a new meaning in light of his later focus on the dimension of care of the self and its relationship to power and knowledge. We can now clearly see that Descartes's *Meditations* are a form of care of the self, an exercise of self-transformation, and an attempt to form an ethical *parrhēsiast*—a subject who has the right and the capacity to use truth to govern. This effort is situated within a general problematization of the deployment of pastoral power. Seen from this angle, it is clear that Descartes's ascetic work is an act of freedom. He frees the body from imprisonment in a *false* system of power and knowledge; he frees it in order to allow it to develop according to a new logic. And he frees philosophy to set for itself the new task of developing "useful" knowledge—medicine—that will see to the government of the body in terms of its natural functioning, its health and perfection. Philosophy will be freed from the prison of an illusionary system of knowledge so that it can govern itself, conduct itself, according to its own proper rules. The mind will no longer wander in an epistemic space defined in terms of signs to be interpreted, signs which function according to the forms of resemblance. The *Meditations* awaken the philosopher from this dream world and allow him to perceive a space that is clear and orderly. To grasp something in its objectivity will no longer require an art of interpretation but rather the clear and distinct perception that will allow the philosopher to analyze it, to perceive the different parts of which it is composed and the order of their arrangement.

This form of philosophical knowledge is a departure from that which preceded it in another fundamental way. Descartes established a relationship between the philosopher and truth no longer mediated by *askēsis*—even if his manner of establishing this relationship was itself an *askēsis*. In order to gain access to the truth, all the philosopher has to do is look at the object and to follow the proper rules in analyzing its parts.[58] Evidence and method are the foundation of knowledge, not *ēthos* and *askēsis*. This represents a transformation not only of the philosopher and the ground of his knowledge, but of the nature of truth itself. The truth gained through analysis is no longer in and of itself a saving power which completes the subject in her very being. Rather, analysis results in knowledge of an object—this knowledge may be useful in one way or another, but it is not in and of itself a saving power: "It is evident that knowledge [*connaissance*] of the Cartesian type could not be defined as access to the truth: rather, it will be knowledge [*connaissance*] of a domain of objects. It is there, if you like, that the notion of knowledge [*connaissance*] of an object comes to substitute itself for the notion of access to truth."[59] What this new schema results in, according to Foucault, is an impoverishment of the relationship between subjectivity and truth.[60] This has important consequences for the way that ethical *parrhēsia* and care of the self will constitute themselves as modes of resistance. At the same moment, political power, as we have seen, takes on a new function: its new operation is no longer to impose the law on abstract juridical subjects. Rather, it will invest individual bodies, controlling them by nurturing them, taking care of them, making them healthy and happy. In other words, politics itself, once it comes to be defined as biopolitics, is pastoral in nature. Biopower takes over the activity of care of the self. It defines its ethical material in terms of the productive biological substance of life; it establishes a relationship to the rules which one might call rational choice ("I will follow these rules because they are in my best interest as an economic, biological being—following the rules both maximizes my possibility for personal pleasure and biological survival"); it develops and deploys a set of technologies for working on the ethical substance—these will be the disciplines; and it defines a *telos,* normalization. In other words, the structure of biopower can be grasped according to the four elements of moral self-constitution that Foucault introduces in the introduction to *The Use of Pleasure.*[61]

In the next chapter I will analyze this ensemble in some detail. The new subject of care perceives itself through this biopolitical grid. In fact, the main function of biopolitics is to institute this mode of care of the self: it is through this definition of care of the self that individuals are able to be produced and controlled; it is within this system of actuality that they will be confined. The displacement of the spiritual relationship between the subject and the truth is crucial given this new mode of political reason—philosophy loses contact with its proper element at the very moment when that element becomes the terrain of new modes of power. Power functions by investing, defining, and caring for the body understood as a bioeconomic entity. The operation of biopower is to define the freedom and truth of the individual in economic and biological terms. Reason is given the task of comprehending the body in these terms and setting the conditions within which it can be free. Reason itself must be free, both from illusion and from repression, to follow its own rules, which lead to knowledge and happiness.

This notion of freedom is imposed upon the subject as its very relationship to itself—the disciplinary work on bodies, space, and time is the means by which this relationship to oneself is invested in individual bodies. The formation of the disciplines marks the moment where *askēsis* itself was absorbed within biopolitics. As we shall see, biopolitics and discipline, by taking over and defining life, space, and the body at the level of their being, have confined subjectivity as well by defining and limiting its relationship not only to itself but also to the truth. The definition of freedom in biological and economic terms relegates ethical *parrhēsia* to the role of critiquing repressions in order to free the individual—but the freedom of the individual itself understood in biological and economic terms is already a biopolitical construction. The biopolitical project simultaneously reduces life to biological and economic terms and political reason to the administration of bioeconomic life. The fact that government should aim at setting the conditions for individuals to live the life they desire, and that doing so is perceived in both economic and biomedical terms, seems *normal* to us.[62] But such an idea is a radical departure from the experience of the body, of politics, and of government which predominated before the Cartesian moment. The rise of biopolitical government was originally a scandal because it represented such a dramatic break both with the previous form of political rationality and with the pastoral government of souls. The idea that government should conform to biology and economy rather than to spiritual salvation or to the deployment of the law was radical. The embodied subject would no longer be the site of a spiritual struggle for salvation. The political ruler would no longer ground his rule in a virtuous *ēthos,* and the object of his rule would no longer be an abstract juridical subject. The object of political control appeared within a new framework defined in naturalistic biological and economic terms.

This new development, almost paradoxically, makes possible a new spiritualization of politics and political discourse. Politics and political discourse take the form of messianic programs for the spiritual salvation of populations defined in bioeconomic terms.[63] In other words, the displacement of pastoral power by biopower does not result in a total elimination of the themes of conversion and salvation. Rather, it results in the possibility of articulating these in bioeconomic terms, in political terms. However, this also means that resistance can take the form of counter-practices of political spirituality. This explains Foucault's admiration for the spiritual roots of the Iranian revolution, as well as the dangerous ways this spirituality can be captured by totalitarian projects.[64] This leaves one with the question: Can philosophy develop spiritual practices of resistance that avoid the traps of totalitarianism?

Clearly this new subject of care will have important consequences for the way in which philosophy will define itself as a form of ethical *parrhēsia.* Philosophy first became a form of ethical *parrhēsia* and care of the self in the figure of Socrates. The purpose of philosophy was to institute a care of the self as a spiritual transformation that resulted in a subject capable of political and ethical life. This movement resisted a *dispositif* of power and knowledge founded upon the neglect of the self. Therefore, the self, the self as subject, arose, according to Foucault, as an art of resistance. The philosopher was a practice of resistance to modes of power and knowledge which controlled individuals, confined them, imposed upon them false ways of life. The mode of subjectivation that philosophers deployed in order to resist falsehood and neglect was not simply *logos*—it required *ergon.* The philosophical life, the body of the philosopher, the space he inhabited, was the site of this resistance, it was the terrain that had to be reclaimed in order to win access to the truth. The rise of a new form of power which functions not through a neglect of the life of bodies and the space they inhabit, but through a precise, detailed, and constant knowledge and control of life, the body, and space takes over the terrain carved out by philosophical practices of the self. Contemporary with the rise of this form of power, Descartes displaces the notion of access to the truth as a spiritual *askēsis*. Consequently, philosophy will no longer be able to perceive its activity in terms of spiritual exercise. By defining the relationship between the subject and truth in terms of method and evidence, Descartes does not eliminate the spiritual foundation of this relationship, but rather neglects it, obscures it, such that it will no longer be perceived as the element within which philosophy exists. He makes possible an academic discipline of philosophy. The modern, institutional, academic and theoretical activity of philosophy is quite foreign to the activity of care of the self, the practice of the *bios philosophicos* and of ethical *parrhēsia* we saw in part 1. In the following chapter, I will turn to Foucault's interpretation of Kantian *parrhēsia* and its relationship to the rise of disciplinary power in order to see the displacement of philosophical care of the self taking place at the same moment when the disciplines claim the care of the self as their proper activity. These two movements—the rise of the disciplines and the fall of philosophical *askēsis*—structure the way Kant experienced himself as a subject of power, knowledge, and care. His attempt to define a *parrhēsiastic* practice struggled within the confinement of this space.

8

Toward a Critique of the Present

With the appearance of the disciplines and biopolitics we have, in a sense, come full circle. In Athens in the fifth century B.C., self-neglect lay at the foundation of political domination. Socrates and Plato initiated a resistance against this domination (rhetorical flattery) by inventing a philosophical art of the self. This philosophical art was both a care of and a knowledge of the self and an ensemble of technologies of life through which individuals would be recalled to the vocation of caring for their souls. Through a series of reversals, struggles, resistances and conquests, the modern self, the subject itself, has become an effect of power. Modern "man" cannot be charged with neglecting himself, with a lack of self-knowledge. However, it may be that the very form of our attention to our selves, the multitude of practices and technologies of the self and of life combined with the preponderance of scientific knowledge about individuals, in fact, preclude a considered practice of care as a practice of freedom.

In the previous chapters I developed Foucault's reading of Descartes. That reading situates Descartes on the border between two different experiences of the relation between the subject and the truth. The *Meditations* opens within the experience of spirituality. But the *askēsis* Descartes performs in order to gain access to the truth leads to a new kind of subjectivity, the cogito. The cogito has direct and immediate access to the truth in the form of evidence. Thinking and living become two distinct domains. The proper conduct of the mind will become a methodological problem. The career of thinking, the practice of philosophy, will no longer be lived as an embodied, true life that is *other* than the ordinary. At the same time, the conditions begin to fix themselves in which life, in particular the life of the body with its own proper biological determinations, will become a problem of scientific, medical concern. The body as a bio-economic substance will more and more become caught in the net of physical determinations, a strict causal field that is nonetheless transparent to reason. Reason is thereby set over and against the body and nature in order to know and control them. Life and the body will be defined in medical and economic terms and not in ethical and political terms. They will be conceived of as a natural, organic process rather than as a spiritual, ethical practice. With this new *dispositif* beginning to organize itself, Descartes was forced to reinvent the *parrhēsiastic* subject by fashioning a new relation of the subject to the truth—that is, a new kind of subjectivity and a new experience of truth. The philosopher-scientist will be the one who can properly tell the others the truth in order to govern them, to help them in the proper conduct of their thoughts and their lives. The proper conduct is defined by the order imposed by reason itself: it analyzes and arranges things to establish a rational order where there was natural disorder.

Foucault's archaeology of Kantian thought will lodge it within this general framework of the problem of governmentality. What both Descartes and Kant contribute to is the coming to pass of the Cartesian moment: the moment in which the subject ceased to experience herself openly and fully within the tradition of spirituality. For Foucault, the movement away from this experience had several consequences. First, the practices of the self which organize a mode of subjectivity were absorbed by new techniques and relations of power: disciplinary techniques; they were given a new teleology: normalization; they defined a new ethical substance: biological, economic productivity; and they set up a new relationship to rules of conduct.[1] The *parrhēsiastic* relation as the anchor point of an ethics was displaced by this new grid of power, knowledge, and subjectivity. Second, philosophical efforts to resist modes of government were no longer able to draw upon spiritual practices. Because philosophy was now defined as a form of thinking disconnected from a bodily practice, and the body was defined biologically rather than ethically, because one's way of life no longer served as access to the truth, philosophy was not able to oppose itself to power as an alternate practice of the true life. Third, because of these two developments, the critique of power and government did not adequately respond to the way in which power predominately functions, that is, to the spread of the disciplines, of biopower and normalization. However, despite this limitation, Foucault will still find in Kant resources for his own philosophical self-fashioning. Kant, like Plato, the Hellenistic philosophers, and Descartes, attempts to define an art of government, a care of the self, and a form of ethical *parrhēsia*. The dialogue Foucault initiates with Kant began as early as 1960 with his translation of *Anthropology from a Pragmatic Point of View*.[2] His *thèse complémentaire* offered, along with the translation, an extended introduction to Kant's text. The argument of this introduction is ambitious, going far beyond the text itself to set up the general problematic of "anthropology" as Foucault will develop it in *The Order of Things*. The latter work can be seen as culminating in its brief but crucial archaeology of Kantian thought. Together these two projects take up Kant in an attempt to question the foundation of our thought and its involvement with the privileged form of man (who is simultaneously the subject of all meaning and values and the object of foundational knowledge). Beginning in the late 1970s, Foucault returns to Kant but with a different purpose in mind: the archaeology of an Enlightenment *ēthos*. This chapter will explore the tension between Foucault's two seemingly contradictory projects. I will attempt to show that by bringing them together a rich and unified, though complex, path of thinking reveals itself.

Foucault writes that the essay "What Is Enlightenment?" is a reflection by Kant on the contemporary status of his own enterprise: "it is the first time that a philosopher has connected in this way, closely and from the inside, the significance of his work with respect to knowledge, a reflection on history and a particular analysis of the specific moment at which he is writing and because of which he is writing. It is in the reflection on 'today' as difference in history and as motive for a particular philosophical task that the novelty of this text" lies.[3] Kant's essay is in this sense "journalistic"—not merely because it appears in a journal, but more profoundly because it is an account of what is happening at the moment. As Foucault sees it, this text shows that for Kant thinking was an urgent task. The philosopher had to diagnose what was happening as it was happening. For Kant this meant understanding his own actuality: the Enlightenment.

In other words, Kant initiated a new philosophical question and with it a new philosophical *ēthos*. The question which appears in this text is: "What are we in our actuality? . . . What are we today?"[4] For Kant, attention to the present situation in its singularity was an essential philosophical task. This mode of attention is already in itself a certain ethic, a mode of care of the self, and it calls for particular virtues, capacities, and techniques. Moreover, the very appearance of this philosophical attention to the present has a spontaneous effect on the essence of that present. As soon as the question—Who are we today?—is raised, it becomes a definitive part of one's actuality and that actuality itself is transformed. In other words, as soon as Kant posed it, the question immediately became an essential aspect of the Enlightenment as a historical event, as a modern critical attitude, and as a singular fact of our own present. The critical philosopher was defined by the project of diagnosis, which meant grasping the present as difference, as a unique event. He had to forge critical tools and adopt a critical attitude or *ēthos*, that is, he had to deploy a particular practice of the self in order to constitute himself as a philosopher. Enlightenment is inseparable from its reflection on itself.

In this chapter I will develop Foucault's reading of "What Is Enlightenment?" and his view of its relation to (a) the present moment to which it responds, (b) the Kantian project at large, and (c) Foucault's own project. I will show that Foucault's experience of Kant is essential to his attempt to fashion a critical voice and ethic. Foucault's care of the self is, through Kant, a care of the present. However, Foucault's understanding of the present or of actuality diverges from Kant's in important ways. Because of Foucault's understanding of history and his commitment to the practice of genealogy, he is forced to critique Kant's transcendental philosophy and the particular way that Kant defines maturity or autonomy. Andrew Cutrofello's *Discipline and Critique* is an indispensable reference for working out the relationship between Kant and Foucault.[5] In this book Cutrofello shows, on the one hand, that a Foucauldian-style genealogy allows one to rethink the categorical imperative as a strategic principle of care of the self; and on the other hand, that such a reading provides Foucault with a normative, "transcendental" basis for his ethic of resistance to forces of domination.[6] He argues that genealogy allows us to see precisely how Kant, even as he tries to free himself from heteronomy/domination, is caught up in an experience of subjectivity, reason, and the body which is framed by disciplinary relations of power. On the one hand,

> Kant subscribes to the juridical model of power, and he fashions critique on a juridical model so that it might serve as an instrument for resisting domination. Hence, the political stakes of critique consist primarily in a battle of laws. At the same time, Kant recognizes the emergence of disciplinary power, which, however, he continues to construe on a juridical model. As the key to critical philosophy's struggle with disciplinary power, Kant invokes a new form of discipline. Thus the juridical battle between power (heteronomy) and critique (autonomy) becomes a struggle between two sorts of discipline—a discipline of domination (heteronomy) versus a discipline of resistance (autonomy).[7]

Because Kant lacks a genealogical awareness of the rise and nature of discipline, he thinks of the subject, reason, and power in juridical terms of laws and rights. On the other hand, his failure to grasp the problem of heteronomy genealogically causes him to think of it in "metaphysical" terms rather than social-political ones:

> In "What Is Enlightenment?" Kant contrasts critical living with dogmatic living, suggesting that to allow "a doctor to judge my diet for me" would be a sign of "immaturity" in the sense of living uncritically. Kant's care of the self—his practice of ethical ascetics—purports to be a way of living critically. However, the aim of his program is not, primarily, to free his body from the heteronomous influence of external forces of domination—such as, for example, the coercion of medical technologies. For Kant, the primary threat to freedom comes, precisely, from our own bodies.[8]

Cutrofello shows that Kant's reliance on a juridical model of reason and power, and his belief that the source of heteronomy is the body rather than external relations of power, are the result of his ungenealogical approach. "Because he lacks any genealogical understanding of the juridical, Kant cannot question the political stakes of his construal of freedom as law-obeying autonomy. He construes the problem of discipline as a way of overcoming nature, instead of as a way of overcoming political forces of domination."[9] Cutrofello's aim is to develop what a Kantian care of the self would look like. Referring to the notion of discipline as it appears in Kant's work as well as in his life, he shows convincingly that Kant practiced a deliberate philosophical life in the form of an "ethical asceticism."[10] Through a genealogical critique of Kant's juridical model of reason/power and his perception of heteronomy in a metaphysical light, Cutrofello shows that it is possible to free Kant's categorical imperative and ethical ascetics from those unnecessary limitations in order to construct more effective disciplines of resistance.

My argument here takes up Cutrofello's hypothesis about Kant's mode of critical reasoning and care of the self. His attempt to show that the limitations of Kant's thought are themselves intrinsically effects of discipline and biopower is convincing, and I will refer to it and develop it in what follows. However, rather than explore Kant's practice of care and his discipline of resistance, I will show how and why Foucault appropriates Kant's critical attitude while rejecting his transcendental philosophy. Then, returning to the material from the first three chapters of this book, I will show that Foucault's final research project was an attempt to present an alternative ethic of resistance, not by posing universal laws or limits to power or freedom, but by offering alternative possibilities of ethical subjectivity, other possible ways of fashioning one's subjectivity in relation to the ethical problems of the present.

Kant and the Present

What is Kant's understanding of his own present? First of all, Kant defines the present as "an age of Enlightenment." Kant claims that the Enlightenment "*is man's emergence from his self-incurred immaturity. Immaturity* is the inability to use one's own understanding without the guidance of another. This immaturity is *self-incurred* if its cause is not lack of understanding, but lack of resolution and courage to use it without the guidance of another."[11] For Kant, the age of Enlightenment is an event or a process. It is the process of emerging or exiting from a given status: immaturity. This event is the becoming mature of mankind: it refers to a collective process—"man's emergence" from immaturity—but it also appeals to individuals who are responsible for their own immaturity and for exiting from it on their own.[12] Therefore, enlightenment is an individual ethic and a collective political movement. It is also the purpose and destiny of humanity to become mature. Furthermore, Kant links this age to a single individual, Frederick the Great: "Our age is the age of Enlightenment, the century of Frederick."[13] Because of the rule of Frederick, the present is the opportune moment (the *kairos*) for the event of enlightenment. According to Kant, right now is the time to exit from immaturity and to learn how to think for ourselves. The answer to the question, Who are we? is to be found in a diagnosis of the precise historical situation in which one finds oneself—in Kant's case, the event of Enlightenment. This moment, this event, defines "who we are" in terms of a task: to exit, to become free, to become autonomous.

Kant defines immaturity as the condition in which one allows others to think for oneself: one relies on authorities such as authors, lawyers, and directors of conscience, for example; and one leans on what Kant calls "mechanical instruments" of the mind, "rules [or dogmas] and formulas."[14] This process, then, concerns the way in which individuals use their own minds, it involves a decision concerning the conduct of one's own thought: Will I employ formulas given to me by others, will I rely on dogmatic interpretations of things? Or will I think for myself, and challenge these formulas and ready-made interpretations of things? Furthermore, this thinking is directly linked to living. The decision about how to govern one's thoughts is simultaneously a decision about how to govern one's life: how to make decisions concerning what one knows, what one can know or ought to know; how one chooses a healthy regime or diet; what one ought to believe, one's faith, and so on. The present is understood, then, in terms of government—of how to be and how not to be governed, of how to govern oneself. Enlightenment is the process by which one resolves, properly and responsibly, the tension between the commands of others and the commands of one's own reason. To become mature is to become autonomous, to become capable of governing oneself according to the decisions and the rules which one, as a rational being, gives to oneself.

How does Kant *respond* to the present as he has articulated it, what stance does he take with respect to this moment? First, it is important to note that in this very concern with actuality is already a response: Kant's attitude is one of solicitude with respect to what is actually happening. Philosophical reflection must attend to its own situation and speak to that situation. In order to reinforce this aspect of Kantian enlightenment, Foucault turns to the "Contest of the Faculties."[15] In this text Kant offers evidence of the progress in "man's" perfection. The evidence, according to Kant, has to do with the French Revolution. However, the Revolution itself is not the evidence that humankind is advancing toward enlightenment. Kant is "concerned only with the attitude of the onlookers as it reveals itself in public while the drama of great political changes is taking place."[16] The progress of mankind toward enlightenment and autonomy is to be gauged by the relation which the spectator takes with respect to the actual moment. Whatever the outcome of the Revolution itself, humanity's progress is reflected in the concern for the event itself. The spectator—Kant himself—defines the Revolution in terms of enlightenment, in terms of the struggle to become free and mature. Enlightenment takes place through the act of defining what is happening in terms of enlightenment. One's response to the present, then, is how one defines one's relationship to what is happening; one's relationship to oneself is defined in one's relationship to what is happening at the moment.

Furthermore, taking a stance with respect to what happens requires making that position public at the very moment when the present is unfolding. Therefore, Kant asserts that enlightenment requires courage, that it is attached to character, to virtue. One must comprehend the essence of the present, what is happening at the moment, and one must develop the courage, the moral virtue, to respond to that moment, to seize the moment and take up the task of enlightenment. Kant also claims that man is not yet living in an "enlightened age" but that he is in the process of, the event of, becoming enlightened, of thinking for himself, of becoming autonomous. Given that the very moment at which Kant is writing is the moment which calls for action, one must possess the resolve, the courage, and expend the effort to act. "The motto of enlightenment is therefore: *Sapere aude!* Have the courage to use your *own* understanding!"[17] This means not simply judging what is happening, but speaking about what is happening, defining one's position publicly with respect to the event of the Enlightenment.

Kant argues that in addition to an individual *ēthos*—developing a "journalistic" attitude and the moral courage to challenge the authority of others—there is a political condition necessary for this event to unfold as it should. "For enlightenment of this kind, all that is needed is *freedom*. And the freedom in question is the most innocuous form of all—freedom to make *public use* of one's reason in all matters."[18] A "pact" between individuals understood as subjects—as free, rational, autonomous beings—and the sovereign who issues commands and requires obedience, must be established. Foucault sees in this another formulation of the problematization of *parrhēsia*.[19] Kant, openly and defiantly, asserts the necessity of free, frank speech. He will argue that freedom—the will both to speak freely and to listen to words freely spoken—is necessary for the process of enlightenment. But far from destabilizing political power, the freedom to publicly critique authority actually contributes to political obedience and social order. To see this, we must understand how Kant understands *parrhēsia*—frankness, critique, resistance—and its relation to government.

To grasp the relationship between *parrhēsia* and the power to which it speaks, we have to look at the unexpected distinction between the public and the private in Kant's notion of the use of reason.

> The *public* use of man's reason must always be free, and it alone can bring about enlightenment among men; the *private use* of reason may quite often be very narrowly restricted, however, without undue hindrance to the progress of enlightenment. But by the public use of one's own reason I mean that use which anyone may make of it *as a man of learning* addressing the entire *reading public*. What I term the private use of reason is that which a person may make of it in a particular civil post or office with which he is entrusted.[20]

The scholar, the intellectual, the individual insofar as he constitutes himself as an intellectual, must be allowed to criticize power in the name of reason, and power must listen to reason. If free public reason is permitted, then private reason can legitimately be made to obey. In the private use of reason, on the other hand, where an individual has an assigned function and "acts as part of a machine," obedience is required. Reason must be used in this setting only instrumentally, as a means for attaining preestablished ends. In this limited setting, "Kant does not ask that people practice a blind and foolish obedience, but that they adapt the use they make of their reason to these determined circumstances."[21] The individual exists in the social-political world as a "part of the machine" and therefore must use reason in order to enable the social machine to function. However, the individual, as a rational being, also exists "as a member of a complete commonwealth or even of cosmopolitan society, and thence as a man of learning who may through his writings address a public in the truest sense of the word, he may indeed argue without harming the affairs in which he is employed for some of the time in a passive capacity."[22] Therefore, enlightenment requires individual virtue, journalistic vigilance, and it requires a political "pact"—a *parrhēsiastic* pact. The nature of the pact is such that individuals are guaranteed intellectual freedom as scholars addressing in their writings the reading public. The individual is therefore something which exists both as a subject of universal reason and as an instrument in the social machine. "Enlightenment is thus not merely the process by which individuals would see their own personal freedom of thought guaranteed. There is Enlightenment when the universal, the free, and the public uses of reason are superimposed on one another."[23] When this is achieved, man's instrumental life, his life as a functioning part of the social machine, will be harmonized with his existence as a subject of universal reason. Because of its aim, as well as its internal limits, the freedom to reason in public increases and legitimates private obedience.

What's more, Kant argues that the *parrhēsiastic* contract is beneficial not only for political obedience but also for the process of enlightenment itself: "A high degree of civil freedom seems advantageous to a people's intellectual freedom, yet it also sets up insuperable barriers to it. Conversely, a lesser degree of civil freedom gives intellectual freedom enough room to expand to its fullest extent."[24] Too much "civic" freedom can hinder intellectual enlightenment; that is, private obedience is good because it encourages intellectual freedom. Civic obedience is a positive force in the development of enlightened citizens. The constraint on action and on the private use of reason will set up the necessary conditions within which intellectual freedom can begin to develop. The individual, who is privately determined according to fixed functions, will have the opportunity to constitute freedom in the form of universal reason; he will be able to develop this reason through "critique," through the recognition that freedom is autonomy, that is, obedience to the laws of reason. Within the "hard shell" of civil constraint the "germ" of "man's inclination and vocation to *think freely*" will grow until "it gradually reacts upon the mentality of the people, who thus gradually become increasingly able to *act freely.*"[25] Civil obedience combined with intellectual freedom results in individuals who are able, eventually, to act freely; once they have been *disciplined* they will be able to obey the laws of reason which they give to themselves spontaneously.

However, only where the sovereign has the power to enforce civic obedience will the opportune moment for the event of enlightenment appear. The age of Frederick, the Enlightenment, is possible because "only a ruler who is himself enlightened and has no fear of phantoms, yet who likewise has at hand a well-disciplined and numerous army to guarantee public security, may say what no republic would dare to say: *Argue as much as you like and about whatever you like, but obey!*"[26] The army represents the repressive power of the sovereign to enforce the law—and it is in large part, according to Kant, this repressive power which ensures the stability and confidence necessary for the sovereign to listen to *parrhēsia* in the form of intellectual critique. The army ensures the civic obedience within which individuals can become enlightened. The army, in a sense, secures the space within which *parrhēsia* and enlightenment can take place: it gives the sovereign the confidence to allow *parrhēsia* and to hear it out; it constrains individuals in the private use of their reason, giving them the discipline required for intellectual freedom. Social order, security, discipline, and the smooth functioning of the social-political machine are all necessary ingredients for intellectual freedom.

Foucault claims that in the background of Kant's notion of enlightenment is his critical project. Critique is the way in which individuals become subjects of universal reason. Kant's three *Critiques* together form the "handbook of reason" and therefore of the Enlightenment.[27] To join this event and take up the task of maturity one must think freely or autonomously; in other words, one must recognize and accept the limits reason imposes on itself as law. Critique, transcendental philosophy, reveals the limits, the conditions of possibility of experience. It defines what it means to think for oneself, to be autonomous and free. Foucault writes:

> Critique for Kant will be that which says to knowledge: Do you really know how far you can know? Reason as much as you like, but do you really know how far you can reason without danger? Critique will say, in sum, that our freedom rides less on what we undertake with more or less courage than in the idea we ourselves have of our knowledge and its limits and that, consequently, instead of allowing another to say "obey," it is at this moment, when one will have made for oneself a sound idea of one's own knowledge, that one will be able to discover the principle of autonomy, and one will no longer hear the "obey"; or rather the "obey" will be founded on autonomy itself.[28]

Critique is the philosophical activity that defines the proper mode of government: one is autonomous when one governs oneself through one's own will by the laws of reason, thus becoming mature.

While Foucault does not explicitly connect his reflections in his own essay entitled "What Is Enlightenment?" to his earlier interpretation of Kant, I contend that it is worth doing so. In fact, I would argue that the earlier interpretation frames his later approach in a way that is evident even if implicit. Foucault's *thèse complémentaire* as well as crucial chapters of *The Order of Things* put forward an interpretation of the relation between Kant's critical project and his anthropology.[29] The central problem which unites these two separate domains of knowledge is what Foucault calls the "analytic of finitude."[30] On the one hand, anthropology seeks to discover in his "concrete forms of existence" a positive knowledge of man's finitude: the empirical study of man as a living being shows his finitude as organic function; the study of man as a laboring being shows his finitude as a needful and value-imposing being; the study of man as a linguistic being shows his temporality and his relation to meaning.[31] It will be man's empirical limits which make him knowable and which make it possible for him to acquire knowledge; it is these limitations which structure the world in which he lives and his necessary modes of inhabiting that world. On the other hand, transcendental philosophy tries to find in the essential finitude of the transcendental subject the limits of reason that constitute through their very nature as limits the conditions under which (or within which) experience and knowledge are possible. Kant's thought is a thought of the *limit*. In anthropology and in transcendental philosophy, the task is to define the human subject as both the origin of knowledge, value, and meaning and as the ultimate object of knowledge. It is through establishing concrete empirical finitude or transcendental finitude as the condition of the possibility of experience that one establishes the nature of man and of knowledge. Therefore, when Foucault argues that the *Critiques* are the "handbook of reason," and that maturity requires recognizing the limits intrinsic to reason which define its autonomy, it is evident that he is referring to his early work on this topic. Critique and transcendental philosophy, in the sense of an analysis of finitude, lie at the heart of the Enlightenment: "The Enlightenment is the age of critique."[32]

In sum, Kant's response to the event of Enlightenment is to fashion a critical *ēthos*, one of solicitude with respect to what is happening, one of courage, one which questions limits but in the name of limits, and one which ultimately seeks to challenge the way in which individuals allow themselves, in their very subjectivity, to be determined heteronomously. But the event of Enlightenment is not contradictory to a certain form of political government. As Foucault puts it:

> It would be . . . easy to show that for Kant himself, this true courage of knowing, that invoked by *Aufklärung*, this same courage of knowing [*savoir*] consists in recognizing the limits of knowledge [*connaissance*]; and it would be easy to show that for him autonomy is far from being opposed to obedience to sovereigns. But it no less remains that Kant affixed the understanding of knowledge to critique in his enterprise of desubjectification in relation to the game of power and truth, as a primordial task, as a prolegomena to any present and future *Aufklärung*.[33]

Individuals must not let others think for them; this is, in effect, to let others determine who they are. Immaturity is the state in which one does not fashion oneself as a subject of universal reason, but rather is subjected to the rules and dogmas, the self-interpretation, which is imposed upon one by external authorities—one is fashioned, subjectified, by others. Therefore, "the essential function of critique would be that of desubjectification in the game of what one could call, in a word, the politics of truth."[34] At the same time, as one frees oneself from heteronomy, one accepts the political restriction of "private reason"—both as a condition of possibility of intellectual freedom and as the result of the definition of freedom in terms of the public use of reason.

Foucault and the Present

So far we have seen how Kant perceives what is happening in the present moment and the way he responds to that moment. Now I want to turn to Foucault in order to see how the actual moment shows itself to him. Foucault argues in both versions of his essay that Kant's text is the source of a new *ethos:* the modern critical attitude. This attitude calls for a permanent "ontology of the present." This ontology is grounded in a way of living and of thinking which understands its own present situation and responds to that situation; in other words, for Foucault ontology is not just a thinking of being, but is a way of being. In particular, it is a way of being which attends to the relations between power and knowledge in order to ask how to be governed and how not to be governed. But while Foucault adopts this critical *ethos,* and in fact suggests that critique is perhaps "virtue in general," Kant's practice of critique is, in his view, not adequate to the task it sets for itself.[35] Why can we not, according to Foucault, fashion ourselves as critical subjects according to the Kantian model (at least as it appears in this reading)? In order to answer this question we must first address a few others: (1) What is Foucault's concept of the present, or of actuality, in general? (2) How does he understand the actuality which Kant addressed? (3) How does he conceive our own actuality? Answering these questions will show why some elements of the Kantian model may remain necessary, even if the complete formulation of his enlightenment/critique cannot be accepted by Foucault. Finally, we can see the way Foucault's approach leads to other models for fashioning oneself as a critical subject.

    1. How does Foucault understand the nature of the "present," of "actuality," in general? I have in fact posed, and attempted to answer, this question throughout this book. The overall structure of what Foucault calls "experience" is the three-dimensional space structured by relations of power, knowledge, and subjectivity. However, these three dimensions of experiential space are to be understood not as static states of being but rather as events and practices, as ways of thinking that must be perpetually reactivated through attitudes, institutions, and relations, and as a dynamic network of forces, tactics, and technologies. The introduction of new modes of power, new epistemic formations, or new practices of the

self has the potential to rearrange the map of possible or necessary experience. Foucault's "history of the present" traces the history of difference, of rupture, out of which our own present emerges, in order to reveal that the present is not a fixed entity but a movement; it is dynamic and tactical rather than natural, determined, and static.[36] This way of thinking and of grasping the actual in its "systematicity," that is, at the level of thought itself, will lead Foucault to a very different mode of critical awareness than that of Kant.[37] While Kant introduced this vigilance as a philosophical project, and linked it to the thought of the present as difference and as event, his critical project is limited by an inability to grasp the fundamental events which have structured his thought from the outside.

2. How does Foucault understand Kant's actuality? For Foucault, the ground of Kantian critical enlightenment is formed by an ensemble of events, the beginnings of which we examined in the previous chapters. These events have to do with the development of new relations of power—discipline, biopolitics, normalization—and a new relation of the self to itself and to the truth—the Cartesian moment. Both of these developments emerge from the critique of pastoral power: its relations, techniques, modes of knowledge, and strategies were simultaneously attacked and appropriated in such a way that they spread across the cultural landscape, transforming that landscape in fundamental ways. Through this struggle these practices and strategies of control, resistance, and care began to organize themselves in new settings, new institutions, with new techniques, relations, and strategies. In this way, according to Foucault, one can link the birth of the critical attitude, and the Enlightenment as an event in the history of thought, directly to the birth of discipline, biopower, and the Cartesian moment. I will first look at the disciplinary background to the Kantian critique, and then turn to the Cartesian moment. Finally, we will be able to turn to Foucault in order to see how he is able to free himself from these practices with the help of his reading of Nietzsche.

The dispersal of pastoral power resulted in the emergence of a general cultural problematic of government: "how to govern children, how to govern the poor and beggars, how to govern a family, a house, how to govern armies, how to govern different groups, cities, states, how to govern one's own body, how to govern one's own mind."[38] On the one hand, this period was defined by a "governmentalization" of society; this was not, as we saw, simply the appearance of a theoretical or intellectual problem, but rather the deployment of new political technologies of individuals through the institutions and relations of the police. The critical attitude, according to Foucault, can be traced to this event: "Now this governmentalization, which seems to me characteristic enough of these societies of the European West in the sixteenth century, cannot be dissociated from the question 'How not to be governed?'"[39] The problem of government is inevitably bound up with the problem of resistance and the formation of the critical attitude, which is

> at once partner and adversary of the arts of government, as a way of suspecting them, of challenging them, of limiting them, of finding their right measure . . . There would have been something that would be born in Europe at this time, a kind of general cultural form, at once a moral and political attitude, a way of thinking, and so forth, and which I would simply call the art of not being governed, or the art of not being governed like that and at this price.[40]

It is this "reflective indocility" which is at the heart of enlightenment.[41] The question for us is, Does Kant's attempt to develop an art of indocility respond to the actual relations of power which constitute his actuality? For Foucault, the answer finally must be: not completely. This is because Kant did not clearly grasp the transformation in the functions of power and of subjectivity that took place through the dispersal of the pastorate.[42] In order to understand the limits of Kant's critical art, we must see the relationship between his thinking and his actuality: an actuality constituted through the formation of the discipline, the development of biopolitics, and the displacement of the ascetic relation between the subject and truth.[43]

Discipline

In *Discipline and Punish* Foucault writes:

> The great book of Man-the-Machine was written simultaneously on two registers: the anatomico-metaphysical register, of which Descartes wrote the first pages and which the physicians and philosophers continued, and the technico-political register, which was constituted by a whole set of regulations and by empirical and calculated methods relating to the army, the school and the hospital, for controlling or correcting the operations of the body.[44]

A new mode of construing human beings as objects of knowledge and power appears in the seventeenth century: the human being as a natural being, as a body in nature, is to be understood as a kind of machine functioning according to laws that are observable and describable. However, this knowledge appears in two settings which put forward apparently contradictory aims. The technico-political goal is to submit man-the-machine to a discipline which will make him function perfectly, usefully, and obediently. The individual will be thoroughly instrumentalized, produced in such a way that her own desires, pleasures, development, happiness, and health will be achieved through her deployment as a functional element of the social machine.[45] On the other hand, according to a strategy which seems to be radically opposed to this, the individual-machine appears for the philosophers as a free subject who stands before other subjects and the sovereign in a contractual relationship. For Kant this means that man "is more than a machine."[46] Even though the body as a natural, physical entity determined by natural laws *is*, in fact, a machine, the individual as a rational being is not. Human beings are not reducible to instruments of the social machine, just as they are not reducible to the natural laws that determine their physical existence. The individual as body-machine must be submitted not essentially to the state and its demands, but to reason and the laws it gives to itself in its freedom. These two seemingly opposed views do, however, share one common aim: the discipline of the body-machine in order to actively realize a concrete image of political or moral perfection, freedom, and truth.[47]

Kant's mode of *parrhēsia* aims at resisting the arbitrary coercion of individuals who are essentially free, rational beings. However, not only does he accept the constraint of bodies—or of private reason and "civic freedom" of action—he strives to legitimate it and claims that it is necessary for and conducive to intellectual freedom, which is the true "inclination and vocation" of humanity.[48] In other words, while "What Is Enlightenment?" articulates a critical *ēthos* of attention to what is happening in the present, it is also ensnared in what Foucault calls the "anthropological sleep" with its oscillation between a positivist or empirical knowledge of man and an eschatological discourse about the realization of the concrete truth of man.[49] In Kant's essay it is easy to hear the eschatological voice: the emergence from immaturity would be the final realization of man's "original destiny."[50] Furthermore, given the empirical nature of man as it is revealed positively, or rather pragmatically, in anthropology, one can discover the modes of legitimate coercion, the proper program for freeing the truth of man from that in his empirical nature which impedes the realization of this freedom and truth. Given the nature of this empirical-transcendental doublet—man as positive nature and promise for the future—Kant is able to accept and even appeal to a strict power over bodies, over the use of reason in its private capacity, because this constraint is necessary for the progress of man. With proper disciplinary control of bodies and actions, humans will be free from the disorder of natural impulses and the heteronomous determination by physical laws, they will be able to emerge from immaturity and exercise their freedom as subjects of universal reason.[51] In this sense, the free subject of reason and its laws is given the opportunity—or is forced—to emerge through the disciplinary control of the individual body as the object of nature and its laws. Foucault argues that this critique of coercive power embraces discipline without questioning the coercive effects and tendencies intrinsic to it as a strategic relation of power, and without questioning its presuppositions about the body as a natural object, presuppositions that are the foundation for this mode of power. Thus, this critique of power in the name of freedom, which simultaneously disciplines the body in the name of freedom, advances and legitimates the spread of disciplinary power. Conversely, the disciplining of the body will be necessary in order to produce individuals who experience their freedom in terms of the universal laws of reason:

> The general juridical form that guaranteed a system of rights that were
> egalitarian in principle was supported by these tiny everyday, physical
> mechanisms, by all those systems of micro-power that are essentially non-
> egalitarian and asymmetrical that we call the disciplines . . . The real,
> corporal disciplines constituted the foundation of the formal juridical
> liberties. The contract may have been regarded as the ideal foundation
> of law and political power; panopticism constituted the technique, uni-
> versally widespread, of coercion. It continued to work in depth on the
> juridical structures of society, in order to make the effective mechanisms
> of power function in opposition to the formal framework that it had
> acquired. The "Enlightenment," which discovered the liberties, also
> invented the disciplines.[52]

In other words, free, autonomous subjects do not simply appear in nature—they must be produced through discipline. It is out of this very discipline that "the man of modern humanism was born."[53] Scientific, medical, "instrumental" knowledge of individual bodies and natures arises as an effect of discipline. But disciplinary power is also the condition of possibility of the very objects to be known: bodies appear as objects through and within disciplinary relations, procedures, techniques, and strategies. The way bodies are made to appear in these settings will condition the kind of knowledge that can be had of them, and this knowledge then functions as an element of the disciplinary control of them. The "anthropos" of the new philosophical anthropologies is fashioned within these relations of power that function simultaneously as modes of producing knowledge. That is, the operation of disciplinary techniques is what first produces individuals as possible objects of scientific knowledge.[54]

Foucault argues that one can see "the gradual extension of the mechanisms of discipline throughout the seventeenth and eighteenth centuries, their spread throughout the whole social body, the formation of what might be called in general the disciplinary society."[55] If in the middle of the seventeenth century, society was transformed through the great confinement, that transformation was in fact only one sign of the more radical shift from sovereign to disciplinary power. The confinement simply excluded all of the disorderly elements so that a society based on order, the order of production, morality, and rational calculation could arise. Classical power-knowledge acts in order to put things in their proper places, to reveal the order that already resides in things; for example, put the mad in the houses of confinement where they belong (because they are confined already at the level of their being) and allow the natural order of society to flourish. The disciplines, however, did not simply exclude the disorderly. The disciplines are not essentially exclusionary practices. They represent the development of techniques by which order—orderly individuals, bodies, minds, hearts—can be effectively produced out of disorder. "The disciplines function increasingly as techniques for making useful individuals. Hence their emergence from a marginal position on the confines of society, and detachment from the forms of exclusion or expiation, confinement or retreat."[56] The disciplines originate in closed and total disciplinary spaces such as those of the army, the monastery, the school, and the hospital and slowly develop relations, techniques, and knowledges that migrate or "swarm" in open spaces, in effect making more and more of social space disciplinary and converting more and more of the time of individual existence to disciplinary time.[57] Therefore, discipline "may be identified neither with an institution nor with an apparatus; it is a type of power, a modality for its exercise, comprising a whole set of instruments, techniques, procedures, levels of application, targets; it is a 'micro-physics' or an 'anatomy' of power, a technology."[58] I would like to sketch some of the elements of this "micro-physics of power" as Foucault presents them in *Discipline and Punish*. This will allow us to see the way they form the background for Kant's enlightenment and the experience of man that informs it. His vision of the body-machine is already an instance of the disciplinary framing of individuals, as is his vision of the relation between this disciplined body-machine and its final truth, its eventual emergence in its truth as a subject of universal reason, as autonomous. Foucault's microphysics of power analyzes the way discipline works *on* space, time, bodies, and groups *through* surveillance, normalization, and examination *in order* to produce a field of objects to be known and a knowledge of these objects—both of which are forms of, and effects of, the procedures and techniques of disciplinary power.[59]

In order to understand discipline, one must see what it does. Foucault analyzes it in terms of the ways it makes "docile bodies," and the "means of correct training" it employs to make useful bodies. These procedures and aims are not separate. One of the innovations of discipline is to combine control and production into the same operation. Therefore the way space, time, bodies and groups are perceived, arranged, and used simultaneously controls them, makes them more controllable, and increases their productive capabilities. "A body is docile that may be subjected, used, transformed and improved."[60] Under the heading of "docility" Foucault analyzes the disciplinary arts of space, time, bodies, and collectives. Under the heading of "training" he analyzes the techniques of surveillance, normalization, and examination. In my outline I shall follow the order of his analysis.

Arts of Space

The disciplinary art of space and of "distributions" is the first and perhaps the simplest of discipline's modes of operation. Discipline does not presuppose an independently existing individual who is brought before it like a court of law; rather, "discipline 'makes' individuals."[61] The individual first appears within the categories established by the social-disciplinary needs and which allow for the isolation and distribution of individuals to their proper places. That is to say, discipline first arises through the formation of an artificial space, which it imposes upon the world as a grid of intelligibility. In its rawest form, discipline requires enclosed, total, disciplinary spaces: the houses of confinement, the monastery, the school, the hospital, the factory, the army barracks, and so on. The production of space as a grid of intelligibility serves numerous purposes. Space is organized in order to make individuals visible, to bring them into the light, to isolate them from each other in order to enhance the ability to know them and control them by making them available for constant observation.[62] Yet it makes them visible within the framework and according to the models that it has established: as detainees, as soldiers, as students. Foucault uses the example of the army, one of the original disciplinary laboratories. The discipline begins with a distinct image of the soldier which it seeks: "The soldier was someone who could be recognized from afar; he bore certain signs: the natural signs of his strength and his courage, the marks too, of his pride, his body was the blazon of his strength and valor . . . movements like marching and attitudes like the bearing of the head belonged for the most part to a bodily rhetoric of honor."[63] This image of the soldier, who rarely exists in nature, serves as a mold in a sense: it is on the one hand the originary reference with respect to which individuals are measured, and on the other hand it is the model that serves to guide the formation of the individual. Disciplinary space will make individuals, first of all, visible with reference to this yardstick and goal.

Furthermore, it does not simply spread out a neutral space; it defines "places." Within the disciplinized area each unit, each individual, must be distributed to its proper place where it can be seen, trained, put to use. Individuals must be experienced individually, that is, in isolation from the group—the group itself must be broken down into its elements to prevent it from taking on a life of its own or to prevent the individuals from disappearing within its shadows.[64] The disciplines arise, therefore, in order to deal simultaneously with groups and individuals. Each site within the grid is defined by a function and each individual who is located at a site takes on that function. However, "the elements are interchangeable, since each is identified by the place it occupies in a series, and by the gap that separates it from the others."[65] The individual is not defined so much by his intrinsic function or nature, but by the place he occupies in a segmented, networked space. One takes on the function of the place to which one is assigned. Again, the individual appears as an individual in disciplinary space with reference to the functional demands placed on him by that space. But discipline "individualizes bodies by a location that does not give them a fixed position, but distributes them and circulates them in a network of relations."[66] Furthermore, one has in this series a "rank": this is one's place in the series of differences which divide one functional site in the network from all of the others. Discipline operates, then, first of all by establishing a grid of functional spaces and by managing the movement or flow of individuals along a series of ranks. Individuals identify themselves by way of this ranking and strive to ascend the series, developing themselves by and for this movement. In other words, individuals first become individual objects of knowledge when they appear in a grid of relations, functions, and ranks imposed upon them. It is in terms of that grid that they can be compared with each other, measured, studied, individuated with respect to each other and with the functional demands placed on them. It is within this schema that they are made intelligible.

Foucault provides, as an example, the disciplinary system of distribution and ranking deployed in a Jesuit *collège:*

> In the eighteenth century, "rank" begins to define the great form of distribution of individuals in the educational order: rows or ranks of pupils in the class, corridors, courtyards; rank attributed to each pupil at the end of each task and each examination; the rank he obtains from week to week, month to month, year to year; an alignment of age groups, one

after another, a succession of subjects taught and questions treated, according to an order of increasing difficulty. And, in this ensemble of compulsory alignments, each pupil, according to his age, his performance, his behavior, occupies sometimes one rank, sometimes another; he moves constantly over a series of compartments—some of these are "ideal" compartments, marking a hierarchy of knowledge or ability, others express the distribution of values or merits in material terms in the space of the college or classroom. It is a perpetual movement in which individuals replace one another in a space marked off by aligned intervals.[67]

Discipline institutes a space saturated by divisions, compartments, functions, and ranks that permit a mass to be decomposed into a number of individuals. In this way the group is worked on, controlled, managed, and used at the level of its individual components. One appears for others and for oneself within this grid of functions and ranks. Educational discipline, for example, is the formation of a technology for the mass production of students, the mass transmission of knowledge. The requirements of mass education—a minimum of expenditure (in terms of time, teachers per student) and a maximum of production (in terms of knowledge imparted, or at least in terms of students ascending through the minimal requirement of ranks)—require a science of discipline. The ability to control individual bodies and make them learn in such a setting, in large groups, cannot happen without the production of docile individuals—individuals who are obedient, who control themselves so that they do not need to be actively controlled by another. Discipline "made the educational space function like a learning machine, but also as a machine for supervising, hierarchizing, rewarding."[68] The educational situation is just one example; discipline in general, as an art of space and distribution, allows for the mass production and regulation of individuals.

> The first of the great operations of discipline is, therefore, the constitution of "tableaux vivants," which transform the confused, useless or dangerous multitudes into ordered multiplicities. The drawing up of "tables" was one of the great problems of the eighteenth century . . . In the eighteenth century, the table was both a technique of power and a procedure of knowledge. It was a question of organizing the multiple, of providing oneself with an instrument to cover it and to master it; it was a question of imposing upon it an "order."[69]

The imposition of an order is what brings individuals into the light of measurements, functions, and ranks according to which they become intelligible and controllable objects. The subject who sets up and orches-

trates this gridlike space must perceive the world as elements to be ordered and arranged in order to suit the functions demanded of it. It is not
enough to know how to recognize the signs of a soldier, for example. One
must possess the technology for taking raw material and forming out of it
an individual who resembles the image one has of a soldier. The disciplinary art of space—and as we will see below, that of time—is structured by
the classical forms of analysis, measurement, and order. Discipline imposes these forms on space and on bodies.

Arts of Time

Discipline also invents arts for grasping acts and bodies in their temporal
dimension. Time is deployed through an array of technologies, beginning
with the timetable. The timetable has "three great methods—establish
rhythms, impose particular occupations, regulate the cycles of repeti-
tion."[70] This art of time was developed within the disciplinized space of
the monastery. "For centuries, the religious orders had been the masters
of discipline: they were the specialists of time, the great technicians of
rhythm and regular activities."[71] Discipline is the rigorous control of time.
It divides time into segments and it allocates these segments to activities,
to functions. Discipline establishes a rhythm based on functionality in
economic terms as well as in terms of control. The art of time satisfies the
disciplinary need to control and account for each moment, to know at
every moment what is being done and what must be done:

> An attempt is also made to assure the quality of the time used: constant
> supervision, the pressure of supervisors, the elimination of anything that
> might disturb or distract; it is a question of constituting a totally useful
> time . . . Time measured and paid must also be a time without impurities
> or defects; a time of good quality, throughout which the body is con-
> stantly applied to its exercise. Precision and application are, with regu-
> larity, the fundamental virtues of disciplinary time.[72]

In addition, discipline does not simply deploy a time which is precisely accounted for, which is broken down into units and which flows according to a functional rhythm. The acts, gestures, and movements of the
body at work, busy learning, or in training, are broken down into the most
minute functional units possible in order to establish a knowledge and a
control, not just over the body and its acts, but over the successive elements of the act itself. Foucault provides an example of this kind of de-

tailed decomposition of the act or gesture in the discipline of marching. The simple act of walking is decomposed into a dizzying series of postures, distributions, angles, joints, and rhythm.[73] This art of time is

> a collective and obligatory rhythm, imposed from the outside; it is a "programme"; it assures the elaboration of the act itself; it controls its development and its stages from the inside . . . A sort of anatomo-chronological schema of behavior is defined. The act is broken down into its elements; the position of the body, limbs, articulations is defined; to each movement are assigned a direction, an aptitude, a duration; their order of succession is prescribed. Time penetrates the body and with it all the meticulous controls of power.[74]

To march properly, to master the art of walking in formation, to establish a perfect concert of moving soldiers, a rigorous temporal decomposition and reconstruction of the simple act of walking is necessary. Through this operation, the temporality of the body in motion is claimed from within the very motion of the body itself by a power imposed on it from the outside. The body itself as a functional whole is comprehended around the "gestures" or actions it is trained to perform. In order to master the art of handwriting, for example, according to this disciplinary model, one cannot simply focus on the fingers, the hand, the arm: the body as a whole is always present in every gesture. In order to perfect the gesture or action, the entire body must be trained and practiced and organized around the gesture. Only through this attention to the body as a whole, the body which extends beyond the act itself, can the body be trained to disappear into the gesture and the gesture be made to flow "naturally" out of the body. "A disciplined body is the prerequisite of the efficient gesture."[75] Through this training, through this production of acts and gestures, this development of capacities, talents, and mastery of actions, the body becomes disciplined. It becomes more efficient, more capable, and simultaneously more docile and manageable. The individual becomes alert to himself through the process of training and exercise, and through the development of his body's capacities. In order to develop his "natural" potentials he must control his body, submit it to the exact program that allows him to master an activity. Indocility results in flawed performance, an awkward, irregular body stumbling through abnormal, incorrect gestures. To be trained is to be docile. A trained body is one that bears the inscription of power in the way it moves, feels, in its capacities and needs; all of these are the body constituted as an effect of power, of training.

Within a disciplinary framework, the attention to time does more than regulate it and use it to impose upon the body a meticulous arrangement of succession and simultaneity within each gesture. Discipline makes of the decomposition of time a productive promise:

> It poses the principle of a theoretically ever-growing use of time: exhaustion rather than use: it is a question of extracting, from time, ever more available moments and, from each moment, ever more useful forces. This means that one must seek to intensify the use of the slightest moment, as if time, in its very fragmentation, were inexhaustible or as if, at least by an ever more detailed internal arrangement, one could tend towards an ideal point at which one maintained maximum speed and maximum efficiency.[76]

Time itself is a resource that can be mined for production. Discipline, to achieve the fertility of time, aims "to teach speed as a virtue."[77] The "need for speed" is a disciplinary effect. The obsession not simply to be able to do something, to do it well, to enjoy doing it well, but to be able to be done with it as quickly as possible and move on to the next thing comes along with discipline.

The Organ-ized Body

These disciplinary technologies of space and time, as we have seen above, arise with the imposition of the classical *dispositif* of order in the form of the table—spatial grids and timetables. They deal with a field of objects that first become intelligible as objects in terms of the table of relations and functions imposed on them. The discipline begins with the image of the end result—the ideal soldier or student, for example—and goes to work on the actual individual as its material. It sets up its shop, its functional space and time, to sculpt the individual body, its form and its temporal dimension. But the work of laying out disciplinary grids of time and space, of working on individuals as raw material, as blank slates, runs up against an obstacle: the body. The body does not simply allow itself to be molded passively like clay. It has a mind of its own, so to speak. It is through the confrontation of disciplinary power with the body to be trained that a new kind of knowledge becomes possible:

> Through this technique of subjection a new object was being formed; slowly, it superseded the mechanical body—the body composed of solids and assigned movements, the image of which had for so long haunted those who dreamt of disciplinary perfection. This new object is the natural body, the bearer of forces and the seat of duration; it is the body sus-

> ceptible to specified operations, which have their order, their stages, their internal conditions, their constituent elements . . . In the exercise that is imposed upon it and which it resists, the body brings out its essential co-relations and spontaneously rejects the incompatible.[78]

In other words, it is through the work of discipline that the body is able to appear in a new way as an object of knowledge and control. The body is not clay or stone, it refuses to bend to the artist's hand without putting up a fight. Discipline has to wrestle with the body which spontaneously refuses to be disciplined. In other words, "nature" as "organism" appears as that which stands against the imposition of order—and order must allow itself to be guided as it guides, to learn from the body, through the body's spontaneous development or resistance, how it is to be made into a perfect instrument. "The body, required to be docile in its minutest operations, opposes and shows the conditions of functioning proper to an organism."[79] Foucault is not suggesting here that nature is that which pre-exists discipline. Nature is defined and experienced as that which resists discipline. He is also not attributing a will to the body, or suggesting that this form of resistance results from the will, the rational decision of the individual. What resists here is to be found in the differentiation of discipline as regulated fashioning and the body as a material which, unlike a canvas or a slab of clay, follows lines of development, movement, and change independent of those demanded by the discipline. In this way, through the struggle of disciplinary techniques with the bodies they apply themselves to, the nature of "man"—his organic life functions, instincts, raw capacities, needs, and faults, in sum, his *finitude*—appears as a positive object of knowledge. In other words, it is through discipline that a new epistemic formation begins to take shape. What resists the imposition of the classical order is the organic functioning of the body; it must be trained precisely because its functions, tendencies, and processes of becoming seem to move in directions of their own and appear as a "spontaneous resistance" to the minute and intense investment of power that takes place through the training of the body. We can see in the agonism of power and bodies the origin of "man," the "anthropos" of anthropology.[80]

In order to deal with the unruly, spontaneously organ-ized body of resistance, disciplinary tables of space and time are complemented by a technique of exercises. One develops a *genetic* temporality of the individual comprehended through a series of graduated exercises resulting in the acquisition of more and more complex skills and capacities.

> Exercise is that technique by which one imposes on the body tasks that are both repetitive and different, but always graduated. By bending behavior towards a terminal state, exercise makes possible a perpetual

characterization of the individual either in relation to this term, in relation to other individuals, or in relation to a type of itinerary. It thus assures, in the form of continuity and constraint, a growth, an observation, a qualification.[81]

That is, individuals become intelligible on the basis of their progression from one stage of exercises, development, and growth to the next: do they advance quickly and easily, ahead of the others; are they on a par with the majority; or are they slow, do they have trouble, do they refuse or fail? Conversely, the individual in this framework begins to organize his consciousness of self: one becomes aware of oneself in relation to the progress one is supposed to be making in these exercises.

The technique of genetic individuality through exercise originated, like the timetable, in the monastic setting:

> In its mystical or ascetic form, exercise was a way of ordering earthly time for the conquest of salvation. It was gradually, in the history of the West, to change direction while preserving certain of its characteristics; it served to economize the time of life, to accumulate it in a useful form and to exercise power over men through the mediation of time arranged in this way. Exercise, having become an element in the political technology of the body and of duration, does not culminate in a beyond, but tends toward a subjection that has never reached its limit.[82]

We can see here that discipline appropriates not only the territory of spirituality but its techniques as well, transposing them to new settings in the service of new aims. If the monastic practice was a resistance to "earthly time"—time saturated by desire, greed, pride, and death—these new practices are a way of taking over time as a source of productivity. In this way they resist other modes of temporality, such as monastic time, which submit a potentially useful body to a temporal organization that wastes the body and its time.[83]

Tactics

Discipline is also a "tactical" technique of bringing the individual units together to produce concerts, functional "wholes" that are greater than the sum of their "parts." Individuals must be produced as cellular, organic, genetic wholes, but they also must be made to function in unison—each one able to hold down a place in relation to all the others so that together they are like one great machine. "The body is constituted as a part of a multi-segmentary machine."[84] Disciplinary tactics forge individuals with an eye toward the place (or places) they must be able to hold in a social organization: a factory, a school, a hospital, an army, a city, and so on. The political metaphor of the body-machine is not, as Foucault tries to show, a simple ideal or ideology—it is a technology. "While jurists or philosophers were seeking in the pact a primal model for the construction or reconstruction of the social body, the soldiers and with them the technicians of discipline were elaborating procedures for the individual and collective coercion of bodies."[85] The disciplines achieve real social-political integration through the deployment of a power which *makes* individuals who experience their very individuality as part of this machine. The disciplines are the anatomo-socio mechanics of the political body-machine. "Discipline is no longer simply an art of distributing bodies, of extracting time from them and accumulating it, but of composing forces in order to obtain an efficient machine."[86] It is through discipline that the body-machine and the social machine are superimposed on one another, not as a metaphor but as an ensemble of practices of knowledge and of control.

Normalization

"The success of disciplinary power derives no doubt from the use of simple instruments; hierarchical observation, normalizing judgment and their combination in a procedure that is specific to it, the examination."[87] All of the segmenting, organ-izing, genetic and tactical procedures outlined above are integrated with the deployment of these simple instruments in all sorts of settings and invest bodies with their effects. Techniques of observation reverse the ancient link between power and visibility. In the classical power relation between the sovereign and the subject, the essence of power is its ability to show itself in the might and glory of the ruler: the might of the sovereign is on display before the subject who remains in the shadows. But in discipline it is the *object* of power that is made permanently visible. The body, its actions, its thoughts, its desires are observed and the body itself is placed in a network in which it observes others as it is observed by them. Space and time are spread out as mechanisms of making individuals visible; in this sense space and time themselves are modes of visualization, permeated by sight, by observation.

Second, the function of judgment in discipline is not essentially "juridical." The disciplinary "judge" is not primarily interested in the ways in which *acts* violate laws, but rather the ways in which *individuals* fail to

fulfill the potential in them and fail to develop according to the preestablished pattern. "The whole indefinite domain of the non-conforming is
punishable: the soldier commits an offence whenever he does not reach
the level required; a pupil's 'offence' is not only a minor infraction, but
also an inability to carry out his tasks."[88] This mode of judging and punishing is "corrective."[89] In addition to the judgment which "punishes,"
there is the one which rewards: the individual who conforms to the rule,
who accomplishes the tasks expected of him, who passes the examination,
who performs all the required exercises quickly and efficiently, is re-
warded. The purpose of judging in this way is to improve the individual,
to force or to induce him onward toward the goal which has been set for
him. Like observation, judgment is in a way built into time and space and
in this way pervades the body. Space is determined by ranks and thus reflects judgments; time defines the progress of the body in its development,
and quick or slow development is already a form of judgment that per-
meates time. The result is a thorough "differentiation that is not one of
acts, but of individuals themselves, of their nature, their potentialities,
their level or their value. By assessing acts with precision, discipline judges
individuals 'in truth'; the penalty that it implements is integrated into the
cycle of knowledge of individuals."[90]

The third instrument of disciplinary power is the examination. It is
the synthesis and culmination of observation and judgment that produces
in a document a written knowledge of individuals. Individuals can in this
way be known with precision as "cases." In the examination, one sees the
birth of a science of the individual:

> One is no doubt right to pose the Aristotelian problem: is a science of
> the individual possible and legitimate? . . . One must no doubt give an
> answer lacking in "nobility": one should look into these procedures of
> writing and registration, one should look into the mechanisms of exami-
> nation, into the formation of the mechanisms of discipline, and of a new
> type of power over bodies.[91]

The examination is linked to documentation, and in this new documentation, the culmination of all the disciplinary techniques, the individual appears in his individuality as an object of knowledge. Discipline
aims at making individuals into objects of power-knowledge, it is essentially "anthropo-logical." This new scientific discourse of the examination
represents one central appropriation of the technology of confession
within a new system of actuality. Foucault makes this clear in his analysis
of the modern *scientia sexualis*. Discipline functions as a hermeneutics of
the self by "combining confession with examination, the personal history

with the deployment of a set of decipherable signs and symptoms; the interrogation, the exacting questionnaire, and hypnosis, with the recollection of memories and free association: all were ways of reinscribing the procedure of confession in the field of scientifically acceptable observations."[92] The examination is not simply the culmination of learning, a way of acquiring knowledge about an individual; it is more important a means for further forming the individual. Furthermore, the individuals are not simply objects of knowledge and power; they discipline and examine themselves, seeing in these activities their own freedom, fulfillment, happiness, and truth. Through the disciplines individuals come to identify themselves in terms of norms, or of the normal. That is, they identify themselves both with the content of the normal as it is defined within the framework of discipline and biopolitics, and with the form of power, the techniques of normalization. In other words, the individual understands herself not just in the *content examined* but also as an *examining subject,* in the activity of examination. Individuals appropriate hermeneutics as their relationship to themselves.

Finally, the disciplines take over the confession/examination as a normalizing practice by shifting it from a religious context to a medical context: "The confession and its effects were recodified as therapeutic operations . . . placed under the domain of the normal and the pathological."[93] The modern form of the examination resituates the hermeneutics of the subject within a disciplinary setting, makes it a technique of normalization. Disciplinary normalization reinscribes the activity of speaking ethical truth and the relationship of spiritual direction in new forms and places these in the hands of new experts:

> If one had to confess, this was not merely because the person to whom one confessed had the power to forgive, console, and direct, but because the work of producing the truth was obliged to pass through this relationship if it was to be scientifically validated. The truth did not reside solely in the subject who, by confessing, would reveal it wholly formed. It was constituted in two stages: present but incomplete, blind to itself, in the one who spoke, it could only reach completion in the one who assimilated and recorded it.[94]

Judgment, observation, and examination along with spatial and temporal control produce a clear and steady knowledge of individuals: the relative merits of each and the potentials and tendencies of each. The purpose of all these distributions, records, and controls is so that individuals "might all be like one another."[95] The aim of all these techniques is to *normalize* individuals.[96] As we have seen, the norm first organizes discipline by serving as an image of the final product of its work: the ideal soldier, worker, or student. But the confrontation of discipline with actual individual bodies results in an "empirical" (or disciplinary) knowledge of the normal. Through comparing individuals with each other, measuring them against the criteria imposed on them all equally, discipline constructs a new figure of the normal, one based on concrete empirical knowledge; the normal arises as the average, the standard which emerges within the practice of the disciplines. The original ideal is transformed into a scientific, quantitative knowledge. This knowledge then serves to perfect the disciplines, fine-tuning them, tailoring them to the nature of the bodies they have to work on. The norm as a mode of power-knowledge arises in the struggle between discipline and bodies. It is within this context that a knowledge of "nature" as organic, as genetic, as space and time, as potential, as desire and passion, as instinct and function, as various types of indocility or abnormality, first emerges. Discipline produces through this struggle and through its techniques of observing, comparing, judging, examining, and documenting, a knowledge of the normal: of the way in which proper development, progress, and adaptation come to pass. A normal body is one which advances and develops its capacities on schedule and results in well-adapted, healthy, productive, and happy life. A body which does not adapt to this scientifically purified disciplinary order, a body which resists this training, which fails these examinations, which does not become happy, or healthy, or productive within the social organism, is abnormal.

"Man" appears as the being who has a nature that must be induced, forced, corrected in order to reach his potential. Man is also, because of his unique nature, the being who is able to discover nature in himself and manipulate it in order to attain his natural destiny. Here we see that the anthropological dualism of positive knowledge and eschatological knowledge is intrinsic to discipline. It is simultaneously positive knowledge of natural finitude and normative knowledge of a promise to be fulfilled.

This new mode of power along with the new objects and knowledge that it produces serve as the background to Kant's reflection on enlightenment and his critical project. Even as Kant resists the political instrumentalization of individuals, he legitimates the spread of discipline. This is because Kant was unable to see that power was beginning to reside more in the norm than in the law, and the law was coming more and more to function in service of the norm.[97] Disciplinary power-knowledge gave rise to an experience of man in terms of natural finitude. It was on the basis of the "analytic of finitude" that the norm and the law came to be thought in concrete terms as fixed positivity and fixed destiny. The law and the norm articulate a regime which "is of a mixed nature: it is an 'artificial' order, explicitly laid down by a law, a program, a set of regulations. But it is also an order defined by natural and observable processes."[98] Finitude—both in the empirical form of the organic, living, speaking body and in the transcendental form of the subject—forms the essential possibility of knowledge, and it forms the possibility of "man" as an object of knowledge. In these forms man appears as both a "positive" nature and as a "promise" to be achieved through knowledge.[99] In this way the analytic of finitude as fixed limit, both positive and prophetic, is a normalizing knowledge. The "technico-political" aspect of this knowledge and power aims at producing/enclosing human being within a norm defined instrumentally. The Kantian-philosophical aspect, on the other hand, aims at enclosing human being within the fixed limits designated by a particular image of free, autonomous, rational being. Both of these reflections on finitude attempt to fix the nature of man as an object and a subject of power and knowledge. They both function as positive knowledge and eschatological program. And they aim at the same end, despite the apparently divergent projects they give themselves: the disciplinary control of the body, of life, of space and time, in the name of freedom, truth, and the perfection of man.

The Cartesian Moment

Another aspect of Kant's historical reality frames the way he is able to problematize his own freedom: this is the Cartesian moment. If discipline is the way individual bodies and the lives they lead are made into objects of power and knowledge, then the Cartesian moment is the transformation in the way individuals organize their own subjectivity, their relationship to themselves as subjects, as thinking beings governing themselves and their relation to the truth. The cogito as a form of subjectivity has access to the truth through the simple act of looking. It bases its knowledge on evidence, and it develops its knowledge by conducting its thoughts according to rules which are founded in its own being. Kant's definition of freedom in terms of intellectual freedom—the freedom of the scholar to address the public through the medium of the journal—reflects this new definition of philosophy as discourse, *logos*. The spiritual transformation of the subject through an embodied *askēsis* no longer clearly appears as the condition of access to the truth, and it is no longer the basis of the subject's capacity to use the truth to govern itself or others. On the one hand, because knowledge is a matter of looking at what is evident and following the proper methods of induction and deduction, then the embodied life of the thinker is accidental and insignificant. On the other hand, because truth is ascertained through the act of seeing clearly what is evident and proper methodological thinking, then the body and the manner of living can inhibit the thinker's ability to think. The body, the control of life, of the private use of reason, therefore, becomes a matter of disciplinary control. Rather than being the access to truth, the practice of a way of living must be designed to make the body disappear, to make it interfere as little as possible in the development of knowledge.

The Cartesian moment and the deployment of disciplinary power are inseparable historically. Both take place in the space opened by the dispersal of pastoral power and the struggle against its deployment. But they are not only historically coincident. They move in the same direction, they serve as anchors for each other. In his 1982 course at the Collège, Foucault links Kant to the Cartesian moment, saying that his thought is essential in the displacement of spirituality:

> It seems to me that what one sees in Descartes in a very clear way . . . is given the final twist in Kant, which consists in saying: that which we are not capable of knowing is precisely the very structure of the subject who knows, which means that we are not able to know it. Consequently, the idea of a certain spiritual transformation of the subject, which would finally give it access to something to which it does not have access at the moment, is chimerical and paradoxical. Therefore, the liquidation of what one might call the "spiritual condition" of access to the truth, this liquidation takes place with Descartes and with Kant; Kant and Descartes appear to me the two central moments.[100]

Kant finalizes the Cartesian rupture of philosophy and spirituality by showing that the subject is the condition of all possible experience and as such lies beyond experience itself: the subject cannot be known, or perceived. The notion of a self-transformation of the subject in its very mode of being through a deliberate work on itself is absurd in such a framework.[101] The subject by its very nature structures all possible experience as an object of knowledge—its fixed forms of sensibility and categories of understanding establish the possibility of truth, of true propositions or judgments. There is no possibility that the subject as such does not possess access to truth. Furthermore, truth is not being: being-in-itself, the thing-in-itself, is never given to the subject. No *askēsis* can give the subject an experience of being, of its own being or of being in itself; we can only know being as it appears for a subject constituted such as we are. In order to acquire knowledge and to advance knowledge, the primary condition is that one comprehend and respect the limits of reason itself. By allowing understanding to function within the limits that reason necessarily imposes upon itself, one can develop a coherent knowledge of a domain of objects.

Despite all this, Foucault believes that the spiritual condition of truth does not completely disappear. Its traces remain in Kant's work and it continues to be a problem philosophically. Foucault lists Schelling, Schopenhauer, Nietzsche, Husserl, and Heidegger as examples of thinkers who, even if obliquely, take up this problem.[102] However, the simultaneous rise of biopolitics, which defines life in biomedical and economic terms, and the Cartesian invention of the cogito, which defines reason in terms of method and evidence, obscure the fundamental relationship between one's way of life—one's way of being-in-the-world—and one's access to the truth. In Kant, the problem of the spiritual condition of knowledge is taken up in the question of discipline—the body, as the source of heteronomy must be submitted to the discipline of reason—and in the question of the relationship between the epistemological subject and the ethical subject. With respect to this latter question, in an interview with Hubert Dreyfus and Paul Rabinow in 1983, Foucault again brings up the relation of Kant and Descartes. Here as well he claims that Kant is working within a problematization handed down to him in part by Descartes and by the opening up of the Cartesian moment.

> After Descartes, we have a subject of knowledge which poses for Kant the problem of knowing the relationship between the subject of ethics and that of knowledge. There was much debate in the Enlightenment as to whether these two subjects were completely different or not. Kant's solution was to find a universal subject, which, to the extent that it was universal, could be the subject of knowledge, but which demanded, nonetheless, an ethical attitude—precisely the relationship to the self which Kant proposes in *The Critique of Practical Reason*.[103]

With Descartes, according to Foucault, the subject's relation to the truth is no longer founded upon her *ēthos*, her way of life. The subject who knows is not clearly identical to the subject who lives and acts. In this admittedly not very clear or rigorous statement, Foucault nevertheless indicates that Kant seeks to establish a relationship between the universal subject of reason and the ethical subject that lives and acts in the concrete world. In order to clarify Foucault's response, Dreyfus and Rabinow re-asked their question in different terms: "You mean that once Descartes cut scientific rationality loose from ethics, Kant reintroduced ethics as an applied form of procedural rationality." Foucault responds:

Right. Kant says, "I must recognize myself as universal subject, that is, I must constitute myself in each of my actions as a universal subject by conforming to universal rules." The old questions were reinterpreted: How can I constitute myself as a subject of ethics? Recognize myself as such? Are ascetic exercises needed? Or simply this Kantian relationship to the universal which makes me ethical by conformity to practical reason? Thus Kant introduces one more way in our tradition whereby the self is not merely given but is constituted in relationship to itself as subject.[104]

In each action one must take up a relationship to oneself as a universal legislator of moral law. This universal subject is the foundation for an ethics in that the universal moral law is built into its very structure as a subject. The subject itself is not brought into being through the practice of a way of life, through an ethics, through an *askēsis* which first gives it access to the truth. Philosophy is constituted as a form of knowledge—the knowledge of reason's limits and the laws that it gives to itself—not as a way of life. It becomes an academic discipline. Life, on the other hand, is made to conform to the laws imposed upon on it, either the laws of universal reason or the discipline of the social machine. Life as the material of an ethical work, which gives one access to the truth and to freedom, is absorbed within the disciplines, biopolitics, and the process of normalization. The disciplinization of philosophy occurs when the body, the life of the philosopher, is separated from the practice of philosophy. Philosophy becomes *logos* and no longer *ergon:* it is seen as the production of discourses rather than as the production of ways of life. The Cartesian moment, biopolitics, and disciplinary power emerge and function together. The social-political project is to define freedom in biopolitical terms: health, productivity, and normalcy. The body therefore must be controlled and disciplined in order to fulfill its productive potentials. On the other hand, according to the Cartesian moment, the freedom to attain truth is defined in terms of method and evidence, the ability of reason to follow its own rules. To do this the subject must control his own body and discipline it, so that intellectual freedom can be attained without interference from the heteronomy of a body that functions according to natural determinations. Biopolitics, discipline, and the Cartesian moment all converge in the definition of the body, of life, as the object of disciplinary control. Because the body is no longer seen as an ethical practice, but rather as a biological process, Kant cannot see that his definition of the body as the source of heteronomy and as the object of discipline converges with the spread and intensification of the very forms of power and government that he attempts to resist. The definition of freedom and government in juridical terms—freedom as autonomy, government of one-self as following the laws which one spontaneously gives to oneself—also prevents him from seeing clearly the way in which the law is set up in ser-vice of the norm, and is used and legitimated by it. In other words, while Kant argues that discipline is necessary in order to control the body so that one can become a mature autonomous legislator of universal law, what is actually happening is that the law has been put in the service of the spread of discipline. The promise of autonomy, of freedom, is what makes one accept, and even demand, the discipline of the body and the control of life. Even if Kantian morality offers a powerful resistance to the reduc-tion of the individual to biomedical and economic terms, its definition of freedom in terms of autonomy not only does not impede the work of disci-pline and normalization, it contributes to it.

The horizon against which Kant's project unfolds remained, for the most part, hidden from him: it functioned as the condition of possibility for his thought. Disciplinary practices set up a field of objects to be known and a subject who both knows and controls that field. The Cartesian mo-ment broke with the ascetic relation between the subject and truth such that it became irrational to think that one could transform one's relation to the truth, that the subject in its very being did not have immediate access to truth. Because of the Cartesian moment, Kant will discover human finitude in terms of necessity rather than in terms of possibility. His project will be, as Foucault sees it, to discover in finitude the essence of man: the a priori condition of the possibility of experience. It will be the receptivity of the body—of the forms of sensibility—and the cate-gories of synthesis which structure every possible object of knowledge. Furthermore, the body, as a natural process operating according to phys-ical determinations, is defined as the source of heteronomy, confinement, and falsehood. The Cartesian moment and the rise of disciplinary power function together: the ascetic ground of thinking slips out of the dimen-sion of spirituality, out of the dimension of the ethical, and into the field of discipline. The art of discipline will take over almost completely the field of the arts of the self and of life. The formation of individuals, of bod-ies, of thinking, acting subjects takes place more and more in disciplinary settings, and it is organized more and more around the "normal" as its gravitational center. Because Kant does not grasp the dimensions of his historical moment at the archaeological level—that of the relations of power, knowledge, and subjectivity—he fails to see the way in which man as subject-object is formed within power-knowledge relations, and he can have no explicit recourse to the ascetic transformation of the subject as a site of resistance to this *dispositif.*

The Nietzsche Effect

For Foucault, Kant's thought speaks in two voices: one which says that thinking is the critique which leads us to the transcendental a priori conditions of possible experience; and one which initiates a critical ontology of the present, an ethic of concern with what is happening at the moment. It is the latter voice that Foucault will listen to, and this will lead him to rethink the way in which Kant fashioned his own critique of the present as transcendental philosophy. As Foucault sees it, the rise of the disciplinary mode of power, the despiritualization of the subject and truth, and the invention of a philosophical *ēthos* of critique are defining elements of our own actuality. But if Kant's attempt to problematize his present and to define and practice a form of *parrhēsia* remains more or less blind to the function of discipline and to the contingency of the Cartesian moment precisely because they function as the conditions of possibility of his thought, how is Foucault able to escape that same blindness? Of course, there are other historical events which bring the Enlightenment into a new focus and cast a certain suspicion upon it: the degradations of industrialization, the colonization and exploitation of much of the world by enlightened Europeans, two world wars, the Holocaust, the atomic destruction of Hiroshima and Nagasaki, and so on. But philosophically, what allowed Foucault to begin to get free of the thought of man was his experience of Nietzsche.[105] He claimed: "I am simply Nietzschean, and I try as far as possible, on a certain number of issues, to see with the help of Nietzsche's texts—but also with anti-Nietzschean theses (which are nevertheless Nietzschean!)—what can be done in this or that domain."[106] This is not the place for an account of the development of Foucault's thought and how he came to Nietzsche. Rather, I wish to indicate some of the elements he appropriates from Nietzsche, both methodologically and substantively, that allow him to perceive the present differently. And I want to show how Foucault, with his new Nietzschean insights and approach, is able to discover a way of thinking which is "anti-Nietzschean" while still remaining Nietzschean.

In Foucault's earliest works, Nietzsche's voice is clearly audible and his name is frequently invoked. Nietzsche is one of those thinkers who managed to think from outside, or from the margin of his epoch. It is in the "dernières paroles de Nietzsche" that the tragic madness of the world—excluded by the classical age and normalized by the eighteenth- and nineteenth-century doctors—can be heard to speak.[107] It is Nietzsche whose thought escapes the anthropological sleep: "The Nietzschean undertaking could be understood as the ending point finally given to the proliferation of the interrogation of man."[108] Nietzsche signals the advent of a reflection on language which announced to the Foucault of *The Order of Things* the "death of Man."[109] There were additional sources which served to open Foucault's eyes to the contingency of anthropological thinking (Bataille and Blanchot, for example), but Nietzsche provided him with the tools for understanding and exploiting this contingency.

The Nietzsche whom Foucault adopts is the "genealogical" Nietzsche.[110] Nietzsche's style of genealogy teaches Foucault a number of things. First, the subject, knowledge, and truth do not reside outside of history as its transcendent "origin." The subject and knowledge, as a correct representation of reality, do not finally emerge when this origin is recovered and purified of the accretions of history, illusion, power, ignorance, and so on. Rather, these things are products of history—the subject itself is a historical artifact. Nietzsche initiates a way of thinking which "reintroduces into the realm of becoming everything considered immortal in man."[111] The second lesson Foucault learns from his experience of Nietzsche is that this realm of becoming out of which subjects and objects emerge is constituted through the clash of opposing forces. It is from Nietzsche (filtered through Heidegger) that Foucault discovers the productive dimension of power and is able to fashion, in part, his "genealogy of the modern 'soul'" as a study of the precise forms, techniques, and strategies of power relations.[112] Third, Nietzsche shows Foucault that this history of power relations is played out on bodies and that the body itself even as it is traversed by power spontaneously resists it: "We believe, in any event, that the body obeys the exclusive laws of physiology, and that it escapes the influence of history, but this too is false. The body is molded by a great many distinct regimes; it is broken down by the rhythms of work, rest, and holidays; it is poisoned by food or values, through eating habits or moral laws; it constructs resistances."[113] Finally, Nietzsche strives to invest his genealogy with a therapeutic function. "Its task is to become a curative science."[114] The purpose of shifting the subject and its knowledge or its possible knowledge from the ahistorical into the realm of becoming, the purpose of tracing that event of becoming as an agonism, and of situating the agonism at the level of the body, is to heal by opening up the dimension of the possible.

This catalog is incomplete, of course. It is meant to show merely the elements Foucault appropriates from Nietzsche in order to plot an escape route from the confinements of the present. Furthermore, this experience of Nietzsche is established at the very beginning of Foucault's career and is articulated in the works of the 1960s and up to 1971. There is nothing to suggest that Foucault returned to Nietzsche in any other way to articulate that experience otherwise. However, one is led to wonder how the Foucault of the 1980s would read Nietzsche. Certainly, Nietzsche's work is suggestive of a rich array of practices of care of the self. But this is not the place to begin an exploration of that type.

In his essay on "What Is Enlightenment?" after having sketched the Kantian art of critique in the name of autonomy and on the basis of transcendental philosophy, Foucault offers an alternative set of critical practices. By way of an abbreviated commentary on Baudelaire, Foucault draws out some important elements of what he calls the "attitude of modernity."[115] The attitude of modernity he defines here, which first arises perhaps with Kant's definition of enlightenment, reflects very clearly the Nietzschean effect on Foucault. First, he says that the modern *ēthos* involves a particular relation to time: it is a "consciousness of the discontinuity of time: a break with tradition, a feeling of vertigo in the face of the passing moment."[116] Faced with time as discontinuity, one seeks in the "perpetual movement" of the present "something eternal that is not beyond the present instant, nor behind it, but within it."[117] One seeks to find within the present moment a real possibility of transcending (or transgressing) that moment: "Modernity is the attitude that makes it possible to grasp the 'heroic' aspect of the present moment."[118] The present appears as containing within it a task, and it is the attitude of modernity, the attention to the moment in its "eternity," that seeks out that task and tries to define it. The task is, however, "ironical" because it does not attempt to "treat the passing moment as sacred in order to maintain it or perpetuate it."[119] Rather, it harbors a power of transformation, which means displacement, not destruction, of the present: this "transfiguration does not entail an annulling of reality, but a difficult interplay between the truth of what is real and the exercise of freedom . . . For the attitude of modernity, the high value of the present is in-dissociable from a desperate eagerness to imagine it, to imagine it otherwise than it is, and to transform it not by destroying it but by grasping it in what it is."[120] The subtlety of this passage has been lost on many readers who think Foucault is engaged in a thoroughly destructive enterprise. The modern *ēthos* does not "annul reality," but transforms it precisely by "grasping it in what it is." Finally, Foucault discovers in Baudelaire's sense of the modern attitude "an indispensable asceticism."[121] To practice the modern attitude one must make "of his body, his behavior, his feelings and passions, his very existence, a work of art."[122] The vertiginous attention to the discontinuity of time; the ironical heroization of the moment as a task; the transformation of life, of the "natural" into art, into something "more than natural": these are the basic elements of modernity as Baudelaire sees it. We know, and we have seen over and over again, how Foucault activates this *ēthos* of modernity in his own thinking. Certainly the feeling of vertigo before the ruptures in time is a sensation Foucault experienced and attempted to convey in his work. Grasping the "eternal" that lies within the present is also precisely what he attempted to do in each of his studies; to seek out those forms, relations, discourses, and practices which inhabit the present in such a way that they constituted it in its essence. The present, through the work of this attitude, appears in an entirely new light. In showing the present to be a work of "art"—the effect of *technē*—he makes it into a possibility for art, for a *technē* of "transfiguration." Finally, a privileged space of art is the very existence of the individual, who is also already a product of art—in our present, the arts of disciplinary normalization. The task of modernity is to take up the self as a work of art: for Foucault, this art of the self is far from indifferent or hostile to ethics, it is the real life and substance of it.

Foucault goes on in this essay to present an outline of the kind of *ēthos* which he has tried to develop and practice and which he wishes to define as a legacy of the Enlightenment (one among many possible forms of this legacy). The project Foucault has inherited from Kant diverges from its original formulation in fundamental ways:

> We must try to proceed with the analysis of ourselves as beings who are historically determined, to a certain extent, by the Enlightenment. Such an analysis implies a series of historical inquiries that are as precise as possible; and these inquiries will not be oriented retrospectively toward the "essential kernel of rationality" that can be found in the Enlightenment and that would have to be preserved in any event; they will be oriented toward the "contemporary limits of the necessary," that is, toward what is not or is no longer indispensable for the constitution of ourselves as autonomous subjects.[123]

In this quote it is clear that Foucault's Kantianism is thoroughly un-Kantian: his attention to the present seeks not to critique it in terms of the fixed and universal limits and laws of freedom and of reason, but to provoke a very different sense of the limit. His way of formulating the task in this essay, developed out of a lecture he gave in Paris in 1983, is almost identical to the closing suggestions in his *thèse complémentaire*. In that text he asks: "Isn't it possible to conceive of a critique of finitude which would be as liberating with respect to Man as it is with respect to the Infinite, and which would show that finitude is not the term, but rather the curve and crux in time where the end is a commencement?"[124] If Kantian thought is a reflection on limit, so is that of Foucault. However, where Kant experiences the limit as the expression of the necessary and in this way the limit *within* which experience becomes possible, Foucault thinks it in terms of the contingent and therefore the limit *beyond* which new possibilities await. For Foucault, human finitude means the perpetually possible: it constitutes a territory beyond the frontier that remains to be explored.

Foucault announces the Enlightenment *ēthos* as, at the very least, a suspicion with regard to "humanism."[125] This is because, as Foucault sees it, humanism "has always been obliged to lean on certain conceptions of man borrowed from religion, science, or politics. Humanism serves to color and to justify the conceptions of man to which it is, after all, obliged to take recourse."[126] Humanism is according to this definition uncritical: it is precisely this which Kant was resisting in his appeal to individuals to think for themselves, to free themselves from the ready-made answers to questions concerning their nature and purpose. Again, the way Foucault phrases his critique of humanism in the passage above recalls his attacks on the form of man which he sees at the basis of our thinking. For this reason, Foucault is "inclined to see Enlightenment and humanism in a state of tension rather than identity."[127] The "antihumanism" expressed in this inclination is clearly both an ontological and ethical statement: humanism substitutes a particular political, religious, or scientific image of man for the undefined activity and possibility of human freedom; therefore it is both ontologically false and ethically dangerous. That Foucault's antihumanism is grounded in a deep concern for ethics and truth is nothing shocking: his entire project, from its earliest forms to its final genealogy of care of the self and *parrhēsia,* could have its source and its impetus in nothing else. Yet the question remains and has been raised frequently: Given this antihumanism and this refusal to define the essence of human being, what sense can one have of ethics and truth, of freedom?

Foucault, then, takes up the project of enlightenment, but in this radically transformed sense.

> If the Kantian question was that of knowing what limits knowledge has to renounce transgressing, it seems to me that the critical question today has to be turned back into a positive one: in what is given to us as universal, necessary, obligatory, what place is occupied by whatever is singular, contingent, and the product of arbitrary constraints? The point in brief, is to transform the critique conducted in the form of necessary limitation into a practical critique that takes the form of a possible transgression.[128]

The critique of limits proceeds archaeologically and genealogically. It defines archaeologically the particular problems—"heroic" tasks—which have presented themselves at unique points in time; and it traces genealogically the transfigurations which thought has, through its "art," developed in response to its present.[129] This research is carried out in the name of freedom: "It is not seeking to make possible a metaphysics that has finally become a science; it is seeking to give new impetus, as far and as wide as possible, to the undefined work of freedom."[130] Foucault reiterates this theme in one of the final lectures of his 1983 Collège course where he describes his project as a "history of inventions which refers itself to the principle of freedom, not conceived of as a right of being, but as a capacity of doing."[131] The concluding paragraphs of Foucault's text on the Enlightenment characterize this critical work as "an attitude, an *ēthos,* a philosophical life in which the critique of what we are is at one and the same time the historical analysis of the limits that are imposed on us and the experiment with the possibility of going beyond them."[132] It is a "work on our limits, that is, patient labor giving form to our impatience for liberty."[133] Critical and experimental, analytical and ethical, it is a theoretical project that is simultaneously a practice or ensemble of practices of the self.

All of this resonates with the well-known preface to *The Use of Pleasure* in which Foucault openly characterizes his work as philosophical, but in an unexpected sense. He defines the style of thinking which resulted in that book as an attempt to "get free of oneself."[134] It was a kind of curiosity which has less to do with accumulating knowledge, with reinforcing beliefs and experiences, and more to do with an experiment.

> But, then, what is philosophy today—philosophical activity, I mean—if it is not the critical work that thought brings to bear on itself? . . . The "essay"—which should be understood as the assay or test by which, in the game of truth, one undergoes changes, and not as the simplistic appropriation of others for the purpose of communication—is the living substance of philosophy, at least if we assume that philosophy is still what it was in times past, i.e., an "ascesis," *askēsis,* an exercise of oneself in the activity of thought.[135]

These reflections point to a critical attitude and practice very different from the one advanced by Kant. The "historical ontology of ourselves" would be the work which attends to the present, seeks out what is "eternal" within it, and which presents itself as a task that is inseparable from an ethic understood as an *askēsis.* But in this questioning and displacement of limits, and in this critique of humanism understood as uncritical adherence to particular images of the human essence, what possibilities can Foucault's project offer for the practice of the self? What would such thinking be like? What kinds of freedom can it create?

Conclusion

A New Poetics of Philosophy

In the preceding chapters, I have assembled a few fragments from what one might call Foucault's unwritten genealogy of philosophy. The thread holding these fragments together is the problematization of *parrhēsia* and care of the self. This genealogy shows that our present philosophical situation begins to take shape at the moment when the ancient philosophical project of care was displaced by the modern scientific project of knowledge; the moment when the ancient imperative, *take care of yourself,* was displaced by the modern imperative, *know yourself.* This genealogy suggests that Foucault offers a coherent story about the history of philosophy and the path that led to where we are. In other words, Foucault's final research appears to provide us with new historical knowledge. More specifically, it seems that this genealogy gives us knowledge about ourselves insofar as we take part in the traditions and institutions of philosophy that emerge from this history. In this way, Foucault's project seems to be determined by the modern imperative, *know yourself.* However, to characterize Foucault's project as such and to expect or demand that it present us with historical, objective knowledge about ourselves and about philosophy, is to forget the way Foucault often described his own work. Especially in the period when he was engaged in his excavations of ancient philosophy, but even before then, he described his project in terms that belong less to the modern project of knowledge than to the ancient project of care. In particular, he described his work as an exercise, an *askēsis.* In the introduction to this book, I argued that we have to take this claim seriously if we wish to grasp the meaning of Foucault's excavations of philosophical life. In other words, we have to experience his work as an exercise rather than as the accumulation and transmission of historical knowledge. In these final few pages I want to retrace the steps we have just taken along the path of philosophy. Now, however, I want to show that they do not ultimately lead us to historical knowledge about philosophy (even if they do provide us with such knowledge), but rather that they are an exercise in philosophical care of the self. Through this *askēsis* Foucault was able to transform his relationship to himself as a philosopher, and if we "hear" his discourse properly it can have the same effect on us. To allow this to happen, we must examine the way his work functions both as a diagnosis and a poetics of the present.

Foucault's genealogy of philosophy clearly forms part of his historical ontology of our selves and our present. As we have seen, the formation of modern philosophy as a discursive practice requires two simultaneous developments. On the one hand, the Cartesian moment opens a chasm within the history of philosophical practices and discourse. The consequence of this moment is that the relation between the subject and truth becomes a matter of method rather than *askēsis*. On the other hand, around the same time that this rupture splits the history of philosophy into two heterogeneous forms, new relations of political power begin to take over the technologies and relations of care of the self. In other words, just at the moment when philosophy ceases to conceive of itself as an *askēsis* and a *poiesis* for becoming a subject who has access to the truth—the moment it ceases to conceive of itself as care of the self—political government arises as an ensemble of relations, institutions, and technologies for producing subjects who are normal: politics starts to take care of people. The modern philosophical *neglect* of the self (life, the body, pleasure, pain, the passions, desire, and so on) as a material to be formed in order to fashion a subject open to the truth, and to the truth of her self, goes along with the movement by which institutions of disciplinary power absorb the poetics of subjectivity, the care of the self. The care of space, time, bodies, and existence is now primarily managed by disciplinary experts (such as doctors, psychiatrists, teachers, nutritionists, life coaches, self-help gurus) within disciplinary institutions (schools, hospitals, health clubs, and so on) and is oriented toward the construction of normal (healthy, well-adjusted, productive, and predictable) individuals and lives. Bodies, space, time, and relations are managed by disciplinary and normalizing procedures; they are arranged in precise ways that induce specific effects. In this way, the Cartesian moment and the advent of biopolitics (power over life, the power to form subjects productively) arise and function together. These developments are irreducible to each other but are always interrelated.

Our present situation is defined by these two events. Modern philosophical subjectivity is constituted by the Cartesian project of knowledge understood as a thoroughly discursive intellectual activity. This mode of philosophical subjectivity—the set of norms, relations, methods, and practices that define us as philosophers—is embodied in modern academic institutions of philosophy; it is incorporated in and through our philosophical activity. It constitutes the strangely invisible background, the given place, the system of actuality within which we think. This arrangement, these forms and relations, seem so inevitable and natural that we tend not to investigate how they got to be the way they are or challenge how they shape the texts we read, the work we produce, the language we use, the thoughts we think, and the lives we lead. In other words, we are formed as readers, writers, speakers, and subjects by the discipline of philosophy, a discipline that is a historical artifact, far from inevitable and far from natural. This *dispositif* of philosophy structures the knowledge we produce, it shapes the way we think and talk and the way we arrange our space and time, the way we inhabit our bodies, and our relations.

Our relation to philosophy, to its history, its texts, to ourselves as philosophers is therefore permeated by the *dispositif* of the Cartesian moment and modern relations of power and knowledge. I have tried to indicate what this means in my presentation of Foucault's reading of Descartes and Kant. In Descartes we see the traces of spiritual exercise in his *Meditations* and in his *Discourse on Method*, but we also see in our own relation to his text the consequence of his project. We no longer approach the *Meditations* as a set of spiritual exercises to be performed, but rather as an argument, as a set of propositions to be assessed in terms of logical validity, methodological coherence, and reference to external reality verifiable through the presentation of evidence. In other words, according to Foucault, what makes us Cartesian is not that we develop theories or ideas about the mind-body problem, the role of evidence, the nature of clear and distinct perception, or even that we deal with these problems. Rather, what makes us Cartesian is that we take up a certain relation to texts as objects of knowledge, to problems as objects of thought, to ourselves as thinking beings. To be determined by the Cartesian moment is to practice philosophy as a discursive activity determined by methods of analysis for manipulating propositions and evaluating them according to evidence and logic. It is in this sense that the Cartesian mode of subjectivity constitutes us as philosophers when we sit down to read a text or take up a problem. Furthermore, this form of subjectivity, this philosophical activity, is not deposited somewhere in our unconscious; it is inscribed in the very institutions of academic philosophy. In order for discourse to count as philosophy it must be produced according to the academic norms of the institutions of philosophy, institutions that are grounded upon the Cartesian moment. One becomes a philosopher through the incorporation of the proper mode of subjectivity, the proper relation to oneself as a thinker, and the proper relation to truth defined as knowledge.

In my presentation of Foucault's complex engagement with the thought of Kant, I illustrated the way modern philosophy constructs a critical project that not only neglects the fact that life has come to be managed and determined by discipline, normalization, and biopolitics, but moreover contributes to this process. Kant defines philosophy on a political model of legislating and judging. Subjectivity, freedom, and the relation to truth are defined as autonomy, self-legislation. Kant defines the danger that autonomy must confront as the heteronomous forces of na-

ture acting in and through our bodies. Therefore, in order to realize the
truth of ourselves, our autonomy, we must submit the body to the strict
control and discipline of reason understood as lawgiver. Politically, this
means we must obey in the realm of the private use of our reason, we must
let ourselves function as cogs in the social machine. Doing so will allow for
the space of free speech—discursive, intellectual freedom—to function
as critical truth and autonomy. However, by defining social-political freedom in these terms, Kant submits the body to the disciplinary, normalizing, and bioeconomic project of modern political power. Furthermore,
Kant establishes the autonomous, well-disciplined critical judge as the
norm articulated by critical philosophy. This autonomous judge, as we
have seen, is made possible on the basis of the disciplinary control of the
body and life. Therefore, in defining philosophical subjectivity as autonomous reason and establishing it as the normative model of human
life, the truth of our selves, Kant's critical project contributes to and even
requires the disciplinary control of life.

All of this articulates part of the historical ontology of the present
and provides a kind of historical knowledge about our selves. As such it is,
like his earlier studies of the prison, medicine, psychiatry, the human sciences, and so on, part of Foucault's diagnosis of the present in terms of
power, knowledge, and subjectivity. Nonetheless, we must recognize that
Foucault's final project does not function in the same way as these earlier
archaeologies and genealogies. First of all, this is because the final project
provides a genealogy of the very discourse that Foucault was speaking and
writing: that is, philosophical discourse. Second, he does not just diagnose the present form of his own discourse; in doing so he *transforms* it.

Foucault's genealogy of philosophy constitutes a new form of philosophical activity, a different relation to philosophy, to its history, and to its
modern practice of subjectivity. Foucault does not take up a Cartesian or
Kantian relation to philosophical texts, to the history of philosophy, or to
the embodied and institutional life of the philosopher. He does not submit texts to analysis and evaluation in terms of logical validity, methodological coherence, or correspondence to an external reality, nature, or
substance. He does not judge them in order to condemn them to falsehood and irrationality or to praise them for their objective truth and rationality. In other words, he does not attempt to consider them as systems
of propositions organized by the *telos* of producing knowledge. His project
does not employ the techniques necessary for the production of knowledge and self-knowledge. Rather, Foucault grasps philosophical texts as
modes of constituting philosophical life or subjectivity. That is, he sees
them through a different lens, not as arguments but as portraits or even
"biographies," not as theories but as technologies and practices. What al-

lows them to appear this way is the application of different technologies of reading, technologies that make possible a different experience of the truths these texts bring about. In other words, Foucault transforms his mode of being a philosopher and his relation to the truth; he practices a new mode of philosophical subjectivity. This practice cannot be reduced to the modern Cartesian project of knowledge; this relation to the truth cannot be reduced to method and evidence, but rather must be understood as an exercise, an *askēsis*.

In this way, Foucault's genealogy directs our attention not just to the discursive practice of philosophy—the production of discourse—but also to the practice of philosophy as a way of life inserted into larger contexts of power and knowledge. Philosophy is an art of living that problematizes. It resists deployments of power, knowledge, and subjectivity by forming arts of living and speaking. In other words, philosophy develops practices of subjectivity, forms of living, and modes of discourse that challenge and transform those that confine thought and life. Excavating philosophy as care of the self opens up a kind of aesthetic appreciation of philosophy. This is not just an attention to the style of discourse that forms texts, but to the style and construction of modes of living toward which these texts gesture, to the techniques they employ or articulate for giving form to life. This is not to say that we should read philosophy as if it were literature or poetry. But rather we can read it as critical reflection on, and artistic transformation of, life. In other words, life is the substance and the product of art; philosophy is both a *poiesis*—a work we perform on ourselves—and a *technē*—a form of reflective awareness about how to work on ourselves.

Philosophical modes of subjectivity, then, are born out of struggle, as forms of resistance and exercises of freedom, in order to establish new connections between subjects and truths. Foucault's project of care of the self is, therefore, not arbitrary. He was not promoting narcissism or developing a new "dandyism." Rather, I have shown that his philosophical poetics is always guided by his problematization of modern forms of power, knowledge, and subjectivity. His final project maintains constant reference to his earlier work, and this problematization shapes the way Foucault reads philosophical texts, just as much as these texts reconfigure how he understands himself as a philosopher.

Philosophy therefore offers critical appraisals of and theories about care of the self, and at the same time, functions as an element of care of the self. In other words, genealogy as care not only transforms our relation to philosophy, but also opens up new philosophical projects. One can discover a whole history of different techniques for constituting ethical subjects and subjects who have access to truth, for constituting different forms of the relation between the subject and truth, between the subject and herself, and between the subject and others. Genealogy opens up new realms of philosophical life. As we saw in the introduction, the history of philosophy offers "a whole rich and complex field of historicity in the way the individual is summoned to recognize himself as an ethical subject."[1]

To continue to activate this new experience of philosophical subjectivity, we would have to remain constantly aware of our present situation in terms of power, knowledge, and subjectivity; continue to search the history of philosophy for techniques and practices that respond to the dangers of the present; and maintain an experimental attitude, a willingness to test practices, to reimagine the meaning and form of our relations to ourselves and to others. The truths that such a philosophical work opens onto are, then, *parrhēsiastic*. They are so in two senses. On the one hand, philosophical truths are diagnostic. Philosophical discourses and lives are true to the extent that they effectively and meaningfully problematize who we are in terms of power, knowledge, and subjectivity. And on the other hand, philosophical truths are etho-poetic. The truth of philosophical discourses and lives is to be experienced in their transformative effects, their power to reveal and resist the intertwining, intensification, and mutual reinforcement of relations of power, knowledge, and subjectivity. The etho-poetic truths of philosophy are the new possibilities it brings into being, the new systems of actuality it fashions. The experience of these truths takes place in the exercises of thought and in the experiments that we perform, in the test (*épreuve*) of resistance and transformation.

Foucault's work also reveals that the subjectivities, practices, and truths that this etho-poetic exercise of philosophy produces and activates can never be taken as final or absolute. *Parrhēsiastic* truth is linked to the problematization it diagnoses and resists. Once philosophical arts of resistance are detached from the problematization that gives rise to them, they lose their truth effects. Cartesian philosophy arose as a form of resistance to practices, discourses, and subjectivity that were dangerous, stultifying, and untrue (pastoral power, the Renaissance episteme). The truth of Descartes's spiritual exercises was that they produced transformative effects and problematized the deployment of power, knowledge, and subjectivity that they confronted. But the mode of subjectivity he practiced has been detached from this problem, linked to new relations of power and knowledge, and now forms the basis of a new problematization. Our modern form of philosophical subjectivity is the sedimentation of previous arts of resistance. But Foucault shows that all forms of subjectivity are technologies, arts of the self that emerged through concrete historical problematizations. This means that no set of practices, discourses, or forms of life can be accepted as final, universal, and true, because they all arise as concrete responses to concrete problems. There is, therefore, no natural form of human life; the most natural thing about us is that the problem of being human always requires new responses and new forms of life. This means that the diagnostic and poetic truths we produce and activate here and now, to the extent that they are true—that they respond to and transform our present modes of being—will form the basis of future problematizations and will have to be resisted and transformed yet again later. For this reason, Foucault claimed "not that everything is bad, but that everything is dangerous, which is not the same as bad. If everything is dangerous, then we always have something to do."[2]

Foucault shows us that philosophy, as care of the self, has no conclusion, no terminus; it can never be fully achieved or finished. Rather, the philosophical art of care of the self is ongoing and experimental. And how could it be otherwise? For the point at which we cease to take care of ourselves is the point at which we cease to be ourselves.

Abbreviations

Unpublished Courses by Foucault at the Collège de France

"CdF81"   "Subjectivité et vérité: Cours au Collège de France, 1981"

"CdF83"   "Le gouvernement de soi et des autres: Cours au Collège de France, 1983"

"CdF84"   "Le courage de la vérité (Le gouvernement de soi et des autres, II): Cours au Collège de France, 1984"

Courses by Foucault Published in France

CdF75   *Les anormaux: Cours au Collège de France, 1974–1975*

CdF76   *"Il faut défendre la société": Cours au Collège de France, 1976*

CdF78   *Sécurité, territoire, population: Cours au Collège de France, 1978*

CdF82   *L'herméneutique du sujet: Cours au Collège de France, 1981–1982*

Other Works by Foucault

BC   *The Birth of the Clinic: An Archaeology of Medical Perception*

DE   *Dits et écrits, 1954–1984* (4 vols.)

DP   *Discipline and Punish: The Birth of the Prison*

DT   *Discourse and Truth: The Problematization of Parrhēsia*

EW1   *The Essential Works of Foucault, 1954–1984*, vol. 1, *Ethics, Subjectivity, and Truth*

EW2   *The Essential Works of Foucault, 1954–1984*, vol. 2, *Aesthetics, Method, and Epistemology*

EW3   *The Essential Works of Foucault, 1954–1984*, vol. 3, *Power*

FL   *Foucault Live: Collected Interviews, 1961–1984*

ABBREVIATIONS

FR   *The Foucault Reader*

HF   *Histoire de la folie à l'âge classique*

HS   *The History of Sexuality,* vol. 1, *An Introduction*

MIP   *Mental Illness and Psychology*

OT   *The Order of Things: An Archaeology of the Human Sciences*

RC   *Religion and Culture*

TS   *Technologies of the Self: A Seminar with Michel Foucault*

UP   *The Use of Pleasure,* vol. 2 of *The History of Sexuality*

Notes

Introduction

1. Michel Foucault, preface to *Anti-Oedipus: Capitalism and Schizophrenia,* by Gilles Deleuze and Félix Gauttari, trans. Robert Hurley, Mark Seem, and Helen R. Lane (Minneapolis: University of Minesota Press, 1983), xiii.

2. Foucault, preface to *Anti-Oedipus,* xiii. Foucault wrote this in 1977. He had not yet made his supposed shift to the question of ethics, the problem of subjectivity, and the arts of the self. And yet he already uses the language that would later become very familiar to his auditors at the Collège de France and elsewhere.

3. I want to insist that by calling Foucault's project an introduction to *the* philosophical life, I do not mean to suggest that for Foucault there is but one form of philosophical activity. To the contrary, Foucault's final research reveals a multitude of different forms of philosophical life, and it gestures toward an open horizon of possibility for creating as yet undiscovered modes of philosophical life.

4. To my knowledge, Ladelle McWhorter's book *Bodies and Pleasures: Foucault and the Politics of Sexual Normalization* (Bloomington: Indiana University Press, 1999) best comprehends and enacts this understanding of Foucault's work and of the philosophical task. Her work has helped me to understand the transformative function of Foucault's work.

5. *UP,* 8.

6. Michel Foucault, "The Masked Philosopher," interview with Christian Delacampagne, April 6, 1980, in *FL,* 305.

7. *UP,* 8.

8. Ibid., 11.

9. Ibid. This passage has a tone and a vocabulary which are decidedly "Senecan." The notion of the voyage of the self outside of itself, resulting in a "cosmic" view (looking down on oneself from above); and the importance of old age not as a period of life but as a characteristic relationship to oneself which is privileged and which is a practice, an *askēsis,* are impossible to ignore.

10. See, for example, *DE,* 1:662–63 (no. 55).

11. See, for example, *DE,* 1:553 (no. 42), 1:581 (no. 47). In this reference Foucault also contrasts structuralism and existentialism in terms of their "penetration" into the concrete existence of individuals in the form of a style of existence.

12. "CdF84," March 14.

13. *UP,* 8. This quote reinforces the idea that Foucault's final works are not

simply *about* care of the self, but more fundamentally, they *are* a practice of care of the self.

14. *CdF82*, 241

15. Foucault does later qualify his remarks. See "Ethics of the Concern for Self" in *FL*, 448. It seems to me that he does not retract the claim that an ethics of the self is unique and essential as a resistance to power, but rather he backs away from the idea that it is the only or the ultimate resistance to modern power.

16. *DE*, 1:553 (no. 42).

17. Ibid.

18. *DE*, 1:581 (no. 47).

19. Ibid.

20. The best-known formulations of this claim are in Foucault's essay on Kant's "What Is Enlightenment?" in *DE*, 4:562–77 (no. 339).

21. I am referring, of course, to *Discipline and Punish* and *The History of Sexuality*, vol. 1. See chapter 5 of the present study.

22. The care of the self is the theme of Foucault's last two published books, *The Use of Pleasure* and *The Care of the Self*, as well as numerous lectures, interviews, articles, and his courses in Paris and elsewhere beginning in 1981 and continuing until his last course in 1984.

23. *UP*, 26–32. This is the basic structure of ethical practice Foucault discovers in his return to ancient philosophy.

24. Andrew Cutrofello, *Discipline and Critique: Kant, Poststructuralism, and the Problem of Resistance* (Albany: State University of New York Press, 1994), 116–35.

25. *CdF82*, 3–4.

26. The archives of the Centre Michel Foucault are held by the Institut Mémoires de L'Édition Contemporaine. The IMEC is housed at L'abbaye d'Ardenne, 14280 Saint-Germain-la-Blanche-Herbe, outside the city of Caen. Audio recordings of most of Foucault's lectures at the Collège de France are available at the Bibliothèque du Collège de France in Paris.

27. See, for example, *CdF82*, 19—but see the entire lecture of January 6.

28. "CdF83," March 2.

29. Michel Foucault, "Truth Is the Future," interview with M. Dillon, November 1980, in *FL*, 301.

30. John McCumber, *Time in the Ditch: American Philosophy and the McCarthy Era* (Evanston, Ill.: Northwestern University Press, 2001), xx.

31. Michel Foucault, interview with Charles Ruas, September 15, 1983, in *FL*, 404–5.

32. *UP*, 32.

Part 1

1. See *The Use of Pleasure* and *The Care of the Self*.

2. Foucault had not adequately elucidated the nature of this crisis prior to his 1983 Collège de France course.

3. Is it that democratic discourse requires that one speak the "truth" or that one speak "truthfully"? The former would mean that one says what is true, and the latter that one says what one truly believes. For Hannah Arendt, politics is the realm of the latter form of truthfulness ("Truth and Politics," in *Between Past and Future* [New York: Penguin Books, 1993], 227–64; I am grateful to Serena Parekh and Andrew Cutrofello for calling my attention to this ambiguity in the concept of political truth and to Arendt's treatment of the problem). It is not clear that the institution of democracy in Athens had either view in mind. For Foucault, what is at stake is the way democracy comes to be problematized with respect to truth and to the subject who speaks. I might add here that rethinking the concept of truth in terms of diagnosis and etho-poetics might alter the problem. It appears that Arendt treats the truthfulness of statements in a rather traditional way: the statement is true if it corresponds either to the state of affairs or to the belief one holds. Neither diagnostic truth nor etho-poetic truth fit this model. Diagnostic truth is "disclosive" rather than "adequate," and etho-poetic truth is transformative and creative rather than objective.

Chapter 1

1. "It was a matter of analyzing, not behaviors or ideas, nor of societies and their 'ideologies,' but the problematizations through which being offers itself to be, necessarily, thought—and the practices on the basis of which these problematizations are formed. The archaeological dimension of the analysis made it possible to examine the forms themselves; its genealogical dimension enabled me to analyze their formation out of the practices and the modifications undergone by the latter" (*UP,* 11–12).

2. *CdF82,* 16, January 6.

3. I have chosen to reconstitute this horizon in its totality based on a synthetic reading of Foucault's several attempts to interpret it. I take these different approaches as successive attempts to articulate a complex historical situation along all of the possible axes of interpretation. Furthermore, it is not clear that Plato's writings elaborate a coherent and systematic theory of philosophical *parrhēsia* so much as a series of experiments which engage the historical situation.

4. See *DT,* 1; "CdF84," February 8, February 1.

5. "CdF84," February 1.

6. Ibid.

7. Ibid.

8. Ibid.

9. Ibid.

10. Ibid.

11. Ibid.

12. *DT,* 8.

13. The opposition between *parrhēsia* and rhetoric is decisive in the problematization of democracy in Athens.

14. "CdF84," February 8.

15. Ibid.

16. See the section "Truth and Power: The Problematization of *Parrhēsia*" later in this chapter.

17. "CdF84," February 8.

18. Ibid.

19. Ibid., February 1.

20. "CdF83," January 5.

21. "CdF84," February 1.

22. Ibid. See also Thomas Flynn's excellent summary of this lecture, "Foucault as *Parrhēsiast*," in *The Final Foucault,* ed. James Bernauer and David Rasmussen (Cambridge: MIT Press, 1988). This work originally appeared as volume 12, nos. 2–3, of the journal *Philosophy and Social Criticism* (1987).

23. "CdF84," February 1.

24. Ibid.

25. Ibid.

26. Ibid.

27. Foucault clarifies what he means by the notion of fiction in the following statement: "As for the matter of fiction, it is very important to me. I am quite aware that I have never written anything but fictions. I'm not saying for all that that this is outside truth. It seems to me the possibility exists to make fiction work in truth, to induce effects of truth with a discourse of fiction, and to make it so that the discourse of truth creates, 'fabricates' something that does not yet exist, therefore, 'fictionalizes.' One 'fictionalizes' history starting from a political reality that makes it true, one 'fictionalizes' a political outlook that does not yet exist starting from an historical truth" (Michel Foucault, "Power Affects the Body," interview with Lucett Finas, January 1–15, 1977 [date of initial publication in *La Quinzaine Littéraire* 247], in *FL,* 213).

28. *HS,* 135–59.

29. *UP,* 5–6.

30. See, for example, *HS,* 59–60. I am going through this development schematically. It has been handled at length elsewhere: see, for example, James Bernauer, *Michel Foucault's Force of Flight: Towards an Ethics of Thought* (New Jersey: Humanities, 1990); and Hubert Dreyfus and Paul Rabinow, *Michel Foucault: Beyond Structuralism and Hermeneutics,* 2nd ed. (Chicago: University of Chicago Press, 1983).

31. *HS,* 17–23.

32. Foucault's first reference to the term *parrhēsia* is in *CdF82,* 132. It will become a main theme of the course and be the central topic of "CdF83" and "CdF84."

33. See chapter 3 of the present study.

34. "CdF84," February 1.

35. Ibid.

36. Ibid.

37. *CdF82,* 241.

38. Ibid., 241–42.

39. "CdF83," January 12; "CdF84," February 8; *DT,* 12–48.

40. Robert J. Bonner, *Aspects of Athenian Democracy* (New York: Russel and Russel, 1933), chap. 4, pp. 67–85.

41. *DT,* 113–16. The aristocratic critique of democratic discourse clearly reflects a desire to establish rigid power relations in the city. It is a desire to set up controls which restrict political discourse to the aristocratic class. Likewise, in modern democracy, normalizing judgments and disciplinary techniques control political discourse by identifying and producing subjects who have the "right" to speak and those who do not—or who cannot because their discourse cannot be taken seriously (the abnormal: the insane, the uneducated, the criminal, and so on).

42. *DT,* 48.

43. Michel Foucault, "Problematics," in *FL,* 420–21. Foucault's experience of "thought" is remarkably similar to that described by Arendt in her essay "On Thinking and Moral Consideration," in *Responsibility and Judgment* (New York: Shocken Books, 2003), 159–89. There she describes thinking as an activity, or a way of being, in which one "unfreezes" frozen thoughts, concepts, or words. For the Foucauldian analyst, this would be the activity or way of being by which one unfreezes the problematics frozen into rigid forms of relations and practices.

44. Foucault, "Problematics," *FL,* 421.

45. Ibid.

46. Ibid.

47. Ibid.

48. Ibid.

49. *UP,* 11.

50. Ibid., 11–12.

51. Foucault, "Problematics," *FL,* 420–21.

52. "CdF84," February 8.

53. "CdF83," January 26; *DT,* 20.

54. *DT,* 20.

55. Ibid.

56. Euripides, *Ion,* trans. K. H. Lee (Warminster, Eng.: Aris and Phillips, 1997); Greek text, Oxford University Press, 1981.

57. Euripides, *Ion,* lines 590–95.

58. Ibid., line 594.

59. Ibid., line 621.

60. Ibid., line 594.

61. Ibid., lines 670–75.

62. Ibid.

63. "CdF83," February 2.

64. Ibid.; "CdF84," February 8.

65. "CdF83," February 2.

66. Ibid.

67. Thucydides, "The Funeral Oration of Pericles," bk. 2, chap. 4 of *The Peloponnesian War,* trans. Rex Warner (Baltimore: Penguin Books, 1954).

68. "CdF84," February 8.

69. Ibid.; see also Euripides' plays *Ion, Hippolytus,* and *The Phoenician Women.*

70. "CdF84," February 8.

71. *DT,* 27; "CdF83," January 19.

72. Euripides, *Ion,* lines 590–95.

73. Euripides, *Orestes,* trans.William Arrowsmith (Chicago: University of Chicago Press, 1958). Foucault's notes in *Discourse and Truth* cite the translation by Philip Vellacott in *Orestes and Other Plays* (New York: Penguin Books, 1983).

74. *DT,* 38–42.

75. Ibid., 38–40.

76. Ibid., 39.

77. Ibid., 40.

78. Ibid., 41.

79. Ibid.

80. Ibid.

81. "CdF83," February 2.

82. According to Foucault's reading, Plato does not simply reject democracy. His problematization of democratic life and speech is subtler than that. While it is true that Plato is a harsh critic of Athenian democracy, and in some ways democracy in general, this fact should not blind readers to his attempt to reimagine democratic *parrhēsia.* See Sarah Monoson, *Plato's Democratic Entanglements* (Princeton: Princeton University Press, 2000).

83. "CdF84," February 8.

84. Ibid.

85. Ibid. Foucault also shows that this perception of democracy and its discursive game is evident in texts of the fourth century such as Isocrates' "On Peace" and Demosthenes' "Third Philippic." Both of these texts show that the democratic assembly will not tolerate any discourse that does not flatter it. See *DT,* 49–53; Foucault refers to Isocrates, "On Peace," paragraph 14; Demosthenes, "Third Philippic," paragraphs 3–4.

86. "CdF83," February 9; DT, 54–55.

87. Plato, *Republic,* trans. Paul Shorey, in *Plato: The Collected Dialogues,* ed. Edith Hamilton and Huntington Cairns (Princeton: Princeton University Press, 1961), 557b.

88. Plato, *Republic,* 561d.

89. Ibid., 557b (my italics).

90. Ibid., 558b.

91. Ibid., 493b.

92. Ibid., 492c.

93. Ibid., 493c.

94. Plato, *Crito,* trans. Hugh Tredennick, in *Plato: The Collected Dialogues,* ed. Edith Hamilton and Huntington Cairns (Princeton: Princeton University Press, 1961), 44d.

95. Plato, *Republic,* 493a–d.

96. Ibid., 493b–c.

97. Ibid., 560b.

98. Foucault does not use the term "biopolitics" in his analysis of the problematization of democracy in fifth-century Athens. This analysis of the *Republic* is my own attempt to develop what Foucault says in "CdF83" and "CdF84." The structural analogy between the three fields of analysis in Plato and those in Foucault is my suggestion. It does, however, fit with Foucault's understanding of Plato's problematization of politics. See the beginning of chapter 3 of the present study.

99. "CdF83," February 9.

100. "CdF84," February 8.

101. Ibid.

102. Ibid.

103. *CdF82*, 4.

104. Ibid., 303.

105. Ibid., 6.

106. Ibid.

107. Foucault would be in agreement, in general, with thinkers such as Charles Taylor, E. R. Dodds, and Bruno Snell who also think that the self as we know it is a modern invention or discovery.

108. *CdF82*, 9.

109. Ibid.

110. Ibid., 82.

111. Ibid., 46–47.

112. Ibid.

113. See Arendt, for example, in "On Thinking and Moral Consideration," in *Responsibility and Judgment.*

114. *CdF82*, 82–82.

115. *EW1*, 226.

116. *CdF82*, 443–44.

117. Ibid., 444.

118. Ibid., 443.

119. Ibid., 79–81, 465–67.

120. Ibid., 16ff.

121. Ibid., 16–17.

122. Ibid., 184.

123. Ibid., 17.

124. Ibid.

125. Ibid.

126. Ibid.

127. Ibid., 18.

128. Ibid., 19.

129. Ibid., 17–18.

130. Ibid., p. 18.

131. *UP,* 72.

132. *CdF82*, 184; see also 19, 180–84.

133. "CdF84," March 14.

Chapter 2

1. Foucault provides interpretations of a number of other works by Plato. In the final lecture of his 1983 Collège course, he presents detailed readings of *Gorgias* and *Phaedrus* that reveal the role of *parrhēsia* in Socratic dialogue. Foucault makes occasional reference to the *Laws* (as we will see below) in the same course, and he offers readings of other letters of Plato. However, I have chosen to focus on the *Seventh Letter,* the *Apology, Alciabiades,* and *Laches* for a few reasons. First, Foucault's interpretation of these four texts lays out the basic themes that he began to develop in 1982 and continued to pursue in 1984. His most detailed philosophical approach to Plato and Socrates is to be found in his sustained interpretation of these texts—the dialogues in particular. The connection to the political context is most evident in the *Seventh Letter* and the *Apology.* The two roads that *parrhēsia* and care of the self follow in later thinkers are apparent in *Alcibiades* and *Laches.*

2. Plato, *Seventh Letter,* trans. A. Post, in *Plato: The Collected Dialogues,* ed. Edith Hamilton and Huntington Cairns (Princeton: Princeton University Press, 1961).

3. "CdF83," February 16.

4. Plato, *Seventh Letter,* 328c.

5. Ibid., 328e.

6. Ibid., 329b.

7. "CdF83," February 16.

8. Ibid.

9. Plato, *Seventh Letter,* 331b–d.

10. See chapter 1.

11. "CdF83," February 16.

12. Ibid.

13. Plato, *Seventh Letter,* 330d–e.

14. Ibid., 330d.

15. "CdF83," February 16.

16. Plato, *Seventh Letter,* 331a–c.

17. "CdF83," February 16.

18. Plato, *Seventh Letter,* 340b.

19. Ibid., 340c.

20. Ibid., 340d.

21. Ibid., 340c–d; "CdF83," February 16.

22. "CdF83," February 16.

23. Ibid.; Plato, *Seventh Letter,* 341c.

24. "CdF83," February 16.

25. Ibid.

26. Ibid.

27. See chapter 1 of the present study for a discussion of the different modalities of veridiction outlined by Foucault.

28. "CdF83," February 16.

29. Plato, *Seventh Letter,* 342b.

30. Plato, *Republic,* 336b–354b.

31. Plato, *Seventh Letter,* 343e.

32. Ibid., 344b.

33. "CdF83," February 16.

34. Plato, *Seventh Letter,* 341c.

35. Ibid., 344c.

36. Michel Foucault, "Self Writing," in *EW1,* 209.

37. Foucault, "Self Writing," *EW1,* 210.

38. See Michel Foucault, "On the Genealogy of Ethics," in *EW1,* 258, for the dismissal of ancient ethics; see *EW1,* 294–95, for the critique of philosophy as retrieval of the past.

39. Foucault, "On the Genealogy of Ethics," *EW1,* 295

40. Foucault, "Self Writing," *EW1,* 212–13.

41. Pierre Hadot, "Réflexions sur la notion de 'culture de soi,'" in *Exercises spirituels et philosophie antique,* 2nd ed. (Paris: Albin Michel, 2002), 329.

42. Plato, *Apology,* trans. Hugh Tredennick, in *Plato: The Collected Dialogues,* ed. Edith Hamilton and Huntington Cairns (Princeton: Princeton University Press, 1961), 17b.

43. Plato, *Apology,* 17a.

44. "CdF84," February 15.

45. Ibid.

46. Plato, *Apology,* 17d.

47. "CdF84," February 15; "CdF83," March 2; see also Burnett, *Euthyphro, Apology, Crito,* 67; and Sallis, *Being and Logos* (Bloomington: Indiana University Press, 1996), 30n.

48. "CdF83," March 2.

49. Plato, *Apology,* 17c.

50. "CdF83," March 2.

51. Ibid.; Plato, *Apology,* 17c.

52. "CdF83," March 2.

53. One thing that should be clear is that if we are to construct something like a Foucauldian ethics of the self, we cannot base it on the quest for the true life understood as a natural life. The concept of the natural, as becomes clear in part 2, has normalizing effects and is one of the main relays in the power-knowledge network of biopolitics. Therefore, if there is such a thing as a *true life,* then it refers to a different concept or foundation of truth. The argument I develop through this book is that Foucault's conception of truth is both diagnostic—the truth is that which discloses power-knowledge relations—and it is etho-poetic—the truth is that which brings about transformations in subjectivity and life.

54. "CdF83," March 2; "CdF84," February 15; Plato, *Apology,* 31c.

55. Plato, *Apology,* 31c.

56. "CdF83," March 2; "CdF84," February 15; Plato, *Apology,* 31d.

57. "CdF83," March 2.

58. "CdF84," February 15.

59. Ibid.

60. Ibid.

61. Ibid.

62. Ibid.

63. Ibid.

64. Ibid.

65. Ibid.

66. Ibid.

67. Ibid.

68. The way *examination* functions as a form of power will be discussed in more detail in part 2.

69. See chapter 1 of the present study.

70. Plato, *Republic,* 560b.

71. "CdF84," February 15.

72. Plato, *Apology,* 29d–e; "CdF84," February 15.

73. "CdF84," February 15.

74. Ibid.

75. Ibid.

76. Perhaps this is a good spot to address a frequent critique of Foucault's philosophical ethics. His notion of care of the self, or as he often called it, the aesthetics of existence, is often criticized as narcissistic and irresponsible. Pierre Hadot, for example, worried that Foucault's interpretation of ancient philosophy as a "culture of the self" could lead to a "dandyism of the 20th century" ("Reflections sur la notion de 'culture du soi,'" in *Exercises spirituals et philosophie antique,* 331). Charles Taylor criticized Foucault for presupposing an irresponsible and arbitrary glorification of freedom, without positing any notion of the good life to guide it ("Foucault on Freedom and Truth," *Political Theory: An International Journal of Political Philosophy* 12 [May 1984]: 152–83). It should already be clear from Foucault's discussion of the political problem in Athens and the formation of care of the self as a resistance to political control, that his approach to ethics is neither narcissistic nor arbitrary. A close reading of Foucault's texts does not yield a nihilistic narcissism. Perhaps one might argue that the very language of care of the self, or aesthetics of existence, reflects a pervasive "aesthetization" and "subjectivizing" tendency in his thought. The term "aesthetics" supposedly refers to a reduction of human activity to the level of pleasure, subjective tastes, and creative freedom unbound by ideas of intersubjective responsibility. Yet the term "aesthetic" is not always, or even perhaps primarily, understood in these senses. Kant, a thinker to whom Foucault returned time and time again throughout his career, defined aesthetics as the experience of a *sensus communis.* It is a space defined in terms of communicability. Aesthetic pleasure cannot be separated as such from the need to communicate that pleasure: "It must be the universal communicability of the mental state, in the given presentation, which underlies the judgment of taste as its subjective condition, and the pleasure in the object must be its consequence" (Kant, *Critique of Judgment,* trans. Werner Pluhar [Indianapolis: Hackett, 1987], 61). Aesthetic experience, aesthetic pleasure, is inseparable from aesthetic judgment, and aesthetic judgment is inseparable from the *sensus communis*—the sense of belonging to a community—and the idea of universal communicability, which founds it (Kant, *Critique of Judgment,* 87–90, pp. 159–62). Kant provides three maxims which define the notion of the *sensus communis* and links it to the idea of universal communicability: "1) to think for oneself; 2) to think from the

standpoint of everyone else; and 3) to think always consistently" (ibid., 160–61). Aesthetics puts us in the domain of expression, not solipsistic pleasure. It is the domain in which we free ourselves from our limited perspective, from heteronomous determinations, and actually sense ourselves as subjects. It seems to me that Foucault's use of the term "aesthetics" in the expression "aesthetics of existence" is closer to this Kantian tradition than to a notion of subjective, that is, purely private, taste. For Foucault, the aesthetics of existence always takes place in, and responds to, a community and defines itself in terms of its attachments to, or ruptures with, that community.

What about the excessive language of the "self" and the "subject"—the care of the *self,* the ethics of the *self*—don't these expressions lead to an egoistic position? To suggest that an ethics founded upon the notion of the care of the self is narcissistic, it seems to me, presupposes an impoverished notion of the self. One only has to look at Aristotle's discussion of friendship to see that a much fuller and richer notion of the self does not cut it off from its relationships to the world and to others. For Aristotle, the self perceives itself in its friend, the friend is "another self" (Aristotle, *Nicomachean Ethics,* 1170b7–9). Or in one of the most interesting discussions in the *Ethics,* he suggests that the happiness of the self cannot be separated from the lives and actions of its children—the life of the child is part of the parent, part of one's self (ibid., 1101a23–1101b9). Foucault, as well, refuses to define the self as something wholly contained within an individual monad. In fact, his analysis of disciplinary power attempts to show how this experience of the self is actually the effect of techniques of separation, isolation, individuation, and differentiation. The definition of the self as an atom is a disciplinary effect. For Foucault, the self is not contained within itself but is always outside of itself—inhabiting its relationships, grasping itself through social and historical practices, knowing itself in terms of discourses produced around and through it. Reading the notion of care of the self as narcissistic requires closing one's eyes to what Foucault meant by "the self."

77. "CdF84," February 15.

78. Ibid. Alexander Nehamas gives an excellent critical though sympathetic reading of Foucault's interpretation in chapter 6 of his book *The Art of Living: Socratic Reflections from Plato to Foucault* (Berkeley: University of California Press, 1998), especially 157–68. He illustrates the technical difficulties with aspects of Foucault's interpretation of Socrates' last words in the *Phaedo,* and his view that the dialogues *Apology, Crito,* and *Phaedo* constitute a "series" expressing a unified philosophical viewpoint.

79. "CdF84," February 15; Plato, *Crito,* 50b–54e.

80. "CdF84," February 15; Plato, *Phaedo,* trans. Hugh Tredennick, in *Plato: The Collected Dialogues,* ed. Edith Hamilton and Huntington Cairns (Princeton: Princeton University Press, 1961), 62b.

81. "CdF84," February 15: Plato, *Phaedo,* 115b.

82. Plato, *Phaedo,* 118a.

83. "CdF84," February 15.

84. Ibid.

85. Ibid.

86. "CdF84," February 22, 29.

87. Ibid.

88. Plato, *Alcibiades,* in *The Dialogues of Plato,* trans. B. Jowett, 2 vols. (New York: Random House, 1920), 2:733–72; *CdF82,* 32–71.

89. Plato, *Alcibiades,* 103a.

90. *UP,* 215; see also 215–46.

91. Ibid., pt. 5.

92. Plato, *Alcibiades,* 124a–b.

93. Ibid., 120b–c.

94. *CdF82,* 51.

95. Ibid., 52

96. Foucault translates the Greek word *khrēsis* into French as *se servir.* This term is perhaps closer to the variety of meanings available to the Greek word than our English equivalent. In English "to serve," "to serve oneself," or "service" might be better than "to use" because "serve" indicates not only making use of something but being of use to something. I have render *khrēsis* as "use" in order to remain consistent with previous translations, such as *The Use of Pleasure.*

97. *CdF82,* 55–56.

98. Ibid.

99. Michel Foucault, *Thèse complémentaire pour le doctorat dès lettres,* University of Paris, Faculty of Letters and the Human Sciences, 1961, 39–40. See also Immanuel Kant, *Anthropology from a Pragmatic Point of View,* trans. Victor Lyle Dowdell (Southern Illinois University Press, 1996), 3–4.

100. Plato, *Alcibiades,* 132b.

101. Ibid., 133a.

102. Ibid., 135e.

103. *CdF82,* 70–71.

104. Ibid., 168.

105. *CdF82,* 77n12.

106. Ibid., 46.

107. Ibid., 49.

108. Ibid., 164.

109. Ibid.

110. "CdF84," February 22.

111. Ibid.

112. Ibid.

113. Ibid.

114. Ibid.

115. Ibid.

116. Plato, *Laches,* trans. Benjamin Jowett, in *Plato: The Collected Dialogues,* ed. Edith Hamilton and Huntington Cairns (Princeton: Princeton University Press, 1961), 123–44.

117. "CdF84," February 22.

118. Plato, *Laches,* 179d.

119. Ibid., 178a–180a.

120. Ibid., 178a–b.

121. Ibid., 200c.
122. Ibid., 183c–184a.
123. "CdF84," February 22.
124. Ibid.
125. Ibid.
126. "CdF83," February 9.
127. Plato, *Laws*, bk. 8, 835ff.
128. Foucault's reading of *Laches*, it seems to me, reflects his general critique of the discourse of normative ethics.
129. "CdF84," February 22.
130. Ibid.; Plato, *Laches*, 184d–187b.
131. "CdF84," February 22.
132. Plato, *Laches*, 186a–187b.
133. Ibid., 186c.
134. Ibid.
135. "CdF84," February 22.
136. Ibid.
137. Plato, *Laches*, 187e–188a.
138. Ibid., 188a.
139. Ibid., 188b.
140. "CF84," February 22.
141. Ibid.
142. Ibid.
143. Ibid.
144. Ibid.
145. Ibid.
146. Ibid.; Plato, *Laches*, 188b.
147. Plato, *Laches*, 188b.
148. "CdF84," February 22.
149. Plato, *Laches*, 188d.
150. Plato, *Republic*, 399a–c.
151. Plato, *Laches*, 189a.
152. "CdF84," February 22.
153. Plato, *Laches*, 189a.
154. *DT*, 65.
155. Plato, *Laches*, 200c–201b.
156. Ibid., 194a.
157. "CdF84," February 22. The same sort of inversion takes place in the Socratic-Platonic reflection on eros: the truth of eros, of love, is that love is the desire, the longing, for the truth; that is, the truth of love is the love of truth.
158. Merleau-Ponty captures this notion of style and discourse and the relationship between them in his analysis of language and art, in "Indirect Language and the Voices of Silence" ("Le langage indirect et les voix du silence"). With respect to style as the meaning of language: "Much more than a means, language is something like a being, and this is why it has the power to make someone present to us: the words of a friend on the telephone give him to us, as if he existed entirely

in his manner of address or of taking leave, of beginning and finishing his phrases, of advancing by way of things unsaid. Meaning [*le sens*] is the total movement of speech." With respect to style as the meaning of actions: "A woman who passes by is not first of all a corporeal shape, a colorful mannequin, a spectacle, she is 'a singular, emotional, sexual expression,' she is a certain way of being embodied, revealed in as a whole in her movement or even in the single clack of a heel striking the ground, the way the tension of a bow is present in each fiber of the wood" (Maurice Merleau-Ponty, "Le langage indirect et les voix du silence," in *Signes* [Paris: Gallimard/Folio, 1960], 69 and 87, respectively).

Chapter 3

1. *CdF82,* 79. Foucault focuses on the first and second centuries A.D. of the Hellenistic and Roman period in order to distinguish this period from ancient Greek philosophy.

2. See the introduction and the section "Foucault's Discovery of *Parrhēsia*" in chapter 1 of the present study.

3. Foucault introduces the term *parrhēsia* in his lecture of January 27, 1982, during his analysis of the correspondence of Fronton and Marcus Aurelius. But he does not return to the term again until February 10—and even here his analysis is cut off by his desire to turn to other problems. He takes *parrhēsia* up in a much fuller way in his lectures on March 3 and 10.

4. In a recent essay, Jean-François Pradeau seems to completely misread Foucault on this point, assuming that Foucault takes Hellenistic and Roman philosophy to be basically hermeneutic in style. As we shall see, this is precisely the opposite of what Foucault says and the entire purpose of his excavations. See Jean-François Pradeau, "Le sujet ancien d'une éthique moderne," in *Foucault: Le courage de la vérité,* ed. Frédéric Gros (Paris: Presses Universitaires de France, 2002), 131–54.

5. See the introduction to the present study.

6. In *The Subjective Life of Power* (Stanford: Stanford University Press, 1997), Judith Butler translates *assujetissement* as "subjectivation" in *Discipline and Punish.* Such a translation suggests—and her essay confirms this—that she sees only one mode of subject-ing individuals, that which is more properly subjection. However, in the 1980s Foucault uses the term *subjectivation* to refer to practices of the self and care of the self. Frédéric Gros—who directed the publication of Foucault's 1982 Collège course—sees a technical distinction in Foucault's work (*CdF82,* 493). According to the *Dits et écrits* index, the term *subjectivation* first appears in 1982, in an essay entitled "Le subject et le pouvoir" (*DE,* 4:223 [no. 306]). In fact, the context does not suggest that the term means something different from *assujetissement,* but rather it refers to any and all practices that lead to the formation of a subject. However, this essay was originally written in English and translated into French—and it is likely to have been written before the 1982 course, which seems to represent the turning point in Foucault's comprehension of care of the self. The next appearance in *Dits et écrits* of the word *subjectivation* is in the essay "Le

combat de la chastité," which clearly draws on Foucault's courses from 1980 to 1981 (*DE*, 4:307 [no. 312]). In this reference it is clear that the term refers to the work by which a subject comes into being through its own activity. Yet, still here, the subjectivation process is one by which the individual connects speaking the truth to self-renunciation. Does this mean it is another form of subjection? The first clear reference to subjectivation in the sense of care of the self, freedom of the self, does not come until 1983 in the article "Self Writing" (*DE*, 4:419 [no. 329]). In other words, the term does not in fact appear to have the regularity of a technical distinction. However, Gros's suggestion that this is so is, to my mind, a very helpful heuristic device for separating what seem to be two different ideas: the subjection of the individual to the truth spoken by an expert, and the subjectivation of the individual by a work on herself. Butler's collapsing of these terms is linked to a flattening of Foucault's work, and the loss of a conceptual distinction which adds a layer to Foucault's diagnosis of the "present" and his etho-poetic response to it.

7. "CdF84," February 29.

8. In fact, I believe that through close examination of Foucault's lecture courses at the Collège from 1976 to 1981 one would be able to follow with some detail the shifts in his thought that link these projects which appear so radically external to each other in the published work. I have not performed such a study, but my experience of these courses—though not exhaustive—suggests to me that this is the case.

9. *CdF82*, 241.

10. Ibid., 220, for example.

11. "CdF83" and "CdF84," in particular February 1, 1984, on the development of his thought.

12. See Michel Foucault, "The Subject and Power," in Dreyfus and Rabinow, *Michel Foucault: Beyond Structuralism and Hermeneutics*, 209.

13. "CdF84," February 8.

14. Ibid.

15. Ibid.

16. Foucault's diagnosis of "true discourses," that is, "scientific" discourse, always had as their target the "human sciences"—the discourses on man. His problem was therefore to understand the links between the discourses that pronounced the truth of man as an object of knowledge and the relationships of power that made man into such an object.

17. "CdF84," February 8.

18. Ibid.

19. I borrow the term "prismatic" from Thomas Flynn because it seems to be the best metaphor for this aspect of Foucault's thought. Flynn has also used the term "kaleidoscopic" to characterize the effect of Foucault's work.

20. "CdF84," February 8.

21. Ibid.

22. *CdF82*, 172–74.

23. Hadot, *Exercises spirituels et philosophie antique*, 323–32.

24. Ibid., 324.

25. Ibid., 325.

26. Ibid., 324.

27. Ibid., 331.

28. Ibid., 330.

29. Ibid., 325.

30. Ibid., 332.

31. *CdF82*, 172.

32. Ibid., 172–73.

33. Ibid., 108–17. These two characteristics are important to Foucault because they reflect an ethics based on a choice rather than on an imperative, and they also reflect an ethics based on a real belonging to some form of community. Such an ethic, for Foucault, is much more viable given our situation—postmodern and disciplinary. But it should be kept in mind that Foucault distinguished ethics—the work on oneself—from morality in the sense of the law. Ethics has to do with the formation of the subject, in a sense, in relation to the law.

34. See chapter 2 of this study, on *Alcibiades;* and *CdF82,* January 6 and 13. Foucault does not seem too interested in marking a differentiation between Socrates and Plato, but perhaps here is one area where such a contrast seems possible in his thought. In his analysis of the *Apology* and *Laches,* Foucault makes it clear that Socratic *parrhēsia* and care are not limited to a specific moment in one's life, and while these are conceived as a preparation for politics, Socrates is willing to engage anyone anywhere in a continuous exercise and examination of himself and others. The "Platonic" theory, detailed in *Alcibiades,* is more restrictive and is linked to the threshold between adolescence and adulthood.

35. *CdF82*, 91.

36. Ibid., 92.

37. Ibid.

38. Ibid., 92–93.

39. Ibid., 93.

40. Ibid., 94.

41. Ibid.

42. Ibid., 94–95.

43. Ibid., 95.

44. Ibid., 96.

45. Ibid., 126; see also 139–40n3–4; and Seneca, *Lettres à Lucilius,* trans. H. Noblot (Paris: Les Belles Lettres, 1945), vol. 2, bk. 5, letter 52, pp. 41–46.

46. See chapter 5 of this study, and Kant and Foucault's essays entitled "What Is Enlightenment?"

47. *CdF82*, 126.

48. *UP,* 26–28.

49. This is similar to what Heidegger and Arendt analyze as clichés and idle talk—representations detached from the world, the ground from which they emerge and to which they point. Again, it is another approach to the Socratic-Platonic problem of semblance and opinion.

50. The Senecan principle of living always as though one were old unifies life.

51. *CdF82*, 128.

52. Ibid.

53. Ibid., 129. A free will is therefore not a will that is able to affirm or deny any proposition or action which is placed before it. Rather, the free will is nothing other than the will to care for oneself: the will to self which is freed from the distractions, the sickness, of *stultitia*. It is therefore not the detached will of a Sartre, but is perhaps closer to the will as it appears in Descartes's Fourth Meditation—the will which sees the truth is free insofar as seeing the truth in itself frees the will to will the truth. In fact, this notion of the free will may be closest of all to the will in the Second Critique (Kant, *The Critique of Practical Reason,* trans. Lewis White Beck), where the categorical imperative is the form of the will itself. Foucault does not think that the Stoic will is autonomous in the Kantian sense; that is, freedom is not necessarily reducible to autonomy understood as legislative. In chapter 8, I look at Foucault's remarks concerning Kant's notion of the will as it appears in his ethics.

54. *CdF82,* 129.

55. Ibid., 130.

56. Ibid., 130–31.

57. Ibid., 131.

58. Ibid.

59. *CdF82,* see, for example, 171–78.

60. Ibid., 174–75.

61. Ibid., 175.

62. Ibid., 175–76.

63. Ibid., 178.

64. Ibid., 177.

65. Ibid., 205.

66. *CdF82,* 197–214. See Hadot's article "Conversion," in *Exercises spirituels et philosophie antique,* 223–35.

67. *CdF82,* 201–8.

68. Ibid.

69. Ibid., 206.

70. Ibid., 209–33.

71. Plutarch, *De la curiosité,* French translation by Dumontier and Defradas; see *CdF82,* 218n42.

72. *CdF82,* 211.

73. Ibid., 211–12.

74. Ibid., 212–13.

75. Ibid.

76. Ibid., 213.

77. Ibid., 213–14. This idea and the use of the archery imagery is reminiscent of Nietzsche's preface to *Beyond Good and Evil:* "But the fight against Plato, or so to speak more clearly and for 'the people,' the fight against the Christian-ecclesiastical pressure of millennia—for Christianity is Platonism for 'the people'—has created in Europe a magnificent tension of the spirit the like of which had never yet existed on earth: with so tense a bow we can now shoot for the most distant goals . . . But we who are neither Jesuits nor democrats, nor even German enough, we good Europeans and free, very free spirits—we still feel it, the whole need of the spirit and the whole tension of its bow. And perhaps also the

arrow, the task, and—who knows?—the goal" (Nietzsche, *Beyond Good and Evil: Prelude to a Philosophy of the Future,* trans. Walter Kaufmann [New York: Vintage Books, 1989], 3).

78. *CdF82,* 225–26.

79. Ibid. See *CdF82,* 234n9. Foucault's source for this is Seneca's account of the Cynic, Demetrius. See Seneca, "Bienfaites," in *Oeuvres complètes de Sénèque le philosophe,* ed. M. Nibard and Firmin Didot, trans. Baillard (1869), vol. 7, bk. 1, p. 246; *CdF82,* 234n9.

80. *CdF82,* 227.

81. Ibid., 169.

82. Ibid., 125.

83. Ibid., 126. Foucault refers to Musonius, fragment 2.3 (see *CdF82,* 139n2). This reference to the "being" of the individual is interesting. In the first lecture and elsewhere, Foucault marks a difference between the concrete existence of the individual and the very being of the subject qua subject. Here he seems to suggest that *hexis*—habit—is the being of the individual, the subjectivity of the individual transformed through care.

84. *CdF82,* 131.

85. *DT,* 69–70.

86. Ibid.

87. *CdF82,* 131–32.

88. Peri Parrhēsias, *On Parrhēsia,* ed. Alexander Olivieri (Leipzig: B. G. Teubneri, 1914). For a helpful compendium of Foucault's sources, see Foucault, *The Hermeneutics of the Self,* trans. Graham Burchell (New York: Palgrave Macmillan, 2005), xxxi–xli (translator's note). This note compiles the French translations of ancient works cited by Foucault along with English translations of those works.

89. *CdF82,* 132.

90. Ibid.

91. Ibid.

92. Philodemus, cited by Foucault, *DT,* 74.

93. *CdF82,* 228–32.

94. Ibid., 230.

95. Ibid., 229.

96. Ibid., 230.

97. Ibid., 231.

98. Ibid., 231–32.

99. *DT,* 71.

100. See chapter 2 of the present study.

101. *DT,* 72.

102. Ibid., 72–73.

103. *CdF82,* 134. It is worth noting the irony in Foucault's choice of the term "normalization" to capture the tendency of power-knowledge relations in the contemporary world: what does it mean for a *normalien* to critique normalization?

104. Ibid., 135.

105. Ibid.

106. Ibid., 137.

107. Ibid., 138.

108. Ibid.

109. Ibid.

110. *DT,* 89–94.

111. Ibid., 92.

112. *DT,* 90.

113. Ibid.

114. Ibid., 91.

115. *CdF82,* 149.

116. Ibid.

117. Ibid., 148–49.

118. Ibid., 185–88.

119. Ibid., 186; Epicurus, *Vatican Sayings,* no. 23. The notion of utility (*khrēsis*) arose first in Foucault's analyses of ancient philosophy in *Alcibiades.* See chapter 2 of this book.

120. *CdF82,* 186.

121. Ibid., 187.

122. Ibid.

123. Ibid.

124. Ibid., 188.

125. Ibid., 189.

126. Ibid., 188.

127. Ibid., 312.

128. Ibid., 304.

129. Ibid., 305.

130. Ibid., 312.

131. Ibid., 309–10.

132. Ibid., 311. While Foucault is drawing on the vocabulary of the period— *prokheiron* and *ad manum*—his interest in this point is striking: the expression *sous le main,* "ready-to-hand," inevitably reminds us of Heidegger's *zuhanden.* Readiness-to-hand is the mode of being characteristic of entities in the everyday world. However, here Foucault is not talking about just any piece of equipment in a world structured according to our projects; he is talking about the "equipment" constitutive of the "subject" (*Dasein* in Heidegger's vocabulary). But it doesn't make sense to speak of *Dasein* in terms of readiness-to-hand because *Dasein* is precisely "that for the sake of which" everything is ready-to-hand (Martin Heidegger, *Being and Time,* trans. John Macquarrie and Edward Robinson [San Francisco: HarperSan-Francisco, 1962], 116–17). Furthermore, if what Foucault is getting at here is the constitution of the conscience, then his project would seem to be radically distinct from that of Heidegger. For *Dasein* and its conscience are fundamentally different in their Being than ready-to-hand equipment. Furthermore, *Dasein* and the conscience in *Being and Time* are not constituted but rather existential—constitutive—of the very Being of human beings: the call of conscience "comes *from* me and yet *from beyond me and over me*" (Heidegger, *Being and Time,* 320). Yet a fundamental characteristic of *Dasein,* as Heidegger's analysis reveals, is not simply the fact that it *has* a conscience, that the call issues from itself and to itself, but more

subtly that *Dasein* is determined by its "wanting to have a conscience" (ibid., 334). Of course, the implications of Heidegger's analysis of conscience are not at all simple or straightforward, but on this point we might find some resonance with Foucault's analysis of spiritual exercises. That *Dasein* hears the call of conscience but wants to have a conscience, is related to the fact that *Dasein* must choose to hear the call authentically, and to maintain its "anticipatory resoluteness" (ibid.; see, for example, 352–58). In other words, *Dasein* must choose to take up an authentic relation to the call; that is, to itself in its finitude. The equipment that the Hellenistic philosophers aimed at putting *sous la main* of the subject (*Dasein*) are essentially modes of being with oneself, modes of being-in-the-world, and modes of being-with-others that maintain the proper (authentic) relationship to the truth of oneself and the world; they forge a conscience in the sense of an organizing and active principle rather than a punishing "superego." Discourse, as ready-to-hand, is not so much a piece of equipment that one takes up the way one picks up a hammer or a pen, but rather it comes forward, responding to the dangers one confronts; it is the concrete form of the resoluteness to accept one's finitude. The discourse produced in the subject through *askēsis* is the support, the foundation upon which the subject maintains the proper relationship to itself, to the world, and to others.

This brief foray into the thought of Heidegger is not meant to reduce Foucault's analysis to a *Daseinanalysis*. Rather, it seems to me that reference to Heidegger's reflection on *Dasein* as being-in-the-world is especially helpful in attempting to understand what Foucault is referring to when he uses the word "subject." It is clear, or should be, that Foucault does not mean a substance, or a detached reality existing independently of the world, of a body, of a historical context. Furthermore, Foucault often uses the term *ēthos* in place of the term "subject." This suggests that the subject is something that doesn't simply exist, but in a way is only by way of its modes of existing—Foucault uses the expression "modes of being of the subject," in the plural. Finally, he uses the term "subject" to indicate three types of entities: the relationship of oneself to oneself; the agent of an action or speaker of a discourse; and the principle of knowledge in the sense of that which "has" a domain of objects of knowledge, that which has access to the truth. *Dasein*, as it is described by Heidegger, is a useful starting place for understanding what kind of being a subject is insofar as it is a relationship to itself, an agent and an openness in which a field of objects become knowable, a mode of disclosing a world. In other words, if we ask what kind of subject can be "constituted" by discourses and practices, then one potential starting point in our answer would be a subject who is not fundamentally a substance, given a priori, but who exists only through her intimate and concrete manner of living in the world, disclosing the world as a meaningful reality. However, it is quite clear that Foucault's analyses of the subject cannot be reduced to Heidegger's analysis of *Dasein*, even if *Dasein* remains an important reference. This is because for Foucault, while the subject does seem to be an individual who is existentially structured by her being-in-the-world and who has a structural unity (the three ecstasies of time), the subject is also constituted by discourses and practices through which her particular mode of being is forged. In other words, the manner of being-in-the-world, the mode of being of the subject, the mode of disclosing the world and oneself, are fashioned by historically concrete practices. And therefore, for Foucault it may be impossible to draw the line between that which is existentielle and that which is existential.

133. *CdF82,* 339, 406–15.

134. Ibid., 341.

135. Ibid., 340–41.

136. Ibid., 339.

137. Ibid., 316–17.

138. Ibid., 319.

139. Ibid., 318–19.

140. Ibid., 320–21.

141. On this point, Foucault refers primarily to Epictetus and Seneca; there are important differences between them, but they both argue that the proper exercise and practice of listening is indispensable for the practice of care of the self. See *CdF82,* 320–23.

142. Foucault points out a distinction between *technē* and *tribē* or *empeiria* in Epictetus. Listening is not strictly speaking an art, a *technē,* because it does not ground itself on knowledge. Rather it is an exercise, a practice, an particular kind of effort, *tribē,* and a certain competence, *empeiria.* Speaking, on the other hand, the activity of the master, is a *technē* because it is grounded on a detailed poietic knowledge.

143. *CdF82,* 324–26.

144. Ibid., 326–31.

145. Ibid., 327.

146. Ibid., 328.

147. Ibid., 329.

148. Ibid., 332–34.

149. Ibid., 333.

150. Ibid., 334.

151. See, for example, *DT,* 98; *Technologies of the Self;* and *Religion and Culture.*

152. *DT,* 108.

153. Ibid., 108–9; Epictetus, *The Discourses as Reported by Arrian,* trans. W. A. Oldfather (Cambridge: Harvard University Press, 1956), 3.12.

154. *DT,* 109.

155. Ibid., 110; Epictetus, *The Discourses,* 3.8.

156. This example appears in many places in Foucault's work.

157. See "CdF84," March 21; *DT,* 101–8.

158. Michel Foucault, "About the Beginnings of the Hermeneutics of the Self," in *RC,* 167.

159. *DT,* 107.

160. Foucault, "Beginnings of the Hermeneutics of the Self," *RC,* 167.

161. *DT,* 103.

162. Foucault, "Beginnings of the Hermeneutics of the Self," *RC,* 167.

163. *DT,* 96.

164. Foucault, "Beginnings of the Hermeneutics of the Self," *RC,* 167.

165. *TS*, 36–37.
166. Ibid.
167. Foucault, "Beginnings of the Hermeneutics of the Self," *RC*, 167.
168. Ibid., 168.
169. *TS*, 35.
170. See chapter 1 of the present study; see also *CdF82*, 79–81, 465–67. The *technē tou biou*—the arts of living—are the techniques, the skills, which one needs to possess and use in order to "produce" a life which is beautiful, good, and just. Rhetoric, for example, would allow one to speak well and convincingly; strategy would allow for effective warfare; economy would permit one to manage one's private affairs; diet or regimen would produce a healthy life; and so on. Care of the self, *epimēleia heautou*, on the other hand, is all of the practices by which one effects a transformation in one's very way of seeing or being in the world; it brings about a new disposition or a new form of perception or self-consciousness.
171. *CdF82*, 81.
172. *DT*, 111–12.
173. Ibid., 112.
174. Ibid.
175. *CdF82*, 201ff.
176. Ibid., lectures of February 10, 17, and 24.
177. Ibid., 295.
178. Ibid., 243–45.
179. See, for example, Epicurus's *Letter to Herodotus* or *Vatican Sayings*, no. 45.
180. Hadot stresses the fact that it is the false opinions, conventional opinions, which lead one astray; one must cleanse one's mind of these false opinions. It is not simply that the body and its appetites must be controlled; it is that the false interpretation of these appetites leads one to injustice and unhappiness (Pierre Hadot, *Qu'est-ce que la philosophie antique?* [Paris: Gallimard, 1995], 178–96).
181. See *CdF82*, 262–95. Foucault also refers to Hadot, and his debt to the latter is plainly evident in these analyses.
182. *CdF82*, 252. See also *CdF82*, 105–8, where Foucault describes how old age is perceived as ideal.
183. *CdF82*, 260–61.
184. Ibid.
185. Ibid., 261.
186. Ibid., 263.
187. Ibid.
188. Ibid.
189. Ibid., 265–66.
190. Ibid., 266.
191. Ibid.
192. Ibid.
193. Ibid., 267–68.
194. Ibid., 269.
195. Ibid., 262–75.
196. Ibid., 277–97.

197. Ibid., 278.

198. Ibid., 278–79, 283–84; see Marcus Aurelius, *Meditations*, bk. 3, sec. 11.

199. *CdF82*, 284.

200. I am translating from the French text of the *Meditations* used by Foucault, translated by Budé, p. 54. See *CdF82*, 298n2.

201. *CdF82*, 278; Foucault refers to several texts in the *Meditations:* bk. 6, sec. 3; bk. 3, sec. 11; bk. 11, sec. 16.

202. *CdF82*, 280.

203. Ibid., 281.

204. Ibid.

205. Ibid., 282.

206. Ibid., 282–83.

207. Ibid.

208. Ibid.

209. *BC*, xi.

210. Ibid., xi–xii.

211. Ibid., 90.

212. Ibid.

213. *CdF82*, 284–85.

214. Ibid., 285.

215. Ibid., 288–89.

216. Ibid., 290.

217. Ibid., 291.

218. Ibid., 291–93.

219. Ibid., 292.

220. Ibid., 293.

221. Ibid., 294.

222. For the distinction between spiritual exercise and intellectual method, see *CdF82*, 281. For that between Stoic and Christian spiritual exercise, see 286–88.

223. Ibid., 286–88.

224. Ibid.

225. Ibid., 298n10.

226. *OT*, 52–56.

227. *CdF82*, 281. This will be the focus of chapter 5.

Chapter 4

1. "CdF84," March 7, 14, 21, 28.

2. Ibid., February 29.

3. Foucault identifies three "vehicles" which have transported Cynicism through history and allowed it to continue to be an essential element of Western culture. (1) The first is Christian asceticism, the Christian witness to the truth. The Christian ascetic, like the Cynic, makes life into the "visible theater of truth." This practice can be found across the entire history of Christianity ("CdF84," February 29). Foucault refers to the Reformation and Counter-Reformation as conflicts

over these practices of truth. (2) The figure of the revolutionary in the nineteenth century was a form of Cynic rejection of convention in the form of political dissension. The "revolutionary life" was an aesthetic, a mode of life, which countered the ordinary life (ibid.). (3) The final vehicle of Cynicism is art, and in particular modern art. Modern art is a Cynic practice in two ways: the "vie-artiste" is an aesthetic elaboration of life as truth. Second, modern art itself is an "excavation, a violent reduction of existence to the elementary . . . art is constituted a space for the irruption of the underside, the lowly, which culture cannot otherwise express" (ibid.).

4. See, for example, James Miller, *The Passion of Michel Foucault* (New York: Anchor Books, 1993), 379; Thomas Flynn, "Foucault as *Parrhēsiast*," in *The Final Foucault;* Gros, "La *parrhēsia* chez Foucault (1982–1984)," in *Foucault: Le courage de la vérité*, 165–66.

5. "CdF84," March 7.

6. Ibid.

7. Ibid.

8. Ibid.

9. Ibid., March 14.

10. Ibid., March 7, 14.

11. Ibid., March 14.

12. Ibid.

13. Ibid.

14. Ibid.

15. Ibid.

16. Ibid.

17. Ibid.

18. Ibid.

19. Ibid.

20. Ibid.

21. Ibid.; see Epictetus, *The Discourses,* 1.14, 2.8.

22. "CdF84," March 14.

23. Ibid.

24. Ibid.

25. Plato, *Apology,* 23b.

26. Ibid., 29e.

27. See, for example, Plato, *Symposium,* trans. Michael Joyce, in *Plato: The Collected Dialogues,* ed. Edith Hamilton and Huntington Cairns (Princeton: Princeton University Press, 1961), 174a.

28. Plato, *Symposium,* 203b–d.

29. The following citations from Seneca are of his *Letters from a Stoic* (London: Penguin Classics, 1969).

30. "CdF84," March 14.

31. Seneca, *Letter 18,* in *Letters from a Stoic,* 67.

32. Ibid.

33. Ibid., 69.

34. Ibid., 69.

35. "CdF84," March 14.

36. Ibid.

37. Ibid.

38. Ibid.

39. Ibid.

40. Ibid.

41. Ibid.

42. Ibid.

43. Ibid.

44. "CdF84," March 21.

45. Ibid.

46. Ibid.

47. Ibid.

48. Ibid.

49. Ibid.; *DT,* 82–87. See Dio Chrysostom, *The Fourth Discourse on Kingship.*

50. *DT,* 82–87.

51. Ibid.

52. "CdF84," March 21.

53. Ibid.

54. Ibid.

55. Ibid.

56. Ibid.

57. Ibid.

58. Ibid.

59. Ibid. Much of Foucault's discussion of the Cynic mode of life is based on a reading of Epictetus's *Discourses,* bk. 3, chap. 22.

60. "CdF84," March 21.

61. Ibid.

62. Ibid.

63. Ibid.

64. "CdF84," March 28.

65. Ibid.

66. Ibid.

67. Ibid.

68. Ibid.

69. *CdF82,* 138.

70. See Miller, *Passion of Michel Foucault,* 379; Flynn, "Foucault as *Parrhēsiast,*" in *The Final Foucault.*

71. See also Gros on this point, "La *parrhēsia* chez Foucault (1982–1984)," in *Foucault: Le courage de la vérité,* 165–66.

72. Philippe Artières, "Dire l'actualité," in *Foucault: Le courage de la vérité,* ed. Gros, 29.

73. "CdF84," February 29, March 7.

74. Ibid.

75. Ibid.

76. Ibid.

77. Ibid.

78. Foucault's discussion of Christian *parrhēsia* closely follows Stanley Marrow's treatment of the problem in, "Parrhēsia and the New Testament," *Catholic Bible Quarterly* 44 (1982): 431–46.

79. "CdF84," February 29, March 28.

80. "CdF84," February 29.

81. "CdF84," March 28.

82. Ibid.

83. Ibid. Foucault refers to Philo of Alexandria for this sense of the word *parrhēsia.*

84. Ibid. Here Foucault is drawing on the Septuagint, the ancient Greek translation of the Hebrew Scripture carried out between 300 and 200 B.C. The name Septuagint is Latin for seventy (LXX) because supposedly seventy scholars did the translation.

85. "CdF84," March 28.

86. Ibid. Foucault suggests that *parrhēsia* in these texts refers more and more to the asymmetric exchange between God and man. It is the joy of opening up one's heart and ascending toward God and the response of God to this openness.

87. Ibid.

88. Ibid.

89. Ibid. Foucault turns to John 5:13–14.

90. "CdF84," March 28.

91. Ibid.

92. Ibid. Foucault sees this notion in the work of John Chrysostom.

93. Ibid.

94. Foucault found another form of ascetic *parrhēsia,* in the work of Gregory of Nyssa, *Traité de la virginité,* French translation by M. Aubineau (Paris: Éditions du Cerf, 1966), bk. 12, 300c–301d; this citation is found in *CdF82,* 24n40.

95. "CdF84," March 28.

96. Ibid.

97. Ibid.

98. Ibid.

99. Ibid.

100. Ibid.

101. Ibid.

102. Ibid.

103. Ibid. This theme was already present in Foucault's 1978 course at the Collège, though he had not yet discovered the experience of *parrhēsia* and the way it organized these struggles and displacements (*CdF78*). In that text as well, he made the claim, again provisionally, that the institutionalization of ethical discourse, of effective discourse about ethical subjectivity, was a response and an attempt to control *parrhēsiastic* life and language. In fact, as early as 1975, Foucault offered a genealogy of a certain strand in the Christian elaboration of ethical subjectivity: the development of the institution of confession (*CdF75,* February 19). The confessional scene controls discourse about ethical subjectivity; confines it within a particular relation, place, and time; and organizes its procedures very precisely.

104. "CdF84," March 28.

105. See chapter 7 of this book.

106. See Michel Foucault, "The Battle for Chastity," in *RC*, 191. Disciplinary control of the body, space, time, action, and association shifts the focus of anxiety. In an unregulated world it is externality that is dangerous; one's actions and relations are possibilities for trouble. But where these are rigorously controlled, the problem becomes one's own body, one's thoughts and passions. The facts of the interior life are now the unregulated and uncontrolled space, time, and activities that have to be ordered and contained.

107. Foucault, "Beginnings of the Hermeneutics of the Self," *RC*, 175.

108. See, for example, the following works by Foucault in vol. 2 of his *Essential Works* (*EW2*): "The Father's No," 5–20; "Speaking and Seeing in Raymond Roussel," 21–32; "Introduction to Rousseau's Dialogues," 33–54; "A Preface to Transgression," 69–87; "Language to Infinity," 89–101; and so on.

109. *EW1*, 199–205. See also Foucault, "Problematics" *FL*, 420–21.

110. *EW1*, 200.

111. Foucault, "Beginnings of the Hermeneutics of the Self," *RC*, 175.

112. Ibid., 176.

113. Ibid.

114. Michel Foucault, "Sexuality and Power," in *RC*, 126.

115. Foucault, "Beginnings of the Hermeneutics of the Self," *RC*, 178.

116. Foucault, "Self Writing," *EW1*, 207.

117. Ibid., 210. This technique of writing was necessary for the hermit, the solitary ascetic. The presence of the other is necessary, the gaze of the other reveals what a unified perspective cannot. In the monastic communities the spiritual guide serves this function. For the hermit, writing performs this task.

118. Foucault, "Beginnings of the Hermeneutics of the Self," *RC*, 179.

119. Ibid.

120. Ibid., 180n.

Part 2

1. *CdF82*, 183.

Chapter 5

1. These texts effectively span the entire career of Foucault's thought: the first, *Histoire de la folie*, appearing in 1961; the second, *The Order of Things*, in 1964; then "My Body, This Paper, This Fire" in 1972; and finally *CdF82*.

2. "The relation to *Order* is as essential to the Classical Age as the relation to *Interpretation* was to the Renaissance" (*OT*, 57).

3. *HF*, chapter 1.

4. *HF*, 38.

5. Ibid., 39.

6. Ibid., 35.

7. Ibid., 44.

8. Ibid., 58.

9. Ibid., 58 (my italics).

10. Michel Foucault, "My Body, This Paper, This Fire," in *EW2*, 393–418.

11. *MIP,* 87.

12. I believe Foucault was able to come to this apprehension of the problem only because of the hard labor which took place in between these two phases of his thought.

13. *CdF82,* 15ff.

14. "CdF83," March 9.

15. René Descartes, *Discourse on Method,* in *The Philosophical Writings of Descartes,* trans. John Cottingham, Robert Stoothoff, and Dugald Murdoch, 3 vols. (Cambridge: Cambridge University Press, 1984), 2:142–43.

16. "CdF83," March 9.

17. Stephen Gaukroger has an excellent discussion of Descartes's treatment of the passions and its relation to Stoic and Augustinian ethics in *Descartes: An Intellectual Biography* (New York: Oxford University Press, 1995). He very rightly cautions us from attributing to Descartes a simplistic reductionism in his approach to the body, the relationship between the body and the mind, and his understanding of medicine in the passage quoted from the *Discourse.* Though his argument is convincing and important, this realization should not prevent us from seeing what is radically different in Descartes's medical ethic: the new possibility of a scientific medical knowledge and technology of the body, its function and health, and its relationship to the soul/mind.

18. What are these opinions? Descartes does not tell us in the *Meditations,* but if we are to judge from the progression of the doubt, one such opinion is the idea that knowledge begins with sense-perception. In the following, we shall link this false opinion to the sixteenth-century episteme which is displaced by that of the classical age.

19. Descartes, *Philosophical Writings of Descartes,* 2:12.

20. Of course, at the moment when Descartes composes the *Meditations* this is not the case. Furthermore, it is not necessary to suppose that the *Meditations* are the process of thinking by which Descartes is led to his certainty in the truth of the method as a way of knowing the world. It is clearly a formalized, ritualized rendition of a way of thinking which will lead to the experience of certainty, evidence, and commitment to the scientific method.

21. Descartes, *Philosophical Writings of Descartes,* 2:12

22. Ibid.

23. Ibid., 8.

24. This is the essence of Foucault's essay "My Body, This Paper, This Fire."

25. See Bradley Rubidge, "Descartes's Meditations and Devotional Meditations," *Journal of the History of Ideas* 51 (1990) 27–49, who argues against such a reading; and Amélie Rorty, "The Structure of Descartes' Meditations," in *Essays on Descartes' "Meditations,"* ed. Rorty (Berkeley: University of California Press, 1986), 1–20, who argues for one. Pierre Hadot, in *Qu'est-ce que la philosophie antique,* also

asserts that the *Meditations* are meant to be taken as spiritual exercises. I treat the relation of Foucault's work to this debate in "Foucault's Cartesian Meditations," *International Philosophical Quarterly,* March 2005. Much of this chapter appears in a slightly modified form there.

26. The notion that the spiritual exercise or meditation is a "genre" of philosophical writing comes from Rorty, "The Structure of Descartes' Meditations," in *Essays on Descartes' "Meditations,"* 1–20. See also Rubidge's discussion of this essay (Rubidge, "Descartes's Meditations and Devotional Meditations," in *Journal of the History of Ideas,* 37–41).

27. Descartes makes this point in his *Principles of Philosophy* (*Philosophical Writings of Descartes,* 1:193) as well as in the *Meditations.*

28. Descartes, *Philosophical Writings of Descartes,* 2:12.

29. Ibid., 2:23.

30. Ibid., 2:36.

31. Ibid., 2:37.

32. *HF,* 58.

33. For Foucault's differentiation between Descartes and the skeptics, see, for example, *HF,* 57–58.

34. See Jacques Derrida, "Cogito and the History of Madness," in *Writing and Difference,* trans. Alan Bass (Chicago: University of Chicago Press, 1978), 31–63. Derrida is responding to Foucault's original 1961 text, *Folie et déraison: Histoire de la folie à l'âge classique* (Paris: Plon, 1961).

35. "Now, the recourse to the fiction of the evil genius will evoke, conjure up, the possibility of a total madness, a total derangement over which I could have no control because it is inflicted upon me—hypothetically—leaving me no responsibility for it" (Derrida, "Cogito and the History of Madness," in *Writing and Difference,* 52–53).

36. The existence of such a text in and of itself shows that any reading of Foucault which sees a radical break between the early Foucault—analyst of all-pervasive power relationships which preclude any role for subjectivity, freedom or resistance—and the later Foucault—sudden champion of unfettered freedom to invent oneself as a work of art—is inadequate to the texts themselves.

37. Foucault, "My Body, This Paper, This Fire," *EW2,* 407.

38. Ibid., 407.

39. Descartes, *Philosophical Writings of Descartes,* 2:12–13.

40. Ibid., 13.

41. Foucault, "My Body, This Paper, This Fire," *EW2,* 401–2.

42. Ibid.

43. *HF,* 57–58.

44. Descartes, *Philosophical Writings of Descartes,* 2:13.

45. Ibid.

46. Ibid.

47. Foucault, "My Body, This Paper, This Fire," *EW2,* 407.

48. Ibid., 405.

49. *CdF82,* 340.

50. Foucault, "My Body, This Paper, This Fire," *EW2,* 396ff.

51. *CdF82*, 341.

52. Foucault, "My Body, This Paper, This Fire," *EW2*, 396.

53. Ibid., 396 (my italics).

54. Ibid. (Foucault's italics).

55. Ibid., 408.

56. Ibid.

57. Ibid.

58. For example, the original distinction between objects of sense-perception as being "distant and weak" or "vivid and near"—that is, two different "places," the far and the near, the confused and the clear—is based on an "existential" foundation; it is determined by the subject's actual presence in the world. This "existential" foundation of space is displaced through the doubt. The subject, now purified of its "actual" conditions, discloses the spatial world in a new light: all space is equal, pure extension.

59. Foucault, "My Body, This Paper, This Fire," *EW2*, 398.

60. Ibid., 398.

61. Descartes, *Philosophical Writings of Descartes*, 2:13.

62. Foucault, "My Body, This Paper, This Fire," *EW2*, 401–3.

63. Ibid., 415.

64. Ibid.

65. Ibid., 406.

66. Descartes, *Philosophical Writings of Descartes*, 2:37.

67. Foucault, My Body, This Paper, This Fire," *EW2*, 406.

68. Ibid., 407.

69. Foucault, "On the Genealogy of Ethics," in Dreyfus and Rabinow, *Michel Foucault: Beyond Structuralism and Hermeneutics.*

70. *CdF82*, 15–20.

71. Ibid., 15.

72. Our mode of living, structured by discipline, functions as the condition of actuality of the cogito, and the cogito as a mode of subjectivity functions as the condition of acceptability of discipline. See chapters 7 and 8 of the present study. Andrew Cutrofello first suggested such a distinction to me over the course of conversations about the function of disciplinary power in Kant.

73. This is not to say that Descartes overlooked, or even could have overlooked, this ascetic dimension of thought. (For example, see the first principle in the *Principles of Philosophy.*)

74. In the next chapter I will turn to a detailed analysis of the nature of this system of actuality.

Chapter 6

1. *CdF82*, 281.

2. The analysis in "My Body, This Paper, This Fire," shows that *askēsis* is called upon to free the subject from the "system of actuality" which resists doubt. What resists doubt is simultaneously what calls for doubt: in other words, Descartes

ought to doubt precisely that which he cannot doubt. What calls for doubt, however, is nothing less than the episteme of the sixteenth century: the play of resemblances which begins with and inhabits the element of the visible. It is not any particular object in this element, but rather the system which holds sway over thinking itself. In other words, the episteme is not a theoretical framework; it is a way of disclosing a knowable world—it is a way of being-in-the-world. "It took nothing less than Descartes's Evil Genius to put an end to this great peril of Identities in which sixteenth-century thought had not ceased to 'subtilize' itself" (Foucault, "The Prose of Acteon" [1964], in *EW2*, 124).

3. See part 1 of this study.

4. Philosophical, and more generally spiritual, subjectivity was defined through the agonism between Cynicism (philosophy as life/action/nature) and Stoicism/Epicureanism (or more broadly, those strands within the Hellenistic and Roman model in which philosophy appears as thought/discourse/reason).

5. Foucault, "The Subject and Power," in Dreyfus and Rabinow, *Michel Foucault: Beyond Structuralism and Hermeneutics,* 214.

6. *CdF78,* 119–26.

7. Ibid., 238.

8. Michel Foucault, "Omnes et Singulatim: Toward a Critique of Political Reason," in *EW3.*

9. *CdF78,* 157–59.

10. See, for example, *CdF78,* 152–53, 233–38.

11. See, for example, *CdF76,* 23, 31, 35.

12. One of the main themes of the 1978 Collège course is the territoriality of sovereignty. See especially the lectures of January 11, 18, and 25. The shift away from political sovereignty and toward political government is marked by a process of de-territorialization (*CdF78,* 113). On the link between sovereignty and justice and law, see, for example, *CdF78,* 99, 112; and *HS,* 135–45.

13. However, this political-juridical form of power could serve many different teleologies. This fact is represented in the unlikely trio that Foucault uses to illustrate this form of political rationality: Plato, Machiavelli, and St. Thomas Aquinas. (For example, see "Omnes et Singulatim.") For Plato, the ruler gives the law to his subjects, and the aim of this law is the perfection of the city, which arises when each one serves the proper function as ordained by the philosopher-king. Foucault turns to Aquinas for a depiction of the Christian theory for which political power is thought of as an art of establishing the "common good," of making the laws which will lead the subjects to moral virtue, or *honestum* (*DE,* 4:151–52, 315; Aquinas, *Summa Theologica,* Q. 92, art. 1). Even here political power is not conceived of as an art of governing, it is not truly a pastoral relation, at least not in the sense that this relation is given in its most fully developed articulation. Finally, Machiavelli conceives of the same basic relationship between prince and subject as do Plato and Aquinas, even if he defines the *telos* differently. For Machiavelli, while the honor and glory of ruling is the prince's true reward, the law the prince establishes and which mediates his relationship to his subjects has the purpose of preserving his power. Therefore, though the ultimate goal of ruling is to maintain power and not necessarily to establish justice or the moral good, the relationship

between the prince and his subjects remains the same—it is the relationship of lawgiver and subject of the law.

14. Foucault, "Omnes et Singulatim," *EW3*, 315.

15. *CdF78*, 238–42.

16. Ibid., 240–41.

17. Ibid., 241.

18. Ibid.,

19. See part 1 of *The Order of Things*.

20. Michel Foucault, "Governmentality," in *EW3*, 213.

21. *CdF78*, 157–59.

22. Foucault, "The Subject and Power," in Dreyfus and Rabinow, *Michel Foucault: Beyond Structuralism and Hermeneutics*, 214.

23. Ibid.

24. Ibid.

25. Ibid.

26. Michel Foucault, "Pastoral Power and Political Reason," in *RC*, 145.

27. Foucault's references for pastoral power in early Christian thought are thinkers such as "Chrysostom, Cyprian, Ambrose, Jerome, and for monastic life, Cassian or Benedict" (*EW3*, 308).

28. *EW3*, 312.

29. Foucault, "Governmentality," *EW3*, 201–2.

30. *CdF78*, 205–13.

31. This will be the subject of the following chapter.

32. "CdF84," February 1.

33. Bernauer, 164–65.

34. *HS*, 59.

35. *CdF75*, 158–59. Foucault analyzed this early form of penance, called "exomologesis," not only in 1975 but again from 1980 through 1982; see "CdF80," "CdF81," and *Technologies of the Self*.

36. *TS*, 41–43; *CdF75*, 159.

37. *CdF75*, 159.

38. *TS*, 42.

39. Ibid.

40. See chapters 3 and 4 of the present study.

41. *CdF75*, 159.

42. Ibid., 160.

43. Ibid.

44. Ibid.

45. Ibid., 161.

46. Ibid.

47. Ibid.

48. Ibid., 162.

49. Ibid.

50. Ibid.

51. Ibid.

52. Ibid.

53. Ibid., 163.

54. Ibid.

55. Ibid.

56. Ibid.

57. Ibid.

58. "CdF83," March 9; *CdF78*, 236.

59. *CdF78*, 152–53, 233–35.

60. Michel Foucault, "What Is Critique?" in *"What Is Enlightenment?"*: *Eighteenth-Century Answers and Twentieth-Century Questions,* ed. James Schmidt (Berkeley: University of California Press, 1996); *CdF78*, 197–98.

61. *CdF78*, 201, 235–38.

62. *CdF75*, 164.

63. Ibid.

64. Ibid.

65. Ibid.

66. Ibid., 164–65.

67. *CdF78*, 235–36.

68. *CdF75*, 164–65.

69. Ibid.

70. Ibid.

71. Ibid., 166.

72. Ibid.

73. Ibid.

74. Ibid.

75. Ibid., 167.

76. Ibid.

77. Ibid., 178.

78. Ibid.

79. See the following chapter.

80. *CdF75*, 165.

81. Ibid., 167–70.

82. Ibid., 168.

83. Ibid., 169.

84. Ibid.

85. Ibid.

86. Ibid., 170.

87. Ibid.

88. Ibid.

89. Ibid., 170–71.

90. *CdF78*, 208–19.

91. *CdF75*, 171.

92. *CdF78*, 208–19.

93. *HS*, 63.

94. See, for example, *CdF78*, 152–53, 233–35; Foucault, "Omnes et Singulatim," *EW3;* and "CdF83," March 9.

95. *CdF75*, 173.

96. Ibid.

97. Ibid.

98. The text which Foucault cites for his analysis of the "confession of the flesh" is one written toward the end of the seventeenth century. However, while this text is a late one and represents perhaps a sort of culmination of this concern, Foucault clearly claims that this new mode of perception of the self, the body, and sin begins in the sixteenth century with the new technology of confession-examination. In an essay on Bataille, Foucault claims that the Christian experience of sexuality as flesh was "a more immediately natural understanding" than our modern psychologized attitude (Michel Foucault, "A Preface to Transgression," in *EW2*, 69).

99. *CdF75*, 176.

100. Ibid.

101. Ibid., 177.

102. Ibid., 177–78.

103. Ibid., 178.

104. Ibid.

105. Ibid. It seems to me that Foucault can be understood here to be making an implicit argument about the source of Descartes's experience of his own embodied subjectivity. Was Descartes's experience of his body fashioned through the practices of direction and confession that he would have experienced at La Flèche, the Jesuit college where he was a student for at least seven years (Gaukroger, 38–62)? If so, then Descartes's thought of the body-machine would have been prepared, not just intellectually, but through the deployment of the body-machine in his very existence through techniques of confession and spiritual direction. "The seminaries had been the point of departure, and often the model, of the grand establishment of the scholars destined to the instruction which we call secondary. The great Jesuit colleges . . . were either the extension, or the imitation, of these seminaries" (ibid.).

106. *OT*, 17.

107. Ibid., 32.

108. Ibid., chap. 1.

109. *CdF78*, March 8.

110. *OT*, chap. 4; *CdF78*, 240–42.

111. *OT*, 71.

112. *BC*, 198; Michel Foucault, *Naissance de la clinique* (Paris: Quadrige/Presses Universitaires de France, 1963), 201

113. Descartes, *Philosophical Writings of Descartes*, 1:113.

Chapter 7

1. Foucault, "Governmentality," *EW3*, 201. This essay is the transcript of a lecture given by Foucault at the Collège as part of his 1978 course.

2. See, for example, Michel Foucault, "About the Concept of the Dangerous Individual," in *EW3*, 184.

3. See, for example, Michel Foucault, "The Political Technology of Individuals, " in *TS*, 148. See also *HS*, 135–45.

4. *TS*, 149.

5. Ibid., 151.

6. Foucault, "Governmentality," *EW3*, 209.

7. *OT*, 54–56.

8. Foucault, "Governmentality," *EW3*, 208.

9. Ibid., 210–11.

10. Ibid., 211.

11. Ibid., 207.

12. Foucault makes the distinction between *zoē* and *bios* in "CdF81," and it is the essence of his argument about biopower in part 5 of *HS*, 135–50. Giorgio Agamben, in *Homo Sacer*, begins his study with this distinction as well, following Foucault's lead.

13. Foucault, "Governmentality," *EW3*, 207.

14. Ibid.

15. Ibid., 214–15.

16. Ibid., 216.

17. Ibid., 208.

18. Ibid., 215–16; see also *CdF75*, March 5, 12.

19. Michel Foucault, "Politics of Health in the Eighteenth Century," in *EW3*, 90–105; Michel Foucault, "Birth of Social Medicine," *EW3*, 134–56.

20. Foucault, "Birth of Social Medicine," *EW3*, 137. This piece is a lecture delivered by Foucault in Brazil in 1974. To my knowledge, this is the earliest time Foucault employs the term "biopolitics."

21. *CdF76*, 242.

22. Ibid., 243.

23. Ibid., 244.

24. Ibid.

25. Foucault, "Politics of Health in the Eighteenth Century," *EW3*, 94.

26. *BC*, 31–32.

27. Ibid., 32–33.

28. Ibid., 33.

29. Ibid., 34–36.

30. Foucault, "Political Technology of Individuals," *TS*, 157.

31. Ibid. The rise of political government does not mean that law and justice are no longer an essential concern of politics. Rather, these problems are displaced by those of governing and of managing life. The politics of justice and biopolitics must coexist, though the relation between these two things will be uncomfortable. One might even say that law and justice are justified by, and grounded in, biopolitics: it is the political capacity to manage and produce life that will give the state the right to make and enforce laws.

32. Ibid., 158.

33. Again, the church does not disappear from the scene, but rather its government of souls must somehow function alongside and overlap a political management of life, of individuals.

34. René Descartes, *Discourse on Method and Meditations on First Philosophy,* trans. Donald Cress, 3rd ed. (Indianapolis: Hackett, 1993), 7; Descartes, *Philosophical Writings of Descartes,* 1:116.

35. *HF,* 75

36. Ibid.

37. Ibid., 63.

38. Ibid., 66.

39. Ibid., 67.

40. Ibid.

41. Ibid.

42. Ibid., 68.

43. Ibid., 68–69.

44. Ibid., 69.

45. Ibid., 70.

46. Ibid., 75.

47. Ibid., 70.

48. Ibid., 76.

49. Ibid., 76–77.

50. Ibid., 86.

51. Ibid., 87.

52. Ibid., 89–90.

53. Ibid., 92–94.

54. Ibid., 94.

55. Ibid.

56. Ibid.

57. Ibid.

58. This relationship is still mediated by *askēsis* on a more profound level: it is the *askēsis* of the doubt which opens up and lays out a world in which the subject and object can come together. For Descartes, this *askēsis* was a necessary spiritual transformation because the space he inhabited prior to it was arranged according to the system of resemblances. The spiritual transformation in order to become a subject in the Cartesian sense will be taken over in the biopolitical technology of the disciplines. In other words, the disciplines forge our relationship to ourselves and to the truth at a profound level, at the level of our being-in-the-world. Our very way of inhabiting space, time, and our bodies is arranged in order to institute a Cartesian relationship between the subject and the truth. The depth of this structure is so great and its truth so self-evident that it cannot be perceived as an *askēsis.* Rather, it is simply the way we live.

59. *CdF82,* 184.

60. "CdF84," March 28. Foucault suggests at the end of his final lecture of the course that the "full and complete" form of the relationship between the subject and truth is only dealt with at the level of the question of life, the practice of life, and the true life as access to the truth. The first lecture, January 6, of his 1982 course also deals with the fundamental notion of spirituality and argues that because we do not raise the question of the spiritual price of knowledge, we remain blind to this fundamental dimension of our subjectivity. He cites in particular

psychoanalysis and Marxism as knowledges that are essentially modes of spirituality, though they cannot admit it because of the normalizing pressure to define knowledge as science. See in particular *CdF82*, 30–31, on this last point.

61. *UP*, 26–28.

62. It may be that the process of normalization is the process of establishing this relationship to oneself; that is, normalization results in subjects who take it for granted that economic and biological health are the ultimate ends to be attained. To argue otherwise is to depart from the norm or to pursue other ends; to define the good in other terms is abnormal.

63. James Bernauer develops this notion in his research on fascism. See, for example, "Michel Foucault's Philosophy of Religion: An Introduction to the Non-Fascist Life," in *Michel Foucault and Theology: The Politics of Religious Experience,* ed. Bernauer and Jeremy Carrette (Burlington, Vt.: Ashgate, 2004), 77–97; and "Confessions of the Soul: Foucault and Theological Culture," *Journal of Philosophy and Social Criticism,* March 2005.

64. Foucault's reports on the Iranian revolution are collected in *DE*, vols. 3 and 4. See Michiel Leezenberg, "Power and Political Spirituality: Michel Foucault on the Islamic Revolution in Iran," in *Michel Foucault and Theology*, ed. Bernauer and Carrette, 99–115.

Chapter 8

1. See the previous chapter and *UP*, 26–28.

2. Michel Foucault, *Thèse complémentaire pour le doctorat dès lettres,* University of Paris, Faculty of Letters and the Human Sciences, 1961. Available at the Bibliothèque Sorbonne, Paris.

3. Michel Foucault, "What Is Enlightenment?" in *FR*, 38.

4. Foucault, "Political Technology of Individuals," *TS*, 145.

5. Cutrofello, *Discipline and Critique.*

6. See Cutrofello, *Discipline and Critique,* especially chaps. 3–6.

7. Ibid., 33.

8. Ibid., 48.

9. Ibid., 63.

10. Ibid., chaps. 4–5.

11. Kant, "What Is Enlightenment?" in *Kant's Political Writings,* trans. H. B. Nisbet (Cambridge: Cambridge University Press, 1991), 54.

12. Foucault, "What Is Enlightenment?" *FR*, 39.

13. Kant, "What Is Enlightenment?" in *Kant's Political Writings,* 58.

14. Ibid., 54–55.

15. "CdF83," January 5.

16. Immanuel Kant, "The Contest of the Faculties," in *Kant's Political Writings,* 182.

17. Kant, "What Is Enlightenment?" in *Kant's Political Writings,* 54.

18. Ibid., 55.

19. "CdF83," January 5, March 2.

20. Kant, "What Is Enlightenment?" in *Kant's Political Writings*, 55.

21. Foucault, "What Is Enlightenment?" *FR*, 36.

22. Kant, "What Is Enlightenment?" in *Kant's Political Writings*, 56.

23. Foucault, "What Is Enlightenment?" *FR*, 37.

24. Kant, "What Is Enlightenment?" in *Kant's Political Writings*, 59.

25. Ibid.

26. Ibid.

27. Foucault, "What Is Enlightenment?" *FR*, 38.

28. Foucault, "What Is Critique?" in *"What Is Enlightenment?"* ed. Schmidt, 387.

29. Foucault, *Thèse complémentaire; OT,* chaps. 7 and 9.

30. *OT,* 312–43.

31. Ibid., 236–49.

32. Foucault, "What Is Enlightenment?" *FR*, 38. Below, I shall try to make a further connection, following Cutrofello, between the anthropological/transcendental project—the thought of man—and the rise of discipline and biopower.

33. Foucault, "What Is Critique?" in *"What Is Enlightenment?"* ed. Schmidt, 387.

34. Ibid., 386.

35. Ibid., 383.

36. Foucault's approach to a history of the present is "futural" in two ways. (1) The way in which Foucault analyzes power-knowledge-subject structures is to show them as "becomings," as events—not ones which are complete, but ones which are in motion. For this reason he considers them from their "strategic" aspect: what they are doing, where they are going (for example, the strategy of disciplinary power, apart from whatever other strategies it is applied to, is an ever-increasing, ever-spreading disciplinization and normalization of the life-world). (2) Foucault's own strategy, or futural interest, is to destabilize the direction of our current experience-event by unveiling its strategic dimension—thus Foucault gives one the possibility of appropriating the future, the possibility of the future as other than the way it is or might be coming about.

37. Foucault will grasp *what-is* at the level of the practices which constitute it as a field of objects, as a "general area" of knowledge. His approach is therefore different from Kant's: Kant begins with knowledge and asks what makes that knowledge true. Foucault asks instead what makes such an area of knowledge possible, what makes it appear as true, what practices allow for these particular statements to be true about these particular objects.

38. Foucault, "What Is Critique?" in *"What Is Enlightenment?"* ed. Schmidt, 384.

39. Ibid.

40. Ibid.

41. Ibid., 386.

42. Cutrofello, *Discipline and Critique*, 33, 48–49.

43. The following is informed by Cutrofello's argument in *Discipline and Critique.*

44. *DP,* 136.

45. If discipline is the work on the body which develops it into a useful, obedient machine, it will be psychology which works on subjects to fashion their de-

sires and experiences of themselves such that they are productive, happy, healthy, and obedient.

46. Kant, "What Is Enlightenment?" in *Kant's Political Writings*, 60.

47. *DP,* 168–69; Cutrofello, *Discipline and Critique*, chaps. 3–4.

48. Kant, "What Is Enlightenment?" in *Kant's Political Writings*, 59.

49. *OT,* chap. 9: "Comte and Marx both bear out the fact that eschatology (as the objective truth proceeding from man's discourse) and positivism (as the truth of discourse defined on the basis of the truth of the object) are archaeologically indissociable: a discourse attempting to be both empirical and critical cannot but be both positivist and eschatalogical; man appears within it as a truth both reduced and promised" (*OT,* 320). Kant's thought shifts back and forth between its transcendental and critical dimension and its empirical dimension. In fact, Foucault argued in his *thèse complémentaire* that Kant's *Anthropology from a Pragmatic Point of View* is caught in this simultaneously empirical-critical mode of thinking. Kant's "What Is Enlightenment?" is marked by the same ambiguity: on the one hand, it is a statement of fact, and it presumes an "empirical" knowledge of man in his immaturity; on the other hand, it is a call to arms and a promise of the future which presumes a concrete image of the destiny and truth of man to be realized through enlightenment. The vision of the "free man" is a kind of reduction of human freedom to a particular image: it is in a sense a form of idolatry. The image of freedom stands in for the being of freedom; the representation of freedom as a particular form or state stands in for the actual, undefined work or activity of freedom.

50. Kant, "What Is Enlightenment?" in *Kant's Political Writings*, 57.

51. Again, the connection I wish to make between Kant's view of private obedience and the emergence of mature, autonomous subjects is based on my reading of Cutrofello. He shows that for Kant, discipline "plays an essential role" in the formation of autonomous subjects. Discipline is necessary "to ensure that reason does not violate its own laws," and "to extirpate the tendencies of our inclinations to lead us into moral error" (Cutrofello, *Discipline and Critique*, 36–37). In addition to the role they play in understanding and in morality, disciplinary practices are essential for producing a healthy and obedient body. Working from several sources, including biographical material, Cutrofello shows that Kant disciplined his body in order to make it healthy and obedient to his rational will (ibid., chap. 4). In an analogous way, discipline appears in the social-political realm of private reasoning and "civic freedom" as the necessary corrective which will extirpate the social upheavals and disorder, the private errors which impede social-political life. In this way social discipline will set the conditions for the development and emergence of autonomous, intellectually free subjects.

52. *DP,* 222.

53. Ibid., 141.

54. In fact, this process is not necessarily "bad"—its intrinsic danger will come from the disciplinary tendency to constantly spread: discipline as a relation of power comes with its own internal strategy. Second, the knowledge-effect which this mode of power produces—the norm, because it is simultaneously juridical

and anthropological, moral and metaphysical—is extremely dangerous in its domination effects.

55. *DP,* 209.

56. Ibid., 211.

57. Ibid.

58. Ibid., 215.

59. This will allow us to understand why Foucault recasts the Kantain notion of the a priori limits—that is, fundamental finitude as the transgressive fundamental finitude—as the possibility of exceeding *these* limits.

60. *DP,* 136.

61. Ibid., 170. See, for example, John Ransom's analysis, "Discipline and the Individual," in his *Foucault's Discipline: The Politics of Subjectivity* (Durham: Duke University Press, 1997).

62. *DP,* 141–43.

63. Ibid., 135.

64. Ibid., 143.

65. Ibid.

66. Ibid., 144.

67. Ibid., 146–47.

68. Ibid., 147.

69. Ibid., 148.

70. Ibid., 149.

71. Ibid., 150.

72. Ibid., 150–51.

73. Ibid., 151.

74. Ibid., 152.

75. Ibid.

76. Ibid., 154.

77. Ibid.

78. Ibid., 155.

79. Ibid., 156.

80. See, for example, *OT,* 218; *Thèse complémentaire,* 113.

81. *DP,* 161.

82. Ibid., 162.

83. It is for this reason that during the French Revolution monasteries devoted to contemplation were shut down: the discipline was not socially useful, it was a discipline which wasted space, time, and bodies.

84. *DP,* 164.

85. Ibid., 169.

86. Ibid., 164.

87. Ibid., 170.

88. Ibid., 178–79.

89. Ibid., 179.

90. Ibid., 181.

91. Ibid., 191.

92. *HS,* 65.

93. Ibid., 67.
94. Ibid.
95. *DP,* 182.
96. Ibid., 183.
97. *HS,* 144: "I do not mean to say that law fades into the background or that the institutions of justice tend to disappear, but rather that the law operates more and more as a norm, and that the judicial institution is increasingly incorporated into a continuum of apparatuses (medical, administrative, and so on) whose functions are for the most part regulatory."
98. *DP,* 179.
99. *OT,* 319–20.
100. *CdF82,* 183.
101. The finitude of man marks his absolute limit: that which cannot be surpassed and that which cannot be transformed. Anthropology also in a way fixes man to his finitude, this time cast as the normal.
102. *CdF82,* 29.
103. Foucault, "On the Genealogy of Ethics," *FR,* 372; also in *EW1,* 279–80.
104. Ibid.
105. One must also recognize here the role of the structuralist movement and avant-garde art and music.
106. Michel Foucault, "The Return of Morality," in *FL,* 471.
107. *HF,* 40.
108. Foucault, *Thèse complémentaire,* 127.
109. *OT,* 305.
110. Michel Foucault, "Nietzsche, Genealogy, History," in *EW2,* 369–92.
111. Ibid., 379.
112. Ibid., 377.
113. Ibid., 380.
114. Ibid., 383.
115. Foucault, "What Is Enlightenment?" *FR,* 39–42.
116. Ibid., 39.
117. Ibid.
118. Ibid., 40.
119. Ibid.
120. Ibid., 41.
121. Ibid.
122. Ibid., 41–42.
123. Ibid., 43.
124. *Thèse complémentaire,* 128.
125. Foucault, "What Is Enlightenment?" *FR,* 43–45.
126. Ibid., 44.
127. Ibid.
128. Ibid., 45.
129. *UP,* 12.
130. Foucault, "What Is Enlightenment?" *FR,* 46.
131. "CdF83," March 3.

132. *FR,* 50.
133. Ibid.
134. *UP,* 8.
135. Ibid., 9.

Conclusion

1. *UP,* 32.
2. Foucault, "On the Genealogy of Ethics," *EW1,* 256.

Bibliography

Works by Foucault

In most cases, where an English translation of a work by Foucault was available, I used it. One important exception to this rule is *Histoire de la folie;* the English translation is of the abridged version that lacks Foucault's reading of Descartes's *Meditations.* Much of the present book relies on currently unpublished material, in particular, Foucault's lectures at the Collège de France in 1983 and 1984. With respect to these courses, I have relied on typed notes I made from audio recordings of Foucault's actual lectures. These recordings are available at the Institut Mémoires de L'Édition Contemporaine (IMEC), which holds the archives of the Centre Michel Foucault. The IMEC is housed at L'abbaye d'Ardenne, 14280 Saint-Germain-la-Blanche-Herbe, outside the city of Caen in Normandy. The audio recordings of these lectures are also available at the Bibliothèque du Collège de France in Paris. For the 1984 course, I also referred to a typescript prepared by Michael Behrent for James Miller. Quotations from the 1984 course are drawn from Berhent's typescript, but are in some cases modified according to my understanding of the audiocassettes. This typescript can be consulted at O'Neill Library of Boston College. Finally, for the 1983 Berkeley course I relied on the manuscript prepared by Joseph Pearson. This course has recently been published under the title of *Fearless Speech* by Semiotext(e).

For excellent and comprehensive bibliographies of Foucault's works, see James Bernauer's *Michel Foucault's Force of Flight* (listed below) and Richard Lynch's online bibliography at www.foucault.qut.edu.au/index.html. The latter is regularly updated and lists all of Foucault's works in English. The Web site where Lynch's bibliography is to be found—*Foucault Resources* by Clare O'Farrell—is a valuable source of information and links to Foucault-related material.

Unpublished Courses at the Collège de France

Only courses discussed in this book are listed below. (For a nearly complete list of Foucault's courses at the Collège de France, including his course résumés, see vol. 1 of *The Essential Works of Michel Foucault, 1954–1984*—though this list does not include Foucault's 1983 and 1984 courses on *parrhēsia*.)

"Subjectivité et vérité: Cours au Collège de France, 1981." Audiocassettes available at IMEC and the Bibliothèque du Collège de France.
"Le gouvernement de soi et des autres: Cours au Collège de France, 1983." Audiocassettes available at IMEC and the Bibliothèque du Collège de France.
"Le courage de la vérité (Le gouvernement de soi et des autres, II): Cours au Collège de France, 1984." Typescript prepared by Michael Behrent.

Courses Published in France

These courses have been published in the series L'Éditions des Cours de Michel Foucault au Collège de France (Paris: Éditions de Seuil, Éditions Gallimard).

Les anormaux: Cours au Collège de France, 1974–1975. Edited by Valerio Marchetti and Antonella Salomoni. 1999.
"Il faut défendre la société": Cours au Collège de France, 1976. Edited by Mauro Bertani and Alessandro Fontana. 1997.
Sécurité, territoire, population: Cours au Collège de France, 1978. Edited by Michel Senellart. 2004.
L'herméneutique du sujet: Cours au Collège de France, 1981–1982. Edited by Frédéric Gros. 2001.

Works in English

Abnormal: Lectures at the Collège de France, 1974–1975. New York: Picador, 2003.
The Archaeology of Knowledge and the Discourse on Language. Translated by A. M. Sheridan Smith. NewYork: Pantheon Books, 1972.
The Birth of the Clinic: An Archaeology of Medical Perception. Translated by A. M. Sheridan Smith. New York: Vintage Books, 1973.
Discipline and Punish: The Birth of the Prison. Translated by Alan Sheridan. New York: Vintage Books, 1979.
Discourse and Truth: The Problematization of Parrhēsia. Notes to the seminar given at the University of California, Berkeley, in 1983. Edited by Joseph Pearson.
Dream and Existence: Michel Foucault and Ludwig Binswanger. Edited by Keith Hoeller. New Jersey: Humanities, 1993.
The Essential Works of Foucault, 1954–1984. Vol. 1, *Ethics, Subjectivity, and Truth,* edited by Paul Rabinow. New York: New Press, 1997.
The Essential Works of Foucault, 1954–1984. Vol. 2, *Aesthetics, Method, and Epistemology,* edited by James D. Faubion. New York: New Press, 1998.
The Essential Works of Foucault, 1954–1984. Vol. 3, *Power,* edited by James D. Faubion. New York: New Press, 2000.
Foucault Live: Collected Interviews, 1961–1984. Edited by Sylvère Lotringer. New York: Semiotext(e), 1996.
The Foucault Reader. Edited by Paul Rabinow. New York: Pantheon Books, 1984.
The History of Sexuality. Vol. 1, *An Introduction,* translated by Robert Hurley. New York: Vintage Books, 1990.

The History of Sexuality. Vol. 2, *The Use of Pleasure,* translated by Robert Hurley. New York: Vintage Books, 1990.

The History of Sexuality. Vol. 3, *The Care of the Self,* translated by Robert Hurley. New York: Vintage Books, 1988.

Madness and Civilization: A History of Insanity in the Age of Reason. Translated by Richard Howard. New York: Vintage Books, 1988.

Mental Illness and Psychology. Translated by Alan Sheridan. Berkeley: University of California Press, 1987.

The Order of Things: An Archaeology of the Human Sciences. New York: Vintage Books, 1994.

Religion and Culture. Edited by Jeremy R. Carrette. New York: Routledge, 1999.

"Society Must Be Defended:" Lectures at the Collège de France, 1975–1976. Translated by David Macey. New York: Picador, 2003.

Technologies of the Self: A Seminar with Michel Foucault. Edited by Luther H. Martin, Huck Gutman, and Patrick Hutton. Amherst: University of Massachusetts Press, 1988.

"What Is Critique?" translated by Kevin Paul Geiman. In *"What Is Enlightenment?":* *Eighteenth-Century Answers and Twentieth-Century Questions,* edited by James Schmidt, 382–98. Berkeley: University of California Press, 1996.

Works in French

L'archéologie du savoir. Paris: Éditions Gallimard, 1969.

Dits et écrits, 1954–1984. 4 vols. Edited by Daniel Defert and François Ewald. Paris: Éditions Gallimard, 1994.

"L'herméneutique du sujet: Cours au Collège de France (1982): Extraits." *Concordia: Revue Internationale de Philosophie,* vol. 12 (1988): 44–68. (The French text offered in this article is based upon a German text, a compilation of the notes of Helmut Becker and Lothar Wolfstetter.)

Histoire de la folie à l'âge classique. Paris: Gallimard, 1972.

Histoire de la sexualité. Vol. 1, *La volonté de savoir.* Paris: Gallimard, Collection Tel, 1976.

Histoire de la sexualité. Vol. 2, *L'usage des plaisirs.* Paris: Éditions Galllimard, 1984.

Histoire de la sexualité. Vol. 3, *Le souci de soi.* Paris: Gallimard, Collection Tel, 1984.

Les mots et les choses. Paris: Éditions Gallimard, 1966.

Naissance de la clinique. Paris: Quadrige/Presses Universitaires de France, 1963.

La peinture de Manet, suivi de Michel Foucault un regard. Paris: Éditions de Seuil, 2004.

Surveiller et punir. Paris: Gallimard, 1975.

Thèse complémentaire pour le doctorat des lettres. University of Paris, Faculty of Letters and the Human Sciences, 1961. Typescript is available at the Bibliothèque Sorbonne, Paris.

Works About Foucault

Adorno, Francesco Paulo. *Le style du philosophe*. Paris: Éditions Kimé, 1996.
Antonaccio, Maria. "Contemporary Forms of Askesis and the Return of Spiritual Exercises," *Annual of the Society of Christian Ethics*, vol. 18 (1998): 69–92.
Artières, Philippe, and Emmanuel da Silva, eds. *Michel Foucault et la medicine: Lectures et usages*. Paris: Éditions Kimé.
Bernauer, James. "Confessions of the Soul: Foucault and Theological Culture." *Philosophy and Social Criticism*, March 2005.
———. *Michel Foucault's Force of Flight: Towards an Ethics of Thought*. New Jersey: Humanities, 1990.
Bernauer, James, and Jeremy Carrette, eds. *Michel Foucault and Theology: The Politics of Religious Experience*. Burlington, Vt.: Ashgate, 2004.
Bernauer, James, and Michael Mahon. "The Ethics of Michel Foucault." In *The Cambridge Companion to Foucault*, edited by Gary Gutting, 141–58. Cambridge: Cambridge University Press, 1994.
Caputo, John. "On Not Knowing Who We Are. Madness, Hermeneutics, and the Night of Truth in Foucault." In *Foucault and the Critique of Institutions*, edited by John Caputo and Mark Yount, 233–62. Pennsylvania State University Press, 1993.
Davidson, Arnold, ed. *Foucault and His Interlocutors*. Chicago: University of Chicago Press, 1997.
Deleuze, Gilles. *Foucault*. Translated by Seán Hand. Minneapolis: University of Minnesota Press, 1986.
Derrida, Jacques. "Cogito and the History of Madness." In *Writing and Difference*, translated by Alan Bass. Chicago: University of Chicago Press, 1978.
———. "'To Do Justice to Freud': The History of Madness in the Age of Psychoanalysis." In *Resistances of Psychoanalysis*, translated by Peggy Kamuf, Pascale-Anne Brault, and Michael Naus. Stanford: Stanford University Press, 1996.
Dreyfus, Hubert, and Paul Rabinow. *Michel Foucault: Beyond Structuralism and Hermeneutics*. 2nd ed. Chicago: University of Chicago Press, 1983.
Eribon, Didier. *Michel Foucault*. Paris: Flammarion, 1989.
Flynn, Thomas. "Foucault as *Parrhēsiast*." In *The Final Foucault*, edited by James Bernauer and David Rasmussen. Cambridge: MIT Press, 1988.
———. "Foucault's Mapping of History." In *The Cambridge Companion to Foucault*, edited by Gary Gutting. Cambridge: Cambridge University Press, 1994.
Gros, Frédéric. *Foucault et la folie*. Paris: Presses Universitaires de France, 1997.
———, ed. *Foucault: Le courage de la vérité*. Paris: Presses Universitaires de France, 2002.
Gros, Frédéric, and Carlos Lévy, eds. *Foucault et la philosophie antique*. Paris: Éditions Kimé, 2003.
Gutting, Gary. *Michel Foucault's Archaeology of Scientific Reason*. Cambridge: Cambridge University Press, 1989.
Han, Béatrice. *Foucault's Critical Project: Between the Transcendental and the Historical*. Stanford: Stanford University Press, 2002.

Lawlor, Leonard. *Thinking Through French Philosophy: The Being of the Question.* Bloomington: Indiana University Press, 2003.

Le Blanc, Guillaume, and Jean Terrel, eds. *Foucault au Collège de France: Un intinéraire.* Bordeaux: Presses Universitaires de Bordeaux, 2003.

Macey, David. *The Lives of Michel Foucault.* New York: Pantheon, 1993.

McGushin, Edward. "Foucault's Cartesian Meditations." *International Philosophical Quarterly,* March 2005.

———. "Foucault's Retrieval of Care of the Self in the Thought of Plato." *Budhi: A Journal of Ideas and Culture* 6, nos. 2–3 (2002): 77–103.

McWhorter, Ladelle. *Bodies and Pleasures: Foucault and the Politics of Sexual Normalization.* Bloomington: Indiana University Press, 1999.

Miller, James. *The Passion of Michel Foucault.* New York: Anchor Books, 1993.

Poster, Mark. "Foucault and the Problem of Self-Constitution." In *Foucault and the Critique of Institutions,* edited by John Caputo and Mark Yount, 63–80. Pennsylvania State University Press, 1993.

Ransom, John. *Foucault's Discipline: The Politics of Subjectivity.* Durham: Duke University Press, 1997.

Raynor, Timothy. "Between Fiction and Reflection: Foucault and the Experience-Book." *Continental Philosophy Review* 36 (2003): 27–43.

Terra, Ricardo. "Foucault lecteur de Kant: De l'anthropologie à l'ontologie du présent." In *L'année 1798: Kant et la naissance de l'anthropologie au siècle des lumières: Actes du colloque de Dijon, 9–11 Mai 1996,* 159–72. Paris: Librairie J. Vrin, 1997.

Watson, Stephen. "Kant and Foucault: On the Ends of Man." *Tijdschrift Voor Filosofie* 47, no. 1 (March 1985): 71–102.

Other Sources

Agamben, Giorgio. *Homo Sacer: Sovereign Power and Bare Life.* Translated by Daniel Heller-Roazen. Stanford: Stanford University Press, 1998.

Arendt, Hannah. *Responsibility and Judgment.* Edited by Jerome Kohn. New York: Shocken Books, 2003.

Aristotle. *Nicomachean Ethics.* Translated by Terence Irwin. 2nd ed. Indianapolis: Hackett, 1999.

Bonner, Robert J. *Aspects of Athenian Democracy.* New York: Russel and Russel, 1933.

Bordo, Susan. *The Flight to Objectivity: Essays on Cartesianism and Culture.* Albany: State University of New York Press, 1987.

Butler, Judith. *The Subjective Life of Power.* Stanford: Stanford University Press, 1997.

Cutrofello, Andrew. *Discipline and Critique: Kant, Poststructuralism, and the Problem of Resistance.* Albany: State University of New York Press, 1994.

Deleuze, Gilles, and Félix Gauttari. *Anti-Oedipus: Capitalism and Schizophrenia.* Translated by Robert Hurley, Mark Seem, and Helen R. Lane. Minneapolis: University of Minnesota Press, 1983.

Delumeau, Jean. *Catholicism Between Luther and Voltaire.* Translated by Jeremy Moiser. London: Burns and Oates, 1977.

Descartes, René. *Discourse on Method and Meditations on First Philosophy.* Translated by Donald Cress. 3rd ed. Indianapolis: Hackett, 1993.

———. *The Philosophical Writings of Descartes.* Translated by John Cottingham, Robert Stoothoff, and Dugald Murdoch. 3 vols. Cambridge: Cambridge University Press, 1984.

Dio Chrysostom. *The Fourth Discourse on Kingship.* Translated by J. W. Cohoon. Cambridge: Harvard University Press, 1949.

Dodds, E. R. *The Greeks and the Irrational.* Berkeley: University of California Press, 1951.

Epictetus. *The Discourses as Reported by Arrian.* Translated by W. A. Oldfather. Cambridge: Harvard University Press, 1956.

———. *Enchiridion.* Translated by George Long. New York: Prometheus Books, 1991.

———. *The Handbook.* Translated by Nicholas P. White. Indianapolis: Hackett, 1983.

Epicurus. *The Essential Epicurus: Letters, Principal Doctrines, Vatican Sayings, and Fragments.* Translated by Eugene O'Connor. New York: Prometheus Books, 1993.

Euripides. *Ion.* Translated by K. H. Lee. Warminster, Eng.: Aris and Phillips, 1997. Greek text copyrighted by Oxford University Press, 1981.

———. *Orestes.* In *Euripides IV,* translated by William Arrowsmith. Chicago: University of Chicago Press, 1958.

Farrar, Cynthia. *The Origins of Democratic Thinking: The Invention of Politics in Classical Athens.* Cambridge: Cambridge University Press, 1988.

Goosens, Roger. *Euripide et Athènes.* Brussels: Palais des Académies, 1962.

Hadot, Pierre. *Exercises spirituels et philosophie antique.* 2nd ed. Paris: Albin Michel, 2002

———. *Qu'est-ce que la philosophie antique?* Paris: Éditions Gallimard, 1995.

———. *What Is Ancient Philosophy?* Cambridge: Harvard University Press, 2002.

Heidegger, Martin. *Being and Time.* Translated by John Macquarrie and Edward Robinson. San Francisco: HarperSanFrancisco, 1962.

Jones, W. T. *The Classical Mind I.* San Diego: Harcourt Brace Jovanovich, 1970.

Kant, Immanuel. *Anthropology from a Pragmatic Point of View.* Translated by Victor Lyle Dowdell. Southern Illinois University Press, 1996.

———. "The Contest of the Faculties." In *Kant's Political Writings,* translated by H. B. Nisbet, 176–90. Cambridge: Cambridge University Press, 1991.

———. "What Is Enlightenment?" In *Kant's Political Writings,* translated by H. B. Nisbet, 54–60. Cambridge: Cambridge University Press, 1991.

———. "What Is Enlightenment?" translated by James Schmidt. In *"What Is Enlightenment?": Eighteenth-Century Answers and Twentieth-Century Questions,* edited by James Schmidt, 58–64. Berkeley: University of California Press, 1996.

Marcus Aurelius. *Meditations.* Translated by Maxwell Staniforth. New York: Dorset, 1964.

Marrow, Stanley. "Parrhēsia and the New Testament." *Catholic Bible Quarterly* 44 (1982): 431–46.

McCumber, John. *Time in the Ditch: American Philosophy and the McCarthy Era.* Evanston, Ill.: Northwestern University Press, 2001.

Merleau-Ponty, Maurice. *Signes.* Paris: Gallimard/Folio, 1960.

Nehamas, Alexander. *The Art of Living: Socratic Reflections from Plato to Foucault.* Berkeley: University of California Press, 1998.

Plato. *Alcibiades I.* In vol. 2 of *The Dialogues of Plato,* translated by B. Jowett. New York: Random House, 1920.

———. *Apology,* translated by Hugh Tredennick. In *Plato: The Collected Dialogues,* edited by Edith Hamilton and Huntington Cairns. Bollingen Series 71. Princeton: Princeton University Press, 1961.

———. *Crito,* translated by Hugh Tredennick. In *Plato: The Collected Dialogues,* edited by Edith Hamilton and Huntington Cairns. Bollingen Series 71. Princeton: Princeton University Press, 1961.

———. *Laches,* translated by Benjamin Jowett. In *Plato: The Collected Dialogues,* edited by Edith Hamilton and Huntington Cairns. Bollingen Series 71. Princeton: Princeton University Press, 1961.

———. *Pheado,* translated by Hugh Tredennick. In *Plato: The Collected Dialogues,* edited by Edith Hamilton and Huntington Cairns. Bollingen Series 71. Princeton: Princeton University Press, 1961.

———. *Phaedrus,* translated by R. Hackforth. In *Plato: The Collected Dialogues,* edited by Edith Hamilton and Huntington Cairns. Bollingen Series 71. Princeton: Princeton University Press, 1961.

———. *Republic,* translated by Paul Shorey. In *Plato: The Collected Dialogues,* edited by Edith Hamilton and Huntington Cairns. Bollingen Series 71. Princeton: Princeton University Press, 1961.

———. *Seventh Letter,* translated by L. A. Post. In *Plato: The Collected Dialogues,* edited by Edith Hamilton and Huntington Cairns. Bollingen Series 71. Princeton: Princeton University Press, 1961.

———. *Symposium,* translated by Michael Joyce. In *Plato: The Collected Dialogues,* edited by Edith Hamilton and Huntington Cairns. Bollingen Series 71. Princeton: Princeton University Press, 1961.

Plutarch. *The Lives of the Noble Grecians and Romans.* Translated by John Dryden. Revised by Arthur Hugh Clough. New York: Modern Library.

Seneca. *The Stoic Philosophy of Seneca: Essays and Letters.* Translated by Moses Hadas. New York: W. W. Norton, 1958.

Snell, Bruno. *The Discovery of the Mind in Greek Philosophy and Literature.* Translated by T. G. Rosenmeyer. New York: Dover, 1982.

Taylor, Charles. *The Ethics of Authenticity.* Cambridge: Harvard University Press, 1991.

Thomson, Douglas. *Euripides and the Attic Orators.* London: Macmillan, 1898.

Thucydides. *The Peloponnesian War.* Translated by Rex Warner. Baltimore: Penguin Books, 1954.

Weber, Max. *The Protestant Ethic and the Spirit of Capitalism.* Translated by Talcott Parsons. New York: Routledge, 1992.

Index

About the Author

Edward F. McGushin is an assistant professor of philosophy at Saint Anselm College and the author of articles on Foucault and continental philosophy.